palgrave advances in
cold war history

Palgrave Advances

Titles include:

H.G. Cocks and Matt Houlbrook (*editors*)
THE MODERN HISTORY OF SEXUALITY

Saki R. Dockrill and Geraint Hughes (*editors*)
COLD WAR HISTORY

Patrick Finney (*editor*)
INTERNATIONAL HISTORY

Jonathan Harris (*editor*)
BYZANTINE HISTORY

Marnie Hughes-Warrington (*editor*)
WORLD HISTORIES

Helen J. Nicholson (*editor*)
THE CRUSADES

Alec Ryrie (*editor*)
EUROPEAN REFORMATIONS

Richard Whatmore and Brian Young (*editors*)
INTELLECTUAL HISTORY

Jonathan Woolfson (*editor*)
RENAISSANCE HISTORIOGRAPHY

Forthcoming:

Jonathan Barry and Owen Davies (*editors*)
WITCHCRAFT STUDIES

Katherine O'Donnell, Leann Lane and Mary McAuliffe (*editors*)
IRISH HISTORY

Palgrave Advances
Series Standing Order ISBN 1–4039–3512–2 (Hardback) 1–4039–3513–0 (Paperback)
(*outside North America only*)

You can receive future titles in this series as they are published by placing a standing order.
Please contact your bookseller or, in the case of difficulty, write to us at the address below
with your name and address, the title of the series and the ISBN quoted above.

Customer Services Department, Macmillan Distribution Ltd, Houndmills, Basingstoke,
Hampshire RG21 6XS, England

palgrave advances in
cold war history

edited by
saki r. dockrill and geraint hughes

First published 2006 by
PALGRAVE MACMILLAN
Houndmills, Basingstoke, Hampshire RG21 6XS and
175 Fifth Avenue, New York, N.Y. 10010
Companies and representatives throughout the world

PALGRAVE MACMILLAN is the global academic imprint of the
Palgrave Macmillan division of St. Martin's Press, LLC and of
Palgrave Macmillan Ltd.
Macmillan® is a registered trademark in the United States,
United Kingdom and other countries. Palgrave is a registered
trademark in the European Union and other countries.

ISBN-13   978–1–4039–3446–8 hardback
ISBN-10   1–4039–3446–0 hardback
ISBN-13   978–1–4039–3447–5 paperback
ISBN-10   1–4039–3447–9 paperback

This book is printed on paper suitable for recycling and
made from fully managed and sustained forest sources.

A catalogue record for this book is available
from the British Library.

Library of Congress Cataloging-in-Publication Data
Palgrave advances in Cold War history / edited by Saki R. Dockrill and Geraint Hughes.
p. cm.
Includes bibliographical references and index.
ISBN-10: 1–4039–3446–0
ISBN-10: 1–4039–3447–9 (pbk.)
1. Cold War—Historiography. I. Dockrill, Saki. II. Hughes, Geraint, 1975–

D840.P26 2006
909.82'5—dc22

2006041678

10   9   8   7   6   5   4   3   2   1
15   14   13   12   11   10   09   08   07   06

Transferred to Digital Printing in 2008

contents

acknowledgements

This book is the outcome of a friendly collaboration between a group of distinguished scholars who are working on specific aspects of the cold war. The editors wish to thank all the contributors who joined us in completing the project. We would also like to thank the staff of the various archives that were consulted in this volume. Saki Dockrill is indebted to the British Academy for grants which enabled her to undertake research in the United States in relation to this project.

Saki Ruth Dockrill and Geraint Hughes
November 2005, London

notes on contributors

Richard J. Aldrich is Professor of Politics at the University of Nottingham and also a Deputy Director of the Institute of Asia-Pacific Studies. During 2004/05 he was a Leverhulme Research Fellow. His recent publications are *The Hidden Hand: Britain, America and Cold War Secret Intelligence* (2001) as well as a two-volume collection of war diaries, *Witness to War* (2004) and *The Faraway War* (2005). Current projects include a study of intelligence and its role in state formation since 1648.

Christoph Bluth is Professor of International Studies at the University of Leeds and Visiting Research Fellow at the Korea Institute for Defense Analyses, Seoul. He was previously Professor of European and International Studies at the University of Reading and is the author of numerous papers and books on international security and cold war history, including *The Nuclear Challenge* (2000), *Germany and the Future of European Security* (2000) and *The Two Germanies and Military Security in Europe* (2003).

Saki Ruth Dockrill is Professor of Contemporary History and International Security at King's College, London, University of London, and was a John M. Olin Fellow at Yale University and recently a Senior Research Fellow at the Norwegian Nobel Institute, Norway. Professor Dockrill is a Fellow of the Royal Historical Society, and an Associate Fellow of the Institute for the Study of the Americas, University of London and has written extensively on defence and security relations in Europe, the USA, and Asia in the cold war. Her main publications include *Eisenhower's New Look National Security Policy* (1996), *Britain's Retreat from East of Suez: The Choice between Europe and the World?* (2002) and *The End of the Cold War Era: The Transformation of the Global Security Order* (2005). Professor Dockrill is currently working on 'Intervention' and 'Global Peacemakers'.

Sir Lawrence Freedman is Professor of War Studies and Vice-Principal (Research) of King's College, London. Sir Lawrence has written extensively on nuclear strategy and the cold war, as well as commentating regularly on contemporary security issues. Elected a Fellow of the British Academy (FBA) in 1995, he was appointed Official Historian of the Falklands Campaign by the Prime Minister, Tony Blair, in 1997. His recent publications include *Kennedy's Wars* (2000), *Deterrence* (2004), and the two volumes of *The Official History of the Falklands Campaign: The Origins of the Falklands War* and *War and Diplomacy* (2005).

Jussi M. Hanhimäki is Professor of International History and Politics at the Graduate Institute of International Studies in Geneva, Switzerland. His most recent publications include *The Flawed Architect: Henry Kissinger and American Foreign Policy* (2004) and, with Odd Arne Westad, *The Cold War: A History in Documents and Eyewitness Accounts* (2003). Professor Hanhimäki is one of the editors of the journal *Cold War History* and also a member of the editorial board of *Diplomatic History* and is currently writing a book on the United Nations and also on the external influences on American domestic politics during the cold war.

Geraint Hughes is a lecturer with the Defence Studies Department at the Joint Services Command and Staff College, Shrivenham, King's College, London, and is currently completing a monograph on Anglo-Soviet relations in the 1960s.

Ian Jackson is Senior Lecturer in International Relations at De Montfort University and is the author of *The Economic Cold War: America, Britain and East–West Trade, 1948–63* (2001) and of the forthcoming book, *The Fall of Bretton Woods: Johnson, Nixon and US International Monetary Policy, 1964–74*.

Lawrence S. Kaplan is University Professor Emeritus of History and Director Emeritus of the Lyman L. Lemnitzer Center for NATO and European Union Studies at Kent State University. Now based in the Washington area, he is a contract historian at the US Department of Defense and is currently a professorial lecturer in history at Georgetown University. Among his numerous publications on NATO are *The Long Entanglement: NATO's First Fifty Years* (1999) and *NATO and the United States: An Enduring Alliance* (1994), and he has also co-edited six volumes based on the proceedings of Lemnitzer Center Conferences.

John Kent is Reader in International Relations at London School of Economics and Political Science (LSE), and has written widely on decolonisation, the Middle East, and British foreign policy and the cold war. Dr Kent is the author of *British Imperial Strategy and the Origins of the Cold War* (1993), edited two volumes of documents on Egypt and the Defence of Middle East, 1945–46 for the British Documents on the End of Empire Project, and published, with John W. Young, *International Relations since 1945: A Global History* (2003).

Wolfgang Krieger is Professor of Modern History at Universität Marburg, Germany. He has been visiting professor at the Institut d'Etudes Politiques, Paris (2005), the universities of Toronto (1999–2000) and Princeton (1991–92). He held fellowships at Oxford and Harvard universities before teaching at Universität München (1987–95) and working at SWP, Germany's foremost think-tank on foreign and defence policy (1986–95). He has published widely on US policy toward Germany since 1941, on US forces in Europe during the cold war, and on the history of intelligence services in the twentieth century.

Patrick Major is Senior Lecturer in History at the University of Warwick and teaches an MA programme on Society and Culture in the Cold War. Dr Major is the author of *The Death of the KPD: Communism and Anti-Communism in West Germany, 1945–1956* (1997) and co-editor with Jonathan Osmond of *The Workers' and Peasants' State: Communism and Society in East Germany under Ulbricht, 1945–71* (2002) and co-editor, with Rana Mitter, of *Across the Blocs: Cold War Cultural and Social History* (2004).

Rana Mitter is University Lecturer in the History and Politics of Modern China at the University of Oxford and is the author of *The Manchurian Myth: Nationalism, Resistance, and Collaboration in Modern China* (2000) and *A Bitter Revolution: China's Struggle with the Modern World* (2004), and co-editor, with Patrick Major, of *Across the Blocs: Cold War Cultural and Social History* (2004) and, with Sheila Jager, of *Ruptured Histories: War and Memory in Post-Cold War East Asia* (forthcoming).

Leopoldo Nuti is Professor of History of International Relations at the School of Political Science, University of Roma Tre, and was a NATO Research Fellow, Jean Monnet Fellow at the European University Institute, a Research Fellow at the CSIA, Harvard University, a Research Fellow for the Nuclear History Program, and most recently, a Senior Research Fellow at the Norwegian Nobel Institute as well as a Visiting Professor at the Institut d'Etudes Politiques in Paris. With a number of other Italian cold war historians, he promoted the creation of the Machiavelli Center for Cold War Studies (CIMA) and has published extensively in Italian, English and French on US–Italian relations and Italian foreign and security policy. Professor Nuti's main publications include *L'esercito italiano nel secondo dopoguerra, 1945–1950. La sua ricostruzione e l'assistenza militare alleata* (Roma: Ufficio Storico dello Stato Maggiore Esercito, 1989), *I missili di ottobre. La storiografia americana e la crisi cubana del 1962* (Milano: LED, 1994) and *Gli Stati Uniti e l'apertura a sinistra. Importanza e limiti della presenza americana in Italia* (Rome: Laterza, 1999). He is currently completing a history of nuclear weapons in Italy during the cold war.

Vladislav Zubok is Associate Professor of History, Temple University, and has written extensively on the Soviet Union in the cold war. Dr Zubok is co-author, with Constantin Pleshakov, of *Inside the Kremlin's Cold War: From Stalin to Khrushchev* (1996) which was awarded the Lionel Gelber Prize, and (with Eric Shiraev) of *Russian Anti-Americanism: From Stalin to Putin* (2000), and is currently completing a project on Soviet behaviour in the cold war, and also on 'Soviet Sixties: Soviet Power and Culture between the Cold War and the West'.

abbreviations, technical terms and foreign words

AFL – American Federation of Labor. The AFL merged with the Congress of Industrial Organisations in 1955 to form the main US trade union federation.

ASW – Anti-submarine warfare.

ABM – Anti-ballistic missile.

ALCM – Air-launched cruise missile.

BBC – British Broadcasting Corporation.

Bildeberg Group – An informal contact group founded in the early 1950s to promote dialogue between American and West European policy-makers.

CAZAB – A counter-intelligence liaison body set up between Canada, the USA, New Zealand, Australia and the UK.

CCF – Congress for Cultural Freedom.

CCP – Chinese Communist Party.

CENTO – Central Treaty Organisation.

CEP – Circular error probable. The technical term used to describe the precision of a missile warhead. The CEP is the radius of a circle, the centre being the point of impact, within which 50 per cent of missiles aimed at the target will fall. CEP is assessed at the maximum range of the weapons system employed, and throughout the cold war both superpowers aimed to reduce the CEP of each ballistic missile system employed.

CFE – Conventional Forces in Europe Treaty.

CIA – Central Intelligence Agency. The US foreign intelligence service.

CIO – Congress of Industrial Organisations.

CMEA – Council for Mutual Economic Assistance (also known as Comecon).

COCOM – Coordinating Committee on strategic trade with communist states.

Comintern – Communist International. The principal coordinating body of the communist movement, which was founded in 1919. Based in the USSR, it was formally abolished in 1943.

Contras – Name given to the US-supported Nicaraguan guerrilla groups which fought the *Sandinista* regime during the 1980s.

CPSU – Communist Party of the Soviet Union.

CSCE – Conference on Security and Cooperation in Europe.

CWIHP – Cold War International History Project.

DCI – Director of Central Intelligence. The head of the CIA.

DFEC – Defence Financial and Economic Committee.

DRV – Democratic Republic of Vietnam.

Dyedovshchina – The nickname given to institutionalised bullying of junior conscripts in the Soviet military.

ECA – Economic Cooperation Administration.

ECSC – European Coal and Steel Community. The precursor to the EEC.

EEC – European Economic Community. Now known as the European Union.

ERP – European Recovery Programme. Better known as the Marshall Plan.

EU – European Union.

FBI – Federal Bureau of Investigation.

FCDA – Federal Civil Defense Administration.

FNLA – Front for the National Liberation of Angola (*Frente Nacionale de Libertacao de Angola*).

Force de frappe – Name given to the French nuclear deterrent.

FRG – Federal Republic of Germany.

GATT – General Agreement on Tariffs and Trade. Now known as the World Trade Organisation.

GCHQ – Government Communications Headquarters. The UK's signals intelligence (SIGINT) service.

GDR – German Democratic Republic.

Gladio – Name given to 'stay-behind' networks established in Western Europe during the late 1940s, intended to provide the nucleus for anti-communist resistance in the event of a Soviet invasion.

glasnost – 'Openness'. The name given to the liberalisation of Soviet politics and the media under Gorbachev.

GNP – Gross National Product.

GRU – Soviet Military Intelligence. Taken from the Russian initials for Main Intelligence Directorate (*Glavnoe Razvyedyvatyelnoe Upravleniye*).

GSFG – Group of Soviet Forces, Germany.

Guomindang – Chinese Nationalist Party.

HUAC – House Un-American Affairs Committee.

Huk – Filipino communist guerrilla movement. Taken from the Tagalog phrase *Hukbalahap* ('People's Anti-Japanese Army'). Originally founded to fight Japanese occupation in the Second World War, the *Hukbalahap* waged a guerrilla war against the pro-American Filipino government from 1946 to 1957.

ICBM – Intercontinental ballistic missile.

IMF – International Monetary Fund.

INF – Intermediate-range Nuclear Forces.

IRD – Information Research Department. The British Foreign Office's covert propaganda wing from 1948 to 1977.

JCS – The US Joint Chiefs of Staff.

JIC – Joint Intelligence Committee. The coordinating body of the UK's intelligence community.

Juche – 'Self-reliance'. The name given to North Korea's policy of autarchic communism.

KGB – The Soviet internal security/foreign intelligence service. Taken from the Russian initials for Committee of State Security (*Komityet Gosudarstvennoe Bezopasnosti*).

KhAD – The State Information Agency. The security service of the communist regime in Afghanistan (*Khedamat-e Etelea'at-e Dawlati*).

Khmer Rouge – The Cambodian Communist Party.

Lao Dong – The Vietnamese Workers Party. The ruling party of the DRV.

LTBT – Limited Test Ban Treaty.

MAD – Mutual assured destruction.

MFN – Most Favoured Nation status. MFN permits a foreign country to export goods to the USA at a reduced tariff rate.

MfS – The East German security service. Taken from the German initials for Ministry of State Security (*Ministerium für Staatssicherheit*). Also known as the *Stasi*.

MI5 – The British internal security service.

MIRV – Multiple independently-targetable re-entry vehicles. An ICBM with an MIRV warhead has the capability to engage a number of targets almost simultaneously.

MPLA – Popular Movement for the Liberation of Angola (*Movimento Popular da Libertação de Angola*). A left-wing guerrilla movement that took power in Angola after the Portuguese withdrawal, and which still governs to this day.

MPSB – Military Production and Supply Board.

Mujahadin – Name given to the anti-communist resistance groups in Afghanistan (translated as 'soldiers of God').

NATO – North Atlantic Treaty Organisation.

NGO – Non-governmental organisation.

NPT – Non-Proliferation Treaty.

NSA – National Security Agency. The US SIGINT service.

NSC – National Security Council.

OAU – Organisation of African Unity. Now known as the African Union.

OEEC – Organisation for European Economic Cooperation.

OKB – Term given to the Soviet strategic weapons research and development bureau (*Opytno Konstruktorskie Biuro*).

Ostpolitik – Term given to the FRG's efforts to improve relations with the USSR and Eastern bloc states from the 1960s onwards.

Pathet Lao – The Laotian Communist Party and guerrilla movement.

perestroika – 'Reconstruction'. Name given to Gorbachev's programme of internal reforms.

Pershing – A US intermediate range nuclear missile, deployed in Europe during the 1980s.

PGM – Precision guided munitions. The military term for a 'smart' weapons system such as the *Cruise* missile.

PHP – Parallel History Project.

PLA – People's Liberation Army. The official name for the Chinese armed forces.

Polaris – A US-designed submarine-launched missile system which, from 1969, also provided the basis for the UK nuclear deterrent.

Politburo – The central decision-making body of the CPSU. Known as the *Presidium* between 1952 and 1966.

PRC – People's Republic of China.

Realpolitik – Term given to the practice of realist, pragmatic power-politics, undertaken purely on calculations of national interest.

Rolling Thunder – The operational name for the US bombing campaign against the DRV from 1965 to 1968.

RSVN – Soviet Strategic Rocket Forces.

SAC – Strategic Air Command. The deterrent arm of the US Air Force.

SACEUR – Supreme Allied Commander, Europe. The general officer (US Army or USAF) in command of NATO land and air forces in Europe.

SACLANT – Supreme Allied Commander, Atlantic. The US Navy admiral in command of NATO naval forces.

SALT – Strategic Arms Limitation Treaty.

Sandinistas – Left-wing Nicaraguan guerrilla movement which seized power in 1979, and which was subsequently targeted by the USA for overthrow.

SAVAK – The Iranian internal security service (1957–79). Taken from the Farsi initials for National Intelligence and Security Organisation (*Sazeman-i Ettelaat va Amniyat-i Keshvar*).

SDI – Strategic Defense Initiative.

SEATO – South-East Asia Treaty Organisation.

SIGINT – Signals Intelligence.

SIOP – Single integrated operational plan. The US contingency plan for global nuclear war.

SIS – Secret Intelligence Service. The UK's foreign intelligence service. Popularly known as MI6.

SLBM – Submarine-launched ballistic missile.

Sputnik – The first space satellite, launched by the USSR in 1957.

throw-weight – A technical term referring to the maximum weight of a warhead that could be placed on a ballistic missile.

UKUSA – Acronym given to the informal agreements on intelligence-sharing concluded by the American and British intelligence communities.

UNCTAD – United Nations Conference on Trade and Development.

UNITA – National Union for the Total Independence of Angola (*União Nacional para a Independência Total de Angola*). Angolan guerrilla movement backed by the USA and South Africa in its war against the MPLA (1975–89).

USAF – United States Air Force.

Viet Cong – The communist guerrilla movement in South Vietnam, an abbreviation of the phrase 'Vietnamese communist' (*Việt Nam Cộng Sản*). Its official name was the National Front for the Liberation of South Vietnam (*Mặt Trận Dân Tộc Giải Phóng Miền Nam*).

VPK – The Soviet Military-Industrial Commission (*Voenno-Promyshlenniya Kommissiya*).

WTO – World Trade Organisation.

Zhdanovshchina – The term given to the purge of Soviet culture and intelligentsia during the late 1940s. Named after Andrei Zhdanov, the *Politburo* member most closely associated with this purge.

introduction: the cold war as history

geraint hughes and saki ruth dockrill

the cold war world

The cold war dominated the international system for nearly 45 years, and exerted a significant influence over the nature and scope of the many military and political conflicts that occurred during those years. In retrospect, the cold war was the major theatre for the West's struggle against communist ideas and about regime change in, and the democratisation of, the communist bloc. The cold war was fought very much on the assumption that 'if your are not with us, you are against us', an assumption that figured more prominently in American society than in its Western European counterparts. While the Soviet leadership in its final years accepted it would be impossible to create a non-Islamic Afghanistan, Mikhail Gorbachev nonetheless believed that a pro-US/Pakistan regime in Afghanistan would be 'totally unacceptable' both to India and to the USSR.[1] Thus, the main tenet of the cold war can be seen as the East–West competition in ideas, arms and spheres of influence.

Propaganda activities, information gathering and spying were part and parcel of winning the hearts and minds of allies and potential allies. The cold war became, to varying degrees, an integral part of the domestic politics of many countries, such as in the form of McCarthyism in the USA during the 1950s or anti-nuclear movements in Europe in the early 1980s. The Western alliance was supposed to have been united during cold war crises, but Europe was seen by the USA as likely to succumb to pitfalls like 'Finlandisation', as America's European allies were often keen to reduce cold war tensions by means of *détente*, cultural exchanges, or negotiations.[2] In the mid-1970s, American right-wing politicians and intellectuals voiced their concern about *détente*, and about the wisdom of Henry Kissinger, who encouraged the US policy of *détente* during the

Nixon years. They believed that: 'we are relying too much on so-called *détente* ... We are not only permitting the Communists to gain one advantage after another, militarily as well otherwise; in many ways we are helping the Communists gain those advantages.'[3]

The main task of fighting the cold war in communist countries was on their home fronts. With the help of the KGB and its offspring in the Warsaw Pact countries, it was important for these countries to control their own societies through an intricate network of intelligence and spying. Not surprisingly, there were also counter-propaganda activities within the Eastern bloc. As the Sino-Soviet split became much deeper after 1969, Radio Free Europe recorded in 1971 that communist China increased its communist European broadcasts by 33 per cent, making 'very aggressive attacks' on Moscow. Similarly, the activities of the Western intelligence agencies, such as of the Central Intelligence Agency (CIA) of the USA, and West Germany's Federal Intelligence Services, were publicly exposed in East Germany, and were used as part of its anti-Western campaign.[4] However, despite jamming by the communist authorities, the West's media could penetrate across the iron curtain. Romania imposed strict restraints on the flow of information (all typewriters were required to be registered with the government to limit clandestine publications by anti-governmental groups), but the Romanians managed to obtain news on the outside world by tuning into Hungarian television. It was well known to the East German leadership that their population watched West German television, and the Czechs enjoyed Austrian and West German broadcasts. This circulation of information, together with increased contacts with the West after the 1970 *détente*, helped to undermine the authoritarian regimes in the East.[5] After all, the beginning of the end of the cold war in Europe was affected by the eagerness of East Berliners to travel freely, by pulling down the Berlin wall, a fact that brought home the importance of the domestic front, which helped to shape the scope and nature of cold war fighting abroad.

At the core of the cold war was the mutually perceived fear of a possible surprise attack by the other side, a fear which was fed by mutual misperceptions, and a lack of understanding of each other. This meant that each side tended to depict the other in the worst possible light, which in turn created a situation whereby both sides misread each other's intentions and overestimated each other's capabilities. The possession of nearly 50,000 nuclear weapons by the two superpowers made the confrontation deadly, while the East–West ideological competition added to the dynamic to expand, and intensify, the cold war worldwide. In the event of a nuclear attack on the USA, its key decision-makers were to be quickly moved to a secret bunker in the heart of the Carolina mountains. At the beginning of his presidency, Dwight D. Eisenhower was taken to this emergency White House through a long tunnel, occasionally interrupted by huge security gates. When he finally reached the bunker, he looked back, and told his national security adviser, Dillon Anderson, that: 'Good God; I did not realise we were this scared.'[6]

After the death of Stalin in 1953, NATO believed that the prospect of a third world war was unlikely except by accident or miscalculation. Nevertheless there was still a great degree of uncertainty in the West surrounding Soviet military intentions. One scholar states that 'On a medical analogy, the West by the 1980s had become well informed about Soviet anatomy and physiology; but the windows to the antagonist's mind remained largely opaque.'[7] Similarly the Soviet Union and the Eastern bloc were aware that NATO's strategy was defensive, but this did not dispel the fear that NATO's strategy could be a 'cover up for a possible surprise nuclear strike'.[8] This also explained why the Kremlin's suspicions of a NATO pre-emptive attack increased in the aftermath of the November 1983 Able Archer exercise.

While at least both sides appreciated the need to avoid a final battle between the two blocs at the cost of the survival of the globe, the West had long believed the Soviet system would eventually decay and decline, and that Western liberal democratic capitalist values would eventually prevail over the East. For Moscow the cold war became an endless race to catch up with, and then equal, the United States in global power and influence. It was remarkable how quickly the Soviet Union exploited power vacuums created by the West – whether it was in the Korean peninsula (after the USA excluded it from its defence perimeter in late 1949), in the Indian Ocean or in the Arabian peninsula (after Britain decided to withdraw from East of Suez in the late 1960s), or in the Third World (where the USA became much less willing to intervene in the aftermath of the Vietnam war). Moscow's pursuit of equality lasted to the end of the Gorbachev era. During the Brezhnev years, the Soviet Union endeavoured to become a global military power equal to the USA. Gorbachev chose instead to adopt a non-military and diplomatic alternative but he too was intent on maintaining Moscow's global influence on a par with that of the United States. During the Malta summit, Gorbachev proposed to George Bush Senior the setting up of a 'Soviet-American condominium', since the USSR and US are simply 'doomed to dialogue, coordination and cooperation. There is no other choice.'[9]

In one important respect, the cold war was therefore a 'credible but ultimately failed Soviet challenge to U.S. hegemony' or to be more precise, a challenge by communism to Western values and systems.[10] The end of the cold war inevitably entailed the disappearance of the Soviet challenge to the West. As far as the West was concerned, the cold war was, in the main, a hell of a waiting game. While it did not necessarily require the collapse of the Soviet Union (which came at the end of 1991), this did contribute significantly to the finale of the cold war.

The cold war was not like the conventional wars that had been fought between the great powers before 1945, but nonetheless it was a global contest and a sort of war. The cold war shared many of the characteristics of modern warfare – ideological differences, large numbers of weapons, war plans, operational manuals, covert operations, psychological warfare, proxy and often bloody battles in the Third World, the formation of alliances, economic and trade pressures and the control of society – but the cold war thankfully did not end in the apocalyptic phase of the third world war by nuclear destruction.[11]

There is no consensus yet amongst scholars and policy-makers as to the prescribed requirements for the end of the cold war or as to the exact timing of that end. Geographically speaking, Europe, as the first theatre of the cold war, was affected most by its end, but many of the regional conflicts in which the superpowers engaged were not necessarily resolved and, more often, conflict continued or recurred. We hope that there will be no more nuclear stand-offs between the great powers, but nuclear weapons after the cold war were scattered around the new Soviet successor states and beyond. The infrastructure of governments that participated in the cold war in a major way has not yet been transformed into a new model suitable for a post-cold war world. Donald Rumsfeld, the US Defense Secretary, recently claimed that the current American armed forces 'resemble nothing so much as a smaller version of their cold war selves, in many ways improved but hardly "transformed"'.[12] The attacks of 9/11 prompted the need for change, but the implementation of detailed and sweeping changes have become the main task, albeit recently faltering, of the second Bush administration. The shadow of the cold war has been a long and enduring one.

the literature of the cold war

Historians argue that a proper understanding and a dispassionate analysis of the past is essential if one is to make sense of contemporary realities – this is as true of international history as it is of any field of historical inquiry. Inevitably, historians are human beings, and their approach to their subject will be coloured as much by subjective factors (such as cultural background, political views, religious beliefs and nationality) as by an objective interest in interpreting past events and understanding them on their own terms. The conscientious historian seeks to avoid the mental trap set by hindsight, and he or she will try to understand the collective mentality (what Germans refer to as the *Zeitgeist*) of the society, state or civilisation they are studying. This approach is as applicable to medieval scholars seeking to explain why from the eleventh to the fourteenth centuries Europeans waged crusades to recover the Holy Land, as it is to their counterparts who debate why it was that American policy-makers in the 1950s and 1960s decided that a communist-led insurgency in a small, South-East Asian country had serious implications for the national security of the USA.

Throughout the past half-century or so the centre of cold war scholarship has been the United States. This partly reflects of the USA's pivotal role in world affairs since 1945 – for better or for worse, American foreign policy decisions have had profound consequences for millions worldwide. The USA played a vital role in defeating the Axis powers in the Second World War, and, with the decline of both the British and Soviet empires its status as a 'hyperpower' (the phrase coined by Hubert Vedrine, the former French Foreign Minister) remains unchallenged. American traditions of open government, press freedom and greater access to official sources (such as the US State Department's publication of its *Foreign Relations of the United States* series) also fuelled academic research into the history of the cold war. The US system was until recently far more liberal than that of its closest West European ally, Britain. For example, in the field of intelligence history, the work done by the 1975 Congressional investigations chaired by Representative Otis Pike and Senator Frank Church did much to put in the public domain information and material on the organisation and operations of US intelligence agencies. In contrast, until the early 1990s the British government denied the existence of either the Secret Intelligence Service (SIS) or the Cabinet Office's Joint Intelligence Committee (JIC), despite clear evidence suggesting otherwise.[13]

When one analyses the historiography of the cold war, it becomes clear that the first studies and debates are American in origin.[14] This is particularly evident in the emergence of the 'orthodox' school of historians in the late 1940s to early 1950s. As noted above, conscientious historians aim to be as dispassionate as possible, but scholarly impartiality is impossible to achieve, and personal political and cultural attitudes and opinions will inevitably shape a historian's work. In this respect, orthodox scholars echoed the US government's mindset, reflecting the 'cold war consensus' that bound American society during this time. They argued that the cold war was caused by Stalin's ideological hostility towards the West and his objective of advancing the cause of world communism. After the Allied victory in 1945, the Soviets spurned US attempts to establish a working relationship with the USSR, opting instead for a foreign policy based upon spreading communism globally. Stalin violated the spirit of the Yalta accords by imposing communist regimes on the East European states. The USA therefore rallied other Western powers in order to 'contain' the expansion of Soviet and (after 1949) Chinese influence. This argument was also expressed in the memoirs written by US officials in retirement. It should be noted that the orthodox scholars were in many respects fighting the cold war in the intellectual sphere. While it would be unfair to portray the orthodox school as the mouthpiece of the administrations of Harry S. Truman and Dwight D. Eisenhower, their views dovetailed with official pronouncements by Washington. Indeed, one of its leading figures, Herbert Feis, was a former State Department official.[15]

In an intellectual climate threatened by Senator Joseph McCarthy's demagogy and the activities of the House Un-American Affairs Committee (HUAC), there were initially very few individuals prepared to question the orthodox thesis.[16] However, a 'revisionist' antithesis to the orthodox school gradually emerged, and historians generally cite the publication of William Appelman Williams' *The Tragedy of American Diplomacy* in 1959 as the point of origin for cold war revisionism. Williams and other revisionists – notably Gar Alperovitz, Lloyd C. Gardner, Gabriel Kolko and Thomas G. Patterson – turned the issue of responsibility for the cause and continuation of the cold war on its head, attributing both not to Soviet expansionism in Europe and Asia, but to American efforts to establish US global economic hegemony. Revisionists generally argued that it was the USA's greed for overseas markets – combined, according to some, with its nuclear monopoly – which forced Stalin to communise Eastern Europe. The establishment of communist rule of Eastern Europe and Moscow's support for revolutionary movements (such as the Chinese Communist Party) was therefore a response to the USA's economic expansionism. In the same way that orthodox scholarship reflected the cold war consensus of the 1940s and 1950s, revisionism was influenced by developments in American foreign policy and social affairs – notably the Vietnam war and the civil rights struggle – that challenged both the assumption that the US system was morally superior, and the view that American foreign policy was inherently benign.[17]

The 1970s saw the emergence of the 'post-revisionist' school. Developments such as the Sino-Soviet split the previous decade undermined the image of a monolithic communist bloc, and showed how tensions between Moscow and Beijing had affected Sino-Soviet relations as far back as the late 1940s. Furthermore, greater access to archival sources revealed the extent to which both orthodox and revisionist scholars had allowed their political viewpoints to shape their work – Robert James Maddox lambasted Alperovitz, Kolko and other like-minded historians for what he regarded as sloppy scholarship and distortions of the documentary record.[18] Post-revisionist scholars like John Lewis Gaddis, Walter LaFeber and Melvyn P. Leffler differed in their assessments on the role played by the respective superpowers in provoking the cold war, but they collectively offered an approach to the study of East–West relations which was more nuanced and better documented than their orthodox and revisionist predecessors.[19] They were also less ethno-centric than their predecessors, and took account of the growth of cold war scholarship worldwide, fuelled by the opening of government papers in Western Europe. In Britain's case, the release of documents dating from the late 1940s, permitted by the 'Thirty Year Rule', allowed scholars to discuss and debate Britain's role in the cold war, drawing attention to the Labour government's role in encouraging US economic, diplomatic and military engagement in Europe (manifested by the Marshall Plan and the North Atlantic Treaty), and the UK's collaboration with the American-led policy of 'containment'.[20] Studies of West European responses to the cold war demonstrated that the USA's alliance partners were not passive actors, and that the West Europeans actively sought US intervention in continental affairs, under a process which Geir Lundestad has dubbed 'empire by invitation'. Furthermore, research based upon Western European archival materials revealed important differences between US and European approaches to relations with the Eastern bloc during the course of the cold war – particularly regarding commercial contacts with communist powers, the German question, the development of NATO and military strategy, and also the conduct of East–West *détente* (notably Willy Brandt's approach to *Ostpolitik*).[21]

Orthodox and revisionist scholars in America had clashed over the issue of American (or Soviet) culpability in causing the cold war, and this debate continues to re-emerge in various guises.[22] Needless to say, there was no analogous controversy in Soviet historiography where – until the advent of *glasnost* in the late 1980s – the parameters of academic research were firmly policed by the ruling Communist Party (CPSU). Soviet historians therefore blamed the aggressive US 'imperialists' and their lackeys for the onset and the continuation of East–West animosity. Certain aspects of Soviet foreign affairs (such as the Molotov–Ribbentrop Pact of 1939 and the invasion of Afghanistan 40 years later) were taboo, and it is not surprising that the standard text on Soviet foreign policy was published under the names of Andrei Gromyko, the USSR's Foreign Minister from 1957 to 1987, and Boris Ponomarëv, the former head of the CPSU's International Department.[23] Power struggles in the Kremlin often required an amendment to the textbooks (as demonstrated by the downfall of Nikita Khrushchev in October 1964 and his subsequent status as an 'unperson'), while the PRC's transition from ally to adversary during the 1960s had its own implications for Soviet historiography. However, there was essentially little development in Soviet and East European scholarship until the latter stages of the Gorbachev era. Even during *glasnost*, however, Soviet scholars challenging the party line did so in the face of bitter resistance from the establishment. For example, General Dmitri Volkogonov's biography of Stalin aroused the fury of fellow senior officers because of its frank portrayal of the USSR's military performance in the first months of its war with Nazi Germany.[24] As far as Eastern Europe was concerned, Polish historians were not free to study the Katyn massacre or the Warsaw rising of 1944, and the same was true for Hungarian scholars and the revolution of 1956.

Following the East European revolutions of 1989 and the fall of the Soviet Union in 1991, formerly inaccessible archival collections in the now defunct Warsaw Pact were opened to scholars. As a result, cold war scholars now have a greater understanding of how developments in East–West relations were seen on 'the other side of the hill'.[25] Despite the collapse of communism, there are still remaining barriers to academic research. In Russia, for example, the Russian Presidential and KGB archives are closed to scholars, although the archives of former Soviet republics can be less restrictive. Historians have also used Soviet documents found in East European archives as a means of circumventing Moscow's official secrecy. Even though communist regimes still hold power in Havana, Beijing and Hanoi, some Cuban, Chinese and Vietnamese sources have been made available to researchers. In this respect, the study of international history has benefited enormously from the work of 'new cold war' historians, Russian and East European scholars, and research bodies such as the *Cold War International History Project* and the *Parallel History Project* on NATO and the Warsaw Pact.[26] To give two examples, historians now have an enhanced understanding of the factors which encouraged China to intervene in the Korean war in 1953, and Cuba to send troops to fight in the Angolan civil war in 1975. In the former case, it is clear that Mao Zedong was influenced both by ideological concerns (including the objective of spreading revolution in East Asia, and of saving a fellow communist state) as well as more traditional national security interests (preventing the Americans from establishing a military presence on China's north-eastern border). Washington assumed that the Cuban intervention in Angola in 1975 was prompted by the Soviets, as this fitted in to the American perception that Cuba was the USSR's proxy. In fact, Fidel Castro had his own motives for assisting the MPLA regime in Luanda, and he made his decision to send troops to Angola without consulting Moscow.[27]

It should, however, be borne in mind that in certain cases access to former Eastern bloc archival materials has served to confirm, rather than challenge, existing interpretations of the policies followed by communist powers. There are few surprises, for example, to be found in Eastern bloc documents concerning the reasons underlying the USSR's suppression of the Hungarian revolution in 1956, the Warsaw Pact intervention in Czechoslovakia in 1968 or the Soviet invasion of Afghanistan in 1979. Furthermore, it should not be assumed that the fall of communism has led to an open house in Western – let alone in Russian and East European – archives. Richard Aldrich reminds us that '[historians] are what they eat', and that their 'diet' of documents is influenced by governments on both sides of the old iron curtain, who can control the release of documents. When British documents dealing with the Suez crisis were released to the public in 1987, scholars discovered that during the late 1950s civil servants had destroyed large numbers of files pertaining to the conflict.[28]

Above all, while recent disclosures shed light on the intentions and attitudes of decision-makers in Washington, Moscow, Beijing and elsewhere throughout the cold war (as opposed to how these were viewed by their adversaries), it is important to avoid the mental trap that hindsight sets for historians. Contemporary perceptions do count, even if they are misconceived, because they shape the making of policy. For example, at the conclusion of the Yom Kippur war of 1973 the Soviet leader, Leonid Brezhnev, used the hot-line to Washington to demand that the USA should force its ally, Israel, to respect the UN ceasefire resolution passed on 21 October. However, the US Secretary of State, Henry Kissinger, concluded that the Soviets were preparing for a unilateral military intervention in the Middle East, and he ordered that US armed forces – including nuclear forces – should be placed on a higher state of alert.[29] During the fall of 1979 Brezhnev and his peers became convinced that Hafizollah Amin, the pro-Soviet President of Afghanistan, was about to break ties with the USSR and align with the Americans. It was this conviction – combined with the objective of defending the communist regime in Kabul against internal revolt – which lead to Soviet military intervention in Afghanistan in December 1979. Both cases show that leaders and senior decision-makers could completely misinterpret the intentions of their adversaries or even their allies. Kissinger's actions at the end of the Yom Kippur war contributed to the decline of superpower *détente*, while the Kremlin's impression of Amin's treachery was a significant factor influencing Moscow's disastrous decision to intervene in the Afghan civil war.[30]

Over the past two decades, the parameters of cold war history have been widened, not only in terms of accessibility of sources, but also in its scope. The revisionists can be thanked for drawing attention to the economic dimensions of the struggle between communism and capitalism, although their conclusions have proved to be contentious. Intelligence has been aptly termed 'the missing dimension' of international history, and its study forms a crucial part of our understanding of the cold war. Both sides devoted considerable effort and resources to espionage directed against hostile – and also friendly – powers. In recent years scholars have taken advantage of 'open government' initiatives (for example, the Freedom of Information Act in both America and the Waldegrave initiative in Britain) to analyse the role of secret intelligence in East–West relations.[31] There is also a growing body of work on the social and cultural aspects of the cold war, and in particular to the interaction between governments and intellectuals on both sides of the iron curtain. The cold war was, in essence, a conflict of ideas, and both Eastern and Western governments sought to persuade their citizens, and other societies, that their way of life was economically, socially, intellectually and ethically superior.[32]

Above all, cold war historiography now encompasses not only the East–West aspect of international history, but the interaction between the rich, developed 'North' and the poor, post-colonial 'South'. The now-familiar concept of a 'Third World' derived from the conflict of interests between the capitalist 'First' and communist 'Second' worlds. It goes without saying that an African or Asian perspective on the cold war often differed sharply from that of an American or a European. For example, when the US Senator Jesse Helms visited the UN Security Council in January 2000 he angered the Namibian delegate, Martin Andjaba, by praising Ronald Reagan's role in spreading freedom and democracy worldwide. The Namibian asserted that throughout his presidency Reagan had implicitly supported the South African *apartheid* regime and had classed the South-West African Peoples' Organisation – which fought for Namibia's independence against Pretoria during the 1980s – as a 'terrorist' movement.[33] Andjaba's rebuke to Helms reminds us that the intervention of the superpowers and their respective allies in Third World conflicts often had a drastic effect on peoples whose awareness – and interest – in East–West rivalry was minimal. The impact of the Arab–Israeli conflict on the cold war demonstrated how local feuds and parochial rivalries could become enmeshed with wider international political disputes. The civil wars in Angola and Afghanistan have outlasted the state of East–West competition and the external interventions which had fuelled and exacerbated them, with calamitous humanitarian results. In Afghanistan's case, the consequences of ongoing conflict, state collapse and international neglect were felt in the streets of New York and Washington on 11 September 2001.

the themes of the book

The cold war has ended and has become history. The aim of this book is to introduce readers to a historiographical overview of the recent works and interpretive discussions of the key concepts of, and approaches to, the study of the cold war. Given the proximity to the contemporary world, the concepts, which will be analysed in this book, could also be of relevance to the understanding of contemporary international relations.

The conventional wisdom about the international system was that a bipolar system would be less stable than a multipolar one. However, the cold war, dominated as it was by the bipolar structure, brought a level of stability in the form of the 'long peace', a term coined by John Lewis Gaddis. There were no industrialised wars between developed societies during the cold war, but this was by no means a foregone conclusion. Indeed, many felt that during the Berlin crisis of 1948–49, the third world war was on its way, and in 1950, Arnold Toynbee stated that 'today it is already apparent that the war of 1939–45 was not the climax of this crescendo movement'.[34] In retrospect, the cold war period seems to have demonstrated that a bipolar structure was preferable to a multipolar one, although the stability of the international system during the period would depend on many other factors, and especially on how one interprets the role of nuclear deterrence, which encouraged both blocs (East and West) to concentrate on their own security and interests. Having said this, the bipolar system was not always stable during the cold war, and some scholars suggest that by the 1970s the world had become multipolar. The economic rise of Western Europe and of East Asia during the 1970s meant that these regional actors were able to play crucial roles in international trade and finance, although the manner in which the cold war ended suggests that the bipolar system led by the superpowers, remained robust, or at least Moscow felt that the Soviet Union and the United States would need to cooperate with each other in order to end the lengthy war. Wolfgang Krieger examines the relationship between the cold war and the international system. His chapter discusses extensively how other international factors – such as economic, cultural and social changes, and the role of the UN – had influenced, and had been influenced by, the cold war.

The concepts of national security and national interests are increasingly seen as obsolete or inadequate tools to understand contemporary international affairs. In the wider domain, however, the cold war dominated thinking about security and national interests, but it is also true that during the cold war the concept of national security was expanded and contributed to the contemporary understanding of 'security' in a wider sense. Jussi Hanhimäki discusses the validity and the limitations of these concepts in understanding the cold war, but he also stresses the more complex nature of these concepts in relation to 'power'. National security and national interests are by no means static, or accepted by all actors as a matter of course. Even within the alliance, East or West, the method of achieving them differed from one to another. Moreover, allied interests and allied security were not necessarily compatible with their own national interests. Hanhimäki reminds us of the importance of noting the interactions of national interest with other factors, globalisation, local interests and culture.

Cold war scholars increasingly attach greater importance to the analysis of ideology in explaining the subtlety of the cold war. How far did the ideological differences between communism and liberal capitalism play a part in promoting the East–West confrontation? Leopoldo Nuti and Vladislav Zubok jointly explain the subject as seen from the East and the West. Ideology was not only a theoretical tool to mobilise the masses and to give justification to what could otherwise be seen to be unjust and illegitimate, but ideology was also used to create a mindset to a better understanding of societies and the structures surrounding them. All in all, ideology can be understood to give a meaning to the international system during the cold war and could work as a driving factor, on its own, in creating the dynamics of the East–West confrontation.

The cold war is also known as a period of alliances. While the East–West confrontation widened in scope, and increased the danger of a superpower nuclear showdown, there emerged the need to assemble resources and brains, and produce some kind of team work. There is the traditional view that states do align with each other in the face of a commonly perceived threat. There is also a concept that states with common characteristics, such as liberal democracies, will naturally combine. Lawrence Kaplan's chapter on alliances examines how NATO and the Warsaw Pact emerged, and the internal tensions within the alliance systems. Equally important was the Sino-Soviet alliance, and other less prominent, but worth remembering, alliances, such as SEATO and CENTO. This chapter explains that cold war alliances were by no means a blueprint for victory, and in some cases, the differing interests of their signatories were skilfully suppressed under the name of the alliance. NATO, however, stands out as the first among equals in terms of its longevity, flexibility, and for what it had accomplished during the cold war, and Kaplan explains why.

The concept of strategy is another important component of the framework of the cold war, not least because the development of nuclear weapons called for a radical revision of strategic thinking. Lawrence Freedman and Geraint Hughes analyse how the traditional concept of strategy was revised, and applied, to the cold war period by tracing the development of such concepts in the USA, as 'deterrence', 'mutual assured destruction', 'second-strike' capabilities, and 'limited war'. Similarly this chapter examines Soviet defence policy and strategies, and how Moscow's military doctrines affected the Warsaw Pact plans for countering NATO. Much ink was spilt over nuclear strategy, and the cold war produced many armchair strategists, some of whom worked closely with governments. This chapter asks how much these strategists did in fact influence the deliberations of official government policies.

Economics had also an important dimension in the cold war. Gorbachev was keen to integrate the Soviet economy closely into the Western-led economic order. During a meeting with Gorbachev in April 1987, US Secretary of State George Shultz (a former professor of economics) stated that 'There are big changes going on in the world economy. ... The central feature is the great growth of the global economy: a general rise in GNP, gigantic expansion in goods and services, a huge increase in trade flows.' Gorbachev listened to the American economist with great interest.[35] Often submerged in the political and diplomatic considerations of the cold war, the economic origins of the cold war were signified by the Marshall Plan. Ian Jackson discusses the differing approaches to the post-war economic order by Moscow and Washington. Within the West, East–West trade was the area where Western Europe and the USA clearly disagreed over the extent of restrictions of trade with the communist bloc. The Europeans wanted more trade with the Eastern bloc than their

American counterparts, as they also believed that East–West trade would help to improve relations between the two blocs. In Washington, the Nixon administration wanted to improve economic relations in the context of *détente*, but Congress remained reluctant to approve any relaxation of trade with the Eastern bloc. Jackson concludes that the fall of the Soviet Union was the result of the shortcomings of its command economy rather than the West's pressure on the Soviet economy. Similarly Christoph Bluth explores the development of the military-industrial complex and its impact in the USSR and the USA, and gives an account of the role of science and technology in the East–West global conflict. This chapter also examines the manner in which technological progress affected the military competition between the superpowers.

Until recently, official secrecy and the lack of material was such that the role of intelligence in international politics was barely studied. Richard Aldrich's chapter on intelligence explains how the history of intelligence has developed in recent years, although it remains hard to explain the exact impact of information on the actual formulation of foreign policy. It is no surprise that a great number of covert operations and secret activities took place during the cold war years. Aldrich's *tour de force* about covert operations and intelligence gathering demonstrates how much effort went into trying to know the enemy, while both sides wished to secure 'plausible deniability'.

The cold war was also concerned with cultural diplomacy, state–private networks, propaganda and popular cultures. The growth of information technology and the diversification of societies ranging from those once imperial states in Europe to newly developing countries in the Third World meant that a cold war culture could easily find its way into the lives of the masses in the form of novels, films and journal articles. Patrick Major and Rana Mitter deal with the 'war of words' and the propaganda conflict between East and West, and the role played by the intelligentsia. Indeed, American cultural projection was not just against the enemy bloc, but also against vulnerable Western European audiences, who might otherwise not enthusiastically embrace American leadership in the post-war world. This chapter also indicates an extent of Western cultural penetration across the iron curtain, resulting in a positive image of Western freedom which developed in the minds of Soviet and East European citizens.

The final chapter deals with the interaction of the cold war with decolonisation and empire. The United States and the Soviet Union both emerged out of revolution and war as anti-imperialist states, although the superpowers themselves developed different hegemonic approaches to their clients states or allies during the cold war. John Kent argues, however, that the Second World War applied significant pressure on the European imperial powers to relinquish their colonies, and he also discusses how the cold war resulted in the USA cooperating with the former imperial powers in order to preserve the solidarity of the Western alliance against the communist onslaught. In this process Britain and France found themselves able to manage the decline of their military power by cooperating with the USA in the Western strategy of containment. The cold war tells us something about the difficulties in the exercise of hegemony over other states in the post-war world. Stalin quickly formed an 'empire by coercion' often with the help of the Red Army, and it was ruled carefully, but ruthlessly, by the Kremlin. The end of the cold war demonstrated how quickly such an coercive empire could collapse as soon as coercion was removed by *perestroika* and *glasnost* and by the renunciation of the Brezhnev doctrine. Decolonisation had opened the way for competition between the superpowers for prestige and influence, but many conflicts in the Third World, where superpowers often acted as patrons of their favoured factions, were left unresolved (such as in Angola and Afghanistan) by the time the superpowers decided to disengage from them in favour of ending the cold war. The European model of Empires were not to be repeated in the cold war, but this did not necessarily smooth the path of the newly emerging countries towards a stable and peaceful statehood.

Overall the book deals with ten key themes relevant to the cold war. These should encourage readers to widen and deepen their interest in the recent past, a period called the cold war.

notes

1. Gorbachev–Najjib (Afghan communist leader), 20 July 1987, Cold War International History Project (CWIHP), Woodrow Wilson Center, USA, *Bulletin*, #14/15 (Winter 2003–Spring 2004), pp.146–8.
2. Fraser J. Harbutt, *The Cold War Era* (Oxford: Blackwell, 2002), p.274.
3. 'Kissinger's popularity fading', 17 January 1975, *The Herald of Freedom*, folder, 29/17, Box. 29, Elizabeth Churchill Brown papers, Hoover Institution Archives, Stanford University, USA.
4. 'Review of East European and Communist Chinese Foreign Broadcasts' May 1971, Folder 22 'Communist Foreign Broadcasting', Box 162, Radio Free Europe (RFE) and Radio Liberty (RL) Corporate Records, Hoover Institution Archives, Stanford University, USA; Paul Maddrell, 'What we have Discovered about the Cold War is what we Already Knew: Julius Mader and the Western Secret Services during the Cold War', *Cold War History*, 5:2 (May 2005), pp.235–58.

5. Tomasz Goban-Klas & Pål Kolstø, 'East European Mass Media: The Soviet Role', in Arne Odd Westad, Sven Holtsmark & Iver B. Neumann (eds), *The Soviet Union in Eastern Europe 1945–89* (Basingstoke: Macmillan, 1994), pp.126–33.
6. Dillon Anderson, 'Recollection of Eisenhower', p.11, Box 1, Dillon Anderson papers, Hoover Institution Archives, Stanford University, USA.
7. Beatrice Heuser, 'Victory in a Nuclear War? A Comparison of NATO and WTO War Aims and Strategies', *Contemporary European History*, 7:3 (1998), p.312; Peter Hennessy, *The Secret State: Whitehall and the Cold War* (London: Allen Lane, The Penguin Press, 2002), p.5.
8. 'East Germany Spy Reports Reveal NATO War Plans', 6 November 2003, *Security Watch*, <http://www.isn.ethz.ch> (accessed 18 November 2003).
9. The Malta Summit, December 1989, *CWIHP Bulletin*, #12/13 (Winter 2001–Spring 2002), p.233.
10. William C. Wohlforth, 'Realism and the End of the Cold War', *International Security*, 19 (Winter 1994/95), p.97.
11. John W. Young, *America, Russia and the Cold War, 1941–1998* (London: Longman, 1999), p.242.
12. Thomas Donnelly, 'Rebasing, Revisited', *National Security Outlook* (December 2004).
13. Christopher Andrew, 'Whitehall, Washington and the Intelligence Services', *International Affairs*, 53:3 (1977), pp.390–404. See also the comments made by the JIC Chairman, Sir Geoffrey Arthur, at JIC(A)(73)36th meeting, 20.9.73, in CAB185/13 (The National Archives, Kew, UK).
14. Martin McCauley, *The Origins of the Cold War 1941–1949* (London: Longman, 1995); Jussi Hanhimäki & Odd Arne Westad (eds), *The Cold War: A History in Documents and Eyewitness Accounts* (New York & Oxford: Oxford University Press, 2003).
15. Feis wrote several books, of which *Churchill–Roosevelt–Stalin: The War they Waged and the Peace they Sought* (Princeton, NJ: Princeton University Press, 1957) and *From Trust to Terror* (New York: W.W. Norton, 1970) are representative of his work. The 'orthodox' view is also expressed in Truman's memoirs, *Years of Decisions* (New York: Doubleday, 1955) and *Years of Trial and Hope* (New York: Doubleday, 1956).
16. It should be noted that McCarthyism did not lead to the complete suppression of critiques of US foreign policy. See, for example, I.F. Stone's *Hidden History of the Korean War* (New York: Monthly Review Press, 1952).
17. For the revisionist school, see Gar Alperovitz, *Atomic Diplomacy: Hiroshima and Potsdam, the use of the Atomic Bomb and the American Confrontation with Soviet Power* (New York: Vintage Books, 1967); Lloyd C. Gardner, *Architects of Illusion: Men and Ideas in American Foreign Policy, 1941–1949* (Chicago, IL: Quadrangle, 1970); Gabriel Kolko, *The Politics of War* (London: Weidenfeld & Nicolson, 1968); Thomas G. Paterson, *Soviet–American Confrontation* (Baltimore, MD: Johns Hopkins University Press, 1973); William A. Williams, *The Tragedy of American Diplomacy* (New York: Delta Books, 1962, revised edition).
18. Robert James Maddox, *The New Left and the Origins of the Cold War* (Princeton, NJ: Princeton University Press, 1973).
19. Three good examples of 'post-revisionist' scholarship are John Lewis Gaddis, *The United States and the Origins of the Cold War, 1941–1947* (New York: Columbia University Press, 1972); Walter LaFeber, *America, Russia and the*

Cold War 1945–1990 (New York: McGraw Hill, 1991, 6th edition); and Melvyn P. Leffler, *A Preponderance of Power: National Security, the Truman Administration and the Cold War* (Stanford, CA: Stanford University Press, 1992).

20. On the British government's Thirty Year Rule, see Richard Crossman, *Diaries of a Cabinet Minister.* Volume I: *Minister of Housing* (Crossman, I) (London: Hamish Hamilton, 1975), 5.8.65, pp.303–4.

21. Geir Lundestad, 'Empire by Invitation?: The United States and Western Europe', *Journal of Peace Research*, 23:3 (1986), pp.263–77. The late 1980s to early 1990s saw an expansion in West European scholarship on the cold war. See, for example, Saki Dockrill, *Britain's Policy for West German Rearmament, 1950–1955* (Cambridge: Cambridge University Press, 1991); John Kent, *British Imperial Strategy and the Origins of the Cold War* (New York & Leicester: Leicester University Press, 1993); Wolfgang Krieger, *General Lucius D. Clay und die amerikanische Deutschlandpolitik* (Stuttgart: Klett-Cotta, 1987); Wilfried Loth, *De Gaulle, Deutschland und Europa* (Opladen: Leske & Budrich, 1991); Pierre Melandri, *Incertaine alliance: Les Etas-Unis et l'Europe 1973–1983* (Paris: Publications de la Sorbonne, 1988); and John W. Young, *France, the Cold War and the Western Alliance, 1944–49* (New York & Leicester: Leicester University Press, 1990). A mere footnote is insufficient to summarise the scope of West European scholarship on the cold war at the time of writing. Nonetheless, works such as William Glenn Gray, *Germany's Cold War: The Global Campaign to Isolate East Germany* (Chapel Hill, NC: University of North Carolina Press, 2003); Ian Jackson, *The Economic Cold War: America, Britain and East–West Trade 1948–1963* (Basingstoke: Palgrave Macmillan, 2001); Klaus Larres & Elizabeth Meehan (eds), *Uneasy Allies: British–German Relations and European Integration since 1945* (New York & Oxford: Oxford University Press, 2000); Effie Pedaliu, *Britain, Italy and the Origins of the Cold War* (Basingstoke: Palgrave Macmillan, 2003); and Georges-Henri Soutou, *L'alliance incertaine: Les rapport politico-stratégiques Franco-allemands, 1954–1996* (Paris: Fayard, 1996) can give the reader an idea of the extensive coverage given to transatlantic, East–West and inter-European relations in the cold war period.

22. See, for example, Michael Cox & Caroline Kennedy-Pipe, 'The Tragedy of American Diplomacy? Rethinking the Marshall Plan' and the responses by various scholars in the *Journal of Cold War Studies*, 7:1 (2005).

23. Andrei Gromyko & Boris Ponomarëv, *Istorii a Vneshnei Politiki SSSR: 1917–1985* (Moscow: Nauka, 1985). This work went through a series of editions. An English-language version, *Soviet Foreign Policy 1917–1980*, was produced by Progress Publishers, Moscow, in 1981.

24. Sergei Goncharenko, 'Sino-Soviet Military Co-operation', in Odd Arne Westad (ed.), *Brothers in Arms: The Rise and Fall of the Sino-Soviet Alliance 1945–63* (Stanford, CA: Stanford University Press, 2000), pp.141–2. On Volkogonov's treatment by the officer corps, see David Remnick, *Lenin's Tomb: The Last Days of the Soviet Empire* (London: Penguin, 1994), pp.401–11. His biography of Stalin, *Triumf i Tragediya* (*Triumph and Tragedy*) was published in English by Weidenfeld & Nicolson in 1991.

25. See, for example, M.E. Sarotte, *Dealing with the Devil: East Germany, Detente, and Ostpolitik, 1969–1973* (Chapel Hill, NC: University of North Carolina Press, 2001).

26. The *Cold War International History Project* and the *Parallel History Project* are both online at <http://wwics.si.edu/> and <http://www.isn.ethz.ch/php/>. The CWIHP publishes working papers and other research work from Russian, East European, Chinese and Vietnamese scholars. See also Jaromir Navratil et al., *The Prague Spring 1968* (Budapest: Central European University (CEU) Press, 1998). Qiang Zhai, *China and the Vietnam Wars, 1950–1975* (Chapel Hill, NC: University of North Carolina Press, 2000); Sarotte, *Dealing with the Devil*; and Westad, *Brothers in Arms, passim*, for good examples of 'new cold war history'.

27. See Chen Jian, *China's Road to the Korean War: The Making of the Sino-American Confrontation* (New York: Columbia University Press, 1994); and Piero Gleijeses, *Conflicting Missions: Havana, Washington, and Africa, 1959–1976* (Chapel Hill, NC: University of North Carolina Press, 2002).

28. Richard Aldrich, *The Hidden Hand: Britain, America and Cold War Secret Intelligence* (London: John Murray, 2002), p.6; Keith Kyle, *Suez: Britain's End of Empire in the Middle East* (London: I.B. Tauris, 2003), pp.3–4.

29. On the 1973 nuclear alert, see Richard Ned Lebow & Janice Gross Stein, *We All Lost the Cold War* (Princeton, NJ: Princeton University Press, 1994), pp.230–49; Jussi Hanhimäki, *Flawed Architect: Henry Kissinger and American Foreign Policy* (New York: Oxford University Press, 2004), pp.312–16; and Victor Israelyan, *Inside the Kremlin during the Yom Kippur War* (University Park, PA: Pennsylvania State University Press, 1995), pp.181–3.

30. Odd Arne Westad, 'Concerning the Situation in "A": New Evidence on the Soviet Intervention in Afghanistan', *CWIHP Bulletin*, 8–9, pp.128–32; William Maley, *The Afghanistan Wars* (London: Palgrave Macmillan, 2002), pp.30–6.

31. Christopher Andrew & David Dilks (eds), *The Missing Dimension: Governments and Intelligence Communities in the Twentieth Century* (London: Macmillan, 1984), p.1. For a historiographical survey of cold war intelligence history, see Raymond Garthoff, 'Foreign Intelligence and the Historiography of the Cold War', *Journal of Cold War Studies*, 6:2 (2004), pp.21–56.

32. See, for example, Frances Stonor Saunders, *Who Paid the Piper? The CIA and the Cultural Cold War* (London: Granta, 1999); the special issue of *Cold War History*, 'Across the Blocs: Cold War Cultural and Social History', 4:1 (2003), edited by Patrick Major & Rana Mitter; and Jeremi Suri, *Power and Protest: Global Revolution and the Rise of Détente* (Cambridge, MA: Harvard University Press, 2003).

33. Barbara Crossette, 'Helms, in Visit to UN, Offers Harsh Message', *New York Times*, 21 January 2000.

34. John Mueller, *The Remnants of War* (Ithaca & London: Cornell University Press, 2004), p.80.

35. George P. Shultz, *Turmoil and Triumph: Diplomacy, Power, and the Victory of the American ideal* (New York: Charles Scribner's Sons, 1993), p.892.

1

the international system

wolfgang krieger

How did the international system change during the cold war? How can this change be assessed within its broader chronological context? In other words, how does this change compare with what happened before and after? And what exactly do we mean by the phrase 'international system'? These are the broad questions which will be examined in this chapter. By mixing thematic approaches with chronological ones, this chapter will focus mainly on issues of political order and of international conflict, although economic, technological and intellectual aspects will at least be touched upon. After all, the cold war was a global struggle for power which impacted on many different spheres of public life.

As we shall see, the term 'cold war' is woefully imprecise, inviting a wide range of interpretations as to its chronology, content and historical significance. Neither is the term 'international system' one which can be used without putting into question a whole range of more or less explicit assumptions which underlie both its colloquial and academic use. Thus our overall question cannot be discussed profitably without referring to public as well as scholarly debates concerning these two terms. Anything less would result in a simple enumeration of events, institutions, norms and practices along the lines of a reference work. The purpose of this chapter, however, is not factual completeness. It is rather to contribute to an understanding of the world we live in and the extent to which it can (or cannot) be explained by historical reflection.

On re-reading many of the 'classics' of cold war history and of political science (particularly those on the subject of international relations), one cannot fail to note how often scholarship itself was an instrument of cold war politics. This is no surprise since the cold war was, among many other things, a battle over concepts for ordering political life both at a national and at a global level. To put it briefly, ideas and perceptions mattered. Obviously, the proponents of Soviet communism wished for a different international order from the believers in liberal capitalism. When interpreting a particular event or structural problem of the international system one could hardly come to a conclusion without departing from a particular set of values. In turn those interpretations would often make assumptions about the future. How would the cold war develop? How would it end? Whose judgements were right? Whose were not?

Therefore the history of the cold war can readily be understood as a series of more or less false predictions of how world affairs would develop. This is true both at the intellectual and at the operational level. The diplomatic and military documents of the early post-war years are filled with gloomy expectations that major war was 'inevitable' within a short time frame. Neither Western leaders nor their contemporaries on the Eastern side could really believe that a period retrospectively called the 'long peace' had begun. They were too preoccupied with their recent historical experience, their thinking was too much shaped by the era of the two world wars to believe otherwise.[1]

Some years later, as the great powers armed themselves with ever more tanks, warships, aircraft, nuclear weapons and missiles, few people were ready to cast aside the 'old wisdom' that more weapons would make war more likely. During the 1960s, when neither the Soviet system nor Western capitalism looked ready to collapse any time soon, theorists concluded that both were essentially two varieties of modernisation which would become ever more alike over time (this being the so-called 'convergence theory'). Neither of the two propositions on 'convergence' or the inevitability of war turned out to be true. In Germany, most people at first could not believe that their country would be divided for long. Two decades later, from the 1960s onward, most people could not imagine that reunification would ever happen in their own lifetime. Indeed, some scholars claimed to have scientific proof that it would never happen, that the international peace order logically required the permanent division of Germany.[2] Neither did many people predict in the late 1950s that the United States would, for four long decades, keep well over 320,000 troops in Europe. By much the same logic most Sovietologists were convinced that Soviet military forces would forever stay where they had once pitched their tents. (It so happens that the Americans are still in Europe today, while the Soviets/Russians went home over a decade ago.[3]) These are only a few examples of mistaken concepts and forecasts, based undoubtedly on 'solid' historical experience, which at one time or another served as a basis for political decision-making as well as for scholarly analysis. As we all know, the end of the cold war came as a surprise to most governments and indeed to most academics. And neither of them did much better with respect to the post-cold war world.

But if the glass was half empty, it was also half full. Cold war history can also be written as a history of international learning, as a process in which a mixture of prudent calculation and historical experience served to avoid costly mistakes. On both sides of the iron curtain we find examples of crises resolved peacefully by wise statesmanship and by examples of prudent restraint in the use of power. Whether the 'long peace' was a product of the growing wisdom of international decision-makers is a good subject for debate, as is the question whether the exponential growth of international institutions and, more generally, of international economic interdependence (or globalisation) has anything to do with it. International organisations have a decidedly positive aura about them – as one can see from the fast-growing numbers of young professionals who wish to work for them. But, in reality, their place in the history of international relations has not been defined with sufficient precision. We do not yet know, for example, why they have not been more successful in reducing Third World poverty or tribal warfare.[4]

explaining the international system

Providing a definition of the term 'international system' is by no means a purely academic matter. The term 'system' somehow suggests that it functions according to certain rules. But this is hardly true. It merely sums up all the actors as well as all the material and immaterial factors which are somehow relevant to the way in which people, organisations and states relate to each other at a global level – hence the term 'international relations'. However, when we speak of an 'international order' (or 'world order') we mean a 'good', that is to say an accepted way of organising those relations. Thus the term 'order' suggests a value judgement about the way in which international relations should be organised. For example, it is obvious why the USSR and the Western liberal-democratic powers could not agree on a particular world order. Neither side could admit that the political system of its opponent was 'good' and therefore deserved a permanent place in the world. Logically, therefore, the cold war international system could at best be one in which 'stability' existed between the two sides, that is to say in which neither side attempted to overwhelm the other by use of force. By the same logic, stability allowed for crises, local (or 'limited') wars, and the 'balance of terror' (or nuclear deterrence combined with very large non-nuclear forces kept in readiness at all times). How then did this system function? To what extent was it substantially different from the international systems before and after the cold war?

Classical 'realist' theories of international relations, such as those formulated by Hans Morgenthau and Raymond Aron, assume that states are the only actors in that 'system', that their most fundamental interaction is about war and peace, and that anarchy or chaos are better terms to describe world affairs.[5] This view seemed to reflect adequately the world situation during the early cold war years. It came to be challenged as international organisations and non-state actors both proliferated and appeared to gain more weight relative to state power.[6] Marxist as well as some non-Marxist writers considered economic factors to be more important than military ones, while other scholars drew attention to the role of small states.[7] 'Geopolitics', based on concepts espoused back in the nineteenth century, claimed that geography largely determined global power issues. Cultural explanations emphasised the importance of ethnicity, religion, and mentalities.[8] In other words, many felt that 'realism' addressed only a fraction of a much more complicated reality and that it overlooked the importance of cooperation between states, even states with all sorts of conflicts between them.

Although the cold war was obviously about a confrontation between two armed camps of states, it generated a progressively subtle 'game' of political understandings and relationships which forced scholars to adapt their terminology and their concepts. In retrospect, it seems that neither the pessimistic emphasis on war and peace ('realism') nor the optimistic concentration on cooperation and institutions ('institutionalism' or 'liberalism') do justice to the complexity of the issues to be addressed.[9] If some people, at the end of the cold war, expected to see a 'new world order' (George Bush Sr.), managed by 'an alphabet soup of international organisations' (to use Henry Kissinger's cynical phrase), the debates rapidly took another direction after 9/11 and after the third Gulf war of 2003.[10]

The historian of international relations should be aware that terminology and concepts can never quite match the varieties of change in world affairs. His or her preoccupation is to dissect that process of change, beginning perhaps with the three general observations. The first is to understand that new elements are often added to the system without displacing older ones. For example, it is common to argue that since the nineteenth century the nation-state came to be seen as the ideal form of political organisation. But in reality, older forms of organisation – from empires to clans – are still relevant political units in the twenty-first century. To speak of the international system as essentially an assembly of states (the 'Westphalian system', which ostensibly dates from the treaties which concluded the Thirty Years War of 1618–48) is simply wrong. Secondly, we must bear in mind that international actors or familiar concepts such as capitalism or religion may retain their familiar names while changing their content. The same is true for states and other international actors. At the same time certain developments or actors acquire different names while remaining much the same. Today's globalisation, for example, does not differ fundamentally from developments within the world economy during the nineteenth century. One could well argue that financial markets were more internationalised before the First World War than they were during much of the cold war. Thirdly, certain forms or instruments of power in international life undergo changes which are not always taken into account in time, either by the political actors or by the analysts. For example, military power lost its value while economic and technological power became more important. One is even tempted to speak of cultural power when one thinks of the impact of popular culture, of the electronic media, or of such new international concerns as the place of women in society and human rights. In the final years of the cold war, the Soviet Union had more military power and more geographical space under its control than ever before. Yet it lacked the power possessed by the more advanced economies and the more attractive 'global' messages. The Pope in Rome still had no divisions – to paraphrase Stalin – but his message presented a serious challenge to the power of the CPSU in Moscow.

How can we identify those gradual, barely visible changes in international relations? One way is to look at statistics (for example, on population growth, trade or migration). But political decision-makers react only slowly or not at all to such numerical or behavioural changes. If we are to understand their learning processes we need to study those critical moments and decisions which indicate that established practices or concepts have become inadequate. This is obviously the case with international crises such as the Berlin blockade or the Cuban missile crisis. Typically, such crises lead to policy changes or even to the establishment of new international institutions or to new treaties. But there are also those 'quiet revolutions', which take place both inside national societies and between them, which are much harder to document and indeed to understand because they are not related to single political decisions or events. How, for example, does one explain those shifts in mentality which appear to underlie the decrease in religious beliefs or the drop in birth-rates since the 1960s? What exactly explains the lack in military enthusiasm in Japan and Germany after 1945? Or why did so many people, during the 1950s, still believe in Soviet-style socialism when the evidence around them should have been sufficient to dissuade them?

explaining the cold war

What exactly do we mean by 'cold war'? Was it truly a period without 'hot' wars? Many in Western Europe tend to make this assumption because they see a sharp contrast between the era of two world wars and the post-1945 decades. But for people in South-East Asia, in certain parts of Africa, in South Asia or in the Middle East, those same years were filled with wars which destroyed human lives on a scale comparable to the world wars in Europe. China suffered some 65 million dead from its communist experiment.[11] The wars in Korea and Vietnam devastated the populations of both the Korean and Indochinese peninsulas.

Even the beginning of the cold war is a matter of some debate. If we assume it started around 1947, as most scholars do, the cold war appears to have been chiefly about territorial problems left unresolved by the Second World War. If, however, we focus on the ideological side of that great power struggle, we cannot but agree with André Fontaine and other early historians who saw the Bolshevist revolution of 1917 as the true starting point of the East–West conflict in which disputes over territories were only secondary concerns.[12] The most famous early explanation, laid down in the 'long telegram' drafted by George F. Kennan, the *chargé d'affaires* at the US embassy in Moscow, in early 1946. Kennan saw Bolshevist ideology as the main driving force to which the West somehow had to find a prudent response.[13] It was this 'orthodox' assessment of the causes of the cold war which 'revisionist' and leftist historians have sought to challenge from the late 1950s onwards.

For the decades after 1945 there is at least a rudimentary consensus how cold war chronology can be divided into well-defined periods. Few will disagree that the years between 1947 and 1953 marked a particularly 'cold' period, followed by a decade beginning with Stalin's death in March 1953 and lasting to the end of the Cuban missile crisis in late 1962 when major war was believed to be less likely but was still seen as a possibility. At that point a 'bipolar system' of the two superpowers, the Soviet Union and the United States, became dominant. It was characterised by a certain confidence that 'the other side' would do anything it could to avoid nuclear war. Despite the frequent wars on a 'regional' scale, world politics became more stable. Around 1975 a number of important changes occurred which some contemporary observers and political activists at the time saw as the beginning of a 'new cold war'. The superpowers were unable to reach any agreements on arms control, while East–West tensions increased, particularly because of competing interests in the Middle East and in the 'Third World'. Finally, the arrival at the Kremlin of a new leadership in March 1985 marked an entirely new course in Soviet foreign policy which prepared the way for an extraordinary number of international understandings and changes in the international system.[14]

Did the cold war really end in 1991, with the collapse of the Soviet Union in December of that year? In most respects it did, though communism remained in power in China, Vietnam, Cambodia, North Korea and Cuba. But some thinkers believe that the Soviet collapse did not fundamentally change international relations from a global perspective. Noam Chomsky and his followers point to the persistence of the gap between rich and poor (the North–South conflict) and the domination of world affairs by the hegemonic power of the United States, which undoubtedly increased after 1991.[15] For Robert Cox, the predominance of neo-liberalist policies, which in his view forms the overarching paradigm of world affairs, dates back to the 1970s and arrived by way of a more or less 'quiet revolution'.[16] In making his argument Cox obviously puts economic power above military power, a view which runs counter to many classical texts on the international system.

The cold war may be over, but we still feel its legacies almost daily. Therefore we still have a big stake in how the cold war is viewed. In turn this makes it both particularly hard to analyse it and particularly important to do so in a critical fashion, that is without being glued to scholarly dogma or established terminology. Perhaps some of the key differences in viewing the cold war international system are found less in what is described than what is left out. In that sense, contemporary opinion may be influenced by today's media-driven politics. People see a crowd of Arab protesters or a burning American flag or an oil-drenched waterfowl or the collapsing Twin Towers of the World Trade Center in New York City – and they 'understand'. Do they comprehend pictures or newsreels of the Berlin blockade, the Korean war, the Berlin wall or the 'mushroom clouds' of nuclear explosions in the same way? And what about those events and shifts in world affairs for which we lack such images?

the roots of the cold war international system

The cold war belongs to a period in history which began long before either 1947 or 1917 and in which ideology was a means for justifying state power. During the nineteenth century, three new political ideologies

– liberalism, nationalism and radical socialism – had become powerful instruments for fighting the old monarchical order. Each was convinced that such change at the national level required a substantially different international system. Liberalism argued that the world would be safer and more prosperous if everyone adhered to democracy, free trade, private property and the rule of law. Nationalism was a force both to fight old social structures and to challenge the multi-ethnic empires which dominated global politics in those days. But by no means did the nation-state become its single political goal. While nationalism helped in creating Cavour's Italy and Bismarck's Germany, it also was a driving force in imperial rivalry and expansion. In 1898 even the United States, with their proud history of anti-imperialism (directed against Britain and Spain), began to acquire an empire and its own overseas sphere of influence. In 1917, the third ideology, social radicalism, produced a Bolshevist Russian empire which threatened to crush the other two ideologies. Far from leading to a united front against this challenge, the forces opposed to Bolshevism became critically divided. The Soviet threat produced a violently anti-democratic nationalist response which came to be known by its Italian name, fascism, because it was in Italy in 1922 that it first took over a national government. When Germany, in 1933, followed the Italian example in Hitler's 'national socialism', or Nazism, fascism was no longer a local response to economic and social crisis but a massive challenge to the international system.

Initially Hitler had focused on transforming Germany into a dictatorship, on overcoming the unemployment crisis and on getting rearmament under way. His demands for a revision of the Versailles peace treaty of 1919 barely exceeded earlier German demands made by democratic governments. But from 1938 his programme of expansionism and racism, outlined in *Mein Kampf* in 1926, was implemented brutally, leading to the assault on the Soviet Union in June 1941. Like Mussolini, who attempted imperial expansion in the Mediterranean and in Ethiopia, Hitler wanted to turn Germany into an empire. He sought to convert Eastern Europe, perhaps as far as the Urals, into a mixture of settlement colonies for Germans and dependent territories under German domination. The liberal powers, Britain, France and the United States, hesitated in their response both to the Soviet and to the Nazi challenge. Since the Soviet Union did not make war on other great powers – unlike revolutionary France in 1792 – it might be tolerated. One might overlook that its declaratory policy insisted that Bolshevist 'achievements' could only be secured if all opposition were overwhelmed, both inside and outside Russia. As to Nazi Germany, it might perhaps be balanced by Soviet power and by Italy. But then the unexpected happened. Hitler formed a coalition with Stalin, which allowed him to conquer East-Central and much of Western Europe. Then his attack on the Soviet Union forced the liberal powers into a coalition with Stalin. Within a few weeks of the German invasion (22 June 1941), the United States, which was giving much support to the British but still refused to enter the war, extended its military aid to Britain's new ally. In December 1941, four days after the Japanese attack on Pearl Harbor, Hitler declared war on the United States. In this way he placed Washington firmly at the side of Moscow. Thus London and Washington never had a chance to refuse a coalition with Moscow, unless of course they were ready to meet Nazi Germany's terms. But given Hitler's brutal racist warfare, on a scale never before seen in history, a compromise with him was out of the question. The only practical option for the Anglo-Saxon powers was to proclaim an idealistic policy for a better world and to make as many concessions to Stalin as necessary in order to win Soviet support for such a new international order.

By 1943, when Soviet forces had gained the upper hand against the Germans, the two Anglo-Saxon powers began to realise fully what lay ahead. Not only was it now likely that the USSR would survive. It was equally likely that the Soviet leaders would use their armies to redraw the map of Europe, perhaps also of the Middle East and of East Asia. Communist expansion might now happen in the clothing of coalition warfare against Germany, Japan and their allies. Those fears are amply documented in the secret papers of British and American leaders, including their military advisers, but they could not be discussed publicly as long as the alliance with the Soviet Union was needed to win the war. The best available strategy to contain Soviet ambitions seemed to lie in a combination of establishing international rules and institutions on the one hand and in making concessions to the Soviets on the other. Based on those assumptions the US President, Franklin D. Roosevelt, and the British Prime Minister, Winston S. Churchill, conducted their coalition diplomacy for a new international system, while Stalin hoped to turn that strategy on its head. He would go along with the programme for a new international order and pocket any concessions offered by the West so long as either or both together did not limit his plans for communist expansion. As soon as the alliance was concluded Stalin's foreign secretary made it clear that the Kremlin intended to retain all territories which the Soviet Union had acquired under its treaty with Nazi Germany in August 1939. In the course of further negotiations, Konigsberg (later called Kaliningrad) with its surrounding territories, the Kurile Islands and Sakhalin peninsula, were added to the Soviet wishlist. This appeared to be sound power politics, but how could it be justified to Western public opinion? How could it be squared with the British-American Atlantic charter (1941) which had promised that no territorial claims would be made?[17]

This tension between *Realpolitik* and international idealism could never be resolved. The most difficult territorial issue was Eastern Poland, since Britain and France had declared war on Germany after the German invasion of Poland. Polish soldiers were fighting alongside Western armies from the first to the last day of the war in Europe. Why should their country cede land to the Soviets who had once collaborated with Hitler in the destruction of Poland? The political strategy pursued by the British and the Americans was one of gradual adjustment to the Soviet territorial demands. Poland was compensated by transferring former German territories and by expelling their German populations. Though put in writing at the Potsdam conference, this transfer was termed provisional, pending a European peace conference. The Americans and British hoped that this would encourage the Soviet government to honour various agreements, among them an accord signed at Yalta on a freely elected Polish government. As we know, this hope was never fulfilled.[18]

Psychologically, as far as Western public opinion was concerned, the Sovietisation of Eastern Europe was not a simple issue of diplomatic betrayal. The wartime propaganda of a suffering Soviet people who bravely defended themselves, led by a firm but benevolent Stalin, was aggressively promoted by communist parties and groupings. They were particularly strong in France and Italy, and had considerable influence on the intelligentsia in Britain and America. Of influence were also the revelations of Nazi atrocities, in particular the liberation of the concentration camps in early 1945, the Nuremberg trials in 1945–46 and a considerable number of further war crimes trials concerning German atrocities on their Eastern front. Though the Holocaust did not become an international *lieu de mémoire* until much later, no one could be unmoved by the sheer scale of the atrocities and by the sufferings of the Soviet people.[19] Even in the USA, where the political left was much weaker than in Europe, there was a strong feeling that rather than being the result of Soviet expansionism, the cold war might have a hidden domestic agenda, that it might be directed against working-class rights, welfare benefits and liberal (left-wing) ideas.

the international system after 1945

It is in this political and psychological context that the new international order was established of which the United Nations, the World Bank, the

International Monetary Fund (IMF), the General Agreement on Tariffs and Trade (GATT) and a number of other institutions and treaties formed the backbone.[20] The Charter of the UN provided a set of norms which outlawed all wars except those conducted in self-defence, individually or collectively, and those military operations which the UN Security Council would mandate in response to an act of aggression. Together with the UN Declaration on Human Rights (1949) those documents laid down the essential norms of the new international system.

But how could liberalism, that is the project of a peaceful, democratic and humane international order, survive in this odd co-habitation with communism? Given the obstacles to 'normal' international relations between the two ideological camps and considering the frightening tensions between them one is surprised to see to what extent the USSR participated in the early negotiations for that new world order. Indeed, the Soviet government was prepared to underwrite political principles which all too obviously contradicted its official ideology and – so far as one can know – Stalin's true intentions. For example, at the Yalta conference Stalin signed the Declaration on Liberated Europe which specified that multi-party, free elections would be held in all liberated countries. With respect to Poland, the document even specified 'free, unfettered' elections. At Potsdam, he formally agreed to principles of political, social, and economic reforms for Germany which specifically prescribed practices of liberal democracy obviously alien to the Soviet system. What is more, the Soviet military authorities tasked with the implementation of those agreements honoured at least some of those principles (at least initially) or deviated from them only in secret. Obviously they wished to present a façade of political respectability. Was this merely an effort to mislead Western governments and public opinion, as some would argue, or did the Soviet leadership appreciate that it had a great deal to gain from such an international system of institutions and practices?

The answer may well lie somewhere in the middle. Stalin may have been undecided on how best to pursue his goals. Recent scholarship no longer assumes that Stalin had a ready-made strategy or overall plan in his desk. There are indications that he improvised a good deal. We have clear evidence that he did not permit Soviet-style coups d'état in Western Europe. In Eastern Europe his preference was for 'voluntary' Sovietisation, achieved by communist election victories and alliances with other political forces. In Germany, he apparently hoped for a withdrawal of Western military forces and for a gradual merger with the Eastern bloc, though a status of 'neutrality' might have been acceptable for a while.[21] While British and American officials noticed early on that their Soviet colleagues were bending or even ignoring the rules, it took their governments two years to admit that Soviet compliance would probably not be forthcoming. Gradually, the West reacted with various forms of diplomatic protest, including the famous speech by President Truman on 17 March 1947 (later dubbed the 'Truman doctrine') which condemned Soviet policy on Greece and Turkey. This was followed by the equally famous Harvard speech of June 1947, made by the Secretary of State, George C. Marshall, in which the USA offered economic aid to Europe (the Marshall Plan). Two years later, after the Berlin blockade, the founding of the Atlantic alliance (eventually called NATO) formed part of a series of measures and institutions which served to answer Moscow's refusal to play by the rules and to keep their promises. Interestingly, however, none of those measures were explicitly directed against the USSR or challenged its status as a great power and empire.

What is surprising in hindsight is not the collapse of the wartime alliance but the very survival of the new international system even though, for several decades, it functioned only in part. While the United Nations failed to establish the kinds of military instruments envisaged in the charter and failed also to ban nuclear weapons (as suggested in 1946 with the Baruch Plan) it survived as a forum for debate on measures of arms control and later as an instrument for peace-keeping activities. The creation of the State of Israel in 1948 and the subsequent efforts to come to an agreement over the Palestinian question were perhaps the outstanding examples of UN activity during those early years. As for the rest, the new international system was off to a slow start as the Soviet Union stuck to its crude mixture of aggressive ideology and imperial expansion. From a pessimist's viewpoint the liberal project of a new international system existed mostly on paper.

crisis management and limited wars: korea and vietnam

How could war be avoided without giving in to Soviet political strategy which would ultimately destroy liberalism? One possible answer, as noted in Jussi Hanhimäki's chapter, was the policy of the 'containment' of Soviet power, as defined by Kennan. Yet even Kennan did not hesitate to suggest that the West, under American leadership, should pursue a vigorous secret policy designed to prevent the creation of further Soviet-type states. Propaganda, financial support for anti-communists, the supply of arms and even armed intervention, that is to say a wide range of covert action measures, would have to be used to prevent the further spreading of Soviet power. And since the Soviets had their own covert action measures, a number of conflicts developed in countries which were not openly placed in either political camp. Thus the cold war confrontation was not one in which war was absent but rather a state of affairs in which each side used all means of fighting so long as they did not provoke a third world war. Their strategies were aimed at 'stability' rather than peace.[22]

As the 'secret wars' and the 'limited wars' came to characterise cold war politics on virtually all sides, the Soviets were at a distinct advantage. They did not have a democratic public at home, critically watching where the money and the soldiers were being sent. Indeed, the Kremlin skilfully exploited those Western weaknesses by lending support to Western peace movements, to anti-colonial activists, and to a variety of left-wing organisations, including of course the communist parties. Soviet intelligence exposed what unsavoury support the West lent to brutal, corrupt right-wing dictators. Their policy of influence was particularly effective during the Vietnam war, not in the least because the USA had little or no support from their own allies. It also played a certain role in Western movements directed against nuclear armaments.[23]

While the two camps fought each other by secret means they also began to establish some informal ways of limiting their confrontation. After all, none of the great powers were prepared to go to war with each other over the unresolved issues of the 1940s. Though neither side was prepared to exclude the possibility of using force, both went to great lengths to avoid at least a direct military clash. This behaviour is perhaps best described as a kind of crisis management which was improved gradually, with each crisis, and which eventually resulted in some formal changes of the international system. The first Berlin crisis of 1948–49 set an important precedent in crisis management. It began as a conflict over economic policies in the four occupation zones of Germany and in the four Berlin sectors but suddenly escalated when the Soviets blocked all land access to the three Western sectors of Berlin. Significantly, they pretended to do 'repair work' on roads and railways rather than admitting that they were imposing an economic blockade. In this way they did not technically violate any written agreements. None existed because in 1945 access to Berlin by land and by inland waterways had been understood to be implicit in the presence of occupation forces. On their part, the Western allied powers responded by organising an airlift of unarmed military transport aircraft which travelled along the air corridors prescribed by the 1945 four-power air agreement. (Even during the Berlin blockade air access was administered by a board of military officers which included Soviet representatives!) In other words, no side directly violated written agreements, though the Soviets clearly acted against the spirit of the Potsdam agreement. Each side was careful not to give the impression of an imminent military attack, though military personnel and equipment were abundantly visible. While the Soviets sought to demonstrate that Berlin was at their mercy, the Western powers were able to show off their superior air capacity which made it possible to keep the West Berliners supplied with food stuffs and fuel. In the end the Berlin airlift turned into a propaganda victory for the West, particularly for the USA, in winning the hearts of the Germans and of many others in Europe. War was avoided and the Soviets returned to the conference table even though two German states were already in the process of being established. Inadvertently Stalin convinced the Europeans of the necessity for the Marshall Plan and of the need to forge a Western defence alliance led by the Americans.[24]

In East Asia, the confrontation took a very different form. The Chinese regime change created a complex set of issues concerning the international status of Taiwan. China's permanent membership on the UN Security Council effectively incapacitated that body because the Soviet Union insisted that this seat be transferred to the Beijing government, instead of leaving it in the hands of President Chiang Kai-Shek (Jiang Jieshi), whose *Guomindang* government had fled to Taiwan (China's seat was not transferred to Beijing until 1971). In the middle of this imbroglio the North Korean communists began an assault across the international demarcation line (along the 38th parallel) in June 1950. In response the United States assembled an international coalition force under UN sponsorship. US strategy was based on the assumption that the feeble North Korean regime would not have undertaken such a dramatic step without political and indeed military backing from Moscow. When the communist Chinese regime sent 'volunteer' forces across the border to fight alongside the North Koreans the war assumed a very different dimension. Was Korea only the testing ground for a wave of communist military offensives elsewhere, particularly in Central Europe? Was the real aggressor sitting in the Kremlin? Surely the Soviets had a certain number of 'military advisers' in Korea. But Western intelligence services could not detect any major preparations for a Soviet attack. Therefore the USA was careful to conduct the Korean war as a 'limited war', that is to say as a conflict without direct great power involvement on both sides. In this way the UN military commander, US General Douglas MacArthur, was left to deal with a thorny issue. How could he conduct combat against the Chinese 'volunteer' forces without bringing China into the war, thereby without involving the Soviets who had signed a Chinese-Soviet friendship treaty in February 1950? Should he bomb Chinese supply lines and send his ground forces across the border to China? From a military standpoint this was the logical way. MacArthur coined the famous phrase that 'in war there is no substitute for victory'. But Truman recalled him, to howling protests from the American political right. While the number of soldiers and civilians killed was immense – perhaps as many as 2 million Koreans (on both sides) and well over 50,000 US soldiers – the Korean war remained a 'limited war'. It was followed by an equally 'limited' one in Indochina, fought between 1946 and 1973 first by France and then by the United States.[25]

It is important to note that this restraint on the part of the West was exercised at a moment when the Soviet Union had performed its first atomic test but was still far from having deployable bombs, let alone any means of delivery at intercontinental distances. Therefore Truman's decision was not so much motivated by a fear of Soviet retaliation, though his British allies did indeed fear a retaliatory Soviet attack in Europe, than by a sense that the international system should somehow be preserved. This was possible because neither the Korean war nor the later conflict in Indochina was in any sense a war of American self-defence. Those wars were not even fought on behalf of or for the protection of an indispensable ally (the defence alliance with Japan was not signed until a year after the end of the Korean war). Rather, they were fought for great power leadership and for a certain idea which the United States had about the international system. Thus America's war in Korea was a global message – made with reference to Europe and to South-East Asia in particular – that the policy of containment allowed for regional wars and that the use of nuclear weapons could not be forecast. To emphasise the latter point the US deployed nuclear-armed bombers both to Britain and to bases in East Asia. Obviously those strategic forces had no tactical purposes either in Korea or in Germany. Their potential targets were in the Soviet Union and in China.

The American war effort in Vietnam was less obviously an effort to contain Soviet power, though Moscow supplied arms to Hanoi. It was even fought at a time when Soviet-American arms control negotiations were under way. In the end it was no longer even directed against Beijing, as President Richard Nixon made his spectacular visit to China in 1972. The Americans ended up fighting a Third World communist country, North Vietnam, which they could not defeat and whose dependence on Soviet and Chinese support did not translate into subservience to Moscow or Beijing. For the United States the Vietnam war began as a proxy conflict in support of the French, whose efforts to reassert themselves in Indochina (1946–54) at first received minimal support from Washington. From 1949 to 1950 US engagement grew rapidly, both financially and with covert support, and was intended both to contain communism in South-East Asia and to bolster the USA's alliance with a key European ally. After partition in the Geneva accords of 1954, which terminated French engagement in Indochina, the US attempted (initially by covert means) to preserve an anti-communist regime in South Vietnam. From the late 1950s the Americans attempted to defeat the Viet Cong's insurgency (which received full backing from Hanoi from 1960 onwards) but essentially they kept alive a corrupt regime with an incompetent military. The myth of 'counter-insurgency' influenced a generation of US leaders, among them President John F. Kennedy, who believed he had the magic bullet for fighting communism. By late 1963 there were 16,000 US 'advisers' in Vietnam. In August 1964, after a naval incident off the North Vietnamese coast in the Gulf of Tonkin, the US Congress gave President Lyndon B. Johnson wide-ranging powers to escalate the war, enabling his administration to order air raids on the North from February 1965. Eventually Johnson deployed ground troops to South Vietnam in the spring of 1965, bringing the peak total to 550,000 in 1968. The US military presence grew because more limited campaigns had failed to defeat the Vietnamese communists, who were supported by the Soviets as well as the Chinese, and to establish a viable non-communist regime in South Vietnam. The result was a crushing political defeat for the Americans and, with 2 million dead, a terrible outcome for the Vietnamese people. In April 1975 the Americans withdrew their last officials by helicopter from the roof of the US embassy in Saigon. All of Vietnam was now communist. But this no longer mattered to the cold war international system. The USA had long before opened an era of negotiations with the USSR and with China.[26]

It is important to remember that both the Korean and the Vietnam wars were fought by coalitions for which America's extensive system of defence treaties provided an indispensable basis, both politically and militarily (discussed in further detail in Lawrence Kaplan's chapter). Beginning with the treaties concluded with the Philippines and Japan in August–September 1951, this alliance system eventually included Australia, New Zealand, South Korea, Britain, France, Pakistan and Thailand. Yet it did not amount to a regional peace order, as NATO did on the European side. At most it supplied the USA with some fighting troops and with a large number of air and naval bases, storage and recreation facilities which were used extensively during those two Asian wars.

nuclear weapons, arms control and the helsinki accords

Despite its crises and wars the cold war international system had a remarkable history of negotiations and of institution-building across the iron curtain. Immediately after Stalin's death in March 1953 the idea of great power cooperation resurfaced. Churchill, who was re-elected Britain's Prime Minister in October 1951, proposed a follow-up summit meeting to the 1945 Potsdam conference where the remaining European issues could be resolved. Truman's successor, Dwight D. Eisenhower, subsequently suggested one scheme for cooperating on civilian nuclear matters (known as 'Atoms for Peace') and another for reducing the fear of surprise attack (the 'Open Skies' proposal). Though neither were successful they signalled a willingness to discuss the new problems of a nuclear-armed cold war. They also assured Soviet leaders that their country was regarded as a legitimate great power and that even its new empire of satellite states might be removed quietly from the list of unresolved issues. At the same time the Soviets accepted for practical purposes the political arrangements which the USA, Britain and France had made with the Germans in the Western zones of occupation by creating the Federal Republic of Germany (FRG) in 1949, and with Japan a few years later.

As noted by Lawrence Freedman and Geraint Hughes in their chapter, the emerging Soviet nuclear arsenal became an issue of great concern in the West. Though there was nothing in international law which prevented a sovereign state from acquiring any weapon it chose to develop and although the USSR as a permanent member of the UN Security Council had a special responsibility to defend the international system against aggressors, there remained the issue of its totalitarian political system. Would the Soviets build up their arsenal only for purposes of deterrence and self-defence or might they, in accordance with their stated ideological goals, regard nuclear weapons as a means to force the export of communism? In the latter case, would it be prudent or even necessary to destroy the Soviet nuclear programme before it could be a threat on a global scale? This last point was indeed raised by some in the United States, particularly by a few senior military figures, but it never became policy. Eisenhower, for example, forbade any of his officials from even considering this option.[27] Therefore the US response to the Soviet weapons programme remained what Truman had decided as early as January 1950, a few months after the first Soviet test. They would build a very large nuclear arsenal, including almost unimaginably destructive hydrogen bombs. And they would equip the armed services with such weapons as fast as delivery systems could be constructed and built. Moreover, the USA would seek to stay ahead technologically and to protect their allies so far as feasible.[28]

The evolution of nuclear strategy and the related technologies and deployments – discussed by Freedman and Hughes, and by Bluth, in the respective chapters – shaped to a considerable degree 'how the cold war was played' (to quote Zbigniew Brzezinski, who served as President Jimmy Carter's national security adviser from 1977 to 1980).[29] After the 1946 failure to ban nuclear weapons by international agreement, the first reaction on the part of the great powers was to acquire those weapons for the simple reasons that they might serve as a deterrent and that ownership would convey international prestige. Thus the Soviet and British programmes came under way as early as 1945–46, even before the cold war was publicly admitted to exist. A decade later the French began work on their own nuclear deterrent. In making this decision, Britain could build on its expertise from the Manhattan Project while France was much further behind and could devote fewer resources to the task. The lack of US support for the development of the French *force de frappe* would eventually lead President Charles de Gaulle to cool off his relations with Washington and to leave the military structures of NATO in 1966.

The primary purpose of nuclear weapons was to threaten any major attacker with the grave risk of a counter-strike of enormous dimensions. It is this idea of an existential guarantee, certainly for a nation and perhaps also for a particular political regime, which has survived into the post-cold war era and which possibly lies at the heart of the Israeli, Indian, Pakistani, North Korean and Iranian nuclear programmes. Whether or not any of those states also intends to annihilate a particular enemy (Iran vis-à-vis Israel for example) is unclear. Surely such an intention cannot be completely ruled out. For the great powers, nuclear arsenals could be seen as an expression of their status as members of the Security Council. But what of the implications for other states? Should they acquire nuclear arms? Should they seek protection (a 'nuclear umbrella') from one of the great powers? Could such protection be trusted? Would the world become more dangerous with the number of nuclear-armed states increasing? One answer was to promote a policy of nuclear non-proliferation, a policy which originated right at the beginning of the nuclear age. When Britain, the USA and Canada began their Manhattan Project, they did so with the intention of excluding their Soviet ally. As it turned out, Soviet scientific competency combined with a substantial spying effort (discussed in Richard Aldrich's chapter) allowed the Soviets to catch up quickly.[30] In turn, the Soviets gave limited support to a Chinese nuclear project but did not allow other communist allies to proceed along that route. Similarly, from the late 1950s the USA gave limited support to the British nuclear programme but sought to discourage other Western powers from developing their own national programmes. Among those, only France refused to submit to US pressure and produced its first test in 1960.

When Soviet–British–American negotiations on non-proliferation began in the mid-1960s, they found common ground in excluding Germany from the nuclear weapons club. The resulting Non-Proliferation Treaty (NPT), which came into force in 1970, implicitly left the door open for France and China to be recognised as club members. All others would henceforth be classified as non-nuclear weapons states. After years of further negotiations nearly all states accepted the NPT. But the refusal on the part of India, Pakistan and Israel sent a signal around the world, in part because Israel was a close military and political ally of the USA. To preserve the notion of equal sovereignty the 'haves' promised to the 'have-nots' that their superiority would be a temporary situation, ending with the eventual abolition of all nuclear weapons. In 1995, when the NPT was turned into a permanent feature of the international system, that promise barely survived.[31]

The existence of nuclear weapons made it difficult for the two superpowers to credibly threaten each other with attack, because of the consequences war would have for both sides. With the exception of the 1962 Cuban missile crisis (discussed in Chapter 5), the USA and the USSR shied away from making specific threats to employ nuclear weapons against each other. It was significant that in the aftermath of this crisis Washington and Moscow signed a number of agreements, which included the establishment of a direct telephone link (a 'hot-line') between the White House and the Kremlin and the conclusion of the Limited Test Ban Treaty (LTBT) in 1963, the NPT and the anti-ballistic missile treaty of 1972. The two superpowers made the public believe that nuclear war was becoming less likely, when in reality the deployment of intercontinental missiles in silos and on nuclear-powered submarines made it much easier technically to launch a devastating first-strike. In the end public sentiment did more to define the international system than did military reality. For much the same reason the Soviet, then Russian, and the US arsenals could be drastically reduced after the end of the cold war. While their remaining stockpiles still exceeded any 'reasonable' needs, they no longer appeared to concern the US or European publics. Eventually nuclear weapons only remained a public issue if owned or aspired to by those outside the circle of 'legitimate' powers of the NPT.

Forcing this type of arms control logic on the allies of the USA and the USSR did not happen easily. During the 1960s, NATO in particular went through seemingly endless transatlantic crises centred around the fear of unequal security among its membership. If nuclear weapons had defensive functions why should smaller states such as France, Germany and Italy renounce part of their right to self-defence? If they did not, as anti-nuclear activists claimed, why deploy US nuclear warheads in Europe? Eventually, in 1966, only France gave a clear answer by leaving the military structures of NATO and requesting the withdrawal of all US forces from her territory. The others grudgingly gave in to Washington, hoping no doubt to save defence expenditures in return for their second-class status.

Although the cold war was a hot and bloody war for much of the Third World, those conflicts had remarkably little impact on the international system. Perhaps one can say that the great powers remained too colonialist in spirit to permit the kind of revolution 'from the villages' which Mao Zedong and other theoreticians of Third World revolutions had envisaged. Surely the anti-colonial rhetoric of both the USA and the USSR had little effect on how each of them dealt with their clients from the poor South of the globe. Each demanded obedience in return for military and civilian aid. Each sought to impose its ideology and its national interests, whereby security concerns and the 'correlation of forces' (a Soviet term for some kind of balance of power thinking à la Moscow) were more important than the strict enforcement of ideology. Local cultures were tolerated so long as they did not interfere with grand strategy as defined by the two supreme hegemons. Initially, a number of other powers sought to maintain a role in this new mixture of colonialism and cold war politics. In the name of anti-communism and 'counter-insurgency' the Netherlands fought to regain Indonesia until 1949. France did the same in Indochina and later in Algeria (from 1954 to 1962), as did the British in today's Malaysia during the 1950s. The British-French attempt to impose their will on Nasser's Egypt in 1956 (the Suez crisis) is surely the best-known case in which the USA told its allies to leave the new 'great game' to Washington. Eventually, American oil interests became interwoven with cold war politics, leading the USA to expand its influence throughout the Middle East, leaving Britain with only a minor role to play in the region. Portugal maintained its own mixture of colonial and anti-communist warfare in Angola and Mozambique until 1974. South Africa did the same in both countries (and also Namibia) until 1989. The USA fought or supported such wars in Latin America, particularly in Guatemala and Nicaragua, from the 1960s through the

1980s. In each case there was some truth in claims of a communist danger, but the raw business and geo-strategic self-interests was only too obvious. Only South Africa's *apartheid* regime was too obnoxiously racist to give even an appearance of anything else, but even there Western support – and later the weakness of Western sanctions policies – was justified by cold war necessity.

To be sure, this expansion of the cold war international system did not come easily and did not always overcome local resistance. Within the Islamic world a strong movement against both Soviet and US hegemony evolved. Iran after the 1979 revolution, Ghadafi's Libya and the fast-growing Moslem fundamentalist groups in several Arab states are obvious examples of this resistance. The war in Afghanistan, after the Soviet invasion of 1979, did much to extinguish those earlier hopes of an Arab nationalism supported by Soviet arms and other aid which the Baathist movement of the 1950s had fostered in Syria and later in Iraq. The USA was quite ready to support such forces, particularly those directed against the Soviets in Afghanistan, without asking for any recognition of Western democratic values or human rights in return. As a consequence, Osama bin Laden's Al Qaeda, once an indirect beneficiary of US clandestine support, grew to become an important terrorist organisation on a global scale, chiefly directed against US influence in the Middle East.[32] When the Soviets became more actively involved in Africa, following the 1973 coup d'état in Ethiopia and the collapse of the Portuguese empire the following year, the USA responded by expanding its covert operations in support of anti-communist 'local' forces (such as, for example, Jonas Savimbi's UNITA movement in Angola). As a result, sub-Saharan Africa became a cold war battlefield. Similarly, Soviet support for various central American civil war parties was countered by Washington. After the US Congress sought to limit such aid to the *Contras* in Nicaragua (the guerrilla groups fighting the left-wing *Sandinista* regime), the administration of Ronald Reagan made a deal with Iran to send money to the *Contras* in return for military equipment Iran needed in its bloody war against Iraq (1980–88). This was in spite of the fact that during this same war, the longest conventional war after 1945, the USA supported Iraq – as did other Western powers and the Soviet Union in different ways and at different times.[33]

If the policies of both Western and Eastern bloc countries towards the Iran–Iraq conflict illustrated the absurdity of applying cold war logic to the Third World, this was by no means the only such case. The original ideological positions of the cold war were utterly compromised when applied forcibly and by clandestine methods to the Third World. Neither

Lenin's Bolshevist variety of communism nor Roosevelt's liberal democracy combined with market capitalism retained any recognisable value during the proxy wars which characterised the cold war confrontation of the 1970s and 1980s.

economic, social and cultural changes in the international system

When the membership of the United Nations increased from 51 founding members in 1945 to 166 in 1991, the UN became to a large degree an organisation concerned with development issues. In 1964, the UN's first UNCTAD conference marked the beginning of its new role in what were later called North–South relations. The World Bank was transformed from an organisation concerned with rebuilding war-torn Europe to a lender for development capital in Africa, Asia and Latin America. Development policy therefore became part of international relations.

But what were the principal concepts for dealing with under-development? Not surprisingly the cold war had a major effect both on the guiding ideas and on their application. At the outset there were two opposing concepts. Liberals assumed that 'freedom from want' (to quote Roosevelt) could be achieved quickly by following the successful examples of industrialisation in the Western world, telescoped into one or two generations. Marxist-Leninists, however, held that poverty was essentially the result of an unequal distribution of riches rather than one of creating wealth and of allocating it efficiently by market forces. They believed that forced industrialisation along the Soviet model, with the state organising and owning capital investment, would produce quick results. As it turned out, both concepts were essentially state-oriented. Both put the emphasis on large infrastructure projects such as dams for irrigation and for hydroelectric plants, airports, harbours, roads and urban construction. Industrial investment was directed toward large industrial plants such as steel mills and cement works. And both concepts underestimated 'local conditions' as well as cultural and social factors. When it became apparent that those factors impeded rapid growth of per capita incomes in most countries, governments were mostly incapable of allocating investment wisely. As a result, huge amounts of money were wasted in corruption. Eventually the West insisted on a market-driven approach with a focus on social improvement. This became the new gospel of development policies which began in the 1980s.

Overall, however, the results were deeply disappointing. While nearly all countries experienced various forms of partial modernisation, high population growth rates and a breakdown of traditional social structures put an end to the most optimistic scenarios. There appeared to be no overall concept which would deliver sufficient wealth to improve everyone's life and which would establish a sound economic basis for robust democratic structures. Nevertheless, development politics generated a vast array of international bureaucracies and NGO (non-governmental organisations) transnational bodies. At least at that level it produced plenty of jobs.

How did those activities and institutions fit into the wider picture of transnational economic politics during the cold war? One must go back at least to the 1930s to appreciate the wider context. After the liberal system of free exchange of goods, capital and labour had been smashed by the First World War, the inter-war years produced various ideologies of self-sufficiency or autarky which cast a long shadow on much of the cold war era. The Bretton Woods system professed to favour market policies, but in reality most countries acted on the belief that political prestige abroad and social stability at home required national, that is protectionist, answers. The attempts to restore the European empires were one expression of this conviction. The creation of economic zones of cooperation, secured by tariffs and trade limitations, was another.

As Alan Milward has argued, European integration which began with the Marshall Plan of 1947 and which was eventually based on the Coal and Steel Community (ECSC) proposed by France in 1951, belonged in that category. It provided for protection and for governmental management in those economic sectors where purely national policies were insufficient.[34] In 1949 the Soviets created the Council for Mutual Economic Assistance (CMEA, or Comecon) as a zone of economic planning and privileged trade with their satellites in Eastern Europe. As to the Americans, their declaratory policy of free trade stood in stark contrast with their strong tradition of self-sufficiency. Their unique economic strength, however, made it possible for them to pursue a parallel strategy of market penetration both in terms of foreign investment by their giant corporations and in privileged access to 'strategic' resources such as oil, uranium and metals.[35] Therefore, the Bretton Woods institutions never came to full fruition. The free exchange of capital, based on the dollar-gold standard, only functioned between 1959, when key Western currencies became fully convertible (Japan followed in 1964), and 1971 when Nixon, under pressure from the financial burden of the Vietnam war, abandoned the gold standard. Free trade under GATT took even longer to materialise.

Eventually, the international system came to be characterised by a separation of economic and politico-military power. Certain countries such as West Germany, Japan and South Korea reached enormous levels of production and wealth but remained 'dwarfs' in the traditional state-based forms of political power. After France and Britain emerged from the trauma of decolonisation they found their place as middle powers, although they possessed permanent seats on the UN Security Council and the elevated status of being 'legitimate' nuclear powers under the NPT. Western Europe saw an extraordinary 'economic miracle', as did some smaller East Asian states (the 'tiger economies'), while the economic predominance of the USA diminished. Latin America, South Asia, China and the Soviet Union fell far behind or stagnated. The Soviet Union and China were great powers but without playing significant roles on the economic stage of fast-growing trade volumes.

The oil crises of the 1970s, resulting from the October 1973 Yom Kippur war and the Iranian revolution of 1979, demonstrated that the USA and Western Europe were now vulnerable to economic and political pressures from Arab oil-producing countries which had no marketable products or services for the growing world economy beyond crude oil and natural gas, and which were insignificant in military terms. But the damage to American power was only temporary because the smaller and medium sized countries within the Western camp were even more defenceless and were thereby forced into a common response under US leadership. Moreover, the Soviets could only benefit from the increase in oil prices to a very limited degree. Their petroleum industry suffered from chronic under-investment. Their production and transportation costs (particularly for Siberian oil wells) were dramatically higher than those of the Persian Gulf states. At best the Soviets could somewhat benefit from the loss of prestige which the capitalist West suffered in the Moslem world. Neither was China in a position to benefit in substantial ways. Its economy had been gravely disturbed by a series of economic disasters – most of them attributable to communist policies – which, after Mao's death in 1976, forced the new leadership into dramatic changes in economic policy (the 'four modernisations' under Deng Xiaoping).

When the enormous Middle Eastern oil-revenues reached the world's financial markets, they came in the form of 'petrodollars'. Much of this money could not be absorbed by the oil states themselves, at least not quickly, and had to be invested in the advanced Western economies if it was to yield satisfactory returns. Again, the communist part of the world simply could not compete for investment opportunities. Neither could it provide those consumer or investment goods which the newly-rich oil barons wished to buy. While the Kremlin leaders benefited somewhat from exporting Soviet oil for much better prices, their communist clients suffered because the 'domestic' price for Soviet oil was gradually adjusted to international levels. In turn this price hike led to soaring state deficits all around Eastern Europe. By borrowing from the West those countries dramatically pushed up their indebtedness in hard-currency denomination. This resulted in a slowdown of investment and, by the late 1980s, led several states to bankruptcy. Their weakened governments would eventually prepare the way for the political revolutions of 1989.[36]

The cumulative effects of the oil crises were felt hardest in the developing countries because their own prices for many of their agricultural products and for various other raw materials dropped dramatically. Many of them lacked the money or even the credit to keep up their declining infrastructure from colonial times, or to modernise their post-independence plants. A few, such as Nigeria and Venezuela, became major oil producers but largely failed to make good use of their new riches for their societies. Others, like Bolivia and later Afghanistan, became ever deeper involved in international drug-dealing. Generally speaking, the great majority of developing countries were poorly equipped and given little opportunity to benefit from the dramatic growth of the global economy which in turn encouraged a renewal of economic liberalism, often called monetarism or neo-liberalism.[37]

The full extent of this revolution in economic policies, both at the national and at the international level, can only be appreciated if one first looks at those older concepts of state interference which preoccupied the wealthy countries of the West during the 1950s and 1960s. At that time the state owned and ran most public services (railways, airlines, utilities, postal services, health services etc.). In some countries, notably Britain and France, the state even owned automobile works, steel mills, coal mines, banks and insurances because they were considered too important for the national well-being to be left to private ownership. In parallel, huge government provisions for healthcare, education, old age pensions, labour market intervention and unemployment relief had evolved into a welfare state which consumed around 50 per cent of GNP, in some cases even more. If one takes into account that in those same countries, before 1914, the state had consumed a share of around 10–15 per cent of GNP, one sees the fundamental change which occurred during and after the First World War. No doubt that increase in state spending was a response to the 'challenge of socialism', including the challenge posed by the Soviet Union. It was thus – at least in part – a result of the pre-1947 cold war to which reference is made above. During the world economic crisis of the 1930s even the United States introduced most of those welfare state provisions, though America was much less threatened by the Soviet example than was Europe after 1918 and again after 1944–45. While the US public sector, after 1945, was significantly smaller than in Western Europe, the pressure for economic protection and for public investment was stronger than many 'internationalist' Americans cared to admit.

In hindsight it may be difficult to believe how many economists and scientists came to believe that the Soviet version of modernity might be equal or even superior to the Western one, citing Soviet advances in space flight (such as the launch of the *Sputnik* satellite of 1957) as well as the quality and superior numbers of scientists and engineers. During the 1960s the proponents of 'convergence theory' argued that the gap between the two systems would eventually diminish, and that capitalism would acquire characteristics of socialism (and vice versa). The habitual forgery of government statistics by the communist regimes, the disheartening testimony of refugees, and reports about the mistreatment of human rights were routinely brushed aside as temporary problems of 'late development' or of the 'mistakes of Stalinism'. It was against this philosophy of the welfare state and the rosy pictures of the Soviet system that both Reagan and the British Prime Minister, Margaret Thatcher, propagated their new policies of cutting back state intervention and welfare provisions during the 1980s. At the same time they espoused a new militancy vis-à-vis Soviet power. Reagan refused to follow the path of merely managing Soviet military power via arms control. His Strategic Defense Initiative (SDI) was as much a political and ideological programme as is was a technical one. Thatcher's neo-liberal rhetoric and policies propagated a modern, individualistic capitalism based on personal liberty. It was nothing less than an intellectual declaration of war on left-wing politics. Her 'bible', Friedrich von Hayek's *Road to Serfdom*, is an anti-communist manifesto which takes economics only as a starting point for a militantly anti-socialist political philosophy.[38]

Interestingly, the Thatcher–Reagan economic vision was followed only guardedly elsewhere in the West. For example, West Germany's Christian-Democrat Chancellor, Helmut Kohl (1982–98), spoke much of a 'spiritual turnabout' (*geistige Wende*) toward traditional values but refused to cut welfare benefits. He did, however, embrace the idea of privatising telephone and public transport services as well as a number of other state-owned businesses and services. Other governments in Western Europe followed suit, even in France where President François Mitterrand began his 14 years in office (1981–95) by nationalising certain enterprises and by increasing state spending. Privatisation and market deregulation became part of the international economic agenda. The GATT (General Agreement on Tariffs and Trade, renamed the World Trade Organisation (WTO) in 1994) oversaw a process in which markets were opened and obstacles to 'fair trading' were removed. The World Bank and the IMF increasingly made their loans contingent on the recipients' adherence to this new creed. As a result a considerable number of threshold countries and even of poor countries suddenly found themselves forced to cut their welfare programmes and subsidies. The European Union (EU) – under the leadership of Commission President Jacques Delors, a French socialist – embarked on a vast programme of privatisation and competition policies which produced a remarkable impetus to private capitalism. From a framework for market restriction and market regulation the EU rapidly transformed itself into an engine for improving international competitiveness, brushing aside traditional economic policies dear to social democrats and labour unions.[39]

To what extent did those changes impact on the international system and its institutions? And how did the communist world respond? Through a series of complicated and drawn-out negotiations the agenda of the GATT (tariff reduction and harmonisation of global trade) was gradually implemented. The Kennedy Round of 1967 cut tariffs for industrial products by half. The Tokyo Round, concluded in 1979, sought to reduce government subsidies. Systematically, all forms of open or hidden discrimination against 'foreign' products and services were being targeted and in large measure eliminated. But other changes, particularly those brought about by the 'computer revolution', took place almost without political or institutional backing. Political actors found themselves driven by the effects of such innovations rather than controlling them. In other words, the international system changed not so much by design as it did by innovation in science and technology. Electronic communication made it nearly impossible for dictatorships to shield their publics from other cultures, other ideas, and from news about their own countries distributed from outside. Radio, television, cassette recorders and copying machines became powerful sources of unauthorised information, used by dissident forces of different sorts. They made obsolete those aspects of state sovereignty which communist leaders (and other dictators) had vigorously defended. Information, capital (legal and illegal) and intellectual property could now be exchanged at a rate never seen before.

If technology made distances less important and borders permeable, a growing international division of labour made countries and societies ever more interdependent. Economic globalisation, which had started with European colonialism as far back as the fifteenth century, built its own structures, now often called networks, which far outstripped the corset of international institutions established in the wake of the Second World War. Aside from private corporations and those older transnational institutions relating to religions, to science and to cultural activities, there arrived on the world stage a new class of actors known as NGOs. Their concerns included human rights (Amnesty International was founded in 1961), ecological concerns (Greenpeace in 1971 and World Wildlife Fund in 1961), and social welfare (*Médecins sans Frontières* (Doctors without Borders) in 1971). Their mission was to challenge the very notion that sovereignty could somehow legitimise the systematic violations of human rights, the isolation of societies and damage done to the global environment. Whether those economic and technical developments, combined with the proliferation of non-state networking activities, would eventually sweep away the traditional nation-state remains open to question.[40]

Fundamental changes in cultural norms also had their impact on the cold war international system. What is often referred to as the transition to post-modernity began to change cold war politics in the West. During the 1960s a younger post-1945 generation no longer felt threatened by communism and began to oppose the 'cold war consensus' which, for example, underpinned US intervention in Vietnam. Increasingly, representatives of this generation rejected the logic of 'mutually assured destruction' which dictated the deployment of ever more sophisticated nuclear missiles. Ecological concerns (expressed by Green parties) and lifestyle issues (such as abortion and gay rights) came to take precedence over the ideas and values which had driven the cold war policies from the 1940s to the 1960s. Those new movements not only imitated each other around the globe but also formed powerful networks of cooperation and exchange. Many of their concerns were eventually enshrined in international agreements and regimes, monitored by international institutions. Waste management, emission control and wildlife preservation are among the better-known examples. Those new technologies and new international concerns essentially came from the rich Western countries who often failed to comprehend that their pet notion of 'sustainable development' had a very different ring in Third World countries. The campaigns for preserving the rain forests are just one example where the daily needs of the local populations were widely disregarded. The idea of limiting growth to save the planet, powerfully propagated by a best-selling study from the Club of Rome (1971), was only one of those eco-pessimist contributions which shaped international debates but paid insufficient attention to the needs and hopes of the world's poor nations.[41]

In the Soviet Union the combination of technological and cultural change came to subvert the political system, too. While Moscow built for itself and for its allies a vast, unconquerable arsenal of weaponry, the performance of its civilian economy increasingly lagged behind. Some modest advances consumer goods and a cautious relaxation of the empire's cultural isolation (admitting pop music and jeans, for example) only alerted the younger generation to all the Western goods and the individual freedom which they lacked. By signing the Helsinki Final Act at the end of the Conference on Security and Cooperation in Europe (CSCE) in August 1975 the Kremlin leadership obtained international legitimacy for the ways in which it had forcibly reordered the political landscape of Eastern Europe. But by conceding to include human rights provisions ('Basket III' of the negotiations) it allowed foreign journalists to work inside the Soviet bloc. Civil rights movements and ecological movements communicated their concerns to the world. The Polish independent labour union 'Solidarity', and prominent dissidents like Vaclav Havel or Andrei Sakharov became familiar figures around the globe, representing a new feeling of 'one world' in which state borders and nineteenth-century ideologies looked redundant.

conclusions

A decade and a half after the end of the cold war the long-term significance of its international system is open to widely divergent interpretations. Our own post-cold war perspectives have changed several times since then, leaving behind them a trail of mistaken notions and predictions. The failure to establish a 'new world order' after 1991 is directly related to them. It took the terrorist attacks of 11 September 2001 to realise how Western covert operations in Afghanistan against the Soviet Red Army (during the 1980s) helped foster radical Islam. It can be argued that the American-British 2003 Iraq war may well be another one of those post-cold war intellectual failures.[42]

Other parts of the cold war's ending were managed remarkably well. New actors were brought into the major cold war institutions, thus enabling them to manage the transition to a new era of global affairs. NATO and the EU expanded into Eastern Europe. The Russian Federation and a new outward-looking China began to play those roles within the United Nations which Churchill and Roosevelt had originally envisaged.

The WTO and the various global summit and conference groupings also welcomed new members. In that sense, international relations became more of a 'system' – with a much thicker web of established rules, procedures and discussion fora – than they had been during the cold war.

At the same time international terrorism, violent ethnic conflicts, and the economic and social backwardness in much of Africa, Asia and Latin America make it all too obvious that those (transformed) global structures hold few answers to the daily concerns of a third of the world's population. While the technologies and the scientific knowledge exist with which to cure most of their sufferings, their states and societies critically lack the requisite political, economic and social structures to implement them. In so many ways neither the suffering countries nor the rich are equipped to deal effectively with the crises of the Third World. It may be utopian to expect an even distribution of wealth around the globe, but even timely and substantial improvements seem impossible in a world which is still marked by so much tragic waste of human, economic and intellectual resources during the cold war era.[43]

notes

1. John Lewis Gaddis, *The Long Peace: Inquiries into the History of the Cold War* (New York & Oxford: Oxford University Press, 1987), *passim*.
2. Jens Hacker, *Deutsche Irrtümer: Schönfärber und Helfershelfer der SED-Diktatur im Westen* (Berlin: Ullstein, 1992).
3. However, some Russian military forces have remained in countries which were once Soviet territories such as Tajikistan and Moldova, which are now deemed part of the 'near abroad'. See Roy Allison, 'Strategic Reassertion in Russia's Central Asia Policy', *International Affairs*, 80:2 (2004), pp.277–93.
4. Bruce Russett & John Qneal, *Triangulating Peace: Democracy, Interdependence, and International Organizations* (New York: Norton, 2001).
5. Any shortlist of readings should include: Hans Morgenthau, *Politics among Nations: The Struggle for Power and Peace* (New York: Knopf, 1986, 6th edition); Hedley Bull, *The Anarchical Society: A Study of Order in World Politics* (London: Macmillan, 1977). For an overview, see Ken Booth & Steve Smith (eds), *International Relations Theory Today* (Cambridge: Polity Press, 1995).
6. See, for example, Karl W. Deutsch, *The Analysis of International Relations* (Hemel Hempstead: Prentice Hall, 1968); Robert O. Keohane & Joseph S. Nye, *Power and Interdependence: World Politics in Transition* (Boston, MA: Little, Brown, 1977); Stephen Krasner (ed.), *International Regimes* (Ithaca, NY: Cornell University Press, 1983); Robert Gilpin, *The Political Economy of International Relations* (Princeton, NJ: Princeton University Press, 1988); Kenneth Waltz, *Theory of International Politics* (Reading, MA: Addison-Wesley, 1979); John G. Ruggie, *Constructing the World Polity: Essays on International Institutionalization* (London: Routledge, 1998).

7. Peter Katzenstein, *Small States in the World Economy* (Ithaca, NY: Cornell University Press, 1985).
8. Samuel Huntington's theory of a future 'Clash of Civilizations', first published in *Foreign Affairs*, 72:3 (1993), is perhaps the most widely known example. This thesis was expanded in *The Clash of Civilisations and the Remaking of World Order* (New York: Simon & Schuster, 1996).
9. See Jean-Baptiste Duroselle, *Tout empire périra: théorie des relations internationales* (Paris: A. Colin, 1992).
10. See Bush's 'new world order' speech (the phrase was used during the State of the Union speech on 29 January 1991), quoted in Lawrence Freedman & Efraim Karsh, *The Gulf Conflict 1990–1991* (London & Boston: Faber & Faber, 1994), p.xliv.
11. Stéphane Courtois et al., *Le livre noir du Communisme* (Paris: Lafont, 1997).
12. Andre Fontaine (translated by D. Paige), *History of the Cold War: From the October Revolution to the Korean War, 1917–1950* (London: Secker & Warburg, 1968).
13. George Kennan writes about his motives for drafting the Long Telegram in his *Memoirs, 1925–1950* (London: Hutchinson, 1968).
14. For an overview, see Odd Arne Westad (ed.), *Reviewing the Cold War: Approaches, Interpretations, Theory* (London: Frank Cass, 2000); David Reynolds, *One World Divisible: A Global History since 1945* (London: Penguin, 2000).
15. Noam Chomsky, *Powers and Prospects: Reflections on Human Nature and Social Order* (London: Pluto Press, 1996).
16. Ken Booth, Michael Cox & Tim Dunne (eds), *Empires, Systems, and States: Great Transformations in International Politics* (Cambridge: Cambridge University Press, 2002).
17. A good introductory text to the Second World War is Gerhard Weinberg, *World at Arms: A Global History of World War II* (Cambridge: Cambridge University Press, 1994). See also Peter Calvocoressi, *Total War: The Causes and Courses of the Second World War*. Volume I: *The Western Hemisphere* (London: Penguin, 1989) for the European war.
18. Antony Polonsky (ed.), *The Great Powers and the Polish Question, 1941–45: A Documentary Study in Cold War Origins* (London: Orbis Books, 1976). Anita Prazmowska, *Britain and Poland, 1939–1943: The Betrayed Ally* (Cambridge: Cambridge University Press, 1995).
19. Peter Novick, *The Holocaust in American Life* (London: Bloomsbury, 2000).
20. The economic institutions are usually referred to as the 'Bretton Woods' system, after the 1944 conference where the respective treaties were worked out. The Soviet Union participated in those negotiations but eventually refused to ratify the agreements and to participate in the institutional activities.
21. Vojtech Mastny, *The Cold War and Soviet Insecurity: The Stalin Years* (Oxford: Oxford University Press, 1995); Norman Naimark, *The Russians in Germany: A History of the Soviet Zone of Occupation, 1945–1949* (Cambridge, MA: Harvard University Press, 1995); Vladislav Zubok & Constantine Pleshakov, *Inside the Kremlin's Cold War: From Stalin to Khrushchev* (Cambridge, MA: Harvard University Press, 1996).
22. Nils P. Gleditsch et al., 'Armed Conflict 1946–2001: A New Data Set', *Journal of Peace Research*, 39:5 (2002); for a starting point on American political strategies, see John L. Gaddis, *Strategies of Containment: A Critical Appraisal of*

Post-War American National Security Policy (New York: Oxford University Press, 2005, 2nd edition); Raymond L. Garthoff, *A Journey Through the Cold War* (Washington, DC: Brookings, 2001); for the Soviet side, see Malcolm Byrne & Vojtech Mastny (eds), *A Cardboard Castle? An Inside History of the Warsaw Pact, 1955–1991* (Budapest & New York: Central European University Press, 2005).

23. For a good starting point, see Christopher Andrew & Vasili Mitrokhin, *The Mitrokhin Archive: The KGB in Europe and the West* (London: Penguin, 1999); volume 2 is scheduled for publication in 2005; Hubertus Knabe, *Die unterwanderte Republik – Stasi im Westen* (Berlin: Propylaen, 1999).

24. Ann & John Tusa, *The Berlin Airlift* (Staplehurst: Spellmount, 1998); William Stiver, 'The Incomplete Blockade: Soviet Zone Supply of West Berlin, 1948–49', *Diplomatic History*, 21:4 (1997), pp.569–602; Zubok & Pleshakov, *Kremlin's Cold War*, pp.51–2.

25. William Stueck, *The Korean War in World History* (Lexington, KT: University of Kentucky Press, 2004); Peter Lowe, *The Origins of the Korean War* (London: Longman, 1995). For a general discussion, see Philip Bobbitt, *The Shield of Achilles: War, Peace and the Course of History* (New York: Knopf, 2002).

26. See David L. Anderson, *The Columbia Guide to the Vietnam War* (New York: Columbia University Press, 2002); and George Herring, *America's Longest War: The United States and Vietnam, 1950–1975* (New York: McGraw Hill, 2002, 4th edition).

27. Much later, in June 1981, a preventive Israeli air strike was carried out against an Iraqi nuclear installation (the Osirak reactor) for this very purpose – the only such case in history so far. It must, however, be pointed out that, at that time, an Iraqi bomb would have had one target, namely Israel, whereas the Soviet atomic arsenal was not built with any such obvious target in sight. On the Osirak raid, see Uri Bar-Joseph, Michael Handel & Amos Perlmutter, *Two Minutes over Baghdad* (London: Routledge, 2003).

28. Robert Bowie & Richard Immerman, *Waging Peace: How Eisenhower Shaped an Enduring Cold War Strategy* (Oxford: Oxford University Press, 1998).

29. Zbigniew Brzezinski, 'How the Cold War Was Played', *Foreign Affairs*, 51 (1972–73), pp.181–209.

30. David Holloway, *Stalin and the Bomb* (New Haven, CT: Yale University Press, 1994).

31. France and China did not sign the NPT until 1992. After 9/11 the USA changed its attitude toward Pakistan (to enlist them for the war against Al Qaeda) and in 2005 they began a new relationship with India, ignoring in both cases their refusal to join the NPT regime. At the same time they stepped up the pressure on other NPT opponents (such as Iran and North Korea). The current state of the Iranian and North Korean proliferation crises was, at the time of writing, still unresolved. For up-to-date information on nuclear proliferation, as well as other contemporary security issues, see <http://www.globalsecurity.org>.

32. Steve Coll, *Ghost Wars: The Secret History of the CIA, Afghanistan and bin Laden, from the Soviet Invasion to September 10, 2001* (New York: Penguin Press, 2004), passim.

33. John Prados, *Presidents' Secret Wars: CIA and Pentagon Covert Operations from World War II through the Persian Gulf* (Chicago, IL: Ivan R. Dee, 1996), pp.337–47, 397–463; Charles Tripp, *A History of Iraq* (Cambridge: Cambridge University

Press, 2002), pp.238–40; Peter Kornbluh & Malcolm Byrne (eds), *The Iran-Contra Scandal: The Declassified History* (New York: New Press, 1993).

34. Alan Milward, *The European Rescue of the Nation State* (London: Routledge, 1992); John R. Gillingham, *European Integration 1950–2003: Superstate or Market Economy?* (Cambridge: Cambridge University Press, 2003).

35. Daniel Yergin & Joseph Stanislaw, *The Commanding Heights* (New York: Simon & Schuster, 1998), and Susan Strange, *States and Markets* (London: Pinter, 1994, 2nd edition) are excellent surveys of the key issues.

36. Mark Mazower, *Dark Continent: Europe's Twentieth Century* (London: Penguin, 1998), pp.368–74.

37. Joseph E. Stiglitz's *Roaring Nineties: A New History of the World's Most Prosperous Decade* (London: Allen Lane, 2003) and *Globalization and Its Discontents* (London: Allen Lane, 2002) offer a good start for those debates.

38. Friedrich von Hayek, *The Road to Serfdom* (Chicago, IL: Chicago University Press, 1944).

39. See Gillingham, *European Integration, passim.*

40. On globalisation, see John Baylis & Steve Smith (eds), *The Globalization of World Politics* (Oxford: Oxford University Press, 2001, 2nd edition); Anne-Marie Slaughter, *A New World Order* (Princeton, NJ: Princeton University Press, 2004); Joseph Nye, *Soft Power: The Means to Success in World Politics* (New York: Public Affairs, 2004); Zbigniew Brzezinski, *The Choice: Global Domination or Global Leadership* (New York: Basic Books, 2004); A.G. Hopkins (ed.), *Globalization in World History* (New York: Norton, 2002).

41. Club of Rome, *The Limits of Growth* (New York: New American Library, 1972) was the first of their studies. For the politics of eco-pessimism, see Børn Lomborg, *The Sceptical Environmentalist: Measuring the Real State of the World* (Cambridge: Cambridge University Press, 2001).

42. James Kurth, 'Ignoring History: US Democratization in the Moslem World', *Orbis*, 49:2 (2005).

43. For one of the most obvious examples, see Stephen I. Schwarz (ed.), *Atomic Audit: The Costs and Consequences of US Nuclear Weapons since 1940* (Washington, DC: Brookings, 1998).

2

national security and national interest

jussi hanhimäki

[We] have about 50% of the world's wealth but only 6.3% of its population. In this situation, we cannot fail to be the object of envy and resentment. Our real task in the coming period is to devise a pattern of relationships which will permit us to maintain this position of disparity without positive detriment to our national security. To do so, we will have to dispense with all sentimentality and day-dreaming; and our attention will have to be concentrated everywhere on our immediate national objectives. We need not deceive ourselves that we can afford today the luxury of altruism and world-benefaction.

In this way George Kennan, who can justly be characterised as having been one of the least sentimental of American foreign policy-makers in the early cold war era, gave his prescription for the overall goals of American foreign policy. Writing in March 1948, he recognised America's tremendous power and the disparity between the United States' material resources and those of the rest of the world. He also clearly believed that the foremost goal of US policy was to maintain the edge it enjoyed. And he was convinced that in doing so American policy-makers needed to forget about the power of ideas, to ignore what, in later years, would be referred to as 'soft power'. As Kennan, at the time the Chief of the State Department's Policy Planning Staff, added: 'We should cease to talk about vague and ... unreal objectives such as human rights, the raising of the living standards, and democratization. The day is not far off when we are going to have to deal in straight power concepts. The less we are then hampered by idealistic slogans, the better.'[1]

Long before Kennan died in March 2005, national security, national interest and the balance of power had ceased to be fashionable terms among historians. Many see them as hopelessly boring concepts, offering few new insights into the past. Indeed, even among diplomatic historians – the group most obviously associated with national security – the past two decades have been characterised by an ongoing debate about the need for new approaches to replace the excessive focus on elite perceptions and decision-making. Among American diplomatic historians – the group that still tends to dominate cold war historiography – this led to a long debate (still ongoing) over the need to include more new approaches in order to avoid a growing irrelevance of the subfield of diplomatic history among the overall context of the historical profession. While Michael Hunt described the crisis as coming to a 'closure' in the early 1990s, any casual reader of, say, the journal *Diplomatic History* will note that a certain self-flagellation continues to the present day. Not even the apparent 'resurgence' of national security as a much talked about concept since 9/11 has been able to reinsert a sense of relevance among the group of scholars that, truth be told, still write history primarily through the lens of national security.[2]

One of the points of this chapter is that while historians in general remain uncomfortable – or bored and disdainful – with talking about such an 'old-fashioned' concept as the balance of power, it is hard to deny that for policy-makers in the United States, the Soviet Union, Great Britain, France, China and elsewhere, the power relationships amongst states mattered a great deal during the cold war. One may find it more exciting to try and uncover the gendered tropes of Kennan's discourse, but one cannot deny the hard reality that to Kennan – whose sexism was undoubtedly beyond the pale – the more traditional measurements of statecraft mattered more than which gendered metaphor he used when talking about the French, the Soviets or the Germans. The frequency of the term 'Soviet penetration' in American discourse is an undeniable fact. But for most language was a tool – and in Kennan's hands a very powerful one – to be used to advance what he thought was the best way of maintaining a balance of power favourable to American national interests, of protecting American national security.[3]

While balance of power theory is clearly no longer in vogue with historians, it has lost – to an extent – its significance among international relations theorists as well. *Realpolitik* is not what it used to be. One reason for this is that the cold war ended in a manner that seemed to contradict realism as an explanatory tool; with one superpower throwing in the towel, giving up its position of power more or less voluntarily. No 'serious' International Relations theorist had thought that such a thing was possible (of course, no historian had either, but we wouldn't want to dwell on that!). Power was and is one of the primary currencies of the international system. Like a businessman that would invest money in return for guarantees of repayment with interest, any statesman – as indicated by Kennan's words above – would jealously guard and try to enhance his country's position of power. When the Soviet Union exited its empire and, within a few years' time, peacefully collapsed, old notions of power – particularly the idea that those who have it will always cling on to it – seemingly lost their meaning.[4]

It is no wonder that as a result of the evident inability for national security, national interest and balance of power to offer adequate explanations to the end of the cold war, there are new trends in present day historiography, in what we have, over the past decade or so, started calling new cold war history. A few years ago, one of its best-known practitioners offered 'three possible paradigms' – ideology, technology, and the third world – as the most promising venues for future analysis of the cold war.[5] This is fine. But it seems that these concepts hardly disclose the prevalence of the old-fashioned national security ideas in cold war history. Indeed, one can make the case that ideology and technology are both, to a large extent, variables of national power; certainly in the case of the cold war this seems to have been the case. The Third World, in contrast, was where much of the second half of the cold war was 'fought'; an arena, broadly speaking, of the then global contest between American and Soviet power, ideas and influence. All of these, undoubtedly, formed core parts of what the leaders in Washington and Moscow considered to be in their national interest. The Third World also became, however, an arena that led to the realisation of the limits of power and the need to define, somewhat like Kennan had in 1948, the limits of national interest.[6]

National interest, national security mattered; a great deal. But they were not the only things that mattered. This chapter will not argue that *Realpolitik* was the only game in town or deny that the various other issues that are discussed in other parts in this book – ideology, culture – were mere tools in an arsenal of cynical policy-makers. Neither does the chapter maintain that 'national security' or 'national interest' have some superior value as tools of analysis. But – by looking at different areas of the world – it does maintain that something called the 'national interest' remains an indispensable part of our understanding about the unfolding, development and demise of the cold war as an international system.

approaches to national security

Perhaps the most promising definition of national security has been provided by Melvyn Leffler. One of the pre-eminent historians of US foreign policy during the cold war, Leffler defines national security policy as 'the decisions and actions deemed imperative to protect domestic core values from external threats'. By demanding attention on both foreign and domestic policy, Leffler maintains, the national security approach to the study of American foreign policy provides 'an overall interpretative framework for studying foreign policy'. In brief, the national security approach – at least when defined as a paradigm for understanding US foreign policy – would bridge the gap between the so-called realists (who study the behaviour of states mainly as a consequence of the distribution of power within the international system) and revisionists-corporatists (who proceed from the assumption that foreign policy is mainly a product of a nation's domestic system). In terms of US policy in the early years of the cold war this meant, Leffler argued in *A Preponderance of Power*, that during the 1940s American policy-makers were driven to a more expansive view of US national security policy because the threat to America's domestic core values came from a new kind of foe: the Soviet Union. Leffler maintained that American officials were 'driven by an ideological conviction that their own political economy of freedom would be jeopardized if a totalitarian foe became too powerful'. In other words, to protect American core values (the 'political economy of freedom') against the Soviet Union (the 'totalitarian foe'), American policy-makers launched a global policy of containment with its various subparts (the Truman doctrine, the Marshall Plan, the 'reverse course' in Japan) and eventually intervened in the Korean War.[7]

The national security approach as defined by Leffler has obvious strengths. Among other things, it recognises that the demarcation between domestic and foreign policy is, as John F. Kennedy famously put it, a 'line drawn in the water'.[8] Moreover, the national security approach is seemingly applicable to almost any country that has the characteristics of a modern nation-state. Countries like Great Britain, Finland, Australia, Japan, Yugoslavia and China were arguably equally consumed in protecting their domestic 'core values' from external threats as were the United States or the Soviet Union. Of course, their methods of protection (i.e. national security policies) varied: very few countries could rely on a formidable military machine – let alone a large nuclear arsenal – for protection in the form of deterrence. Nor could they change the basic facts of geography that might leave some countries more obviously exposed to potential security threats than others; Finland's proximity to the Soviet Union shaped its foreign and national security towards a very peculiar direction, while New Zealand's relative isolation may have translated into a certain sense of 'free security'. In brief, the fact that some powers formed alliances while others did not, hardly contradicts the national security paradigm as defined by Leffler.[9]

Naturally, the national security approach is not a foolproof formula for explaining every fluctuation in the course of the cold war. For example, while it may provide a fruitful way of bridging the gap between rival schools of interpretation among scholars of American foreign policy, the validity of the approach beyond that large but essentially self-contained group is not automatic. What if there was a deep contest over the 'core values' within the borders of a nation? Indeed, the concept is problematic when one looks at entities embroiled in civil wars and the process of decolonisation. Many new states, for example, may have enjoyed the symbols of statehood (own flag, currency, seat of government, membership in international organisations) but often lacked the 'sense' of nationhood. The internal conflicts within much of Africa, the Middle East and Asia offer plenty of cases in point. Moreover, while the national security approach may apply well enough to countries that enjoyed democratic 'core values' – mainly in North America and Western Europe – it is by no means obvious that other forms of government confirm to this analysis. Again, one comes back to the end of the cold war and the evident lack of widely accepted 'core values' inside the Soviet bloc.[10]

However one defines national security and national interest, it seems that one can detect at least two simple ways of categorising their relevance over space and time. There is little to surprise one here: different countries have different national interests and different means of protecting their national security. While some such interests are relatively static – countries rarely move from one place to another – national security policies still seem to be in constant flux: technological innovations, political change and changes in the international context are among the factors bringing about change. What follows is an attempt to review some of the ways in which these two categories apply to the various state actors involved in the cold war.

the superpowers: globalisation of national security

In July 1971, Richard Nixon explained the so-called opening to China to a stunned White House staff in simple terms:

> The reason why it was done is that they are one-fourth of the world's population ... They are not a military power now but 25 years from now they will be decisive ... *Where vital interests are involved, great*

powers consult their vital interests – or else they're played for suckers by those powers that do.[11]

Because of statements like these Nixon and his national security adviser Henry Kissinger have often been considered the foremost – by some almost the only – realists to have been in charge of US foreign policy. Indeed, in John L. Gaddis's influential *Strategies of Containment*, Kissinger and Kennan appear almost at par as the two most capable guardians of an asymmetric – and realist – national security policy. The opening to China and *détente* with the Soviet Union were the two best examples of how they practised what they preached: a policy devoid of excess ideological commitment but still consumed with credibility. And, as they dealt with the Soviets and the Chinese on non-ideological terms, they found that their counterparts in Moscow and Beijing acted in much the same manner. The end result was that the cold war was transformed in a way that, depending on one's angle, either hastened or prolonged its ultimate demise.

Of course, US national interest was hardly invented by Nixon and Kissinger (any more than Brezhnev and Gromyko established Soviet national interests). Conflicting national security interests are at the heart of most prominent interpretations on the respective foreign policies of both the United States and the Soviet Union. For example, it is almost too obvious to mention that in the aftermath of the Second World War both the United States and the Soviet Union viewed the question of Germany as a key issue for the future of their national security; at the minimum, denying complete control of Germany's vast (albeit at the time moribund) military and industrial potential to the other side was a key to America's post-war policy in Europe. Perhaps even more so, the Soviet leadership under Stalin considered pre-empting the revival of the German threat and creation of a security zone in East-Central Europe against such a potential threat to be one of its most important post-war goals. In the end, there was a stalemate – the division of Germany – that satisfied the minimum goals of both Moscow and Washington.[12]

A number of prominent historians of American foreign policy, for example, may differ on whether policy-makers in the Truman administration exaggerated the Soviet threat or not. But few disagree that they considered the policies pursued – from the Truman doctrine and the Marshall Plan to the non-recognition of the PRC and US intervention in the Korean war – as having been the correct course to advance US national security interests as they perceived such interests at the time. Among the scholars who regard national security as an important ingredient in the making of American cold war policies, the consensus tends to be that the majority of policy-makers viewed the world essentially in 'realist' terms. Whether they advocated containment in a symmetric or asymmetric fashion, whether they viewed the Soviet Union primarily as a military or a political threat, the 'wise men' of the 1940s and early 1950s agreed on a basic principle: American national security faced but one significant threat and that emanated from Moscow. Moreover, many of them and their successors – whether Democrats or Republicans, career foreign service officers or politicians – believed that upholding American credibility was important for US national security; hence the many interventions in faraway corners of the world that characterised the cold war. And when one of these interventions went awry – in Vietnam – they searched for a new way of promoting US national security interests: hence *détente*.[13]

Similarly, most historians would probably agree that one cannot even begin to understand cold war Soviet foreign policy without exploring the question of national security or, perhaps more accurately, national insecurity. This was something that Kennan famously acknowledged in his Long Telegram of March 1946 and 'Mr. X' article, printed in the influential journal *Foreign Affairs* the following year; it was something that most biographers of Stalin – whether writing with the benefit of access to Soviet documents or not – would also recognise. While one may disagree about the extent to which Stalin actually worried about his own security and his position of power as opposed to that of his state, almost every aspect of post-war Soviet policy in Eastern Europe can be understood as a reflection of an (often brutally practised) effort to maximise the physical security of the Soviet state. While the Soviets acted differently in, say, Poland and Romania or Hungary and Czechoslovakia, the primary concern – the *leitmotif* – appears to have been much the same. Never again would the Soviet Union be caught unprepared as it had been in June 1941. As in the case of the United States – if from a much weaker overall position – Stalin's Soviet Union viewed the containment of external threats and, if possible, the extension of its socio-economic system, as key to the survival of its 'core values'.[14]

As the cold war matured so too, it seems, did Soviet foreign policy. This was true in at least two ways. First, Soviet leaders continued to place increasing emphasis on what one can consider 'traditional' means for safeguarding their security. Stalin's successor, Nikita Khrushchev, may have spoken much about Third World revolutions and there may have been a moment of euphoric revolutionary nostalgia when Castro's then youthful *fidelistas* gained power in Cuba. But any belief in an unstoppable wave of Third World communist revolutions – or in the USSR's interest in supporting them – remained constrained by the reminder, so vividly in evidence during the Cuban missile crisis, that the Soviet Union's security was not necessarily enhanced (and could be positively jeopardised) by too much involvement in the Third World. The nuclear arms race and the gradual move towards *détente* with the United States were some of the major characteristics of the decade that followed. Vietnam – always a complicated case due to the Chinese role – became more of a burden than an asset for the communist side after North Vietnam's victory in April 1975.[15]

Second, the Soviet leaders – much like their American counterparts – also viewed their security in a more global manner. They intervened – unilaterally or with the help of Warsaw Pact allies – in East Germany, Hungary and Czechoslovakia to protect what can be viewed as threats against Soviet national security and/or its 'core values'. While Moscow's global engagements never matched in scale those of the United States, the Soviet Union became engaged in a game of influence, justified in part by the need to prevent American domination, in the so-called Third World. A part of this game may have been a result of an ideological commitment to the expansion of communism, the other side of that particular coin was straightforward: the existence of more communist states and more Soviet influence – notwithstanding the debacle with China (of which more below) – translated into enhanced security in the form of enhanced support and protection for Soviet 'core values'. Indeed, as one of the doyens of so-called new cold war history puts it: 'using ideas as important elements in constructing our interpretations of Soviet foreign policy history in no way excludes making use of the essential lessons of realism'.[16] The globalisation of the cold war may have reflected a contest of ideologies. But it also reflected the perceived need to enhance national security by the accumulation of like-minded states. And, in the end, it may have led to an imperial overstretch by the Soviet Union, because its 'core values' – the socialist system – could not be sustained.[17]

Still, there is much about superpower behaviour that cannot be explained by simply focusing on questions of national interest. The national security approach – as any 'grand' explanation – presupposes a certain iron logic, an unshakeable rationality, in policy. It leaves little room for personal idiosyncrasies and the possibility that policies that may have been justified as being in the national interest may well have been primarily important as a means of pursuing personal – political or bureaucratic – advancement. Why did Lyndon Johnson delay the decision to send US ground troops to Vietnam until after the 1964 presidential elections? Why did Richard Nixon time his visits to China and the Soviet Union to coincide with the presidential election campaign of 1972? Were some of Henry Kissinger's initiatives driven more by his desire to gain the upper hand in bureaucratic politicking rather than a more 'noble' pursuit of US national interest? Was Reagan a calculating practitioner of *Realpolitik* or 'just' an amateur ideologue that got lucky?

Similar questions must be asked about Soviet policies. Again, conceptions of national security and insecurity help explain much of Soviet policy. Even the most disagreeable Soviet leader, Joseph Stalin, was, Vladislav Zubok and Constantine Pleshakov maintained in their 1996 book, 'closer to a cynical *Realpolitik* than to the idea of world revolution'.[18] Other Soviet leaders were equally driven by – or limited in the choice of their action – by an understanding of national security or insecurity. Khrushchev talked in rash terms about burying the West but was also worried about the supposed irrationality of China's ideological challenge and keen on confirming the Soviet Union's position as a superpower through a tentative *détente* with the United States. And, most of all, how can Gorbachev's policies ever be truly explained as some sort of expression of national interest?[19]

The point, therefore, is not that for the Soviet Union and the United States national security was more important than ideology. Rather, it seems that the whole juxtaposition is artificial. In 2003 Les Gelb and Justine Rosenthal wrote that 'We have passed from an era in which ideals were always flatly opposed to self-interests to an era in which tension remains between the two, but the stark juxtaposition of the past has largely subsided. Now, ideals and self-interests are both generally considered necessary ingredients of the national interest.'[20] Although Gelb and Rosenthal basically referred to the post-cold war – and even more specifically to the post 9/11 – era in *American* foreign policy, their central point could have been made at almost any time during the cold war. And the same, to a large extent, applied to Soviet foreign policy. Ideology was not separable from interests. If anything it was an 'interest' in itself.

allies, stooges and puppets: (in)security systems in europe

Another truism that has emerged from the past quarter of a century of historical research is that despite the imbalance of power that separated the United States and the Soviet Union from the rest of the pack of nations that comprised the cold war international system, neither superpower could simply dictate the terms of policy to its respective allies, or 'puppets'. While it has been evident for a long time that countries like Great Britain and France exercised significant (if not preponderant) influence on the shaping of American policy in Europe, the Middle East and South-East Asia after the Second World War, recent findings from the 'other side' have significantly altered our earlier view of East Europeans as docile stooges of the Soviet Union. As, for example, Hope Harrison has vividly demonstrated, the Soviets chose to erect the Berlin wall because of the growing pressure from their East German 'allies' that do not emerge as the simple puppets or stooges that earlier literature had indicated.[21]

The significance of such observations for this chapter's topic is obvious: the cold war, for all its pervasive influence, did not mean that France and Britain, Poland and Romania, Japan and Germany suddenly ceased to have national interests and national security policies of their own. Moreover, there were countries, such as Switzerland and Sweden that chose to continue along a well-tested national security policy of neutrality. Charles de Gaulle's France in the 1960s and Tito's Yugoslavia in the 1940s may have been the most obvious cases of allies steering a strongly independent course – based heavily on their perception of their countries' national interests – during the cold war. But, as much recent research suggests, they were by far not the only examples, neither in the West nor the East.[22]

There is plenty of evidence for the prevalence of independent national security policies among Western Europeans. With some exceptions, the countries that joined NATO shared, after all, a similar democratic system: their leaders, apparently, judged that the best way of defending their domestic core values was through an alliance with a like-minded nation that held the necessary military and economic assets needed to contain the totalitarian foe from the East. Others may have viewed NATO as a means of preventing another revival of the 'German menace'. In short, to paraphrase the quip attributed to Lord Ismay (NATO's first Secretary-General), it was national security interests – to keep the Germans 'down' and the Soviets 'out' – that necessitated that the Americans stay in.[23] Yet even within the unprecedented framework of transatlantic – and European – cooperation specific national interests prevailed.

The best example of such independence of action, deriving its force from a specific national interest, is, of course, that of de Gaulle's France. From France's own 'opening to China' in 1964 and the President's visit to Moscow two years later, to its development of the *force de frappe* and exit from NATO's integrated military structure, the list of the general's independent initiatives is almost endless. Whether such efforts were directed by illusions of '*grandeur*' or concern over domestic protest that demanded innovative foreign policy, de Gaulle was undoubtedly pursuing his specific vision of what was good for French national interest. If anything, it was easier for a nation like France (or Britain, or any other NATO ally of the United States) to frame its specific foreign policy around a vision of national interest. Lacking (well, for the most part) in imperial and global pretensions, they could focus on pursuing a more tightly defined national security policy. This remains an obstacle to the development of a truly common foreign and security policy within the EU.[24]

While independence had its limits, as the British and the French discovered during the Suez crisis, national interests remained central and were linked – both then and now – to the defence of certain domestic core values that, though similar, were hardly identical to those of the United States. The widespread European criticism of American involvement in Vietnam, for example, reflected a deeply sensed frustration over being relegated to second-class citizens in the global cold war game. But it often also relegated a sense that the globalisation of American policies and the coinciding shift of US focus away from Europe lowered the defences against the threat, to many policy-makers still very real in the 1960s and 1970s, emanating from the East. Seen in this light *détente* was a means of guarding West Europeans' national security interests. Of course, different countries had different interests – Willy Brandt's *Ostpolitik* was in large part geared towards the ultimate goal of German unification. The broad point is, though, that within a 'matured' cold war context, national interest was more openly on display in the policies of America's West European allies than during the early cold war years.

Independent security policy within the Soviet bloc – and avenues open to express specific national interests – was far more circumscribed and, at times, brutally repressed. The danger of 'national deviation' was, after all, the term used to justify the repression in the bloc, particularly after 1947–48. In theory, everything was subjected to a Soviet veto; if a national security interest existed and dictated policy it was Moscow's vision of national security. The East Germans in 1953, the Hungarians in 1956, the Czechs in 1968 bore witness to the overriding demand for uniformity. Nevertheless, even within this system that was devised to serve Soviet security interests there was room for specific national interests to affect policy.[25] For example, as Wilfried Loth has argued, these differences in national interest became increasingly evident after the Warsaw Pact intervention in Prague in August 1968. By the early 1980s, according to Loth, such a joint intervention was no longer possible, because *détente* had increased the differences in national interests among the Warsaw

Pact countries. In the end, the Polish leader General Wojtech Jaruzelski, fearing a possible collapse of 'socialism' and viewing this as a threat to Poland's national security, decided to impose martial law in Poland in December 1981.[26]

Indeed, one of the ironies of the cold war in East-Central Europe was that – much as was the case in Western Europe – as the balance of power between the superpowers became more recognised and stabilised within the context of *détente*, the countries that were part of the Soviet system pursued their own national interests in more assertive ways. The difference was that, unlike in the West, the 'core values' of the political elite in the East were not the same as those shared by the majority of the population (a fact Jaruzelski, among others, clearly recognised). By the late 1980s, this particular credibility gap began to threaten – and eventually contributed to the collapse of – the post-war Soviet bloc system. The gap had been opened, though, several decades earlier by a growing confrontation between the two largest socialist states.

china: a special case?

Since the final victory of Mao's armies in 1949, the PRC has represented a major force in international politics. Indeed, a strong argument has been made that China's role in determining the course of the cold war was central. While 1949 heightened America's security concerns and greatly propelled the division of the world; the Sino-Soviet conflict in the 1960s transformed Soviet security policies and the so-called opening to China in the early 1970s brought about a new era of tenuous stability into international relations. In the ensuing endgame of the cold war, Deng Xiaoping's China – by choosing the road to economic modernisation – greatly eroded the viability of socialism as an alternate system. In short, events in China propelled the major transformations of the cold war international system.[27]

The irony is that while the impact of China's choices on the course of the cold war may have been revolutionary, its policies can quite easily be viewed as reflecting a fundamentally conservative perception of China's national interest rather than a series of ideologically driven obsessions. Interventions and military aid to North Korea or Vietnam, for example, may have reflected a desire to support revolutionary movements. But they were also aimed at regimes within China's 'near abroad', within the PRC's immediate security zone. Alternatively, it has also been argued that Chinese policies after 1949 were driven by a need for greater internal unity after decades of civil war. Demonising the West, and the United

States in particular, as counter-revolutionary agents provided a natural vehicle for mobilising the incipient need for such internal unity. Later, the Soviet Union – useful as an ally in the first decade of the PRC's existence – emerged as such a 'useful threat'; today, one could argue, Japan has once again claimed a role of an external enemy (as seen in, for example, the controversies over Second World War textbooks) that may be needed to prevent globalisation from destroying a sense of Chinese unity.

In this sense, it is relatively easy to argue that the national security approach actually applies quite well to the supposedly special case of China. This is not to argue that Mao and others were not true revolutionaries or that ideology did not matter. But ultimately, once in power even Mao would find himself considering seriously the imperatives of such seemingly 'capitalist' and 'imperialist' notions as national interest and national security. If the Soviets embraced what Zubok and Pleshakov call a revolutionary-imperial paradigm, then the Chinese were driven by a revolutionary-nationalist paradigm. In terms of national security and foreign policy this translated into a degree of flexibility often downplayed in recent literature that tends to (over) emphasise the significance of ideological considerations. In later years, and increasingly since the end of the cold war, the nationalist part has become prevalent in Chinese discourse and what passes for popular politics in a Chinese political system still dominated by the Communist Party.[28]

Indeed, the survival of communism in China may owe a great deal to the ability of post-Mao elites to emphasise a sense of Chinese national interest. Unlike the Soviet Union, China did not 'purchase' its cold war security via the imposition of its own imperialism in neighbouring states. Rather, China's national security and national interest was based upon a historical sense of having been wronged by external powers. Whatever the problems resulting from communist rule, Mao's successors could claim a gradual progression in this regard. A resurgence of Chinese nationalism and a sense of a truly 'Chinese' national interest was one of the by-products of China's emergence as an increasingly important player in international affairs after the 1970s. Ironically, at the time of writing, this development is a troubling one in the eyes of many Western observers.[29]

global insecurity: cold war in the third world

It has already been pointed out repeatedly that national security and national interest, while important determinants of foreign policy choice to most countries, were not the sole factors explaining the course of the cold war. In particular, the case of the so-called Third World presents a conundrum to anyone wishing to analyse them as a whole. Nor is the purpose here to argue that countries as different as Cuba and Pakistan, Indonesia and Peru, should be examined as one group. It is simply to suggest that the idea of a national interest should never be overlooked even in parts of the world where – aside from a desire to remove as much of the external influence as possible – a true national interest is difficult to discern. In particular, it would be difficult to apply the national security approach to more than a select few of Third World countries, simply because so many of them were embroiled in extended internal conflicts over their own future. But a few general points should be made.

First, it is obvious that to many countries and their decision-makers, the Third World mattered as a national security issue. It was, for example, against the American national interest – and in contrast in the Soviet national interest as defined in the 1950s and 1960s – to have Cuba dominated by Castro. For the United States, access to the Persian Gulf region emerged as an increasingly important national security issue during the second half of the cold war; hence, a contest of influence in the Middle East between the United States and the Soviet Union – a contest largely 'won' by the United States but not without its unhappy long-term consequences – became one of the defining themes of the 1970s and 1980s.[30] Moreover, the old imperial countries – France and Britain in particular – attempted to maintain their influence in the former colonies through various forms of association. For example, the establishment and existence of the British Commonwealth was hardly a predominant cold war security issue. But it caused many a cold war-related agonising reappraisal between London and Washington.[31]

Second, there were many so-called Third World countries that utilised the existence of the cold war to the benefit of their national interest and national security policy. Pakistan is one example of an ally of the United States that was able to maintain a formidable, partly US-funded, military machine and not make serious concessions with regards to its internal politics. A number of Latin American states did the same, although there is a difference that needs to be noted. In Latin America, the United States never fully came to terms with supporting dictators that did not have much else to offer than military rule and opposition to communism. There were efforts – Kennedy's 'Alliance for Progress' foremost among them – to enforce positive social change in Latin America. Yet, in part because of the spectre of another Cuba in the Western Hemisphere, American policy-makers usually concluded that immediate national security considerations demanded continued support for strong rulers.

National interest – or the perception thereof – ultimately came first, often with debilitating consequences to Latin American democracy.[32]

Third, the logic of national interest seems to lose much of its explanatory power when one considers the many military conflicts that emerged in the process of decolonisation. After all, it would be difficult to argue that, say, Congo or Angola had a clear national interest in the 1960s or 1970s. Emerging from a civil war, the new leaders – such as Mobutu Sese Seko or Agostinho Neto – initially had a strategy for survival against internal and external threats. In some countries – such as Vietnam – the presence of large foreign contingents defined the conflict in clear terms while allowing one side to present the other as a stooge of 'imperialism'. The conflicts themselves were in a sense rooted in different visions of national interest that, in turn, were defined by the overall context of the cold war system. It became clear to many newly emerging states that in order to safeguard their national security and newly gained independence, membership in the UN or other international or regional sub-groupings (such as the Organisation of African Unity, or OAU) was hardly enough.[33]

In terms of the national security approach there was little obvious logic to any of this, showing the limits of the usefulness of any theory designed as a tool for understanding the behaviour of one nation. But it seems that neither external involvement in nor the internal debacles within various post-colonial states could have been shaped without the various players seriously considering their present or future, national interest. That they lacked internal agreements on such interests and were constantly being subjected to the national security policies of external players only exacerbated and prolonged many of the Third World's security problems.

conclusions

National interest and national security did, in short, matter a great deal. We cannot even begin to understand why the United States kept its troops in and gave economic aid to Western Europe and Japan or why the Soviet Union exercised hegemonic influence in East-Central Europe, without taking into account their respective national security considerations. There was, as there always tends to be, continuity and change. The Soviet Union, for example, acted in a number of ways like its imperial Russian predecessor. Yet it did not simply follow a Tsarist course; revolution mattered, construction and expansion of the community of socialist states was an important goal.

When set against some recent findings about the importance of culture and the complexities of ideology for the unfolding of the cold war, one can draw at least one general and somewhat trite conclusion: the more things changed, the more they stayed the same. That is to say, the more the cold war pervaded people's consciousness and became part of the daily lives of a great number of people on the planet, the harder did policy-makers work to adapt their respective country's national security policy to meet the needs of change. But one thing remained obvious: whether one was in Washington or Moscow, Prague or Bonn, Paris or Beijing, the policy-makers made sense of their world and drew conclusions based upon an understanding that their nation – whatever its internal structure – had a distinctive national interest. The difference between democracies and dictatorships – be they right-wing or left-wing – was essentially in the way in which the rulers of totalitarian states tended to equate national interest and national security with their own personal interests and security. The other major difference had to do with the means at each nation's disposal: whether they possessed nuclear weapons and overseas bases, what their economic resources were, and – equally importantly – how they were viewed abroad by friend and foe alike. One curious thing about the cold war was how it did ultimately become a war in almost all fronts aside from the outright military one between the two major protagonists. Unlike in previous periods of history, national interest and national security could thus be pursued in any number of ways, while culture, propaganda, economic incentives, military assistance (or deprival thereof) could all be viewed as part of the ever-growing arsenal at the disposal of strategic planners.

In the end, one can only close by stressing three basic points. First, national security and conceptions of national interest mattered a great deal during the cold war. They were taken into account when countries and their leaders fashioned policies that affected the course of the cold war. National interest was, in other words, a highly relevant factor that would be foolhardy and mistaken to ignore in any account of the cold war. Second, national interest, alone, does not explain everything. In some cases it may have been wholly irrelevant to the developments under way. The case of new states – which at times developed into failed or failing states – that emerged during the process of decolonisation is one example of the inadequacy of the national security approach as an overall interpretative framework for cold war history. Third, and perhaps more important, the increasingly global and ultimately almost total nature of the cold war meant that the concept of national interest and national security was constantly in a flux, depending on external events, the internal political situation in any given country, and the process of technological and economic change.

In understanding the cold war as an international system or in reviewing any period, crisis or policy one cannot, nor should one, shy away from the seemingly old-fashioned terms national interest or national security. There was, of course, much more to the cold war than rational statesmen designing rational policies, based on careful calculations of power and interest. But historians of the cold war should keep in mind – a fact that at times seems to have been forgotten in our effort not to become too isolated from the mainstream of the historical profession – that something called the 'national interest' remains an indispensable part of our understanding about the unfolding, development and demise of the cold war as an international system. The relevance of national security as a conceptual tool for understanding the cold war remains indispensable.

notes

1. PPS/23: 'Review of Current Trends in US Foreign Policy', *Foreign Relations of the United States 1948*, Vol. 1, No. 2, p.524 (these volumes hereafter cited as *FRUS*). Soft power is, of course, a term popularised by Joseph Nye. See his *Paradox of American Power: Why the World's Only Superpower Can't Go It Alone* (New York: Oxford University Press, 2003).

2. These debates are well summarised in chapters 1–4 in Odd Arne Westad (ed.), *Reviewing the Cold War: Approaches, Interpretations, Theory* (London: Frank Cass, 2000), *passim*. Michael Hunt, 'The Long Crisis in U.S. Diplomatic History', *Diplomatic History*, 16 (1992). In fact, those American diplomatic historians that do have an impact on the debate of the actual course of US foreign policy are those who emphasise a 'realist'/national security framework, John Gaddis and Melvyn Leffler. See, for example, Gaddis, 'Grand Strategy in the Second Term', *Foreign Affairs* (January/February 2005); Leffler, 'Think Again: Bush's Foreign Policy', *Foreign Policy* (September/October 2004). For limitations of space, I have not included extensive footnotes with this chapter, but the ones cited will give interested readers numerous links to further sources.

3. For engaging efforts to encode George Kennan's discourse see Frank Costigliola, '"Unceasing Pressure for Penetration": Gender, Pathology, and Emotion in George Kennan's Formulation of the Cold War', *Journal of American History*, 83 (1997), pp.1309–39. Also, see Costigliola, 'The Nuclear Family: Tropes of Gender and Pathology in the Western Alliance', *Diplomatic History*, 21 (1997), pp.163–83; Robert D. Dean, 'Masculinity as Ideology: John F. Kennedy and the Domestic Politics of Foreign Policy', *Diplomatic History*, 22 (1998), pp.29–62; Emily S. Rosenberg, '"Foreign Affairs" after World War II: Connecting Sexual and International Politics', *Diplomatic History*, 18 (1994), pp.59–70; and Westad, *Reviewing the Cold War*, especially chapter 7 by Yale Ferguson & Rey Koslowski.

4. Some examples of the rejection of 'neo-realism' include Peter J. Katzenstein (ed.), *The Culture of National Security: Norms and Identity in World Politics* (New York: Columbia University Press, 1996); Alexander Wendt, *Social Theory of International Politics* (New York: Cambridge University Press, 1999). See also Richard Ned Lebow, William C. Wohlforth, Yale Ferguson & Rey Koslowski, and Douglas J. McDonald's articles in Westad (ed.), *Reviewing the Cold War*; Francis A. Beer & Robert Harriman (eds), *Post-Realism: The Rhetorical Turn in International Relations* (East Lansing, MI: Michigan State University Press, 1996); Ted Hopf, *Social Construction of International Politics: Identities and Foreign Policies, Moscow, 1955 and 1999* (Ithaca, NY: Cornell University Press, 2002); Martin J. Medhurst, et al., *Cold War Rhetoric: Strategy, Metaphor and Ideology* (East Lansing, MI: Michigan State University Press, 1997).

5. Odd Arne Westad, 'The New International History of the Cold War: Three (Possible) Paradigms', *Diplomatic History*, 24:3 (Fall 2000), pp.551–65.

6. For a major re-evaluation of the Third World as a cold war arena see Odd Arne Westad, *The Global Cold War: Third World Interventions and the Making of Our Times* (Cambridge: Cambridge University Press, 2005).

7. Melvyn Leffler, 'National Security', in Michael J. Hogan (ed.), *Explaining the History of American Foreign Relations* (Cambridge: Cambridge University Press, 2004), pp.202–13. Last quote from Leffler, *A Preponderance of Power: National Security, the Truman Administration, and the Cold War* (Stanford, CA: Stanford University Press, 1992), p.14. For the various interpretative struggles among historians of American foreign policy see the other essays in Hogan's book.

8. John F. Kennedy, *The Strategy of Peace* (London: Hamish Hamilton, 1960).

9. For the links between US domestic and foreign policy see Jussi M. Hanhimäki, 'Global Visions and Parochial Politics: the Persistent Dilemma of the "American Century"', *Diplomatic History*, 27:4 (2003), pp.423–47.

10. For various early critiques of Leffler see Lynn Eden, 'The End of U.S. Cold War History?', *International Security*, 18:1 (1993), pp.174–207; William O. Walker III, 'Melvyn P. Leffler, Ideology, and American Foreign Policy', *Diplomatic History*, 20:4 (1996), pp.663–73. See also the articles by Gaddis, Leffler, Lundestad and Stephanson in Westad (ed.), *Reviewing the Cold War*.

11. Memorandum for the President's Files, 'Briefing of the White House Staff on the July 15 Announcement of the President's Trip to Peking', 19.7.71, in <http://www.gwu.edu/nsarchiv~/NSAEBB/NSAEBB66/ch-41.pdf>.

12. One of the most comprehensive accounts of the complexities revolving around the division of Germany and its central role in the origins of the cold war is Marc Trachtenberg's *A Constructed Peace: Making of European Settlement, 1945–1963* (Princeton, NJ: Princeton University Press, 1999).

13. The symmetric–asymmetric containment formulation is most clearly expressed in John L. Gaddis, *Strategies of Containment: A Critical Appraisal of American National Security Policy During the Cold War* (New York: Oxford University Press, 2005, 2nd edition). On Kissinger and *détente* see: Raymond Garthoff, *Détente and Confrontation: American–Soviet Relations from Nixon to Reagan* (Washington, DC: Brookings, 1994); and Jussi M. Hanhimäki, *The Flawed Architect: Henry Kissinger and American Foreign Policy* (New York: Oxford University Press, 2004).

14. In addition to Leffler – who has not worked with Soviet archival materials – books that tend to support the primacy of security–insecurity considerations

in early cold war Soviet foreign policy include: Vojtech Mastny, *The Cold War and Soviet Insecurity: The Stalin Years* (Oxford: Oxford University Press, 1995), *passim*; Vladislav Zubok and Constantine Pleshakov, *Inside the Kremlin's Cold War: From Stalin to Khrushchev* (Cambridge, MA: Harvard University Press, 1996). For a recent study on a more specific case see Iliya Gaiduk, *Confronting Vietnam: Soviet Foreign Policy Toward the Indochina Conflict, 1954–1963* (Stanford, CA: Stanford University Press, 2003); see also Gaiduk, *The Soviet Union and the Vietnam War* (Chicago, IL: I.R. Dee, 1996).

15. The literature on these issues is massive, growing and still fairly recent. Much of the recent findings have made it to the pages of such journals as *Cold War History*, *Cold War International History Project Bulletin*, *Diplomatic History* and *Journal of Cold War Studies*. Some of the most detailed works include Timothy Naftali & Alexander Fursenko, *One Hell of a Gamble: Khrushchev, Castro, Kennedy, and the Cuban Missile Crisis, 1958–1964* (New York: Norton, 1999); Piero Gleijeses, *Conflicting Missions: Havana, Washington, and Africa, 1959–1976* (Chapel Hill, NC: University of North Carolina Press, 2002), *passim*; Westad, *Global Cold War*. William Taubman's *Khrushchev: The Man and His Era* (New York: Norton, 2003) is a more-or-less definitive biography of the Soviet leader. For an engaging and insightful book that mixes social and diplomatic history to reinterpret the origins of *détente* see Jeremi Suri, *Power and Protest: Global Revolution and the Rise of Détente* (Cambridge, MA: Harvard University Press, 2003), *passim*.

16. Odd Arne Westad, 'Secrets of the Second World: The Russian Archives and Reinterpretations of Cold War History', *Diplomatic History*, 21:2 (1997), p.268. See also Melvyn Leffler, 'Inside Enemy Archives: The Cold War Reopened', *Foreign Affairs* (1996), pp.120–35. For an example of an article that deals with a little-known aspect of Soviet imperial policy see Larissa Effimova, 'Stalin and the Revival of the Communist Party of Indonesia', *Cold War History*, 5:1 (2005).

17. See Geir Lundestad, 'Imperial Overstretch: Mikhail Gorbachev and the End of the Cold War', *Cold War History*, 1:1 (2000), pp.1–20; and Vladislav Zubok, 'Gorbachev and the End of the Cold War: New Perspectives on History and Personality', *Cold War History*, 2:2 (2002), pp.61–100; Hannes Adomeit, *Imperial Overstretch: Germany in Soviet Policy from Stalin to Gorbachev* (Baden-Baden: Nomos, 1998).

18. Zubok & Pleshakov, *Kremlin's Cold War*, p.282.

19. For the post-Khrushchev era see Matthew J. Ouimet, *The Rise and Fall of the Brezhnev Doctrine in Soviet Foreign Policy* (Chapel Hill, NC: University of North Carolina Press, 2003).

20. Les Gelb & Justine Rosenthal, 'The Rise of Ethics in Foreign Policy: Reaching a Values Consensus', *Foreign Affairs* (May–June 2003), p.7.

21. Hope Harrison, *Driving the Soviets up the Wall: Soviet–East German Relations, 1953–1961* (Princeton, NJ: Princeton University Press, 2003). See also Mary Sarotte, *Dealing with the Devil: East Germany, Detente, and Ostpolitik, 1969–1973* (Chapel Hill, NC: University of North Carolina Press, 2001), *passim*; Avril Pittman, *From Ostpolitik to Reunification: West German–Soviet Political Relations since 1974* (Cambridge: Cambridge University Press, 2002).

22. For alliances in general see Lawrence Kaplan's chapter in this volume, as well as Vojtech Mastny, 'The New History of Cold War Alliances', *Journal of Cold War Studies*, 4:2 (2002), pp.55–84.

23. Lord Ismay allegedly declared that NATO's role was 'to keep the Americans in, the Russians out, and the Germans down'. This quote has, however, never been adequately cited and is possibly apocryphal.

24. Maurice Vaisse, *La grandeur: politique etrangere du General de Gaulle, 1958–1969* (Paris: Fayard, 1999); see also Suri, *Power and Protest*; Frederic Bozo, *Two Strategies for Europe: De Gaulle, the United States, and the Atlantic Alliance* (New York: Rowman & Littlefield, 2001). See also Piers Ludlow, 'No Longer a Closed Shop: Post-1945 Research in the French Archives', *Cold War History*, 2:1 (2001); Tamara Keating, *Constructing the Gaullist Consensus: A Cultural Perspective on French Foreign Policy toward the United States in NATO* (Baden-Baden, 2004). For one recent essay that deals with the Anglo-American special relationship see Nigel Ashton, 'Harold Macmillan and the "Golden Days" of Anglo-American Relations Revisited, 1957–63', *Diplomatic History*, 29:4 (2005), pp.691–724.

25. One example of this is discussed in Sheldon Anderson, *Cold War in the Soviet Bloc: Polish–East German Relations, 1945–1962* (Boulder, CO: Westview Press, 2000).

26. See Wilfried Loth, 'Moscow, Prague and Warsaw: Overcoming the Brezhnev Doctrine', *Cold War History*, 1:2 (2001).

27. Chen Jian, *Mao's China and the Cold War* (Chapel Hill, NC: University of North Carolina Press, 2001). Other influential recent studies include Qiang, *China and the Vietnam Wars, passim*; Michael Sheng, *Battling Western Imperialism: Mao, Stalin and the United States* (Princeton, NJ: Princeton University Press, 1997); Shuguang Zhang, *Mao's Military Romanticism: China and the Korean War* (Lawrence, KS: University of Kansas Press, 1996); Odd Arne Westad (ed.), *Brothers in Arms: The Rise and Fall of the Sino-Soviet Alliance 1945–63* (Stanford, CA: Stanford University Press, 2000), *passim*.

28. Suisheng Zhao, *A Nation-State by Construction: Dynamics of Modern Chinese Nationalism* (Stanford, CA: Stanford University Press, 2004); Alastair I. Johnston, *Cultural Realism: Strategic Culture and Grand Strategy in Chinese History* (Princeton, NJ: Princeton University Press, 1995).

29. For example, Peter Hays Gries, *China's New Nationalism: Pride, Politics, and Diplomacy* (Berkeley, CA: University of California Press, 2004).

30. Due to current events the Middle East continues to attract much 'presentist' writing. Two recent examples of books that deal with the Middle East in a 'serious' historical light are Salim Yaqub, *Containing Arab Nationalism: The Eisenhower Doctrine and the Middle East* (Chapel Hill, NC: University of North Carolina Press, 2005); Douglas Little, *American Orientalism: The United States and the Middle East since 1945* (Chapel Hill, NC: University of North Carolina Press, 2004).

31. The 'special relationship' remains one of the pre-eminent obsessions of the British historical profession. For useful relatively recent overviews see: John Dumbrell, *A Special Relationship: Anglo-American Relations in the Cold War and After* (New York: Macmillan, 2001); and Jonathan Holloway (ed.), *Twentieth Century Anglo-American Relations* (Basingstoke: Palgrave Macmillan, 2001).

32. In addition to those already cited, some recent work include Piero Gleijeses, 'A Brush with Mexico', *Diplomatic History*, 29:2 (2005), pp.223–54; Lester D. Langley, 'The United States and Latin American Revolution in the 1960s', *Diplomatic History*, 28:2 (2004), pp.277–80; Stephen G. Rabe, *The Most Dangerous Area in the World* (Chapel Hill, NC: University of North Carolina Press, 1999); Eric Roorda, *The Dictator Next Door: The Good Neighbor Policy and the Trujillo Regime in the Dominican Republic, 1930–1945* (Durham, NC: Duke University Press, 1998); Greg Grandin, *The Last Colonial Massacre: Latin America in the Cold War* (Chicago, IL: University of Chicago Press, 2004).

33. Aside from Vietnam, Angola and the Congo, one country that has attracted much attention recently is Indonesia. See Andrew Roadnight, *United States Policy Towards Indonesia in the Truman and Eisenhower Years* (Basingstoke: Palgrave Macmillan, 2002); Robert J. MacMahon, *The Limits of Empire: The United States and Southeast Asia since World War II* (New York: Columbia University Press, 1999); Paul F. Gardner, *Shared Hopes, Separate Fears: Fifty Years of U.S.–Indonesian Relations* (Boulder, CO: Westview, 1997). For a general overview of various African states' search for foreign policy see Stephen Wright (ed.), *African Foreign Policies* (Boulder, CO: Westview, 1998).

3
ideology

leopoldo nuti and vladislav zubok

The role of ideology in cold war historiography and, more in general, in the development of the contemporary international system, has been a source of academic dispute. Hans Morgenthau, the father of modern realist thinking in international relations, believed that ideas can be reduced to structure. According to this explanation, ideologies occupy a secondary place to the power relationship, which remains the basic conceptual tool to analyse the international system. Yet, according to other schools of thought, ideology has its own sphere of influence: beliefs and principles that regulate human behaviour constitute a factor that cannot be reduced to material and institutional considerations. This is particularly true for the contemporary world: whether one agrees or not with Karl Dietrich Bracher, who defined the twentieth century as the century of ideologies, it is undeniable that throughout the past century most political systems felt an increasing need to surmount their political activities with an ideational justification.[1] Modern political systems, in other words, require ideological means to boost their legitimacy: large groups are more easily mobilised under vague value-laden slogans than geopolitical and pragmatic security considerations, and modern societies can sustain high levels of mobilisation and deprivation for a long time only if duly motivated. The First and Second World Wars demonstrated the uses and abuses of ideologies by various political regimes. The growing politicisation of the masses transformed the political landscape in Europe and elsewhere. New global visions of the international order began to challenge the old elitist notion of an international system based on the balance of power.

Historians realised, accordingly, the need to reintroduce ideology into their debates in order to come to grips with the transformations of the twentieth century. Bracher, among others, defines ideology as a

Weltanschauung, a vision of the world, which implies a significant amount of simplification and of exploitation of political ideas in order to mobilise and control large masses of population. This interpretation is a useful conceptual tool to understand the history of the twentieth century, but it can be applied mostly, if not exclusively, to those political systems which used ideas as a straightjacket to discipline their societies.

A different interpretation comes from the work of a number of sociologists and anthropologists. Clifford Geertz, in particular, has defined ideology as an instrument which serves the purpose of rendering 'otherwise incomprehensible social situations meaningful, to so construe them as to make it possible to act purposefully within them'. For Geertz, ideologies are 'maps of problematic social reality and matrices for the creation of collective conscience'.[2] From this perspective, ideology can be regarded as the cognitive framework through which individuals as well as entire societies interpret and attribute a meaning to the world that surrounds them. Here ideology loses most of its negative connotation, present in Bracher's definition, and becomes a conceptual tool to investigate the mindset of politicians and other actors of the international system. It is no longer a superfluous, irrelevant superstructure that obfuscates the realities of 'hard' power. Rather, it is a component of the international system as real as the – supposedly more 'realistic' – power-based relations between the states.

Both interpretations affected recent historiography of the cold war, expanding its scope far beyond narrow diplomatic history, and its realist and neo-realist interpretations. There is a new understanding that ideological and cultural factors not only accompanied the 'basic, structural' causes of the global confrontation, but also played an autonomous role in that historical drama. It may appear that researchers have finally returned to the much earlier traditional interpretation of the cold war as primarily an ideological contest, or rather the clash between the democratic 'free world' and the totalitarian countries guided by the ideology of Marxist-Leninism in its various permutations. In reality, however, the rediscovery of ideology in the cold war does not mean the return to the totalitarian model. Rather, it means further development of those approaches that emerged because the 'totalitarian' model no longer dominated the field. By stressing the meaning of ideology as the cognitive process through which individuals shape their image of the world and make sense of the reality that surrounds them, historians have begun to re-evaluate the importance of the ideological dimension as the mental framework used by policy-makers to look at themselves and at their international policies.

As in any transition from theoretical discussion to empirical research, there is a natural difficulty in exploring the role of ideological factors in the cold war. To begin with, was there a common Western view of the cold war and of the Soviet Union? Was there, in other words, anything even vaguely resembling a cohesive Western ideology, mirroring the Soviet one? Bracher seems to believe that in the period between 1945 and 1950, the rejection of the totalitarian experience and the widely shared appreciation of liberal democracy united the Western Europeans and the Americans and were widely supported on both sides of the Atlantic.[3] Yet according to Melvyn Leffler, in the early years of the cold war there was no such a common view – or at least it would be misleading to emphasise its importance. Leffler believes that it was a simplification 'to frame international politics in the initial post-war years as a struggle between tyranny and American freedom'. He then evokes specifically Lundestad's concept of 'empire by invitation' by the Europeans. He warns that it should not be understood in terms of the appeal of American ideology of market capitalism and democracy; nor should it 'be understood to mean that those soliciting or accepting American assistance had the same motives or concerns as did the United States or shared the same values as did Americans'.[4]

Thus, if one looks beyond the many official statements of faith in liberal democracy and free-market capitalism, and starts searching for less fuzzy concepts than a generic anti-communism and a deep distrust and dislike of the Soviet Union, its regime and its practices, it is difficult to come up with a common Western creed that could mirror the view of the world that characterised the Soviet Union and its leaders. Differences of mentality and the gradations in threat perceptions complicated the transatlantic relationship throughout the cold war. The US and Western European leaders learned this at their own expense during the many crises that beset their alliance. While in Europe this divergence was more subdued, as the perception of a Soviet threat there was more palpable, in the rest of the world the USA often found itself at odds with the British and the French. 'Out-of-area issues', as they became known in NATO jargon, beleaguered the Atlantic alliance almost from the start.[5] As Frank Ninkovich put it, 'abroad, American globalism was welcomed when it accorded with the self-interest of the allies, but it seemed eccentric and utopian when they derived no immediate benefit from it'.[6] This difficulty in squaring interpretations of non-European events, moreover, was only one of the many discrepancies in the Western European and American approaches to the confrontation with the Soviet Union.

The discussion of ideological factors in the cold war has only begun to map out this phenomenon. In our chapter we will deal with the most controversial and interesting issues to emerge. First, we summarise what the historiography says about the specific content and peculiarity of 'American ideology' in US foreign policy, in particular during the cold war. Second, the chapter covers ideological perceptions and projects that existed during the cold war in Western Europe. Third, we will look at an amalgam of ideologies that existed within the Soviet bloc and, more broadly, under the umbrella of world 'communism'. Finally, we deal with the recent views of Soviet ideology and its evolution during the cold war, especially with regard to the ultimate changes in Soviet behaviour that led to the unexpected and peaceful end of the global confrontation.

what was american ideology about?

A common tenet of cold war historiography is that the USA always had a much more ideological approach to the Soviet Union than its European partners. US policy, in other words, has generally been regarded as strongly influenced by ideals, morality and principles, whereas the Western Europeans featured a supposedly value-free, more traditional inclination to pursue a realistic approach, fully attuned to the old-fashioned belief in the principles of the balance of power. This may as well have been the case, but if one tries to move beyond this initial generic assumption one soon finds out that there has been little, if any, scholarly consensus on how much US foreign policy itself was influenced by such an ideological outlook and on what was its actual weight in the day-by-day policy-making process. Nor has there been any agreement whether the presence of an ideal dimension – as opposed to a supposedly hard-nosed, realistic one – was beneficial or detrimental to the fortunes of American diplomacy. Particularly, in the early years of cold war studies, the most important historical schools paid little – if any – attention to the ideological dimension of the conflict.

Ironically, the most remarkable proof of the strength of ideological influences on the early US cold war policies can be found in the writings of American 'realists'. Historians, political scientists and policy-makers who had been trained according to the realist school of foreign policy, from Hans Morgenthau to George Kennan to Henry Kissinger, decried the presence of an idealistic component in US international behaviour as an obstacle to the implementation of a more practical, down-to-earth version of diplomacy.[7] Ideology, from a realist point of view, was a mix between an encumbrance and an almost inescapable vagary forced upon otherwise wise and sensible statesmen by the whims of American public opinion. According to realism, great powers pursue their national interests without being unduly concerned with moral issues and lofty principles, and the USA should stick to this rule. Kennan himself expressed this notion in a much-quoted paragraph – 'We should cease to talk about vague objectives such as human rights, the raising of living standards, and democratisation. The day is not far off when we are going to have to deal in straight power concepts. The less then we are hampered by idealistic slogans, the better.'[8] From this perspective, the typical American belief in representing a unique chapter in the history of mankind, and the insistence on viewing the USA as the last bastion of liberty in a world besieged by obscure forces bent on extinguishing the last sparkle of hope for civilisation, constituted more a liability than an asset. According to another realist, Walter Lippmann, the American habit of regarding a new variation to the old game of power politics behind a Manichean vision of a fight to death between good and evil negated any legitimacy to the other side and its interests, thereby making impossible the conduct of 'normal' diplomacy. Lippmann believed that US foreign policy was substantially correct in its response to Soviet expansionism, but its implementation was hampered by the need to hide what was essentially more or less traditional conduct behind a universal moralist language that could appeal to, and be recognised by, American public opinion.

In another irony, the revisionist scholars, themselves not alien to various, often radical ideological views, largely overlooked the impact of ideological factors on US foreign policy. Following in the footsteps of William Appleman Williams' *The Tragedy of American Diplomacy*, they insisted that the real rationale of American foreign policy was its economic drive to expand and dominate foreign markets in order to support a cycle of perennial capitalist growth. In this perspective, ideology has been assigned a much less meaningful role, namely that of an instrument more or less consciously manipulated by the elites to align public opinion behind their economically-determined choices.

The so-called post-revisionist 'synthesis' stressed the importance of the US *perceptions* of the Soviet threat, thereby opening a path towards the study of the policy-makers' mindset. It also admitted that different interpretations of the correlation of forces and the balance of power could emerge from different economic beliefs (Keynesian or anti-Keynesian), and this in itself could be the key variable in understanding the genesis and the development of the cold war.[9] Summing up the previous disputes, Michael Hunt wrote in his pioneering study on American foreign policy ideology:

Twentieth century US foreign policy has been depicted in terms of the pursuit of overseas markets essential to stability and prosperity at home. It has also been treated as an extended struggle between clear-eyed realists on the one hand and fuzzy-minded moralists, opportunistic politicians and a mercurial public on the other. These approaches, whatever their merits, are by themselves incomplete, for they deal inadequately with one of the most notable features of American policy. *And that is the deep and pervasive impact of an ideology with its roots in the eighteenth and nineteenth centuries. The power and persistence that ideology acquired has not been sufficiently appreciated.*[10]

From this perspective, Hunt and other scholars have reached the conclusion that the cold war was the only way in which American political culture, steeped in a deeply revered image of the USA and its role in the world, could conceive and portray the struggle against the Soviet Union. Far from being either an instrumental device for the pursuit of economic expansion or a mere appendix to what was above all a quintessential power struggle, ideology was thus essential to understand the very nature of the American engagement in the bipolar confrontation.

Not surprisingly, scholars who looked at the ideological roots of American foreign policy, sharply differed in their attitudes. Some of them developed a benevolent view. Frank Ninkovich, for instance, regards the cold war as the basic continuation of the deepest Wilsonian conviction that in the contemporary world a *national* foreign policy made no longer sense, and that only a *global* attitude could attempt to regulate and control the forces that shaped modernity. He therefore gives a positive reading of US ideology as the instrument that has allowed American foreign policy to forge a course of action commensurable to the challenges of a new, globalised, international environment.[11] Tony Smith has focused on the many attempts to export democracy that have been carried out by US foreign policy at several stages of cold war, looking with sympathy at the efforts of the Kennedy administration to promote democracy in the Third World and in Latin America, at the human rights campaign of Jimmy Carter, and at the highly rhetorical tone of the Reagan administration, in particular in its first mandate.[12] A similar favourable interpretation has been offered by Walter Russell Mead, who has reached the conclusion that the interplay between the different shades of American ideology has given its foreign policy an unprecedented flexibility, thus enabling it to adjust with great success to an array of very different circumstances. The ability to combine the idealistic Wilsonian aspirations with the practical, aggressive, even cynical outlook of the Jacksonian approach, in particular, seems to Mead a very powerful amalgamation to deal with a large number of international problems.[13]

On the other side, there were negative evaluations. Hunt himself argued that, unless it managed to shed some of its old ideological assumptions, US foreign policy was bound to stumble into an endless repetition of Vietnam-like mistakes. Another critical appraisal came from Michael Latham, who analysed the Kennedy administration's emphasis on modernisation and development as the key concepts of its policy toward the Third World and Latin America. Latham describes the deep-seated conviction of the Kennedy intellectuals, reinforced by the social sciences theories of the time, that the USA possessed the intellectual key to socio-economic progress of the non-developed countries. The application of US concepts of economic development would transform and enrich Third World societies, thereby undermining the appeal of communist ideology and preventing revolutions and insurgencies. According to Latham, however, such a theory and practice reveal a common pattern with some century-old typical American assumptions. They can be better understood merely as a modern reformulation of the traditional habit of the Americans to 'carve out a redemptive mission for themselves and portray themselves as a progressive force carrying out a moral task'. The emptiness of this illusion, the author concludes, is demonstrated by the ultimate eventual failures of all the examples he analyses, from the Peace Corps to the Alliance for Progress.[14]

Perhaps the most radical variation of this critical assessment of US ideology is the one formulated by Anders Stephansson. In a number of works he has reached the conclusion that the cold war was a US project, as the United States did not know any other way of relating their policies to the outside world than by painting a vision of themselves as engaged in an 'uncompromising, Herculean struggle' against an enemy which – being the negation of freedom itself – could not have any 'possible legitimate interests or concerns'. Stephansson argues that the famous National Security Council paper NSC-68 (April 1950), with its vision of a radical confrontation with the USSR, epitomises this global American view, and that Paul Nitze, its main author, was one of the foremost interpreters of US cold war ideology. For Stephansson, therefore, the cold war must be defined according to the duration of this irredeemably antagonistic attitude, which he believes lasted from 1945 to 1963, when the search for a new kind of relationship with the former enemy replaced the previous view of unremitting hostility.[15]

The new 'ideological' emphasis in American cold war historiography is not without problems. There is a paradoxical risk to use ideology as an all-encompassing notion that may embrace every single aspect of US foreign policy, thereby reducing to zero both its explicative function and the importance of other factors. In order to avoid this danger, we find it useful to refer to Martin Seliger's explanation of ideological behaviour adapted to international politics by Douglas MacDonald. This explanation distinguishes between a fundamental (normative, ends-oriented) dimension of ideology and a technical one (empirical, means-oriented). Following this distinction, MacDonald places both the fundamental and the operative dimensions of ideological behaviour along a continuum, which allows him to cancel 'the typical dichotomy posited between "progressive internationalist" (that is, strongly emphasizing moral prescriptions) and "conservative internationalist" (that is, strongly emphasizing technical prescriptions) approaches to international politics among American political elites', since *both* are defined as 'different dimensions of the same phenomenon of ideological behaviour in service to final goals'.[16] Such a definition allows distinguishing between those periods and moments when the USA developed a more forceful, idealistic foreign policy, and those when they adopted a more 'traditional', balance of power-oriented interpretation of the international system. One can also conclude that American foreign policy was shaped by *both views* – a more traditional view of international relations, based on such calculations as the balance of power and its configuration, and a more idealistic view which was shaped by a deep belief in the moral and ideal mission of the United States and which perceived therefore the confrontation with the Soviet Union in terms of a clash between two contrasting visions of the world. Following MacDonald's paradigm, moreover, it becomes possible to solve what may otherwise appear like intractable contradictions by assuming that US policy-makers were influenced by their image of the exceptional role of the United States even when they – like Dean Acheson – were particularly concerned with traditional diplomatic concepts, such as the configuration of power in the international system. These concerns, as Melvyn Leffler correctly points out, were based on the beliefs that a society which 'attributed primacy to the protection of civil liberties and individual rights ... would be difficult to sustain either in a world dominated by trade blocs or, worse yet, in a world dominated by the Kremlin's power'.[17]

western european ideologies: national and transnational

To what an extent were these US attitudes and views shared by its Western European allies? Was there, in other words, a fully cohesive Atlantic point of view on the ideological struggle against the Soviet Union, or was there a separate Western European cold war ideology, different from the American one, which may warrant a distinct investigation? These questions are not easy to answer not only because it is problematic to lump together the differing attitudes of the Western European states, but also because historians have not paid much attention to the cultural and ideological dimension of the cold war in Western Europe. Compared to the long and vibrant discussion on US foreign policy, research on the mental landscape of Western European policy-makers has just got off the ground. Besides, historians have been primarily preoccupied with investigating the impact of American concepts and ideas on the Western European outlook. By contrast, they dealt little with West European reactions to the Soviet Union, with their image of the enemy. The limited attention dedicated to the ideological space occupied by Soviet Russia in the Western European mindset could lead, as David Caute warned, to a one-sided, distorted picture of the cold war as being 'instigated exclusively by a belligerent, expansionist USA and its client states'.[18]

Basic foreign policy attitudes of the Western European countries in the cold war could probably be best described as a combination of ideological adversity towards the communist regime and of a more traditional concern with the unprecedented expansion of Soviet power and influence in East-Central Europe. Yet, in comparison with the United States, Western Europeans seemed to frame their enemy image in somewhat more traditional terms, without resorting to global moralist language. While in most cases Western European political elites welcomed an American intervention to restore the balance of power on the continent, they did not advocate a major overhaul of the entire international system. To quote just one – highly significant – example, most Western European governments would have probably been satisfied with a US military guarantee or with a steady flow of military supplies, without necessarily going as far as setting up the Atlantic Pact or its permanent organisation, NATO, two years later. Nor did the Western Europeans easily accept the logic of economic cooperation that the Truman administration tried to impose upon them as a precondition for the implementation of the Marshall Plan: the literature on the subject is replete with examples of European governments dragging their feet in implementing the American prescriptions to think about the continental economic recovery rather than their own national benefits. In the mindset of Western European politicians the balance of power *inside Europe*, and the future of colonial possessions (for those countries who had them) outside, along with national security, remained the prevalent framework in which they understood the international system and formulated their policies. Retaining their imperial possessions, in particular, was regarded for a long time after the war as paramount by British and French policy-makers (not to mention the lesser European powers) in order to retain a great power status. This was an objective which often conflicted with American anti-colonialist sentiment.

As early as the 1980s, an international research group made up of British, French, German and Italian historians reached the conclusion that up to the mid-1950s 'power' was probably the most significant concept to explain the international conduct of the Western European states.[19] By and large, the historical literature on the foreign policies of the Western European governments has reflected this attitude, and it has – more or less consciously – followed what may be described as a realist interpretive paradigm. Only recently have some studies demonstrated a growing concern with ideological matters and, in Great Britain, a clear attempt to counter Soviet ideological propaganda through a host of different initiatives, particularly the setting up of a specialised section in the Foreign Office (the Information Research Department, or IRD) charged with developing all sorts of ideological and cultural countermeasures.[20] Similar initiatives were also discussed in France and Italy, where the need to counter the heavy propaganda barrage of the communist parties was deeply felt, and special attention was dedicated to propping up the governments with strong anti-totalitarian ideological campaigns.[21] All these studies, however, seem to fall more under the category of the analysis of covert operations and psychological warfare rather than outline a more ideological dimension of the Western European approach to the cold war.

Within this predominant realist paradigm, however, one can find many nuances. The diversity of Western European politics and governments was reflected in a variety of attitudes towards the Soviet Union, the political status quo and the international system. On a state by state basis, their actions varied according to national political agendas and to the political orientation of the governments. A number of them vigorously challenged European status quo. France under the Gaullist government after 1958 attacked the concept of the transatlantic solidarity which left only a secondary role for France (especially in comparison with Great Britain and West Germany). De Gaulle came with the vision of 'Europe from the Atlantic to the Urals' and attempted to locate French diplomacy in the centre of the developing European *détente*. West Germany proclaimed in 1957 the Hallstein doctrine, denied the legitimacy of the state borders in the East and continued to call for the full revision of the cold war order, based on the division of Germany. However, by the late 1960s West Germany, along with other Western European countries, began to envelop a web of commercial and cultural relations with Eastern European countries and the Soviet Union, according to its own national interests. Behind this new, less confrontational approach lay the hope that in the long run the communist regimes would develop a vested interest in this cooperation and would therefore adopt a more cooperative foreign policy, eventually perhaps even shedding their more unpalatable domestic features. While different in many ways, the two more visionary versions of this approach – de Gaulle's and Brandt's – both hoped that a policy of peaceful transformation would gradually lead to the melting away of the blocs and of the cold war itself. In the case of Brandt's *Ostpolitik*, however, some of its critics had the impression that in its shift from full frontal revisionism to gradual change West Germany was actually adapting itself to acceptance of the status quo.

A deeper understanding of Western Europe's position might also emerge from the expansion of what so far has been a rather neglected field of studies, namely the role of transnational political forces and movements. Perhaps because of the assumption that Western European politicians acted upon a realist set of foreign policy assumptions, cold war historians have paid relatively little attention to the ideological debate of European policy-makers and to the activities of political parties at the transnational level. There are very few studies, therefore, that focus on the link between the cold war and the two main European political families, the centre-right Christian Democratic and the Socialist ones. While David Hanley's assertion that the scholarship on Christian Democracy is non-existent may be a bit extreme, he certainly has a point.[22] Very little work has been done on the international relevance of these political forces during the Cold War, since it is only in the 1990s that historians and political scientists have begun to explore them in a comparative perspective in order to assess their transnational impact on the evolution of the international system.[23] Even in the latter case, however, historians have tended to concentrate on the significance of the Christian Democratic parties for the process of European integration, rather than for the broader international system or for the evolution of the cold war.[24]

More attention has been focused on the development of the international policy of the Catholic Church, although here the availability of sources remains a problem.[25] As Ennio Di Nolfo's pioneering study of US–Vatican relations has demonstrated, already in the Second World War Pope Pius XII sought to alert the United States to the impending Soviet threat, which he perceived in very strong, almost apocalyptical terms.

The Catholic hierarchy therefore played an important role in shaping the ideological parameters of the anti-communist and anti-Soviet ideological crusade, later widely used by Catholic circles in the United States, as well as in Italy. Vatican views of the post-war communist threat have also been explored to a certain depth, and some other studies have elucidated the subsequent difficult path the Catholic Church followed to work out an understanding with the communist regimes.[26] These writings, however, still do not offer a full picture of the influence of the Catholic Church in shaping the European cold war mindset, and the topic seems to warrant further and deeper investigations.

The same is true for the other large family of European political forces, namely the socialist parties. Even if the situation here may not be as bleak as for the Christian Democrats, since the socialists were genetically linked to the communists and therefore had to define their identity either in alliance with, or in opposition to, their communist offspring, most comparative studies on the European democratic left focus on its domestic policies. Donald Sassoon's monumental history of the socialist parties in the twentieth century, for instance, has some fascinating sections on the international attitudes of a number of European socialist forces, but is far more interested in describing their domestic policies.[27] Some comparative work has also been done on the attitude of the socialist forces towards Europe and European integration, rather than on the international system in general, particularly in the case of the early post-Second World War years.[28]

Finally, in the overall study of the problems related to the resilience of communist parties in Western Europe, scholars have examined the difficult relationship inside the left and the complex ties between socialists and communists. While providing important information and background material, however, in general most of these studies do not elucidate the possible linkage between the foreign policy of a leftist, socialist government and the ideological debate carried out at the international level among the socialist parties. They rarely discuss, in other words, whether a socialist orientation shaped – or failed to – the cold war policies of the Western European governments whenever the moderate left was in power: at most, there are passing references to the need to appease the left-wing electorate with some rhetorical gestures. In short, there is no overall, transnational analysis of how the non-communist left gradually came to adopt a cold war point of view and adapted itself to seeing the USSR as an enemy and the United States as an ally, nor do we have an updated study of the Socialist International.[29] Some work has been done, but at a national, rather than comparative, level: Hugh Wilford's book on the British left discusses in depth the interrelationship between US cultural and propaganda policies and the activities of the British Labour Party,[30] while in the case of Italy, Leopoldo Nuti's work on the Kennedy administration and its attempt to help shape a modern, social-democratic Italian left has tried to weave into a single narrative the multiple strains of US–Italian political, cultural and ideological relations. As for Euro-communism, the failed attempt to retool the Western European communist parties (in particular those of France, Italy and Spain) into a more effective and modern political force, there is also ample scope for new research. In spite of the importance of the initiative, which if successful clearly might have had an obvious direct impact on the evolution of the international system, the large work done in the 1970s and 1980s by political scientists has not been followed up by cold war historians, who only recently have begun a more in-depth investigation of its possible implications.[31] What is still largely missing from the studies on the European socialist and communist parties, therefore, is an attempt to weave together the national cultural, theoretical and political perspectives into a single overall narrative of the ideological world of the Western European left throughout the cold war and of its impact on the evolution of the international system.

Finally, in what seems to be a most promising field of study, increasing attention has been paid to the influence of less traditional political forces, such as those transnational networks that throughout the cold war advocated various forms of arms control, human rights and the development of a less confrontational relationship between the blocs. Lawrence Wittner's work on the anti-nuclear movement and the seminal study by Matthew Evangelista, in particular, have highlighted the influence and the impact of these non-conventional political ideas; Mary Dudziak has developed an interesting analysis on how the ideological dimension of US foreign policy, and in particular the defence of civil rights and the freedom of the individual, had a profound impact on American society and contributed to the Civil Rights movement in the American South; and Jeremi Suri has built an interesting case for the study of how the need to contrast the rising tide of new political forces shaped and influenced the origins of *détente*, whose roots he describes as far more influenced by the fear of new ideological challenges than by any shift on the balance of power.[32]

ideas of european integration

If by ideology we accept the Seliger–MacDonald definition of a set of principles in service to the construction of a particular world order,[33] or at least understand it as an ideational blueprint 'for constructing an international political order', then there is little doubt that during the cold war the most original and influential ideological Western European contribution lay in the gradual development of the notion of European integration. This was a conceptual project to renovate the political structure of the continent – or at least of its Western half – and rid it of the flaws that beset it in the past. True, building a new Europe was not a global ideological project comparable to the ones developed by the United States and the Soviet Union. At the same time, the concept of European integration fits MacDonald's definition because of its transformational nature and its indubitable goal to alter the status quo.

The European project began before the cold war and, as we can see today, went far beyond it. Its origins can be traced to an independent set of causes and ideas that preceded the Second World War. Besides, it can be – and indeed was, at least in its early steps – regarded at once both as a tool for fighting the cold war more effectively as well as a way to moderate its impact or even to escape from it by overcoming some of its features and eventually bring about a different constellation of power. For the United States and many European statesmen with a strong Atlanticist orientation, the construction of Europe meant above all the strengthening of the West by bringing together some of the most powerful European states of the time into a single cohesive bloc; others, however, also saw the construction of Europe as a way to redeem the continent from the horrible mistakes of its past, from the seemingly inevitable logic of its decline or from the apparent stringencies of an impending bipolar order, which clearly limited the freedom of manoeuvre of some of its prominent states. With the passing of time, this latter vision was also tinged to an increasing extent by the willingness to prove a certain European *otherness* in comparison to the United States – a process that has certainly accelerated, albeit it is not yet predominant – in the aftermath of the cold war.

This vision of Europe as an ideological project is only partially reflected in the way it has been studied. A large part of the historians who have worked on European integration have clearly done so from the militant perspective of Federalism. Europeanism as a creed, particularly in its federalist variant, has therefore produced a large body of scholarship which has studied the process of integration from a singularly activist and teleological perspective – one that seemed prone to place great emphasis on the role of ideals, but also to judge actions and individuals according to the degree by which they served the ultimate goal of the cause. The history of European integration therefore has often been portrayed as a morality play, a narrative with saints and sinners, visionary innovators fighting a dramatic battle against the ever-resurgent Hydra of the national state. As this early approach attached perhaps even too much importance to the role of ideas in shaping a new Europe, it gradually evoked a different response, in particular due to the work of Alan Milward. Milward and his disciples, therefore, have stressed the importance of economic factors in shaping the national strategies of those policy-makers who conceived the European project, thereby denying much of the importance to the ideal intentions held in such high esteem by earlier scholars.[34] Closed in by the zeal of the Europeanists on one side and the economic reductionist slant of the Milward revisionists on the other, the field of European integration studies has often been reduced to a rather secluded discipline, and it is only in the recent past that it has begun to develop its process of emancipation from the limitations of the previous approaches. The recent literature, in fact, seems more prone to investigate the cultural and ideological dimensions of European integration without the zeal of the earlier approaches, and in turn this trend might turn out to be one of the most significant contributions to a new narrative of cold war mentalities.[35]

a western ideology?

It is necessary to ask whether during the cold war there was any serious attempt at shaping a Western – as compared to a national or to a distinctly Western European – ideology, and whether such ideology ever had any impact on the evolution of the international system. The increasing concern of historians for the cultural dimension of the cold war has spurred a whole trend of studies in this direction, and several interesting works have begun to illuminate what was until the 1990s a thoroughly neglected dimension. For example, the Congress for Cultural Freedom (CCF) was intended to present an image of a benign, progressive and democratic Western world in competition with the forces of communist totalitarianism. The creation of the CCF reflected widespread concerns that West European intellectuals could be seduced by the Soviet model, which presented itself as a system based on economic and social justice. As noted in Chapter 9, some scholars are sharply critical of the CCF's reliance on CIA support, concluding that the Congress and other anti-communist intellectual groups were simply tools used by Washington to shape an American-oriented Europe. Other scholars are more sympathetic towards the CCF and its affiliates. Michael Hochgeschwender argues that the Western intelligentsia who rallied behind the anti-communist cause acted out of principle, and do not deserve to be considered to be CIA stooges.[36] A similar assessment has been reached by Volker Berghahn, who has focused on the role of non-governmental American philanthropic institutions such as the Ford Foundation in promoting a positive image of the USA in Western Europe, and in forging transatlantic bonds. While openly recognising the role of Allen Dulles and the CIA in supporting some of these supposedly private initiatives, Berghahn refuses to portray them as the result of a 'conspiracy', stating that they derived from:

> [the] experience of a generation of Democrats and New Dealers who came out of the Second World War and saw nothing illegitimate in this kind of activity. And, indeed, it may be argued that these and many other programmes not only fostered intellectual and cultural understanding across the Atlantic and helped to soften negative images of the USA in Western Europe, but also began to pave the way that eventually led to *détente* and the de-escalation of the East–West arms race.[37]

Other transatlantic initiatives have also been the object of interesting research. Particular attention is being increasingly dedicated to what has been perhaps – at least before other organisations such as the Trilateral Commission were created – the single most important network of influential politicians and personalities, namely the so-called Bilderberg group created between 1952 and 1954 by the Polish expatriate Joseph Retinger and the Dutch Prince Bernhard zur Lippe-Binnenfeld. While until not long ago the Bilderbergers were mostly the object of journalistic investigations which emphasised their presumed semi-conspiratorial and secretive nature, they are now the object of fresh analyses that try to stress their importance in forging a common Western perspective on the cold war, mending transatlantic rifts, locating possible future points of tension in order to prevent them, and above all providing a clearinghouse where year after year a larger number of key figures from both sides of the Atlantic could discuss their common problems and gradually shape a sense of unity and purpose.[38]

Much work has also been done on the trade unions relations between the USA and Western Europe, particularly stressing the importance of the early US efforts to use the AFL and the CIO to export to their Western European counterparts an American model of industrial relations based on the non-political activity of the unions, and closely linked to a uniquely American working ethos and such new concepts as productivity. This is an aspect of the shaping of a common transatlantic perspective which has been studied quite in depth, once again mirroring all the previous debates about the interconnection between the US unions and the CIA, about their influence (or lack of) with their European counterparts, and about their more or less passive role in receiving the suggestions and the support of the Americans.[39]

Less research has been done on some of the most famous networks such as the Trilateral Commission, or the Aspen Institute – not to mention less well known ones such as the Atlantic Institute, Intercom, or the short-lived but influential series of the so-called Harpsund meetings.[40] The latter, in particular, between 1963 and 1966 played a crucial role in bringing together members of the social-democratic left from Sweden (Arne Gejier), Germany (Willy Brandt, Erich Ollenhauer) and the UK (Harold Wilson) with such prominent American figures as Walter and Victor Reuther and Hubert Humphrey, helping the construction of a leftist Western identity firmly set into an Atlantic framework. As one of the few historians who have written on the subject has noted, the meetings were 'an assertion that an influential Transatlantic Left might yet play a role in reshaping the social life and economic performance of the capitalist democracies in the 1960s and beyond'.[41]

By and large, the research carried out in the field of transatlantic political and cultural relations is still in a rather early stage. Yet one can already see a clear divide among those historians. On one side stand those who regard the combined result of all these networks and initiatives as a success. They emphasise shaping a common Western ideology or identity that helped to reduce the nationalist stereotypes and to forge a limited Western identity. They also recognise that this common identity was the product as much of the US efforts as of the Europeans themselves. On the other side are those scholars who regard the American role as paramount in setting the ideological stage, thus playing a hegemonic role in framing the European intellectual debate according to its own political agenda. While the first trend seems to apply the 'empire by invitation' paradigm to the field of a transatlantic ideological discourse, and presents a more complex web of influences rather than a one-way street of American ideas steadily flowing across the Ocean, the latter group seem to prefer a somewhat reductionist approach that ultimately turns the whole analysis of the transatlantic cultural discourse into a projection of American power. Whatever one's assessment is, there seems to be some agreement that, in the words of Dominik Geppert, there was a certain amount of 'political, social and cultural convergence of Western nations that gradually took place in the 1950s and in the 1960s, [and that it] was not created by the anonymous forces of what has been called "progress" or "modernity". It was rather, at least partly, the result of very conscious efforts by small elites on both sides of the Atlantic to promote liberal values in politics, economics, society and culture.'[42]

communism, nationalism and the cold war geopolitics

During the decades of the cold war, communist ideology was an official guiding doctrine by many states in Europe, Asia, Africa and Latin America. The Western cold war propaganda often, especially during the 1950s, used graphic images of the spread of 'communism' around the globe. John Foster Dulles believed that Stalin's work *The Economic Problems of Socialism*, a crude adaptation of Marxist-Leninist theoretical tenets to the post-Second World War period, was the best guide to interpret Soviet international behaviour. Yet it became clear, especially after Stalin's death, that there was no such thing as a uniform 'communist ideology' that could override other interests and motives of communist states. In every 'communist' country ideas of Marxism-Leninism transformed into a 'national' version; they conflicted, or co-existed and blended with nationalism in various combinations that reflected geopolitical realities, the character of ruling elites, and other non-ideological factors.

The impact of communism on the small states of Eastern Europe, of course, should begin within the context of Soviet empire. Poland, Czechoslovakia, Romania, Hungary, Bulgaria and the German Democratic Republic (GDR) became 'people's democracies', designed to remain within the Soviet military and economic bloc after 1945. The ruling elites in these countries heavily depended on Soviet military and economic support to stay in power. From the 1960s to 1980s most studies on Eastern European countries assumed that the communist ideology was only a cynical veneer for the regimes that were imposed by the Soviet Union during the late 1940s. Yet the 'new cold war' historiography, with access to the archives of these countries, as well as the former USSR, reveals a more complex interaction of ideological, geopolitical, social and economic components. Recent documentary publications in the *Annals of Communism* series de-emphasise the role of ideology and idealistic intentions among the *Comintern* (Communist International) figures who began to Sovietise Eastern Europe. The publication of the diary of Georgy Dmitrov (the head of the *Comintern* and Bulgaria's first communist leader), along with other materials of the Communist International, allowed some researchers to characterise this organisation as a 'vast bureaucratic apparatus' whose participants were cynical and squabbling pragmatists, 'outwardly loyal' to both the Communist cause and the Soviet master, Joseph Stalin.[43]

In contrast, some Russian researchers point to indigenous roots of the early communist regimes in Eastern Europe, including the voluntary emulation of the Soviet model by idealistic elite groups.[44] The debate on this issue continues.

Historical research proves that in each country of Eastern Europe communist ideology had to deal with powerful antidotes. First, there was a strong presence of 'European identity' among the intellectual elites, and general population. This identity in Hungary, Poland and Romania had the historic component of Russophobia, the fear of 'barbarians from the East'. Educated classes, as well as the remains of the 'bourgeoisie' generated sympathies with Western countries, such as France, Great Britain and (after 1945) the United States. These sentiments grew, despite (or perhaps because of) the virulent official anti-American and anti-NATO propaganda. Second, there were national identities and aspirations, determined by these countries' previous historical memories and domestic political and social culture. The ruthless suppression of 'nationalist deviations' in Eastern Europe under the banners of the struggle against 'Titoism' after 1948 was a product of Stalin's wrath with the Yugoslav leader, Marshal Tito, and his autonomous brand of communism. The Soviet leader was, however, also aware that local nationalism constituted a threat to Soviet domination in the region. After Stalin's death and Nikita Khrushchev's denunciation of his 'cult of personality' the communist elites in Eastern Europe chose expeditiously to change colours: they blamed the terror and excesses of the past on 'the Moscow factions', which in some cases meant that 'cosmopolitan cadres' (or communists of Jewish origin) became scapegoats for the purges of the late 1940s to early 1950s. The 'national communisms' that developed after 1956, be it Wladyslaw Gomulka's 'Polish communism' or Janos Kadar's 'Goulash communism' (which incorporated consumer-oriented reforms, allowing some market activities) were the policies of those communist leaders who sought to remove from their regimes the stigma of political dependence on the Kremlin and to buy legitimacy through material concessions to population.

For several decades Eastern European regimes adapted themselves to the realities of Soviet military presence within their borders and considerable resistance to Soviet domination in the society. As the recent studies of imperialism and colonialism demonstrate, there is a continuum of reactions to conquest/domination that cannot be reduced merely to resistance and compliance. Beside adaptation, Eastern Europe's 'people's democracies' demonstrated various types of evolution determined by the Soviet factor, but also by domestic choices. In Czechoslovakia, for instance, there remained an indigenous base for transformation of Soviet-style communism into a more social-democratic regime. The 'Prague Spring' of 1968 was a spontaneous mass movement under the slogan of the 'communism with a human face'. After its death under the tracks of Soviet tanks the option of emergence of democratic left ideological paradigms in Eastern Europe came to naught. The next most successful democratic movement in Eastern Europe, the Polish Solidarity (1980–81), despite some influence of social-democratic ideas on the core of its intellectual leaders, followed mostly traditional Catholic and conservative nationalist ideas.

In his study of Romanian communism, Vladimir Tismaneanu stresses the interplay of ideology with elites' choices, and specific historical circumstances, to emphasise diversity and polycentrism within the Warsaw Pact. He draws another comparison between the Romanian case, and the Polish, Czech and Hungarian cases. In the latter countries communist elites developed 'national models' that appealed to pre-Stalinist strands of socialism; elements of these elites supported democratisation and liberalisation, and came to the 'round-tables' with the anti-communist opposition in 1988–89. By contrast, the leadership of Gheorghe Gheorghiu-Dej and then Nicolae Ceauşescu moved to a 'national Stalinism' that left no room for democratisation and liberalisation. While Soviet and European communism moved beyond Stalinism, the Romanian leadership built 'national Stalinism' as the only and last redoubt against change. At the same time, by demonstrating independence from the Soviet Union and the Warsaw Pact and playing diplomatic games with the United States, the Western European countries and the PRC, the Romanian rulers sought to capitalise on the idea of 'Romanian identity' (mixed with 'Dacian' mythology) and to conceal the Soviet origins of their regime.[45]

The situation was radically different in the countries where the communist regime emerged as a result of victory in a coup or civil war, in the historical period characterised by decolonisation and the search for independent models of modernisation. There the ruling groups and their leaders could combine revolutionary legitimacy and personal charisma with powerful nationalist appeal. The studies on revolutionary China, Vietnam and other Third World states of 'socialist orientation' (using their Soviet denomination) reveal an extreme prominence of ideological factors as an independent variable. The Leninist theory of imperialism and colonialism retained its appeal for radical anti-colonial groups in the Third World until the late 1970s; quite a few nationalist regimes in Africa and Asia admired the Soviet example of seemingly successful industrialisation, modernisation and independence. Odd Arne Westad shows in his works that this ideological factor was much feared by the United States, and in the end came to be a decisive factor affecting Moscow's decision-making, for instance on Cuba and Africa.[46]

Yugoslavia presents the first case of a communist regime where ideology became the vehicle for charismatic revolutionary leaders to maintain economic and geopolitical independence from both rival blocs and superpowers. Since the Soviet–Yugoslav split Josip Broz (better known as Tito) began to practise the 'Yugoslav communism' that, despite many overlaps with the Stalinist model, also had many important deviations from it. The Yugoslav government was the first communist nation-state to practise the strategy of survival between the two military blocs, allowed from the 1960s considerable elements of a market economy, and eventually became involved in the 'non-aligned' movement. Tito even became the leader of this movement since 1961. The study of non-alignment has barely begun, but the access to Tito's archives can generate fruitful departures in this area.[47]

The studies of the People's Republic of China provide the most important insights into the role of communist ideology inside and outside the cold war framework. Sino-American scholars, among them Chen Jian and Shuguang Zhang, convincingly show that Mao's 'revolutionary romanticism' played a considerable role in the PRC's decision to intervene in the Korean war.[48] Westad believes it is impossible to understand the rise and fall of the Sino-Soviet alliance without considering ideological issues.[49] During the 1950s–1960s Mao Zedong and the Chinese leadership challenged the 'seniority' of the Soviet 'big brother'. They used ideological themes for international propaganda and domestic mobilisation, in order to prove the PRC, not the Soviet Union, now stood on the forefront of the global revolutionary movement and developed a more radical model for the construction of communism. There is new evidence that the more pragmatic elements in the CCP leadership attempted to combine the ideological criticism of the Soviet Union with economic cooperation, but the 'Cultural Revolution' of the 1960s led to an irreparable breach in Sino-Soviet relations. The impact of the Cultural Revolution on the CCP elites and politics still remains to be studied.

The Chinese ideological alternative to Moscow's communism exercised strong influence during the 1960s–1970s over a number of radical regimes around the world, including Albania and the *Khmer Rouge* in Cambodia. The recent availability of Albanian archives may help researchers to show how the adoption of the 'Maoist model' corresponded with Enver Hoxha's decision to break with the Soviet Union, its long-time protector against Yugoslavia. In Cambodia Pol Pot and Heng Samrin, the leaders of the

Khmer Rouge, launched their extremist and genocidal form of 'national communism' between 1975 and 1979 (capped by the extermination of virtually all urban middle classes and professionals, as well as a significant portion of peasants). The *Khmer Rouge*'s efforts to return Cambodia to 'Year Zero' were directly inspired by Mao's ideology.[50]

At the same time, ideological emulation in all these cases seemed to be greatly facilitated by geopolitical factors: Albania preferred a faraway ally to the Soviet Union, and the *Khmer Rouge* relied on Beijing's assistance against the Vietnamese communists. Cuba under Fidel Castro represents another case, when geopolitical and economic realities greatly influenced the choices of a revolutionary elite straddled between the need for ideological emulation, on one hand, and the nationalist post-colonialist aspirations for independence on the other. After Khrushchev's humiliating retreat during the Cuban missile crisis Soviet–Cuban relations became extremely strained, and parts of the Havana communist leadership (including Che Guevara) opted for the Maoist model against the Soviet one. Unfortunately for the Cuban leadership, it had no room for choice. The unrelenting hostility of the USA and the inability of the PRC to give any economic and financial assistance forced Havana, from 1968, to adapt itself to the role of a permanent economic and political client of the Soviet Union. However, as recent scholarship suggests, they did not agree to become Soviet marionettes in every way. In Africa, first in Angola, then in Ethiopia, the Cubans used every possible leverage, among them ideological, to conduct their own policy. Animated by the strong sense of revolutionary romanticism and solidarity with African radical anti-imperialist liberation movements, the Castro leadership and the younger generation of Cuban military elite successfully pursued interventionist and militant policies in Africa – helped by their allies in the Soviet military and the KGB.[51]

'National communism' in North Korea and Vietnam emerged from the wars of reunification. Kim Il-Sung managed to turn the terrible travail of the Korean war, where his regime was completely dependent on Chinese military assistance and Soviet economic help, into a source of domestic nationalist pride, and attraction for radical intellectuals in the free market, but initially authoritarian and corrupt South Korea. After Khrushchev's denunciation of Stalin and proclamation of 'peaceful coexistence' Kim developed his ideology of *Juche* (or 'self-reliance'). This set of ideas justified Kim's absolute power, as well as an autarkic and militaristic model of modernisation and mobilisation. It emulated Stalinism and Mao's Cultural Revolution, yet also appealed to historically strong Korean nationalism and sensitivity to any forms of dependence on the neighbouring giant, China.[52] Ho Chi Minh and Vietnamese communists first led anti-colonial war with France, then sought to reunify the country by a 'revolutionary war' against the South Vietnamese regime and the United States. When the Vietnam war with the USA began, the elite of the *Lao Dong* (the Vietnamese communist party) was ideologically closer to the Chinese communists than to the Kremlin apparatchiks. Yet, the need to receive Soviet military assistance along with the historic Sinophobia (similar to that shown by the Koreans) made them balance, quite skilfully, between the two communist giants. Also, the Vietnamese communists blamed, with some justice, the division of the country on the decisions made in Moscow and Beijing. Hence the North Vietnamese leadership managed to receive large-scale assistance from both communist countries without becoming a geopolitical satellite of either of them.[53]

By the 1980s both the Soviet model and the alternatives to it within the 'communist' ideological field exhausted their potential and appeal. The rise of new powerful ideological currents, above all Islamic fundamentalism, punctuated the impotence of communist ideas. At the same time, just when communism existed in polycentric mode at the height of its global reach, its demise revealed a variety of possible choices and evolutions. The transformation of the PRC is the best example. The launching of Deng Xiaoping's reforms in 1978 under the pragmatic slogans was hardly related in any way to the bipolar confrontation. Deng was sobered by his personal experience during the Cultural Revolution, and he found a remarkably successful link between the existing 'Chinese communism' and the new opportunities for the modernisation of Chinese economy and society. This model combined the Communist Party apparatus' control over politics and ideology with rapid development of the market economy, funded by foreign investments. The Chinese reforms produced the most amazing economic 'miracle' of the last century, the transformation of China.

The cold war ideological context played a secondary but quite significant role in this transformation. It is obvious that communist ideas per se were virtually replaced by state interests and the ideas of national greatness, just as it had happened earlier with the 'Yugoslav model' under Tito. It is also apparent that the Chinese 'miracle', like the Yugoslav model, would have been impossible without the advantageous position the PRC had in the cold war international system. From the 1970s the United States shifted from regarding this country as an enemy to treating it as an ally against the Soviet Union. On the ideological American screens the PRC no longer registered as a national threat, but gradually began to figure as a preferred target for profitable investments. Also serendipitous for Beijing were the currents of global capital investments from the wealthy First World into Asian 'tigers' (Taiwan, Hong Kong, Singapore, etc.) – which would later reach out to southern regions of the PRC, and then turn the whole country into a new 'world factory'.

what was the soviet cold war ideology?

The study of ideological sources of Soviet international behaviour has begun only recently for the obvious reason that Soviet archives were inaccessible until after the collapse of the USSR. At the same time, a number of American and West European 'realists', beginning with George Kennan in his famous *Foreign Affairs* article, 'Sources of Soviet Conduct', and continuing with the proponents of the 'totalitarian school' (including Hannah Arendt, Merle Fainsod and Zbigniew Brzezinski), speculated about the ideological origins of Soviet policy.[54] In essence, the totalitarian approach said that Marxist-Leninist ideology was an inherent and fundamental raison d'être of the Soviet state and the party regime. Exporting the Soviet variant of 'socialism' and providing support to 'anti-imperialist' movements and forces abroad, as this school explained, served several purposes: constant legitimation of the Soviet domination over its satellites, above all the countries of Eastern Europe, the confirmation of the Communist Party of the Soviet Union's (CPSU) right to control the Soviet state and society, justification of the mobilisational modes of industrialisation and modernisation, and the constant suppression of pluralism and dissent.

The totalitarian school always contained serious ambiguities in interpreting Soviet cold war behaviour. A serious issue was where and how ideological notions and preconceptions made the Soviet Union such a threat to Western Europe and the United States. There was never an agreement on this issue. Kennan firmly believed in the prudence of the Soviet leadership and concluded that containment would hold the Kremlin in check (the fact that their ideology was not time-constrained made them infinitely patient, unlike Hitler and the Nazis). However, NSC-68 (Spring 1950) adhered to the much more alarmist intepretation, depicting the global communist threat as a clear and present danger, so much so that it required quadrupling of the US defence budget even before the outbreak of the Korean war. During the 1960s and 1970s a few influential American historians of the Soviet Union and Soviet foreign policy adhered to the 'ideological' interpretation of Soviet history. Some scholars (such as Adam Ulam) were less deterministic and considered, as Kennan did, the role of Marxist-Leninist ideology in conjunction with Russia's 'Europeanised' history; others (such as Martin Malia) considered ideology to be an overarching factor of Soviet aggressiveness and xenophobia, and treated history and personalities as of secondary importance.[55]

The totalitarian approach to Soviet ideology conceded that, despite the ideological foundations of the Soviet regime, its leaders were fully capable of conducting a 'realist' foreign policy. Some American authors, most notably Kissinger, implied that Soviet foreign policy, beginning with Stalin's, was more realist in the traditional European sense of the term than the external policies of the United States.[56] This raised a fundamental question. If Stalin and other Soviet leaders could act as 'realists', were they apparently free from the tenets of communist ideology? Could one then talk about ideology for 'imperial' and 'domestic' consumption that did not affect Kremlin decision-making? Was there more than one ideology inside what was commonly called 'Soviet or communist ideology'?

Scholars of the totalitarian school sought to answer these questions by asserting that power and desire for more power remained at the core of Soviet ideology. Therefore, they were convinced that the next generation of Soviet leaders, instead of being 'liberalised' by the post-Stalinist experience and *détente* in the 1960s–1970s, would behave more assertively, even aggressively in the international affairs in the 1980s.[57] Most recently, these views have been reaffirmed by a number of younger scholars. They claim that the peculiar ideological-geopolitical worldview made the USSR's security and survival conditional on the eventual changes of regimes and socio-economic orders of other countries around the world. While this worldview became the foundation of Stalin's 'realism', it was radically different from the traditional *Realpolitik*. Nigel Gould-Davies wrote that Stalin's conceptual world had basic assumptions and categories that were 'fundamentally different from our own [i.e. British and American]'.[58]

Since the 1960s a number of American scholars have claimed that the old image of the Soviet state as an ideological monolith was obsolete. It became commonplace to consider Soviet society after Stalin's death as 'post-totalitarian', with the citizenry being less vulnerable to the political domination of the CPSU. Stephen Cohen suggested that inside the party-state there were at least two ideological currents – hard-line Stalinists and 'reform' communists – in deep conflict with each other.[59] Recently Robert English concluded on the basis of archival research and numerous interviews that since the Second World War there was a growing split inside the educated society and the political class between the 'old thinkers', essentially the supporters of Stalin's xenophobic isolationism and imperial expansionism, and the 'new thinkers', who sought to destroy the iron curtain and reconnect the Soviet Union to the outside world, above all to Western Europe. These 'new thinkers', the key sophisticated intellectual minorities, had been flourishing in the 'oases', i.e. academic institutes, research centres of the military-industrial complex, and even in the expertise-oriented departments of the central party apparatus. The supporters of this approach also implied that even during Stalin's years in power there were 'oases' free from the control and pressure of the official ideology. As David Holloway wrote in his book on the Soviet atomic project, science, related to the military-industrial complex, was a most important 'oasis'. The regime's need to build security and increase military power was, in other words, stronger than ideological tenets. In one example, Soviet physics was spared the fate that befell other disciplines, most notably biology, as a consequence of the purge inspired by Trofim Lysenko and other scientists who placed ideology above scholarly integrity. Soviet nuclear physicists were protected from the likes of Lysenko and other self-appointed guardians of ideological purity because without their expertise the USSR could not build the bomb.[60]

The 'oasis' approach better matches the complex situation with the cultured, scientific and engineering elites in the military-industrial complex, with professional diplomats, intelligence services, and academicians in think-tanks. Their access to classified information and their regular access to foreigners necessitated their ability to deal with them effectively. Their approach towards the proclaimed ideological goals of Soviet foreign policy was becoming increasingly critical or cynical. One can mention the evolution of Andrei Sakharov. Until the early 1960s he was the one of the chief designers of Soviet thermonuclear bombs and did not question Soviet foreign policy, acting on his conviction that it was simply necessary to preserve the balance between the Soviet Union and the United States. By 1968, however, Sakharov challenged Soviet ideology by arguing that the interests of humanity and the dangers of nuclear war necessitated 'convergence' between the Soviet Union and the West. Another example is the evolution of Anatoly Chernyaev, eventually a foreign policy adviser to Mikhail Gorbachev. A long-time official of the International Department of the CC CPSU, he had full access to international information and the vantage point to observe, compare and reappraise Soviet foreign policy. By the 1970s, especially after the Soviet invasion of Czechoslovakia in 1968, he lost any illusions in Leninist ideology and the 'world communist movement'. He was also repelled by the chauvinist and militarist components in Soviet domestic and foreign policy. Similar evolution can be found among many high-placed experts in the privileged academic institutions and think-tanks, notably the Institute of World Economy and International Relations, later the Institute for the US and Canada (ISKAN).[61]

The 'oases' approach to Soviet ideology, however, could not answer important questions. Where was the place of ideological factors, for instance, in the specific tissue of Soviet foreign policy, combining pragmatism and caution with puzzling miscalculations and aggressive moves, such as the Berlin crises and the Korean war, or the Cuban missile crisis? A number of scholars sought explanation in the leaders' personalities and their specific motivations. Vojtech Mastny and John Gaddis argued that the cold war was, to a great extent, the product of Stalin's deep insecurity and authoritarian miscalculations.[62] Vladislav Zubok and Constantine Pleshakov wrote that Soviet ideological amalgam ('the revolutionary-imperial paradigm') remained the fundamental framework for Soviet decision-making during most of the cold war, yet its specific interpretation was very much influenced by the perceptions, notions and experience of the successive Kremlin leaders.[63] This makes it necessary to understand how the concepts and notions conceived at the top of the decision-making pyramid were interpreted and implemented at its bottom. Also, these views became contested by the majority of Russian scholars in the emerging Russian historiography of the early cold war. They claim that, in fact, the Marxist-Leninist ideological precepts had little to do with Stalin's practical policies, in particular in Eastern Europe. Russian historians believe that Soviet foreign policy was driven, the regime and Stalin's personality notwithstanding, by the quest for security and 'geopolitical interests'.[64]

Another potentially promising direction of research studies ideology, in combination with propaganda and mass culture, as a polyphonic phenomenon, constructed by state agents and state media according to specific needs and in response to changing international and domestic circumstances. The influence of French social history, as well as sociolinguistics, produced a number of research projects on Soviet political culture and 'power discourse'. Stephen Kotkin's study on the 1930s, Jeffrey Brooks' research on Soviet media during the 1940s, David Brandenberger's book on the emergence of 'National-Bolshevism' and 'Russo-centrism' during the 1930s, the monograph by Slava Gerovich on Soviet scientific debates on cybernetics during the 1950s–1960s – these works do not deal with the cold war and foreign policy. Yet they convincingly demonstrate that, for all personal free-thinking or cynicism, all members of Soviet leadership, elites and publicly active society had been reading, writing and thinking ideologically. Gerovich demonstrates that the boundaries between the official ideology and professional activities were not fixed. The philosophical core of Marxist-Leninist ideology, dialectical materialism, allowed any kind of combinations of notions. It was essential for the practitioners in any field to master the language of ideology (Soviet 'newspeak') to be able to pursue their agendas and make careers. Obviously, Soviet foreign policy-making cannot be an exception. Norman Naimark in his seminal study of Soviet occupational policies and attitudes in East Germany concludes that the Soviets constructed the only kind of society they knew; Soviet ideology thus was 'diluted' in the collective experience and political culture of the occupational forces.[65]

Also, such an approach to ideology helps to understand why, until the very end of the Soviet Union, there was no substantial opposition to the regime with anti-communist ideology. Unlike in Central European countries (e.g. Poland), Marxism and 'dialectical materialism' dominated Soviet intellectual discourse; even many dissidents began as the advocates of communism with 'a human face'. Already by the mid-1940s Soviet newspeak emerged that all Soviet people understood, yet foreign communists and socialists could not make much sense of it. Even Soviet diplomats and experts in foreign propaganda communicated in Soviet newspeak when they discussed professional problems among themselves. The premium on mastering the ideological language was high. Even a simple dissertation on US domestic history (not to mention foreign policy) could not be defended and published if not couched in the appropriate ideological lexicon. One of the authors of this chapter confronted this problem when he wrote his diploma at the end of the 1970s at the MGU on the domestic policies of the Truman administration and later a Ph.D. in the early 1980s at the ISKAN on the evolution of the Democratic Party and the presidency of Jimmy Carter. Thus the Soviet ideology remained a constant presence even inside the 'oases of free thinking'.

The new research suggests that Soviet ideology, albeit to a lesser extent than American and Western European ideologies, also was a polyphonic and complex phenomenon. In the late 1940s Soviet ideology included several components. First was the domestic ideological component represented by the campaign against the 'genuflection before the West' and 'rootless cosmopolitanism'. This was overseen by Stalin's chief henchman on ideology and cultural affairs, Andrei Zhdanov (hence the description of this period of Soviet cultural history as the *Zhdanovschina*). The second component was embodied in the notion of the 'two camps', as espoused at the conference of international communist parties convened at Szklarska Poreba, in Poland, in September 1947. Henceforth, the USSR portrayed itself as the leader of progress and peace, and the United States as the leader of the 'Anglo-Saxon' bloc, bent on racial domination and warmongering. Both components of this early Soviet cold war ideology had clear instrumental nature, adapted to internal mobilisation and external bloc-building needs. At the same time, in accordance with MacDonald's definition, Soviet ideology represented a compromise between a fundamental (normative, ends-oriented) dimension of ideology and a technical one (empirical, means-oriented). In other words, the USSR's political and military elites came to hold these ideological tenets as fundamental beliefs and foreign policy guidelines. The same can be said about another component: the much-propagated image of the Soviet Union as liberator of Eastern Europe from fascism. It was used to justify the presence of Soviet troops there and, subsequently, the suppression of popular revolutions in the GDR, Hungary and Czechoslovakia. Yet the same image was a deep-held conviction of the majority of Kremlin rulers and the military elites.

The expansion of Soviet economy, substantial rise of living standards, and especially the growing popularity of the Soviet model of modernisation in the Third World helped to boost ideological beliefs in Soviet society, especially among the young cohorts. At the same time among the educated elites the grip of Soviet ideology lost its power after Khrushchev's denunciation of Stalin in 1956. The new studies show that other events and developments produced splits in Stalinist ideological amalgam. The 'anti-cosmopolitan' campaigns of 1949–52 produced numerous people who began to view the regime, and the party-state, as their enemy. Sociologist Vladimir Shlapentovkh, in his book combining the approaches of 'totalitarian' school and intellectual history, concludes that the Soviet ideological monolith began to erode after Stalin's death, when some intellectuals began to resist ideological pressures and formed a new Soviet 'intelligentsia' that began the movement for liberalisation and openness to the West.[66] There were emerging two ideological poles, one rooted in the 'internationalist' and 'humanist' promises of the Bolshevik revolution, another based on 'Russo-centric' reinterpretations of Stalinism. Yitzhak Brudny concludes that since the mid-1960s there was 'a steep decline in the mobilisational power of the Marxist-Leninist ideology and the consequent erosion of the ideological basis of the regime's legitimacy'.[67] Xenophobic patriotism required complete isolation from 'the West', but the pragmatic requirement of competing with (and eventually overtaking) the USA economically required Western ideas, technology, trade and cultural contacts. While the Soviet state had to allow a limited 'parting of the iron curtain' – allowing foreign tourists to visit the USSR, and authorising the far more limited visits of Soviet citizens abroad – the process of erosion of Soviet ideological mentality accelerated.[68]

Soviet ideology remained the dominant public discourse, but the elements of duplicity, double-think and cynicism grew. The political leadership and elites increasingly regarded ideology as a tedious ritual on which their life and career no longer depended. By the mid-1960s Yuri Andropov already could tell his advisers: 'Think and write without regard [to ideology]. I will know myself what to report to the *Politburo*.'[69] Ideas borrowed from various strands of Russian nationalism since the late 1960s began to spread through the ranks of Soviet bureaucracies. The ideologues of this movement, who spread their views through several literary journals, rejected the 'revolutionary' Marxist component of the ideological paradigm. They viewed communism as a transitional phase towards the triumph of Russia as a world power. At some point, Russian nationalists believed, the communist shell would be tossed off and the 'great Russia' would re-emerge in the world.[70]

Increasingly scholars studying the end of the cold war acknowledge the role of the collapse of Soviet ideology and the rise of Gorbachev's reformist ideology. The totalitarian school influenced some of the first accounts on this subject. William Odom and Jack Matlock, both policy practitioners and veterans of the cold war, concluded in their works that the end of the confrontation occurred only when the Soviet leadership shed its fundamental ideological conceptions, among them the view that the conflict between East and West represented an international 'class struggle', and the notion of 'imperialism as the highest stage of capitalism'.[71] Another approach, represented by Archie Brown, Robert English and other scholars, describes a different dynamic. Instead of the ideological collapse, there was an 'ideological revolution', with the emergence of 'new thinking' after Gorbachev's rise to power.[72] The rejection of the entrenched Soviet ideology threatened Soviet domination in Eastern Europe and domestic control in the multinational Soviet Union itself. However, it did not necessitate the rejection of geopolitical 'realism', reflected in the futile use of force to preserve the integrity of the Soviet state. That rejection still needs to be explained, and most evidence highlights Gorbachev's personality as a key factor. Nonetheless, it was the adoption of key tenets of Gorbachev's ideas on foreign affairs (such as a rejection of the use of force to maintain hegemony over Eastern Europe, and the concept of a 'common European home') which contributed to the largely peaceful demise of communism in Europe in 1989–91.[73]

conclusions

Ideologies and ideological notions mattered in the cold war much more than previous generations of political scientists believed. Either as cognitive frameworks or in their capacity as power-projecting tools, or – if one wants to take a purely instrumental approach – as mere propaganda instruments, ideas were an essential component of the cold war world, which cannot be reduced to any assumed 'realist' structure – be it conceived in purely economic or power-based terms – without losing an essential dimension of the narrative. Some preliminary important conclusions can already be drawn from a decade and a half of post-cold war research. First, cold war ideologies were dynamic and pluralistic amalgams, playing both instrumental and fundamental worldview functions not only in the Soviet Union, but also in the United States and Western Europe. Second, there is no single approach or school that provides an all-encompassing analytical tool for the study of ideologies in the West and the East. Both 'camps' on the opposite sides of the great ideological divide between communism and capitalism remained polycentric; geopolitical interests, historical phobias, nationalist aspirations and particular leadership characters were the crucial 'correcting factors' that affected the 'purity' of ideological doctrines and preferences. Third, further study of the ideological phenomenon requires an international and perhaps inter-disciplinary approach. In conclusion, a systematic study of the ideological dimension of the cold war promises to be one of the most fruitful and rewarding fields for the expansion and enrichment of historical research into the East–West confrontation which lasted from the late 1940s to the early 1990s.

notes

1. Karl Dietrich Bracher, *The Age of Ideologies: A History of Political Thought in the Twentieth Century* (London: Macmillan, 1985).
2. Clifford Geertz, 'Ideology as a Cultural System', in *Interpretation of Cultures* (New York: Basic Books, 1977, 1st edition).
3. Bracher, *The Age of Ideologies*, p.264.
4. Melvyn P. Leffler, 'New Approaches, Old Interpretations, and Prospective Reconfigurations', in Michael J. Hogan (ed.), *America in the World: The Historiography of American Foreign Relations since 1941* (Cambridge: Cambridge University Press, 1995), p.84.
5. On 'out-of-area' issues, see Elizabeth D. Sherwood, *Allies in Crisis: Meeting Global Challenges to Western Security* (New Haven, CT: Yale University Press, 1990), and Douglas T. Stuart & William T. Tow, *The Limits of Alliance: NATO and Out-of-Area Problems since 1949* (Baltimore, MD: Johns Hopkins University Press, 1990).
6. Frank Ninkovich, *The Wilsonian Century: U.S. Foreign Policy since 1900* (Chicago, IL: Chicago University Press, 1999), p.225.
7. The classic reference here is to George Kennan's *Memoirs, 1925–1950* (London: Hutchinson, 1968), *passim.*

8. PPS 23, as cited in Hanhimäki's chapter, is also in Anna Kasten Nelson (ed.), *The State Department Policy Planning Staff Papers*, Vol. II: *1948* (New York: Garland, 1983), p.122.
9. John L. Gaddis, *Strategies of Containment: A Critical Appraisal of American National Security Policy During the Cold War* (New York: Oxford University Press, 2005, 2nd edition), *passim*.
10. Michael H. Hunt, *Ideology and US Foreign Policy* (New Haven, CT: Yale University Press, 1987), p.225. Emphasis added to original.
11. Frank Ninkovich, *The Wilsonian Century: US Foreign Policy since 1900* (Chicago, IL: University of Chicago Press, 1999), *passim*.
12. Tony Smith, *America's Mission: The United States and the Worldwide Struggle for Democracy in the Twentieth Century* (Princeton, NJ: Princeton University Press, 1994).
13. Walter Russell Mead, *Special Providence: A History of US Foreign Policy* (New York: A Century Foundation Book, 2001).
14. Michael E. Latham, *Modernisation as Ideology: American Social Science and 'Nation Building' in the Kennedy Era* (Chapel Hill, NC: North Carolina University Press, 2000). Latham follows the pioneering work of Robert Packenham, *Liberal America and the Third World: Political Development Ideas in Foreign Aid and Social Science* (Princeton, NJ: Princeton University Press, 1973).
15. Stephansson has put forward his thesis in many articles and essays: see for instance his 'The Cold Was Considered as a US Project', in Federico Romero & Silvio Pons (eds), *Reinterpreting the End of the Cold War: Issues, Interpretations, Periodizations* (London: Frank Cass, 2005), pp.52–67; or 'Liberty or Death: The Cold War as US Ideology', in Odd Arne Westad (ed.), *Reviewing the Cold War: Approaches, Interpretations, Theory* (London: Frank Cass, 2001), pp.81–100.
16. Douglas MacDonald, 'Formal Ideologies in the Cold War: Toward a Framework for Empirical Analysis', in Westad (ed.), *Reviewing the Cold War*, p.193.
17. Melvyn Leffler, *A Preponderance of Power: National Security, the Truman Administration, and the Cold War* (Stanford, CA: Stanford University Press, 1992), pp.13–14.
18. David Caute, 'Foreword', in Giles Scott Smith & Hans Krabbendam (eds), *The Cultural Cold War in Western Europe 1945–1960* (London: Frank Cass, 2003).
19. Ennio Di Nolfo (ed.), *Power in Europe? II. Great Britain, France, Germany and Italy and the Origins of the EEC, 1952–1957* (Berlin & New York: Walter de Gruyter, 1992).
20. On the IRD, aside from the analyses in the work of Wilford and Frances Stone Saunders referred to below, see W. Scott Lucas & C.J. Morris, 'A Very British Crusade: The Information Research Department and the Beginning of the Cold War', in Richard J. Aldrich (ed.), *British Intelligence, Strategy and the Cold War* (London: Routledge, 1992); Phillip Deery, 'Confronting the Cominform: George Orwell and the Cold War Offensive of the Information Research Department, 1948–50', *Labour History*, 73 (November 1977); *IRD: Origins and Establishment of the Foreign Office Information Research Department, 1946–48* (FCO Historians' History Notes, No. 9, August 1995). See also Richard J. Aldrich, 'Putting Culture into the Cold War: The Cultural Relations Department (CRD) and British Covert Information Warfare', in Scott Smith & Krabbendam (eds), *Cultural Cold War in Western Europe 1945–1960*.

21. For the parallel developments of *Paix et liberté* in France and *Pace e libertà* in Italy, see Irving Wall, *L'influence americaine sur la politique francaise, 1945–1954* (Paris: Balland, 1991), and Richard Kuisel, *Seducing the French and the Dilemma of Americanization* (Berkeley, CA: University of California Press, 1992). For Italy, see Maria Guasconi, *L'altra Faccia Della Medaglia: Diplomazia Psicologica E Sindacale Nelle Relazioni Italia–Stati Uniti Durante La Prima Fase Della Guerra Fredda (1947–1955)* (Messina: Rubbettino, 1998).

22. David Hanley, 'Introduction: Christian Democracy as a Political Phenomenon', in *Christian Democracy in Europe: A Comparative Perspective* (London: Pinter, 1994), p.1. An excellent example of how the issue has been studied at the national level is Guido Formigoni, *La democrazia cristiana e l'allenza occidentale (1943–1953)* (Bologna: Il Mulino, 1996), which analyses in depth the ideological roots of the foreign policy of the Italian Christian Democrats.

23. Wolfram Kaiser, 'Christian Democracy in Twentieth-century Europe', *Journal of Contemporary History*, 39:1 (2004), pp.127–35.

24. Philippe Chenaux, *Une Europe Vaticane? Entre le Plain Marshall et les Traités de Rome* (Paris: Ciaco, 1990); Stathis Kalyvas, *The Rise of Christian Democracy in Europe* (Ithaca, NY: Cornell University Press, 1996); Emiel Lamberts, *Christian Democracy in the European Union, 1945–1995* (Leuven: Leuven University Press, 1997); Roberto Papini, *L'Internationale Démocrate-Chrétienne: La Coopération Internationale entre les Partis Démocrates-Chrétiens de 1925 à 1986* (Paris: Editions du Cerf, 1988). Michael Gehler & Wolfram Kaiser, 'Toward a "Core Europe" in a Western European Bloc: Transnational Cooperation in European Christian Democracy, 1925–1965', in Thomas Kselman & Joseph A. Buttigieg (eds), *European Christian Democracy: Historical Legacies and Comparative Perspectives* (Notre Dame, IL: University of Notre Dame Press, 2003), pp.240–66; Michael Gehler & Wolfram Kaiser, 'Transnationalism and Early European Integration: The NEI and the Geneva Circle 1947–57', *The Historical Journal*, 44 (2001), pp.773–98.

25. See many of the essays in the collective volume by Diane Kirby, *Religion and the Cold War* (Basingstoke: Palgrave Macmillan, 2002).

26. Ennio Di Nolfo, *Dear Pope. Vaticano e Stati Uniti. La corrispondenza segreta di Roosevelt e Truman con Papa Pacelli dalle carte di Myron Taylor* (Roma: Inedita, 2003). A general study of the Vatican's relations with Moscow is Andrea Riccardi, *Il Vaticano e Mosca, 1940–1990* (Roma: Laterza, 1992), while Alberto Melloni edited what is perhaps the most in-depth investigation of the international repercussions of a deeply significant religious event such as the Second Vatican Council: Alberto Melloni (ed.), *Vatican II in Moscow (1959–1965)* (Leuven: Bibliotheek van de Faculteit Godgeleerdheid, 1997). The memoirs of Cardinal Casaroli trace the slow development of the Church's own *Ostpolitik*: Agostino Casaroli, *Il martirio della pazienza. La Santa Sede e i paesi comunisti (1963–1989)* (Torino: Einaudi, 2000).

27. Donald Sassoon, *One Hundred Years of Socialism: The West European Left in the Twentieth Century* (London: Fontana Press, 1997). See also Dietrich Orlow, *Common Destiny: A Comparative History of the Dutch, French, and German Social Democratic Parties, 1945–1969* (Oxford & New York: Berghahn Books, 1999).

28. Robert Ladrech, *Social Democracy and the Challenge of European Union* (Boulder, CO: Lynne Rienner, 2000); R. Ladrech & Philippe Marliére (eds), *Social*

Democratic Parties in the European Union: History, Organization, Politics (London: Macmillan, 1999); Walter Lipgens, 'Views of Socialist and Trade Union Associations on the Postwar Order in Europe', in W. Lipgens (ed.), *Documents on the History of European Integration*, Vol. 2: *Plans for European Union in Great Britain and in Exile 1939–1945* (Berlin: William de Gruyter, 1986); Wilfried Loth, 'Socialist Parties between East and West', in Antonio Varsori & Elena Calandri (eds), *The Failure of Peace in Europe, 1943–1948* (London: Macmillan, 2002); and also Loth's *Sozialismus und Internazionalismus. Die franzosischen sozialisten und die Nachkriegsordnung Europas 1940–1950* (Stuttgart: Deutsche Verlag, 1977); Michael Newman, *Socialism and European Unity: The Dilemmas of the Left in Britain and France* (London: Junction Books, 1983); Marta Petricioli (ed.), *La sinistra europea nel secondo dopoguerra, 1943–1949* (Firenze: Sansoni, 1981).

29. Josef Braunthal, *Geschichte der Internationale*, vol. 2 (Bonn: 1978).

30. Hugh Wilford, *The CIA, the British Left and the Cold War* (London: Frank Cass, 2003).

31. R. Godson & S. Haseler, *Eurocommunism: Implications for East and West* (New York: St Martin's Press, 1978); P. Filo della Torre, *Eurocommunism: Myth or Reality?* (London: Penguin, 1979); P. Lange & M. Vannicelli, *The Communist Parties of Italy, France and Spain: Postwar Change and Continuity* (Cambridge: G. Allen & Unwin, Center for European Studies, Harvard University, 1981); R. Tökes (ed.), *Eurocommunism and Détente* (New York: New York University Press, 1978); J. Barth Urban, *Moscow and the Italian Communist Party: From Togliatti to Berlinguer* (Ithaca, NY, & London: Cornell University Press, 1986); S. Hellman, 'PCI Strategy and the Question of Revolution in the West', in S. Avineri (ed.), *Varieties of Marxism* (The Hague: Martinus Nijhoff, 1977); D. Blackmer & S. Tarrow, *Il comunismo in Italia e Francia* (Milano: Etas Libri, 1976); A. Macleod, 'The PCI's Relations with the PCF in the Age of Eurocommunism', *Studies in Comparative Communism*, 13:2/3 (1980). For some recent historical articles, see S. Pons, 'L'Italia e il PCI nella politica estera dell'URSS di Breznev', *Studi Storici*, 42:4, pp.929–51; Olav Njolstad, 'The Carter Administration and Italy: Keeping the Communists Out of Power Without Interfering', *Journal of Cold War Studies*, 4:3 (Summer 2002), pp.56–94; Laura Fasanaro, 'L'Eurocomunismo nelle carte della SED', *Mondo Contemporaneo*, 2:3 (forthcoming).

32. Lawrence S. Wittner, *The Struggle against the Bomb*, Volumes I–III (Stanford, CA: Stanford University Press, 1992–2003); Matthew Evangelista, *Unarmed Forces: The Transnational Movement to End the Cold War* (Ithaca, NY: Cornell University Press, 1999); Mary L. Dudziak, *Cold War Civil Rights: Race and the Image of American Democracy, Politics and Society in Twentieth-Century America* (Princeton, NJ: Princeton University Press, 2000); Jeremi Suri, *Power and Protest: Global Revolution and the Rise of Detente* (Cambridge, MA: Harvard University Press, 2003).

33. MacDonald, 'Ideologies in the Cold War', p.183.

34. On the history of European integration there is obviously such a large body of literature that it can't be mentioned here. For one of the best examples of Alan Milward's work, see his *The Reconstruction of Western Europe 1945–51* (London: Methuen, 1984) and *The European Rescue of the Nation State* (London: Routledge, 1992), *passim*.

35. See for instance some of the essays published in vol. 8, no. 2 of the *Journal of European Integration History* (2002), or the work of René Girault on the construction of European identity, for instance his edited volume *Identité européenne au XXe siècle* (Paris: Hachette, 1994).

36. The strongest indictments of the CCF can be seen in Frances Stonor Saunders, *Who Paid the Piper?: The CIA and the Cultural Cold War* (London: Granta Books, 1999), and W. Scott Lucas, *Freedom's War: The US Crusade Against the Soviet Union, 1945–56* (New York: New York University Press, 1999). Other analyses include Peter Coleman, *The Liberal Conspiracy: The Congress for Cultural Freedom and the Struggle for the Mind of Postwar Europe* (London & New York: Macmillan, 1989) and what is in our opinion still the best and most balanced assessment, Pierre Grémion's *L'intelligence de l'anticommunisme: Le Congrés pour la Liberté de la culture à Paris, 1950–1975* (Paris: Fayard, 1995). See also W. Scott Lucas, 'Beyond Freedom, Beyond Control: Approaches to Culture and the State–Private Network in the Cold War', in Scott Smith & Krabbendam (eds), *Cultural Cold War*, p.60. Wilford, *British Left*, p.193; Michael Hochgeschwender, 'A Battle of Ideas: The Congress for Cultural Freedom (CCF) in Britain, Italy, France and Germany', in Dominik Geppert (ed.), *The Postwar Challenge: Cultural, Social and Political Challenge in Western Europe, 1945–1958* (Oxford: Oxford University Press 2003), p.323.

37. Volker Berghahn, 'A Public–Private Partnership? The Cultural Policies of the US Administrations in Western Europe and the Role of the Big American Foundations', in Geppert (ed.), *Postwar Challenge*, p.316. See also Berghahn's seminal work, *America and the Intellectual Cold Wars in Europe: Shepard Stone between Philanthropy, Academy and Diplomacy* (Princeton, NJ: Princeton University Press, 2001).

38. For two examples of the polemical, pamphlet-like literature, see, for instance, J. Marrs, *Rule by Secrecy: The Hidden History that Connects the Trilateral Commission, the Freemasons, and the Great Pyramids* (London: HarperCollins, 2000); G. Virebeau, *Le monde secret de Bilderberg: comment la haute finance et les technocrates dominent les nations* (Paris: H. Coston, 1986). On Retinger, see J. Pomian (ed.), *Joseph Retinger: Memoirs of an Eminence Grise* (London: Sussex University Press, 1972); for his role in setting up the Bilderberg group, see Roberto Ducci, *I capintesta* (Milano: Rusconi, 1982), pp.265–85. Among the new research on the Bilderberg group, see Valerie Aubourg, 'Guy Mollet et le groupe de Bilderberg: le parcours original d'un Européen, 1952–1963', *Histoire(s) Socialiste(s)*, 1 (1999), pp.14–33; idem, 'Organizing Atlanticism: The Bilderberg Group and the Atlantic Institute, 1952–1963', in Scott Smith & Krabbendam (eds), *Cultural Cold War*, pp.92–105.

39. Anthony Carew, *The International Confederation of Free Trade Unions, International and Comparative Social History, 3 and Index* (New York & Bern: P. Lang, 2000); and by the same author, *Labour under the Marshall Plan: The Politics of Productivity and the Marketing of Management Science* (Detroit, MI: Wayne State University Press, 1987), and Walter Reuther, *Lives of the Left Index* (New York & Manchester: Manchester University Press, 1993); Ronald Filippelli, 'Luigi Antonini, the Italian-American Labor Council, and Cold War Politics in Italy, 1943–1949', *Labor History*, 33:1 (1992); Ronald L. Filippelli, *American Labor and Postwar Italy, 1943–1953* (Stanford, CA: Stanford University Press, 1989); Ted Morgan, *A Covert Life: Jay Lovestone, Communist, Anti-Communist,*

and *Spymaster* (New York: Random House, 1999, 1st edition); Ben Rathbun, *The Point Man: Irving Brown and the Deadly Post-1945 Struggle for Europe and Africa* (Washington, DC: Minerva Press, 1996); Federico Romero, *The United States and the European Trade Union Movement, 1944–1951* (Chapel Hill, NC: University of North Carolina Press, 1992).

40. A scholarly interpretation can be found in S. Gill, *American Hegemony and the Trilateral Commission* (Cambridge: Cambridge University Press, 1990). For the Harpsund meetings, see Carew, *International Confederation* and Walter Reuther, *Lives of the Left*, pp.113–15. See also Carl Soberg, *Hubert Humphrey: A Biography* (New York: W.W. Norton, 1984), pp.219–21, and Adolf Sturmthal, *Democracy Under Fire: Memoirs of a European Socialist* (Chapel Hill, NC: University of North Carolina Press, 1989), pp.191–5.

41. Nelson Lichtenstein, *The Most Dangerous Man in Detroit: Walter Reuther and the Fate of American Labor* (New York: Basic Books, 1995), pp.359–60.

42. Dominik Geppert, 'Cultural Aspects of the Cold War', *Bulletin of the German Historical Institute London*, 24:2 (2002), p.70.

43. Leonid Gibianskii, 'Sowietisierung Osteuropas – Character und Typologie', in Michael Lemke (ed.), *Sowietiesierung und Eigenstaendigkein in der SBZ/DDR (1945–1953)* (Cologne, 1999); *The Diary of Georgy Dmitrov, 1933–1949* (New Haven, CT: Yale University Press, 2003).

44. T. Volokitina, T. Islamov, G. Murashko & A. Noskova (eds), *Vostochnaia Evropa v dokumentakh rossiiskikh arkhivov, 1944–1953* (Moscow-Novosibirsk: Sibirsky khronograf, 1997); T.V. Volokitina, G.P. Murashko, A.F. Noskova & T.F. Pokivailova, *Moskva I Vostochnaia Evropa. Stanovleniie politicheskikh regimov sovetskogo tipa, 1949–1953. Ocherki istorii* (Moscow: ROSSPEN 2002).

45. Vladimir Tismaneanu, *Stalinism for All Seasons: A Political History of Romanian Communism* (Berkeley, CA: University of California Press, 2003).

46. Odd Arne Westad (ed.), *The Fall of Détente: Soviet–American Relations during the Carter Years* (Oslo: Scandinavian University Press, 1997).

47. Lubodrang Dimic (ed.), *Great Powers and Small Countries in Cold War, 1945–1955*. Proceedings of the International Scientific Conference, Belgrade, 3–4 November 2003 (Belgrade, 2005).

48. Chen Jian, *Mao's China and the Cold War* (Chapel Hill, NC: University of North Carolina Press, 2001), *passim*; Shuguang Zhang, *Mao's Military Romanticism: China and the Korean War* (Lawrence, KS: University of Kansas Press, 1996), *passim*.

49. Odd Arne Westad, *Decisive Encounters: The Chinese Civil War, 1946–1950* (Stanford, CA: Stanford University Press, 2003).

50. David P. Chandler, *Brother Number One: A Political Biography* (Boulder, CO: Westview Press, 1999); Ben Kiernan, *The Pol Pot Regime: Race, Power, and Genocide in Cambodia under the Khmer Rouge, 1975–79* (New Haven, CT: Yale University Press, 2002, 2nd edition); Ben Kiernan, *How Pol Pot Came to Power: Colonialism, Nationalism, and Communism in Cambodia, 1930–1975* (New Haven, CT: Yale University Press, 2004, 2nd edition).

51. Piero Gleijeses, *Conflicting Missions: Havana, Washington, and Africa, 1959–1976* (Chapel Hill, NC: University of North Carolina Press, 2002), *passim*; see also Piero Gleijeses, 'Havana's Policy in Africa, 1959–76: New Evidence from the Cuban Archives', *CWIHP Bulletin*, 8–9 (1997), pp.5–20.

52. Thomas J. Belke, *Juche: A Christian Study of North Korea's State Religion* (Living Sacrifice Book Co., 1999). A book with a strong Christian perspective, it is nonetheless one of the few studies entirely devoted to the Juche idea. See also Jae-jin Seo, *Comparative Study of Marxism-Leninism and Juche Ideology: Focusing on the Influences in Forming the Political System and the Theory of Open Reform* (Korean Institute for National Unification, 2002); and Kim Hyong-soo, 'The Juche Ideology and Stalin', *Life & Human Rights in North Korea*, 19 (Spring 2001).

53. On the Vietnamese side, see Robert K. Brigham, *Guerrilla Diplomacy: The NLF's Foreign Relations and the Viet Nam War* (Ithaca, NY: Cornell University Press, 1999); Mark Philip Bradley, *Imagining Vietnam and America: The Making of Postcolonial Vietnam, 1919–1950* (Chapel Hill, NC: University of North Carolina Press, 2000); Luu Van Loi, *Fifty Years of Vietnamese Diplomacy, 1945–1995*, Vol. 1: *1945–1975* (Hanoi: The Gioi, 2000). The Soviet perspective is in Ilya V. Gaiduk, *Confronting Vietnam: Soviet Policy toward the Indochina Conflict, 1954–1963* (Stanford, CA: Stanford University Press, 2003).

54. George Kennan (writing anonymously as 'Mr X'), 'The Sources of Soviet Conduct', *Foreign Affairs*, 25 (1947), pp.566–82; Hannah Arendt, *The Origins of Totalitarianism* (London: Allen & Unwin, 1958); Zbigniew Brzezinski, *The Permanent Purge: Politics in Soviet Totalitarianism* (Cambridge, MA: Harvard University Press, 1956); Merle Fainsod, *How Russia is Ruled: Smolensk under Soviet Rule* (Cambridge, MA: Harvard University Press, 1954).

55. Adam Ulam, *Expansion and Coexistence: Soviet Foreign Policy, 1917–1973* (New York: Holt, Rinehart & Winston, 1974); Martin Malia, *The Soviet Tragedy: A History of Socialism in Russia, 1917–1991* (New York: Free Press, 1995).

56. Averell Harriman, *Special Envoy to Churchill and Stalin, 1941–46* (New York: Random House, 1975), p.46; Henry Kissinger, *Diplomacy* (New York: Simon & Schuster, 1994), p.398.

57. See Adam Ulam, *Dangerous Relations: The Soviet Union in World Politics* (Oxford: Oxford University Press, 1983); Pipes describes the impact of his historical studies on policy recommendations in his memoir: *Vixi: Memoir of a Non-Belonger* (New Haven, CT: Yale University Press, 2003).

58. Nigel Gould-Davies, 'Rethinking the Role of Ideology in International Politics during the Cold War', *Journal of Cold War Studies*, 1 (Winter 1999), p.92; Douglas MacDonald, 'Ideologies in the Cold War', *passim*.

59. Stephen F. Cohen, *Rethinking the Soviet Experience: Politics and History since 1917* (Oxford: Oxford University Press, 1985).

60. David Holloway, *Stalin and the Bomb* (New Haven, CT: Yale University Press, 1994), *passim*.

61. Robert D. English, *Russia and the Idea of the West: Gorbachev, Intellectuals and the End of the Cold War* (New York: Columbia University Press, 2000); Anatoly Chernyaev, *Moia zhizn I moie vremia* (Moscow: Mezhdunarodniie otnosheniia, 1995).

62. Vojtech Mastny, *The Cold War and Soviet Insecurity: The Stalin Years* (Oxford: Oxford University Press, 1995), *passim*; John Lewis Gaddis, *We Now Know: Rethinking Cold War History* (Oxford: Oxford University Press, 1997), *passim*.

63. Vladislav Zubok & Constantine Pleshakov, *Inside the Kremlin's Cold War: From Stalin to Khrushchev* (Cambridge, MA: Harvard University Press, 1996), pp.275–82.

64. See Vladimir Pechatnov's piece in Ralph B. Levering, Vladimir O. Pechatnov, Verena Botzenhart-Viehe & C. Earl Edmondson, *Debating the Origins of the Cold War: American and Russian Perspectives* (Lanham, MD: Rowman & Littlefield Publishers, 2002); also see: Tatiana Volokitina, Galina Murashko, Albina Noskova & Tatiana Pokivailova, *Moskva I Vostochnaia Evropa. Stanovleniie politicheskikh rezhimov sovetskogo tipa, 1949–1953, Ocherki istorii* (Moscow: ROSSPEN, 2002).
65. Norman Naimark, *The Russians in Germany: A History of the Soviet Zone of Occupation, 1945–1949* (Cambridge, MA: Harvard University Press, 1995), *passim*.
66. Dmitry Shliapentokh, *Intellectuals and the Political Power: The Post-Stalin Era* (London: I.B. Tauris, 1990), pp.20–8.
67. Yitzhak Brudny, *Reinventing Russia: Russian Nationalism and the Soviet State, 1953–1991* (Cambridge, MA: Harvard University Press, 1998), p.58.
68. Walter L. Hixson, *Parting the Curtain: Propaganda, Culture, and the Cold War, 1945–1961* (New York: St Martin's Press, 1997).
69. Alexander Bovin, *XX vek kak zhizn. Vospominania* (Moscow: Zakharov, 2003), p.141, pp.145–6.
70. Brudny, *Reinventing Russia*, pp.59–60, pp.127–9; Nikolai Mitrokin, *Russkaia partiia. Dvizheniie russkikh natsionalistov v SSSR 1953–1985* (Moscow, 2003), pp.548–9.
71. William E. Odom, *The Collapse of the Soviet Military* (New Haven, CT: Yale University Press, 1998); Jack F. Matlock, Jr., *Reagan and Gorbachev: How the Cold War Ended* (New York: Random House, 2004).
72. Archie Brown, *The Gorbachev Factor* (Oxford: Oxford University Press, 1996); English, *Russia and the Idea of the West, passim*.
73. William C. Wohlforth, *Cold War Endgame* (University Park, PA: Pennsylvania State University Press, 2003). Vladislav Zubok, 'Gorbachev and the End of the Cold War: Perspectives on History and Personality', *Cold War History*, 2:2 (2002), pp.61–100.

4

alliance

lawrence kaplan

The word 'alliance' has always been susceptible to multiple interpretations. It could apply to such cognate relationships as a coalition, *entente*, pact, or bloc as well as to a formal treaty. These variations require scholars to describe alliance in sweeping language as Robert Osgood did in defining it 'as a formal agreement that pledges states to co-operate in using their military resources against a specific state or states and usually obligates one or more of the signatories to use force, or to consider (unilaterally or in consultation with allies) the use of force in specified circumstances'.[1]

In the absence of a single accepted definition of alliance, its range can extend from a blanket alignment, referring to all kinds of international cooperation, to the more specific military cooperation in an alliance against a third power. An *entente* also encompasses military collaboration but it is usually an agreement without the specific obligations of an alliance. Reasons for contracting an alliance are almost as varied as the definition itself. Combining against a threat from a stronger power may be the most common justification of an alliance. This could take a defensive form, as in the case of the North Atlantic Treaty Organisation (NATO) in 1949, or offensive as in the case of the Franco-American alliance of 1778. *Ententes* can evolve into a full-scale alliance, as the Anglo-French-Russian *entente* of 1907 did in 1914. Ideological factors also can play a role in making an alliance, as they did in the Sino-Soviet alliance of 1949 to counter the perceived capitalist threat from the West.

The distinctions between ideological and pragmatic reasons for making alliances are often blurred. Occasionally without the benefit or even a wish for an alliance coincidental coordination of actions could place adversaries on the same side; both the United States and the Soviet Union condemned the Anglo-French invasion of Egypt in 1956, as Ole Hosti observed. It should be recognised that 'an alliance is a formal agreement

111

between two or more nations to collaborate on national security matters'.[2] George Modelski concluded that there is a considerable literature on the working of an alliance – 'on intra-alliance consultations and restraints. But paradoxically, we learn very little about what alliances in fact are.'[3]

The historian is compelled to illustrate by example. The classic case of an alliance, one that involved a number of states with binding obligations, was the Achaean League of Greece in the third century BC. In many ways it served as an unintended model for NATO, the primary case study in this chapter. Initially, it was a confederation of 12 cities (the precise number of nations in the original NATO). It had a federal constitution that left internal affairs to the constituent city-states, each having equal power in a council that met at least twice a year. The council was responsible for all matters of foreign policy, management of the army, and collection of federal taxes. The chief executive was commander-in-chief of the army, serving a one-year term but eligible for re-election every other year. Wars with other city-states weakened the league over the years, with its dissolution at the hands of Rome in 146 BC.

Alliances of this scope and magnitude were not to appear again until NATO was established in the twentieth century. Nor would there be less ambitious alliances until the rise of the city-states at the end of the Middle Ages. As Sidney Fay noted, alliances in the Italian Renaissance 'formed and dissolved with kaleidoscope rapidity'.[4] Less rapid but equally unreliable were alliances among the new nation states of the sixteenth century. From that time until the world wars of the twentieth century the concept of a league of allies, each surrendering certain prerogatives of sovereignty, was not to be found. 'Concerts' such as that following the defeat of Napoleon in 1815 reflected a common goal – the suppression of revolutionary actions – but without binding actions to effect this result.

Alliances to maintain the balance of power in Europe flourished in the sixteenth through to the eighteenth centuries, a time when England allied with any country that could prevent a single continental power from dominating Europe. The balance of power, as Hans Morgenthau saw it, was 'a protective device of an alliance of nations ... against another nation's designs for world domination'.[5] In the sixteenth century England joined with France and the Ottoman empire to prevent Spain's Charles V from controlling the continent. A century and a half later France under Louis XIV evoked a similar reaction from rival powers. The alliances created in those years lasted just long enough to curb the ambitions of a potential conqueror, with smaller nations joining one or the other parties for protection, creating what Stephen Walt has called the 'bandwagon effect' forcing insecure states to accept the domination of a powerful aggressor, as Holland and Spain did in Napoleon's Europe.[6] But the more prevalent balancing impulse were combinations to pursue common interests, and these led to alignments that were subject to dramatic changes in their composition. Arguably, the most startling was the so-called diplomatic revolution of 1756, following the War of the Austrian Succession, that witnessed the termination of the longstanding conflict between Bourbon France and Hapsburg Austria. Until this time Britain had been on the side of Austria in its customary role of containing French expansion. As a consequence of the new combination of Austria and France, Britain joined Prussia, France's former ally, to cope in the Seven Years War (1756–63) with the new Franco-Austrian alignment.

Witnessing the shifting alliances of European monarchies from across the Atlantic was the emerging American nation in rebellion not just against a putatively tyrannical mother country, but against the system of alliances that served the dynastic interests of European monarchs. Ironically, to secure its independence the former colonists allied with Britain's enemy, France, to wage a successful war of independence in the late eighteenth century. Not only did the United States fail to distance itself from the corrupt Old World but it concluded an entangling alliance with an old adversary that engaged France, but with the stipulation that Americans could not leave the war without French approval. Good fortune combined with shrewd diplomacy permitted the new nation to make peace with Britain that secured more territory than its military activities merited. Yet the experience of alliance with a European power, no matter how necessary, nurtured the concept of non-entanglement that was not altered until the twentieth century.

The tradition of isolationism was modified but not abandoned when the United States participated in the First World War. It helped to account for the nation's refusal to accept President Woodrow Wilson's League of Nations, the ambitious effort to provide the world with a collective security system that would end the balance-of-power politics that had caused wars over the centuries. Its decision deepened isolationism in the 1920s and 1930s. The United States stood aside as Europe failed to restrain the aggressive actions of fascist Italy and Nazi Germany until the Japanese attack on Pearl Harbor in 1941 brought the nation once again into a world war. Although the United States had not formally abandoned its traditional attitude toward entangling alliances after victory in the Second World War, it did help to create the United Nations, a new League of Nations, in which it played a leading role. Like its predecessor, it could not assure peace. Any one of the five permanent members of the Council (the victors of the Second World War) had the veto power, which could frustrate UN actions if the nation charged with violating the Charter was one of the permanent members. Referring to the failed League of Nations, J.L. Brierly judged in 1946 that 'what we have done is to exchange a system which might or might not have worked for one which cannot work, and that instead of limiting the sovereignty of states we have actually extended the sovereignty of the Great Powers'.[7]

It was the failure of the second attempt in the twentieth century to establish a concert of nations to maintain collective security that inspired the creation of the North Atlantic Treaty in 1949, and in its wake the Sino-Soviet treaty as well as the Warsaw Pact, the South-East Asia Treaty Organisation (SEATO) and the Central Treaty Organisation (CENTO). The first three were major actors in the cold war and each of them had elements of ideological affinities and perceptions of a common threat. Only the Atlantic alliance through NATO had the intention and capability to construct as well a new order in a Europe that intended to liberate Western Europe from its destructive past.

nato and the western powers

NATO, the first and most enduring of these alliances, was initially the consequence of a need to preserve countries from the grip of Soviet-led communism. Western Europe turned to the United States for economic recovery, offered through the implementation of the Marshall Plan in 1947. However, economic aid was not enough. If ever the time seemed ripe for a formal abandonment of the USA's abstention from entangling alliances with Europe, it was in the dark winter of 1947–48. Efforts to come to terms with the Soviet Union over the future of Germany had failed, leaving an impasse over the German question that portended continuing conflict with the Soviets that could erupt into a deadly new war. The British and French were convinced, as were the vulnerable smaller nations of the West, that American political and military involvement was vital if Europe was to have a sense of security that would ensure its economic recovery. British and French leaders, particularly their respective foreign ministers, Ernest Bevin and Georges Bidault, recognised the obstacles imposed by the isolationist past, and proceeded cautiously to entangle the United States in a Western European defence pact. In a major speech in the House of Commons on 22 January 1948, Bevin spoke of treaties to be made with France, Belgium, the Netherlands and Luxembourg (the latter three known as the Benelux countries) that would culminate in a European union. The process actually had begun with the Treaty of Dunkirk in 1946 when Britain and France bound themselves to suppress any revival of

German aggression. But this narrow alliance was broadened two months after Bevin's address to encompass the Benelux countries in the Brussels pact, a treaty of collective self-defence. Its Article IV unequivocally stated that '[if] any of the High Contracting Parties should be the object of an armed attack in Europe, the other High Contracting Parties will, in accordance with the provisions of Article 51 of the Charter of the United Nations, afford the party so attacked all the military and other aid and assistance in their power'. Ideally, the Europeans wanted the United States to join this Western Union. Still, by demonstrating to sceptical Americans that they were prepared to defend themselves and pool their resources they hoped to break down the barriers to American participation.

In retrospect, Soviet behaviour rather than European plotting pushed the United States out of its isolationism and into a European alliance. The Czechoslovak coup, the warnings to Norway, the efforts to manipulate Italian elections, and the Berlin blockade combined to push the nation closer to Europe. But not close enough in 1948. An articulate minority in the Senate was convinced that membership in a European alliance would enmesh America in the politics of the Old World. The visceral suspicion that Europeans would take advantage of America's beneficence was not confined to isolationists. The military establishment was also uneasy. Military assistance would deplete their stocks, already at risk from a tight military budget. Nor were its leaders happy with recommendations for new commitments implied in a close association with the European allies that would overextend their military resources. But the strongest opposition emerged from the ranks of former isolationists, converts to internationalism, who feared that an Atlantic pact would subvert the UN Charter. Senator Arthur Vandenberg, chairman of the powerful Armed Services Committee, was their most prominent spokesman and had to be convinced that any such treaty would be in conformity with the Charter and not revive the discredited balance-of-power system.

It required long and contentious negotiations in Washington in the summer of 1948 with the Brussels Pact members before a pact could be concluded, and even then the presidential election of that year delayed a final American response. When the treaty was signed on 4 April 1949, it had elements that discomfited the five members of the Brussels Pact. One was the enlargement of the membership to include such countries as Norway and Denmark in the north and Portugal and Italy in the south. Their presence would mean that the core members would receive less military aid than if the alliance had been confined to the United States, Canada and the Western Union. Their primary concern, however, was over the language of what the Canadian statesman, Escott Reid, has called the 'pledge': namely, the guarantee that the United States would come to the aid of any member under attack. They preferred to replicate the clear phrases of the Brussels Treaty's Article IV. Instead, they had to accept Article V which did not accept an automatic response to an external attack. Rather than assuring that the allies, notably the United States, would have to commit 'such military or other action ... as may be necessary' in defence of the victim, the final text settled for 'such action as it [member nation] deems necessary, including the use of armed force'. While this language appeased the US Senate, the allies had to be comforted with the including 'forthwith' should any assistance be needed. They could hope that as the United States became accustomed to its new relationship with Europe, it would treat an attack on London and Paris as the equivalent of an attack on New York or Chicago.

Given the long gestation of the alliance from July 1948 to April 1949, it was obvious that there was no instant obliteration of transatlantic history. The title itself (referring to the 'North Atlantic') reminded sceptics that the United States was not really joining a European alliance. Iceland, like Canada, assumed an importance it otherwise might not have had. Both sides of the Atlantic had to overlook deviations from the treaty's preamble which assured that the treaty was 'founded on the principles of democracy, individual liberty and the rule of law'. Portugal, which was ruled by a right-wing dictatorship until 1974, did not meet this standard any more than Italy fitted into the geography of the North Atlantic. Greece's membership of NATO was not affected by its experience of military rule (1967–74), and the same was true with Turkey, despite the frequent intervention of its armed forces in civilian politics. In these cases, the West's geopolitical interests took precedence over considerations of democratic propriety. Nor were the many references to the UN Charter to be taken as anything more than a device to make the treaty palatable to Vandenberg and his followers. If NATO were genuinely a regional organisation under the aegis of the Charter's Articles 53 and 54 its proceedings would have to be reported to the Security Council where the Soviets held a seat. So in reality the only Charter article specifically identified in the treaty was Article 51, permitting individual and collective defence, without involving the Security Council. The alliance was intended to have a life of 20 years, but not the 50 years of the Brussels Treaty – longer than Americans wanted but shorter than Europeans had anticipated. It was obvious that the treaty was born of compromises necessary to meet the perceived common threat.

The Brussels Pact powers provided a useful model for developing institutions to implement the alliance. The North Atlantic Treaty's

Article 9 mandated a Council. Under its authority subsidiary bodies were quickly established. Regional planning groups were supported by a Military Production and Supply Board (MPSB) and a Defence Financial and Economic Committee (DFEC). More significant were the military arrangements: a Defence Committee (composed of defence ministers), a Military Committee (composed of chiefs of staff), and its Standing Group (composed of military leaders of the three major powers in the alliance). For the most part these were replicas of the Western Union committees which added NATO operations to their regular activities until the NATO groups completed their organisation.

This elaborate infrastructure existed only on paper in NATO's first year. There was little coordination among them. And it did not seem to matter. The Europeans seemingly had won their major objective: entangling the United States in a European alliance. The sense of security this provided permitted them to turn their attention to Article 3, extracting military aid as quickly as possible. Fear of a Soviet invasion was never a critical issue. Rather, it was fear of Soviet intimidation of vulnerable governments and exploitation of domestic communist parties to take power by constitutional means that most concerned them in 1949. The allies achieved this objective as well, but not before the senior partner insisted on monitoring the distribution and use of the supplies and equipment in each of the recipient countries. These bilateral arrangements disturbed the allies, particularly when reciprocal assistance to the United States included base rights. Moreover, the Europeans were expected to endorse a strategic plan that would have the USA evacuate its troops from most of Europe before returning to liberate Soviet-occupied allied territory. This short-term defence plan, reminiscent of the experiences of the Second World War, was so unacceptable that it was replaced by a medium-term plan in the spring of 1950 that would have Europe defended at the Rhine. While this concession left the Netherlands, Denmark and Norway unprotected, it was the best the allies could get at that time. The tensions of the first year were manageable.

What transformed the alliance was a traumatic event on the other side of Eurasia – the outbreak of war in Korea. Assuming that the Soviets orchestrated the North Korean attack against South Korea in preparation for a similar communist attack against West Germany, the United States not only rallied quickly to the support of South Korea, but felt the need to meet a comparable crisis in Europe. The result was a reorganisation of the alliance, putting, as many believe, the 'O' in NATO. Massive military aid followed, and was accompanied by NATO's expanding its membership to include Greece and Turkey in February 1952 – an idea that had been rejected in 1949 – and ultimately West Germany in May 1955 – an idea that was almost unthinkable in 1949. On the assumption that NATO was in immediate danger of a Soviet attack, the southern flank needed to be secured, and German troops and resources had to be tapped if the Soviets were to be deterred or defeated.

Although there was always a military component to NATO, the reorganisation resulting from the Korean war was as extensive as it was dramatic. By the end of 1950 a Supreme Allied Command in Europe (SACEUR) was headed by General Dwight D. Eisenhower and headquartered in Paris with subordinate commands ranging from Norway to Turkey. Similarly, a Supreme Atlantic Command (SACLANT) serving the ocean would have its headquarters in Norfolk, Virginia. Plans were made at the Lisbon meeting of the North Atlantic Council in February 1952 to mobilise 50 divisions, spearheaded by four new American divisions authorised by the US Congress in the aftermath of the Korean war. To match the military changes the office of secretary-general was established at the Lisbon meeting. Traditionally, the secretary-general has been a European, while the supreme allied commanders have always been Americans.

There were no significant changes in the NATO structure or in the composition of the membership over the course of the cold war, except for the addition of Spain in 1982. Drawing in Spain did complete the adherence of the Iberian peninsula, but Spain's presence was less a military factor than evidence of the evolution of the alliance into a vehicle for the movement toward European unification that was separate from opposition to communist expansion but integral to one of the objectives of the alliance.

American domination of NATO was particularly prominent in the first decade as Western Europe continued its recovery from world war. The NATO method of governance was by 'consensus', but it was inevitable that consensus for the most part would be driven by US priorities until Europeans acquired the power to press interests that were not necessarily those of the superpower. Yet dissent frequently appeared even in the early years of the organisation. The smaller nations expressed resentment over lack of consultation by the larger members in 1956, and more successfully in the so-called Harmel initiative in 1967 (named after the Belgian foreign minister, Pierre Harmel) when NATO gave *détente* equal billing with defence as its primary objectives.

France from the outset had opposed what it regarded as an Anglo-American condominium in control of the alliance, and withdrew from the organisation military structure, but not from the alliance itself, in 1966. Greece also withdrew its military support but unlike France returned six years later. Its displeasure was directed not against the United States but against Turkey over the Turkish invasion of Cyprus in 1974. Germany, the potential focus of battle in the event of a Soviet assault, was essentially more favourably disposed toward the American presence and its leadership than the other allies. West German leaders identified the United States as its primary supporter when memories of its Nazi past still haunted its neighbours. Yet those memories faded and as its economic strength grew, the Germans wanted a share in the nuclear capabilities that the British and French as well as the United States possessed. Moreover, they were unhappy with a military strategy that made it inevitable that a war between NATO and the Warsaw Pact would be fought on German territory, West or East.

When the cold war ended with the implosion of the Soviet Union and the disintegration of the Warsaw Pact in 1991, NATO remained intact. Whatever the difficulties the next decade would bring, the alliance survived and believed that it still had missions to fulfil. None of the foregoing tensions culminated in the departure of any ally from alliance even if some of them were never resolved. The smaller nations were mollified by US willingness in the 1960s to share nuclear information; France's decision to leave the integrated military structure did not preclude informal collaboration over the next generation; and the end of the cold war dissolved Germany's concerns about nuclear warfare on its territory.

In NATO's first 40 years there was inevitably a shift in the transatlantic balance as Europe recovered from the devastation of the Second World War and became less dependent on the American partner. By the time that the Soviet empire had imploded the two initial objections of the alliance had been achieved: coping with and ultimately surmounting the challenge of Soviet communism, and moving steadily toward the unification of Europe. Important as the alliance was to the history of both the United States and its European allies its historiography has had a chequered past. In the United States it has suffered from the perception among American historians that the North Atlantic Treaty was a by-product of the Truman Doctrine, a lesser event among the many dramatic changes in American foreign relations after the Second World War. Piecemeal, it appealed as a subject of study to political scientists more than to historians for the lessons it could offer to particular political science models. Political scientists arguably have made greater contributions to NATO historiography than historians, although Marc Trachtenberg and Thomas A. Schwartz have gone some way to redress this imbalance.[8]

While many universities had created centres of foreign policy studies in the past half-century, the Lyman L. Lemnitzer Center for NATO Studies (now NATO and European Union Studies) at Kent State University stands alone among universities in the special place it has given to the Atlantic alliance. Monographs published by the Center for the most part have dealt with the beginnings of the alliance.[9]

The memoirs of such important participants as Canada's Escott Reid and Britain's Nicholas Henderson have illuminated the formation of the alliance.[10] NATO studies in Europe have been extensive, with centres in Oslo and Florence leading the way. British scholars like John Baylis and John W. Young have offered insights into the role of Ernest Bevin in the creation of alliance,[11] while Pierre Melandri, Frederic Bozo and other French scholars have analysed their own country's relationship with fellow North Atlantic Treaty powers.[12] The Military History Research Office in Potsdam has produced monographs and sponsored conferences for the past 20 years on the military role of NATO.[13] Since the 50th anniversary of the signing of the treaty, there has been increased interest in its history, notably among European scholars as NATO archives in Brussels have been become available through 1972. Gustav Schmidt has edited a massive history of NATO, based on two conferences held in Brussels and Bonn in 1999, while Mark Smith has written about the hitherto overlooked topic of NATO's expansion during the cold war – most studies of NATO enlargement tend to focus on the admission of former Warsaw Pact states after 1997. As noted in the Introduction and in Chapter 5, the work of the Parallel History Project (PHP), inspired by Vojtech Mastny, should encourage future scholarly research into the histories of both NATO and the Warsaw Pact. The PHP's primary emphasis lies with the Eastern bloc, but the products of the conferences it has sponsored (which are soon to be published) will aid the study of both of the European cold war alliances.[14]

the rise and fall of the warsaw pact

NATO was the archetype of cold war alliances, even though the alliances that followed differed markedly from the original. The Warsaw Pact is a case in point. If NATO was an association of like-minded nations for mutual benefits, the Warsaw Pact organisation claimed a similar status. But in effect it was an instrument of the senior partner. NATO's members chose of their own will to enter into the alliance, and no actions could be taken without the approval of each nation. In contrast, members of the Warsaw Pact were under the domination of the Soviet Union.

The pact was made with nations of Eastern Europe, all of which were communist regimes linked to the Soviets through bilateral agreements. In this context there was no need for a restructuring of the relationship. But when the Soviet Union tried and failed to prevent West Germany from joining NATO, it established the Warsaw Pact as a counter-NATO. The Treaty of Friendship, Cooperation and Mutual Assistance signed on 14 May 1955 created the Warsaw Treaty Organisation, mirroring the language of the North Atlantic Treaty.[15] The Warsaw Pact's Article 4, the equivalent of NATO's Article 5, obligated each member to come to the aid of any ally attacked by 'any State or group of States with all means deemed necessary including the use of armed force'. Articles 5 and 6 provided the mechanisms for implementing the treaty – a Unified Command and a Political Consultative Committee. The final clause of the treaty stipulated that the Warsaw Pact would dissolve itself if NATO should do the same. The pact was initially another instrument in the Soviet effort to undermine NATO and drive the United States out of Europe.

The Warsaw Pact provided other functions for the Soviet Union. It served as legal justification for stationing its troops in the territories of its subordinate allies – Albania, Bulgaria, Czechoslovakia, East Germany, Hungary, Poland and Romania – even when this arrangement was not carried out, as was the case with Bulgaria, Romania (after 1958) and Albania after 1961. At the same time the Warsaw Pact could pose as a defensive organisation against an aggressive NATO, a position that helped to mobilise popular support in Poland and East Germany. This rationale particularly appealed to Poland, which still feared West German ambitions to recover territory ceded after the Second World War. For the GDR membership of the Pact reinforced its status in the alliance and calmed its fears about a rearmed West Germany that could have access to nuclear weapons.

The Warsaw Pact's military structure bore a superficial resemblance to NATO's. Just as a US Army or Air Force General was always in charge of SACEUR, so a Soviet General was the supreme military commander of the Pact's military forces. But the resemblance ends there. The Warsaw Pact's unified command allowed little initiative to its members. A Soviet Marshal was commander-in-chief of the Joint Armed Forces, with Generals from the lesser nations serving as deputies. While the deputies commanded forces from their own states, the staff of the Joint Armed Forces was situated in Moscow. The Soviets expended little effort to develop the military power of the member states. In essence, this alliance replaced the bilateral agreements before 1955 and provided a more effective means of controlling the political as well as military lives of the partners. Although the ideal of consensus as a prerequisite to decisions was never fully realised in NATO, it did not exist in its counterpart. When a perceived threat to the fabric of communism arose in Hungary in 1956 Soviet forces suppressed the uprising under the treaty's article. Twelve years later the reform movement in Czechoslovakia was put down by the USSR and other Warsaw Pact states (excluding Romania), and inspired the Brezhnev Doctrine that denied the right of any communist country to change its political system.

Soviet control was never complete. Witness Romania's slipping from the Warsaw Pact's military sphere even as it remained an ideological partner, Albania's defection from the Pact in favour of its ties to China, and particularly the ability of Poland's 'Solidarity' movement to survive in the face of opposition from Warsaw as well as Moscow. The loyalty of allies in the event of war was always suspect, and the rapid dissolution of the Pact under the liberalisation of the Gorbachev regime in Moscow sharply contrasts with NATO's history after the cold war. If NATO owes its heritage to the Achaean League, with its sharing of authority, the Warsaw Treaty Organisation resembled the Delian League which Athens exploited in the fifth century BC to convert an alliance of free Greek city-states against Persian aggression into a permanent relationship under Athenian domination.

The historiography of the Warsaw Pact inevitably is considerably sparser than NATO's. During the cold war Western scholars could examine it only from the outside, and Warsaw Pact historians had no more access to documents than their NATO counterparts. Nothing would be printed that was not in accord with official doctrine. Consequently, Western scholars writing in the midst of the cold war often missed the nuances that differentiated the roles of the Pact's members in their relationship to the Soviet Union. Nevertheless, perceptive studies were produced in this period, which included those written by Thomas W. Wolfe, Charles Gati, Daniel N. Nelson and Robin Remington.[16] The end of the cold war opened a path for more authoritative treatments of the Warsaw Pact as the new democracies in Eastern Europe, along with Russia itself, were expected to make the archives available to scholars. But the path was more difficult than anticipated. Many of the records were in disarray, and access in some of the allied countries was minimal. Western scholars and their governments made efforts to provide financial as well as technical help to struggling archives. At a conference held in Washington in March 1994 the Office of the Secretary of Defense and the US Army Centre of Military History gathered historians and archivists from most of the former Warsaw Pact members to discuss the possibilities of archival cooperation in making knowledge of the inner workings of the Pact available to scholars.[17]

While the results of this conference were mixed, momentum was building through the activities of the PHP Cold War International History Project (CWIHP) at the Woodrow Wilson International Center for Scholars in Washington in the later 1990s and especially through the establishment of two new journals, *Cold War History* and the *Journal of Cold War Studies*, also served by international editors. As noted above, the PHP's work on Warsaw Pact sources has led to the publication of a volume of translated documents, edited by Malcolm Byrne and Vojtech Mastny, entitled *A Cardboard Castle*. The editors also provide an insightful introductory essay that comprises the most important history to date of the Warsaw Pact, revealing the tensions and conflicts inside the alliance.[18]

the sino-soviet alliance

The Sino-Soviet relationship reflects another element in the composition of alliances. Like the Warsaw Pact and NATO it can claim an organisation built around a defence against potential aggressors. But unlike both alliances there was no organisation to cement relations. It was a marriage of ideological convenience, based in 1949 on a perception that the capitalist West under American leadership was a common threat to international communism. Although Stalin initially supported the *Guomindang* after the war, the weakness of Chiang Kai-Shek's regime combined with the growing strength of the Communist Party (CCP) demonstrated the logic of aiding the latter in the Chinese civil war, and in supporting the People's Republic after its establishment in October 1949. Mao's willingness to respect the seniority of Moscow as the centre of the communist world was an important ingredient in the match. From China's perspective fear of American hostility made the Soviet Union a vital factor in its sense of security. By the late 1940s the CCP saw the world divided into two camps, and regarded its revolution as part of the Soviet-led international proletarian movement. By firmly implanting itself in the Soviet camp China would inhibit American intervention in East Asia.

Dependence on the Soviet Union as the senior partner seemed validated when China entered the Korean war in November 1950. The psychological more than material support was important as China was locked in combat with the United States. This situation lasted less than a decade. By the end of the 1950s Mao had begun to challenge the apparently risk-averse partner, asserting that the Soviets were not sufficiently confrontational in their relations with the West. Their diverging positions over Vietnam in the early 1960s confirmed Chinese suspicions about Khrushchev's inadequate leadership of international communism. The Soviets responded by exploiting conflict between Mao and his colleagues, and reducing economic and military aid to Beijing in 1960 at a time when the impact of Mao's ambitious plans for economic growth (the 'Great Leap Forward') made such assistance a test of friendship. But when Khrushchev recalled all Soviet experts from China Mao was able to use the dispute with Moscow as a diversion from the failure of his economic programme and as a measure of China's loyalty to a more genuine communism than the Soviets demonstrated.

In essence the alliance was over in the 1960s, the victim of China's competition for leadership of the communist world. It failed to win over the Warsaw Pact – only Albania hued to the line that Moscow was betraying the movement by its apparent accommodation with the West. But it is noteworthy that the United States was slow in recognising the dimensions of the split between Moscow and Beijing. Despite information that was available to Western scholars and diplomats, the United States gave only lip service to the break, and seemed unaware in the 1960s of the opportunities possible in exploiting the division in the communist camp. Only in the 1970s did the United States play the 'China card' when Nixon achieved *détente* with Beijing with the help of Kissinger's diplomacy. By the 1980s when Soviet SS-20 missiles were targeted at Chinese as well as European cities the PRC sought informal relations with NATO, applauding the Atlantic alliance's opposition to the Soviet bloc. Not until late in the 1980s, long after the abandonment of Mao's doctrine of continuous revolution, did Moscow and Beijing move toward more normal relations. By the 1990s the Soviet Union had disappeared and both Russia and China were working to develop a capitalist economy.

It is not surprising that there the historiography of the Sino-Soviet alliance required considerable time to elapse before scholars could approach this subject. Memoirs by Chinese policy-makers did not appear until the 1990s, and are not available in English. Among the more useful works in English is that by John W. Garver, and Gordon H. Chang's study of the triangular relationship between the USA, the USSR and the PRC.[19] Zubok and Pleshakov's study of the USSR's role in the cold war from 1945 to 1964 shed light on the decline of Sino-Soviet relations, symbolised by the acrimonious meeting Khrushchev had with Mao in Beijing in 1958. Michael Chang's work emphasises the role of ideology in the Sino-Soviet alliance, while Odd Arne Westad has edited a valuable study re-examining the evolution of relations between the USSR and China from 1949 to 1963.[20]

seato and cento

More ephemeral were the alliances in the Middle East and East Asia, created by the United States to contain the Soviet expansionism in those areas. Pakistan's membership of both CENTO and SEATO linked the two alliances. But the attempt to replicate the NATO experience in Asia failed. The United States joined with Australia, France, New Zealand, Pakistan, the Philippines, Thailand and the United Kingdom to sign the South-East Asia Treaty Organisation (SEATO) in Manila in 1954. Like NATO and the Warsaw Pact it contained both political and military features, with the military predominating. Basically, the Manila Pact was to provide US nuclear protection to vulnerable states in South-East Asia from both direct Chinese aggression and indirect Soviet-inspired communist insurgents in Vietnam. While it purported to be a mutual assistance pact, it was the inspiration for the American-inspired protocol in aid of the struggling government of South Vietnam after the peninsula's division at the Geneva conference of 1954. The resemblance to NATO was intentional. SEATO was one of Secretary of State John Foster Dulles' building blocks in the containment of communism. But it lacked the elements that made NATO distinctive. SEATO was an American device to avoid a unilateral military commitment to the defence of South Vietnam, and its organs, such as its secretariat-general, were only window dressing. The major partners, Britain and France, had little interest in establishing an Asian NATO. When the Vietnam war exposed the inability of the United States to use SEATO as a surrogate, its irrelevance became clear. The alliance dissolved without fanfare in 1977.

The Central Treaty Organisation (CENTO), a successor to the Baghdad Pact of 1955, was designed to serve as a geographical bridge between NATO and SEATO. Composed of Britain, Turkey, Iran and Pakistan, it lacked an American presence. Dulles wanted to encourage a sense of regional identification as well as to extend an arc around the Soviet Union. The linkages among the alliances were represented by NATO's Turkey and SEATO's Pakistan as members of CENTO. Yet CENTO had even less meaning than SEATO as a defence organisation. When Iraq defected from the Baghdad Pact in 1958 the surviving members took the name of CENTO. The change made little difference in function. CENTO terminated informally when Iran withdrew in February, and Pakistan in June 1979. It had in any case been superseded by the bilateral treaties the United States had concluded with Iran, Pakistan and Turkey that pledged military action against an aggressor (the US–Iranian relationship was, of course, destroyed by the Islamic revolution of 1979). With Turkey in conflict with its NATO partner Greece over Turkey, and Pakistan with India over Kashmir, CENTO was even less credible than SEATO as an effective alliance.

If SEATO and CENTO played a role in the conduct of the cold war, it was in the projection of American power around the rim of Eurasia. The results were periodic deterrence of aggression from the Soviet Union and the PRC and fitful resistance to communist penetration in critical areas. The 'bandwagon' effect was at work in lining up members of both alliances. For a time SEATO's intervention appeared possible in the Laotian crisis of 1961–62. The language of these treaties echoed that of the North Atlantic Treaty, including pro forma obeisance to the UN Charter. But its Article IV, dealing with a military response to aggression, required only that 'the Parties consult immediately in order to agree on the measures which should be taken for the common defence'. Both SEATO and CENTO lasted a generation but like the Franco-American alliance of 1778, its longevity did not signify continuing relevance. Although there are some studies on both alliances, neither has attracted significant historiographical interest.[21]

conclusions

NATO stands alone in the history of the cold war because of the unique qualities that informed its creation. Despite some obvious anomalies in its composition, it was an alliance of democracies into which the hegemon was lured to perform functions that the Europeans could not do by themselves in 1949. The primary initial impulse was protection against the spread of communism, led by an apparently aggressive Soviet Union. Secondary, but ultimately as important, was the role the United States played in helping Western Europe turn its back on its history of internecine wars. Without realising what the outcome would be, the United States set in motion the unification of Europe, by supporting, or not opposing, such European initiatives as the ESCE in 1950, the Treaty of Rome in 1957, and the steps leading to the formation of the EU in the 1990s.

There were conflicts of interests and transatlantic misunderstandings throughout the first half-century of NATO's history, and they persist today in the Franco-German confrontation with America and Britain over Iraq and in the rival NATO–EU rapid response forces. Nevertheless, the most striking difference between NATO and other alliances has been its flexibility. America during the cold war had been the driving force in securing a consensus for NATO decisions, but it was rarely able to impose its will upon unwilling allies. The smaller members' objections were not swept aside; the Harmel report of 1967 that promoted *détente* as well as defence was their product, and the Nuclear Planning Group of 1966 was the result of a successful effort to have their views heard on nuclear matters. The larger allies, particularly France and Germany, had their influence augmented by their roles in the European Community, and subsequently in the European Union.

The alliance's flexibility was manifested by its survival after the cold war when it identified crisis management as one of NATO's key responsibilities at the summit meeting of the North Atlantic Council in Rome in 1991. This objective was designed to replace containment of Soviet expansion as a primary function of the alliance. At the important summit session at Prague in 2002, NATO recognised out-of-area responsibilities that had involved the alliance in Iraq and Afghanistan. NATO's experience in the Balkans in the 1990s and in South Asia in the twenty-first century suggests shortcomings as well as successes in seeking new functions for NATO. Conceivably, tensions over future crises could terminate the alliance, or make its existence irrelevant. No essay on this alliance should conclude without the observation that under the terms of Article 13 of the North Atlantic Treaty any member could withdraw from NATO after a year's notice. France did withdraw from its military structure in 1966, as did Greece in 1974, but Greece rejoined in 1980 and France remains a *de facto* participant in 2005. At the time of writing, no member has chosen to take advantage of Article 13.

notes

1. Robert E. Osgood, *Alliances and American Foreign Policy* (Baltimore, MD: Johns Hopkins University Press, 1968), p.17.
2. Ole Holsti et al. (eds), *Unity and Disintegration in International Alliances* (Lanham, MD: University Press of America, 1973), p.4.
3. George Modelski, 'The Study of Alliances: A Review', *Journal of Conflict Resolution*, VII (December 1993), p.709.
4. Sidney B. Fay, 'Alliance', in *Encyclopedia of the Social Sciences*, 15 vols (New York: Macmillan, 1937), 2:3.
5. Hans Morgenthau, *Politics among Nations: The Struggle for Power and Peace* (New York: Knopf, 1986, 6th edition), p.169.
6. Stephen Walt, *The Origins of Alliances* (Ithaca, NY: Cornell University Press, 1987), pp.19–20.
7. J.L. Brierly quoted in H.F. Hinsley, *Power and the Pursuit of Peace: Theory and Practice in the History of Relations between States* (Cambridge: Cambridge University Press, 1963), p.335.
8. Marc Trachtenberg, *A Constructed Peace: Making of European Settlement, 1945–1963* (Princeton, NJ: Princeton University Press, 1999), *passim*; Thomas

A. Schwartz, *Lyndon B. Johnson and Europe: In the Shadow of Vietnam* (Cambridge, MA: Harvard University Press, 2003).

9. See, for example, Lawrence S. Kaplan, *The United States and NATO: The Formative Years* (Lexington, KT: University Press of Kentucky, 1984) and E. Timothy Smith, *Opposition Beyond the Water's Edge* (Westport, CT: Greenwood Press, 1999).

10. Escott Reid, *Time of Fear and Hope: The Making of the North Atlantic Treaty* (Toronto: McClelland & Stewart, 1977); Nicholas Henderson, *The Birth of NATO* (London: Weidenfeld & Nicolson, 1982).

11. As represented in John Baylis, *The Diplomacy of Pragmatism: Britain and the Formation of NATO, 1942–1949* (Kent, OH: Kent State University Press, 1993) and John W. Young, *Cold War Europe* (New York: St Martin's Press, 1996).

12. Pierre Melandri, *Incertaine alliance: Les Etas-Unis et l'Europe 1973–1983* (Paris: Publications de la Sorbonne, 1988), *passim*; Frederic Bozo, *La France et l'OTAN* (Paris: Masson, 1991).

13. See, for example, Norbert Wiggershaud & Roland G. Foerster (eds), *The Western Security Community: Common Problems and Conflicting National Interests during the Foundation Phase of the North Atlantic Treaty* (Providence, RI: Berg, 1993).

14. Gustav Schmidt (ed.), *A History of NATO, The First Fifty Years*, 3 vols, (Basingstoke: Palgrave Macmillan, 2001); Mark Smith, *NATO Enlargement during the Cold War: Strategy and System in the Western Alliance* (Basingstoke: Palgrave Macmillan, 2000); Jeremi Suri, *Power and Protest: Global Revolution and the Rise of Detente* (Cambridge, MA: Harvard University Press, 2003), *passim*. Routledge is due to publish a volume with the working title of 'War Plans and Alliances in the Cold War'. Another volume, edited by Andreas Wenger, Christian Nuenlist & Anna Locher, provisionally entitled 'NATO in the 1960s: Challenges Beyond Deterrence', is due to be published by the Centre for Security Studies in Zurich in 2006.

15. The Warsaw Treaty Organisation is sometimes abbreviated as the Warsaw Pact. To avoid confusion with the World Trade Organisation, which is discussed in Chapter 1 by Wolfgang Krieger, this alliance will be referred to as the 'Warsaw Pact' throughout this book.

16. Thomas W. Wolfe, *Soviet Power and Europe, 1945–1970* (Baltimore, MD: Johns Hopkins University Press, 1970); Robin A. Remington, *The Warsaw Pact: Case Studies in Communist Conflict* (Cambridge, MA: MIT Press, 1971); Daniel N. Nelson, *Alliance Behavior in the Warsaw Pact* (Boulder, CO: Westview Press, 1986); and Charles Gati, *The Bloc That Failed: Soviet–East European Relations in Transition* (Bloomington, IN: Indiana University Press, 1990).

17. William W. Epley, *Proceedings of the International Conference on Cold War Military Records and History* (Washington, DC: Office of the Secretary of Defense, 1996).

18. Readers are encouraged to consult *Cold War History*, published by Frank Cass/ Taylor & Francis; and the *Journal of Cold War Studies*, published by Harvard University Press. Malcolm Byrne & Vojtech Mastny (eds), *A Cardboard Castle? An Inside History of the Warsaw Pact, 1955–1991* (Budapest & New York: Central European University Press, 2005), *passim*.

19. John W. Garver, *Chinese–Soviet Relations, 1937–1945: The Diplomacy of Chinese Nationalism* (Oxford: Oxford University Press, 1988); Gordon H. Chang,

Friends and Enemies: The United States, China, and the Soviet Union (Stanford, CA: Stanford University Press, 1990).

20. Vladislav Zubok & Constantine Pleshakov, *Inside the Kremlin's Cold War: From Stalin to Khrushchev* (Cambridge, MA: Harvard University Press, 1996), *passim*; Michael Chang, *Battling Western Imperialism: Mao, Stalin, and the United States* (Princeton, NJ: Princeton University Press, 1997); Odd Arne Westad (ed.), *Brothers in Arms: The Rise and Fall of the Sino-Soviet Alliance 1945–63* (Stanford, CA: Stanford University Press, 2000), *passim*.

21. George Modelski, *SEATO: Six Studies* (Melbourne: Australian National University Press, 1962) and Leszek Buszynski, *Failure of an Alliance Strategy* (Singapore: Singapore University Press, 1983) are among the few studies dealing with SEATO. For CENTO, see Magnus Persson, *Great Britain, the United States, and the Security of the Middle East* (Lund, Sweden: Lund University Press, 1998) and Reza Akrami, *Zusammen Arbeit zwischen den Staaten des CENTO* (Bonn, 1970).

5

strategy

lawrence freedman and geraint hughes

The requirements of strategy during the cold war were quite distinct from any other period in the history of conflict. There had been previous periods when a high degree of great power antagonism existed but none when the consequences of war threatened to be so severe. The fear of a nuclear holocaust meant that neither the Western nor the Soviet side was inclined to attempt resolution through war, although both had to make contingency plans for the outbreak of an East–West conflict, occurring either by accident or design. The provisions and plans for all-out war led to a number of unnerving moments, and a degree of arms racing, but the basic inhibition against resort to war held. As a result, when the cold war concluded after some four decades, this was not with a decisive military clash but with the internal collapse of the Soviet bloc.

There is insufficient space to list all the studies relating to cold war strategy, particularly regarding American strategy. There are the studies either by – or about – the generation of civilian strategists (notably Bernard Brodie, Hermann Kahn, William Kaufman, Thomas Schelling and Albert Wohlstetter) whose works influenced the public debate on the role of nuclear weapons in US defence policy which took place during the 1950s, and some of whom also had an input in the policy-making process under Kennedy.[1] Secondly, there are numerous works relating to the conduct of defence policy by successive US administrations from Truman to Reagan, and the perceptions of the Soviet 'threat' that influenced the decisions made on procurement, force structures and doctrine.[2] Students of American defence policy can also consult the US government's *Foreign Relations of the United States* volumes, as well as material made available online by the George Washington University's National Security Archive.[3] Thirdly, there are several studies covering the strategic concepts and planning instituted by the USA's West European allies, which had a wider impact on the development of NATO's strategy for containing Soviet expansion by collective defence in peacetime, as well as its plans for resisting any Warsaw Pact attack. Furthermore, two of the USA's European allies – Britain and France – were nuclear powers, and both countries had their own deterrence doctrines, whether these were based on 'interdependence' with the USA and NATO (as was the case with the British), or on the theoretical use of nuclear weapons for purely national interests (the justification for the French *force de frappe* since the 1960s).[4]

There is less material available covering the Soviet side, although the collapse of both the USSR and the Warsaw Pact has made this subject easier to research. During the cold war, some Western scholars and 'think-tanks' produced carefully researched assessments of the Soviet/ Warsaw Pact 'threat', based on whatever evidence was available in the public domain – from the Soviet and Western media, or from official government sources. These tended to be more analytical and more careful in their conclusions than politically-inspired pronouncements which, for example, included the volumes entitled *Soviet Military Power* published annually by the US Department of Defense during the 1980s.[5] Even after the cold war's end, the Russian government retains a considerable amount of primary source material on Soviet military planning and defence policies. Fortunately, East European archives do offer scholars an indirect means of researching this subject, and the documentary evidence available does offer a means for scholars to reassess pre-1991 studies of Soviet national security policy and strategy. As noted above, both the Cold War International History and Parallel History Projects have also contributed to the study of Soviet and Eastern bloc strategy – the latter has recently published a documentary history of the Warsaw Pact from its foundation in 1955 to its collapse in February 1991.[6]

By strategy, we refer to the interaction of military means with political ends. This is a dynamic relationship in which each element has to be adjusted to the requirements of the other. The story of strategy in the cold war is to a considerable extent the story of apparently absolute military power becoming geared to limited political ends. There are levels of military preparedness where civilian contributions might be expected to play a marginal role. Armies, navies and air forces have their core competencies which are their responsibilities to develop and refine, and their roles are tested on the tactical level of war-fighting. The more, however, the military-political interface becomes important, the more civilians contribute. In the classic Clausewitzian definition, strategy was the use of battle to fulfil the ends of war which, as Clausewitz famously instructed us, are politically determined.[7] During the cold war, it was argued that between tactics and strategy there is an intermediate, or operational, level. This was largely a matter of scale and level of command, drawing together a number of battles rather than a number of smaller-scale engagements. It was of interest during the cold war because it was a level in conventional warfare to which the Soviet Union paid far more attention than the United States. In the nuclear sphere, however, because of the wide political implications of a single nuclear detonation and the existential consequences of a series of nuclear exchanges, there was no special reason why the military had any greater expertise than the civilian. Indeed the civilian strategists set the terms of the debate on nuclear operations, including the large question of whether it was even helpful to think of nuclear weapons in operational terms. In doing so they sought to link operations to the wider questions of policy, including the conduct of the cold war without a 'hot war', as well as the possible course of an East–West conflict. What they did less well was relate this to the level of analysis beyond strategy, that is grand strategy, where all the instruments of policy, economic, cultural and diplomatic as well as military, come together in a fundamental sense. At this level there are questions to be asked about the changes in the international system and how states, or groups of states, are likely to be affected by these changes and how they should best respond. Grand strategy helps identify where, if at all, force or threats of force have a role to play in meeting the objectives of policy. Strategy then considers the alternative forms of force that might be used and how they might meet the ends of policy, and also how these ends might have to be adjusted to fit the means available. The strategy is then realised at the operational and tactical levels of war-fighting.[8]

In this chapter we explain why nuclear strategy acquired an operational focus for both sides in the cold war, accepting that this eventually came to embrace the conduct of arms control negotiations, which provided an alternative (and far less dangerous) arena in which to struggle for comparative advantage. We will also examine the evolution of NATO's planning for peacetime deterrence and its contingency preparations for the complete breakdown of East–West relations, which many expected would lead to a conflict between NATO and the Warsaw Pact in Central Europe. From the 1960s onwards, Western governments perceived that in such a scenario they would face two extremely difficult tasks – ensuring that Western Europe was not overrun by the numerically preponderant Soviet bloc, while preventing the escalation of any continental clash into a cataclysmic global thermonuclear holocaust. Throughout the cold war, NATO's strategic debates were shaped by almost constant wrangling between the alliance's members over how to ensure effective collective defence against the USSR and its East European allies. This chapter will also examine Soviet national security policy, and how the USSR's military doctrine affected Warsaw Pact plans for a conflict with NATO.

characteristics of cold war strategy: the theoretical and policy-making context

One of the key features of cold war strategy, at least on the Western side, was the involvement of civilian defence intellectuals in public debates concerning defence policy. In his *Evolution of Nuclear Strategy* Lawrence Freedman has described the two types of civilian scholars who influenced US thinking on strategy. The 'classical' strategists had backgrounds in politics and history and were preoccupied with the role of force in the international system. It was the classical strategists, such as Bernard Brodie, Henry Kissinger, Robert Osgood in the USA, as well as Michael Howard in Britain and Raymond Aron in France who saw how the risks of nuclear annihilation were challenging traditional concepts of the role of force. As Brodie famously observed at the start of the nuclear age, 'everything about the atomic bomb is overshadowed by the twin facts that it exists and its destructive power is fantastically great'.[9] Soon there was a third fact: this power was accessible to more than one state, immediately raising the prospect of nuclear use prompting a response in kind, and so rendering any political gains looking paltry in the face of wholly disproportionate costs. The classical strategists posed questions of limitation and restraint in the face of a global confrontation between two deeply antagonistic power blocs. So pressing did this issue become that the global confrontation itself became somewhat taken for granted. By the early 1950s the broad outlines of the cold war had already been settled, and the key issues became how to cope with the pace of technological change, especially in the military sphere, with hydrogen (fusion) bombs following the first atomic (fission) bombs, missiles taking over from aircraft as the most reliable means of delivery, submarines offering themselves as platforms, and claims that developments in radar and interception might allow the defence to neutralise the extraordinary leaps forward being made in offensive means. Attempts to develop concepts of limitation and restraint required constant attention to the changing properties of weapons systems and their relevance for prospective nuclear engagements.[10]

This required a different sort of theory and analysis. Here the classical strategists became customers of the 'new strategists',[11] who became, to varying degrees, nuclear specialists. Although they deployed analytical power rather than firepower, they had no compunctions about displacing military professionals from the policy-making process. The main home of the nuclear specialists was the RAND Corporation of Santa Monica, California, a number of whose analysts moved into top positions in the Pentagon after January 1961 under the patronage of Kennedy's Secretary of Defense, Robert McNamara. In this case, the involvement of these 'whizz-kids' in policy decisions received a less than enthusiastic welcome from the US Joint Chiefs of Staff (JCS). The first wave of these new strategists also drew on classical strategy, but over time these links became weaker. Their starting point was the properties of nuclear weapons and the need to think through future scenarios in which their use became a possibility, even a reality. The more specialised they became the more they moved beyond technical matters and more into issues of organisation, command and control, doctrine, and arms control. Consideration of international relations became a different discipline altogether, with some strands focused on how nuclear weapons affected the timeless issues of war and peace, while others considered the course and impact of decolonisation or the impact of the changing nature of the international economy.[12]

Prior to the cold war, debates about military issues were mainly professional. In peacetime civilians largely took interest to bemoan the wastefulness of military expenditure and the dangers of arms racing or, alternatively, to encourage patriotism and often adventurism. In wartime, there was the tendency for 'armchair generals' to emerge, but during the inter-war period the main participants in strategic debates (for example, J.F.C. Fuller and Basil Liddell Hart in Britain, General Heinz Guderian in Germany, Giulio Douhet in Italy, Billy Mitchell in the USA) were either serving or former soldiers. However, the cold war differed from previous great power conflicts because it was a struggle for comparative advantage in which the political stakes were as high as any war but battle was not joined, except in the Third World. There was no obvious means for bringing the underlying conflict to an end, short of a potentially catastrophic war on the one hand or an ideological capitulation on the other. It was such a defining and enduring feature of the international system that it was hard, even fruitless, to think outside this framework. Until the very end there was no confidence that it would be possible to move on to a quite different international system that would be shaped by something other than this conflict between two superpower-led, ideological blocs. This meant that strategic thinking could be unusually long term. The association between military strategy and battle became severely attenuated. The traditional focus on battle required mastering the military sciences, not only the art of moving large armies to dealing with fortifications and directing firepower, but also the capacity to adjust to the inherent uncertainties and consequent surprises of battle. During the cold war all this was played out in slow motion. Developments such as the introduction of new weapons systems could take more than a decade, by which time the adversary had set in motion its own countering move, and preparations had begun for the move after that. None of this involved real engagement with the enemy, except through proxies (such as the wars between Israel and its Arab enemies), and so could not be decisive. The anticipation of the enemy's likely attitudes and behaviour, and changes in the broader political context, had to stretch out years ahead.[13]

In terms of actual operations the starting point was the experience of the Second World War, with led to thoughts of large armies fighting their way across Central Europe and getting reinforcements across the sea against packs of hostile submarines, while airmen took forward the concept of strategic air bombardment but this time with bombs of extraordinary destructive power. As time passed, planning for a major war became increasingly formulaic. There were new possibilities for using firepower with great precision but also unfamiliar combat conditions, especially as systems became geared to fighting without respite, day and night, in all climates. The difficulty with conventional strategic debate, however, for much of our period, was it presumed irrelevance for it was assumed that any conventional engagements would be a preliminary to the main business of nuclear war.

Yet governments recoiled from the prospect of nuclear war. So the purpose of nuclear strategy soon came to be less how to employ nuclear weapons, but how to give a sufficient impression of preparing to employ them that the other side dare not assume that this would not happen. This developed into the study of 'deterrence' and is now considered to be the major contribution of the cold war to strategic thought. This pushed strategy into the area of perceptions and bluff, and while previous generations of strategists had been aware of the importance of these factors, they would never have had so little to say about war itself. Deterrence itself was also a perfect complement to a situation in which political relationships had congealed. It fitted naturally to a grand strategy of containment: holding the line between the communist and capitalist worlds that had emerged in the aftermath of the Second World War. Containment meant that no further Soviet encroachments were to be tolerated; but nor was there to be an effort to liberate those already under Soviet rule. Deterrence warned against further aggression but did not threaten military initiatives. It conveyed the right balance of restraint and resolve. It also, too much for its own good, turned out to be an extremely elastic concept, which got more stretched during the course of the cold war as a great variety of policies, often contradicting each other, were offered as contributions to deterrence. It became what might now be called the 'master narrative'.[14]

The basic problem with nuclear deterrence was that it depended on threats of dubious credibility. If initiating a nuclear war was far too dangerous then why should threats be taken seriously? On the other hand, if a way was found to fight a nuclear war at tolerable levels of danger would there not be some temptation to try it out, especially as such ways could well depend on achieving surprise? The enormous destructive power of individual weapons meant that a tolerable level of danger would require reducing the victim's capacity for retaliation to almost zero. One way forward was to develop a 'tactical' category of nuclear weapons, with relatively low destructive yields which would theoretically limit collateral damage. Unfortunately the number of weapons required to destroy important targets could mean that the level of destruction was still intolerably high. No conviction was ever developed that 'tactical' use of nuclear weapons would stop there: over time it came to be assumed their use would turn a conventional battle into an all-out strategic exchange. It was in this context that the tragic metaphor of 'escalation' was developed to demonstrate how once nuclear use began the conflict would be carried inexorably upward to utter catastrophe. Strategists such as Kahn fought against this idea, insisting that there was nothing inevitable about escalation and that even nuclear wars could be fought in a controlled fashion. Such confidence might have turned out to be warranted in the event of an actual conflict, but it might not. In the mindset of Western policy-makers tactical nuclear use was after the critical threshold, beyond which control over events could well be lost, and not before it.[15]

The alternative approach was to mount a disarming first-strike, depriving the enemy of the capacity for retaliation. Considerable analysis went into calculating the combination of offensive and defensive capabilities necessary to mount such an attack, but after the early 1960s, and in particular with the introduction of submarine-launched missiles, few really believed this was physically possible. At worst they feared that the other side might think it feasible. Indeed from this time on, while mainstream strategists generally accepted the reality of a mutual capacity to assure the destruction of the other, with varying degrees of unease and qualification, attempts to find a way out of the resulting conundrum relied on attempts to manipulate the adversary's perceptions and sense of options. Even if they could not physically prevent retaliation perhaps they could paralyse, disrupt or in some way intimidate the enemy decision-makers. Again the answer was that perhaps they could, but the methods could not be proven – the first time they would be tried would be quite an experiment – and so the outcome was hardly guaranteed and the risks seemed too high. The response of a scared and appalled political leadership to news of the first attack could range from a vengeful impulse to hurt the attacker as much as possible, whatever the consequences, to a despairing passivity. No means of controlling events to be sure of avoiding the worst outcomes resulting from the first use of nuclear weapons were developed. The tension between a certain strategic reliance on the threat of Armageddon and the desperate reluctance ever to implement such a threat was never resolved.[16]

If nuclear war was to be fought and won then somehow ways had to be found of conducting it that allowed for a conclusion far short of the ultimate catastrophe. The problem was that any nuclear use, even if it did not quite mean the 'end of civilisation as we know it', would still feel catastrophic. And while it might be the case that this would lead to an early readiness to surrender or even a tacit agreement on the limits within which such a war might be fought, the prospect was so extraordinary, so beyond historical experience, that no type of response could be guaranteed. The harsh reality was that by the 1960s both sides had a capacity for 'assured destruction'. As a strategy this seemed to be the most terrible of all, as it suggested that both sides would give themselves up to utter nihilism, but as a description of a likely, even if not the most likely, outcome should any nuclear war begin it seemed spot on. By the mid-1960s McNamara was explaining the logic of 'mutual assured destruction' (MAD). Despite continued efforts to challenge the logic of MAD, no American military or civilian strategists could ever point to a credible strategy for using nuclear weapons that would spare the United States terrible destruction. In the 1970s there was much ado about complex scenarios whereby the Soviet Union might gain the upper hand in such a war by attacking only America's land-based missiles. The weapons left would allow for a massive response, but only against cities, and that, it was suggested, might be an escalation too far for the Americans, as this would invite back retaliation in kind.[17] However, before mounting such an onslaught a Soviet leader would find it hard to be confident of a passive American response. The core objective of military strategy – identifying a route to a decisive victory in war – could not be found.

As a consequence, in the nuclear age strategy (at least on the Western side) became not so much a matter of war-fighting, but of war prevention.

Much of the study of nuclear strategy is therefore the study of the non-use of nuclear weapons. In a famous observation, after he had retired as Kennedy's and Johnson's national security adviser, McGeorge Bundy noted how:

> In the real world of political leaders, a decision that would bring even one hydrogen bomb on one city of one's own country would be recognised in advance as a catastrophic blunder ... Political leaders, whether here or in Russia, are cut from a very different mould than strategic planners. They see cities and people as part of what they are trying to help – not as targets.[18]

Bundy's point was valid. All presidents soon concluded that all nuclear options were terrible. Truman, who was the only president actually to authorise the use of nuclear weapons, was appalled by the idea that he should do it again in Korea. Eisenhower allowed himself to appear unperturbed by the nuclear dilemma. Kennedy went to considerable lengths during the great crises of his presidency to avoid resort to nuclear weapons.[19] Johnson sought to develop further the non-nuclear options for major war. Nixon might have felt it helpful if at times his opponents thought him crazy enough to employ nuclear weapons, but he was uncomfortable with thoughts of mass destruction and could claim the promotion of arms control with the Soviet Union his major achievement, a path which his successor, Gerald Ford, continued.[20] Carter showed deep hostility to nuclear weapons, and was reluctant to approve new programmes. Reagan, whose administration was initially assumed to be quite reckless in its nuclear thinking, was in fact the most anti-nuclear of all, an abolitionist who came out of the closet as the cold war was drawing to a close.[21]

In the USA's case, the development of strategy was not just determined by successive incumbents of the White House, their nominees as Secretary of Defense, or by the JCS, but by inputs from Congress, defence intellectuals and 'think-tanks' such as RAND, and (periodically) by press pundits and popular opinion. The situation in the USSR was not analogous. While the Soviet General Staff and the military-industrial complex had significant roles to play, the parameters of strategic debate were set by the Kremlin. Marxism-Leninism shaped defence policy and military doctrine, and the supremacy of the party line was demonstrated in July 1961 when Sakharov was publicly dressed down by Khrushchev for daring to express concerns over the Soviet thermonuclear weapons programme.[22] There was some scope for debate and dispute regarding national security matters within the policy-making elite, particularly during the 1970s and 1980s; but in general CPSU General Secretaries from Stalin to Gorbachev moulded Soviet military policy and planning with their own ideological beliefs, concepts, whims and prejudices.

The USSR's relationship with its Warsaw Pact allies was also fundamentally different from that the USA had with its NATO partners. Even before the Warsaw Treaty was signed in April 1955 the Albanian, East German, Polish, Czechoslovak, Hungarian, Romanian and Bulgarian armed forces were reconstituted, organised, equipped and trained on Soviet lines, and fully integrated into the USSR's order of battle. The Soviets also maintained a military presence in Eastern Europe, including the 21 divisions of the Group of Soviet Forces in Germany (GSFG). Soviet troops served two roles – to prepare for war against the West, and to ensure the continued allegiance of Moscow's 'fraternal' allies. This aim was openly expressed in the 'Brezhnev doctrine', which originated with a speech the Soviet leader made in Warsaw in November 1968, three months after the suppression of the 'Prague Spring'. It was not surprising that Soviet forces were stationed in the four countries (East Germany, Czechoslovakia (after 1968), Poland and Hungary) where communist authority was challenged by internal unrest. Of the Warsaw Pact's founders, only Albania – which was geographically isolated from the rest of the Pact and comparatively unimportant to Soviet security – was permitted to break ranks with the USSR in the 1960s.[23]

The East Europeans did occasionally express their own strategic preferences. During the mid-1950s the Poles lobbied for reforms which would give the East Europeans a voice in Warsaw Pact decision-making, and Czechoslovak officials made similar complaints during 1968. From 1965 Ceauşescu sought to assert Romania's sovereignty against the Warsaw Pact. Nonetheless, the USSR determined the political and military strategy of the Warsaw Pact in a manner which the Americans could not employ with NATO. While the USA established the Nuclear Planning Group in 1966 to keep non-nuclear NATO members informed of US strategic doctrine, the Soviets did not have an analogous relationship with the East Europeans. Although Warsaw Pact forces were armed with nuclear-capable delivery systems, Moscow did not introduce a 'dual key' system of warhead access which NATO operated from the mid-1950s. Furthermore, Eastern Europe's leaders (including Ceauşescu) remained ideologically wedded to the defence and preservation of the 'Socialist Commonwealth', and for all their complaints they accepted Soviet suzerainty.[24] For their part, Warsaw and Prague regarded the Soviets as guarantors against the re-emergence of militaristic nationalism in Germany, and during the early

1960s the Poles were often more vehement than the USSR in denouncing NATO proposals for nuclear sharing involving the Federal Republic of Germany (FRG).[25]

Soviet defence policy took into account Clausewitz's dictum that war served political ends, and translated this into the Marxist-Leninist worldview. The USSR's military doctrine was split into its 'military-political' and 'military-technical' components; the former containing the ideological assumptions shaping strategy and the latter dealing with the organisation and the deployment of Soviet military forces in accordance with political goals. Until the late 1980s, the CPSU stipulated that the final triumph of communism over capitalism was inevitable, and that if a third global conflict broke out it would be because of the USA and other 'imperialist' powers waging a war of aggression against the USSR. While the 'military-political' aspect of Soviet doctrine was defensive, the 'military-technical' part was not. Based on pre-1941 doctrinal debates and the experience of the Second World War, Soviet cold war military planning stressed the importance of achieving strategic surprise, and focused on seizing the initiative in the event of war, launching offensives deep into the enemy's territory. The emphasis placed on nuclear weapons varied, but the essentially offensive posture of Soviet military doctrine remained constant from the late 1940s to the advent of *perestroika*. As such, Soviet society was heavily militarised, and the USSR maintained the world's second largest armed forces (numbering 3,658,000 in 1979), funded by an estimated 15–20 per cent of the USSR's GNP. On paper, this was a formidable military machine, and was a source of concern in Western capitals throughout the cold war.[26]

from the second world war to cuba, 1945–62

During the late 1940s American and British policy-makers became alarmed by the apparent preponderance of Soviet military power in Europe, backed by an army of 175 divisions. Both the USA and UK retained their occupation forces in Germany, which after 1949 became officially committed to Western Europe's defence. For Washington and London, the decision to maintain a military presence on the European continent represented a substantial shift from pre-war defence policies, and it came as an unwelcome surprise to Moscow. Stalin saw Soviet hegemony over the East European states as vital to the security of the USSR, and the imposition of communist regimes in the region was mainly intended to create a *cordon sanitaire* to prevent another Operation *Barbarossa*. Yet the USSR was not initially prepared for the breakdown of relations with the USA and Britain. Stalin had demobilised the armed forces after the end of the Second World War, and by 1948 it appears that the USSR had only 800,000 troops in Eastern Europe – facing roughly the same number of American, British, French and other West European personnel.[27] Stalin himself adopted a schizophrenic approach to military affairs. On the one hand he presided over the creation of the USSR's nuclear and strategic weapons programme, but at the same time he also downplayed the impact of atomic weapons on war-fighting. Soviet military planners presumed that a third world war would be merely fought on a more intense and destructive level than that of 1939–45, and Stalin's simplistic concept of the 'permanently operating factors' influencing victory in total war – the strength, equipment and morale of forces, the calibre of their command, and domestic preparations for war – inflexibly governed Soviet doctrine.[28]

During the late 1940s, American plans for war with the USSR were based on a scenario similar to that of the Second World War. The assumption was that the Soviets would swiftly conquer all of Western Europe (save possibly the UK), and that the initial Western response would be a strategic air offensive, with nuclear bombers, against the USSR. After a few years the Americans would then have mobilised their conventional forces for the liberation of Europe. These plans did not see any significant revision until after the signing of the North Atlantic Treaty of 1949. The conclusion of the Treaty was not initially viewed in Moscow as a serious threat. Stalin believed that 'contradictions' and rivalries between the capitalist powers would eventually undermine the Atlantic alliance, and he underestimated the extent to which the North Atlantic Treaty derived from a general West European interest in a US security guarantee.[29]

The attitudes of both sides changed with the outbreak of the Korean war in June 1950. The conflict provoked a shift in Stalin's thinking. Not only was he informed by Kim Il-Sung in January 1950 of North Korea's preparations to invade the South, but in the winter of 1951 he envisaged the possibility that an East–West war would break out on terms he thought favourable to the USSR.[30] As Lawrence Kaplan notes in his chapter, the sudden assault by North Korea against the South raised European fears of similar communist aggression against Western Europe. The conflict in the Korean peninsula provoked an extensive rearmament programme by the USA and the UK, and efforts to give the North Atlantic Treaty military substance. The Lisbon goals of December 1952 committed NATO members to a substantial build-up of conventional forces in preparation for a war with the Soviet bloc. After months of prolonged debate, NATO also agreed to rearm the FRG and admit it to the alliance (1955). This was inevitably a controversial decision, given that the Second World War was but a recent memory, but it made military sense not only because of the Soviet presence in the German Democratic Repbublic (GDR), but because the East Germans already had an army in the guise of a paramilitary police force.[31]

Moreover, it is worth noting the impact of China's intervention on Washington's strategic calculations. The commander of US and UN forces in Korea, General Douglas MacArthur, wanted to expand the war into China, while the USA's allies feared that nuclear weapons would be used against the Chinese, with unpredictable consequences. The British privately wondered whether the Americans would escalate their war effort and launch a preventive war against the USSR, aimed at destroying Soviet military power while its nuclear capability was in its infancy. Truman had, in fact, specifically ruled out such an approach, and he became so exasperated with MacArthur's insubordination and criticisms of Washington's handling of the war that he dismissed him in April 1951. Despite its nuclear supremacy, the USA had become bogged down in a seemingly intractable conflict of attrition in Korea, much to the dismay of the American public. Eisenhower criticised the Truman administration's mishandling of the Korean war during the 1952 presidential election, and after his victory he implicitly threatened the use of nuclear weapons if the communist side did not agree to a peace settlement. Eisenhower therefore saw the July 1953 armistice as proof that atomic weapons could be employed as both a political tool of coercion and as a means of offsetting the supremacy in manpower of the communist states.[32]

It is now clear that one of the main factors behind the Korean armistice was Stalin's death in March 1953, and the intention of his successors to alleviate tensions with the West. Both the Austrian state treaty and the Soviet withdrawal from Finland in 1955 were partly intended to promote neutralist sentiment within Western Europe. Vojtech Mastny has shown that the establishment of the Warsaw Pact in the same year was itself a political tool, as it was intended to serve as a model for a European security system. This explained why very little thought was given to the military aspects of the Pact, which led it to be initially derided in the West as a 'cardboard castle'. It was not until the Berlin crisis of 1958–61 that the Soviets made serious efforts to upgrade the armed forces of their East European clients, to organise joint exercises and manoeuvres, and to prepare the Pact for potential military operations against NATO.[33]

It was under Eisenhower that the United States began to come to terms with the military meaning of containment. To the classical strategists there was a logic at work that had to be recognised. The assumption of previous wars, that they would be fought with all available means to unconditional surrender, was now challenged by the existence of nuclear weapons. Korea prompted the classical strategists to stress the importance of limitations in war. The basic idea was that so long as objectives were kept limited it should be possible to keep the means employed correspondingly restricted. Following the first Soviet test of August 1949 there was already recognition that the American nuclear advantage was transitory. This assessment helps explain the strong reaction to the speech by Eisenhower's Secretary of State, John Foster Dulles, delivered in New York in January 1954. Dulles never actually used the phrase 'massive retaliation', but his comments concerning the Eisenhower administration's strategy of '[depending] primarily upon a great capacity to retaliate instantly by means and at places of our own choosing' seemed to fly in the face of logic, linking nuclear deterrence to minor challenges to American interests. From this point on the strategists argued that the US should develop military capabilities appropriate to the various categories of threat. Critically this meant having conventional forces capable of responding to any challenge around the globe at an appropriate level.[34]

The logic to this position was unassailable, and it was picked up by Kennedy as he campaigned for the presidency in 1960. Part of the context was the assumption that the Soviet Union was steaming ahead in the missile race, which rendered dependence on nuclear threats even less wise. To Kennedy this dependence on a massive but essentially unusable capability meant that he risked being deprived of real options in the face of the slightest challenge. The talk of Soviet 'salami tactics' supposed that the natural strategy for Moscow was to pose a series of relatively modest challenges, for which the United States lacked a proportionate response but for which nuclear weapons would be wholly disproportionate. The need, therefore, was for the United States and its allies to follow a 'flexible response', which required a build-up of conventional forces. 'Flexible response' did have a nuclear aspect, manifested by the expansion of the US intercontinental ballistic missile (ICBM) force and the introduction of the submarine-launched *Polaris* system. Initially McNamara also hoped to devise a war-fighting strategy based on destroying counter-force (Soviet missile and bomber bases) rather than counter-value (urban) targets. However, he and his advisers soon abandoned these efforts, concluding that the USSR would view them as evidence that the Americans were planning for a first strike.[35]

McNamara also had trouble persuading his European counterparts to build up their conventional force levels. The 1952 Lisbon goals had been abandoned because alliance members were not prepared to pay the economic price for long-term rearmament. Having initially boosted defence expenditure after Korea, the British settled for a long-term policy of retrenchment, based on a reliance on the UK's nuclear arsenal – this approach being enshrined in the 1957 defence review. In November 1954 NATO members adopted a strategy of 'massive retaliation', as outlined in MC48. Alliance war planning was now based on an asymmetric response to the Soviet bloc threat, and involved the almost instantaneous use of nuclear weapons to resist any communist aggression.[36]

In the same way that the Eisenhower era experienced extensive debates over 'massive retaliation', Stalin's demise prompted increased discussion within the military on the role of nuclear weapons in the event of war. After assuming sole authority in the Kremlin in 1957, Khrushchev imposed his own ideas on Soviet strategy. He saw nuclear weapons and ballistic missiles as a means of deterring attack by the USA and its allies, and enabling him to reduce the burden of military expenditure on the Soviet economy by cutting ground and naval forces. Not only were tactical nuclear weapons integrated into the Soviet order of battle, but Khrushchev planned to make the newly established Strategic Rocket Forces the mainstay of the USSR's defence. In 1962, Marshal V.D. Sokolovsky published his treatise on *Military Strategy*, which declared that war-fighting now had a more instantaneous and devastating character, in which 'a strategy of deep nuclear-missile strikes' combined with conventional operations would be employed to 'inflict a simultaneous defeat and destruction of the enemy's economic potential and armed forces throughout the whole depth of his territory, for the accomplishment of war aims within a short time span'.[37] These concepts can be seen in planning documents from the Czechoslovak Defence Ministry, dating from 1964, which portray the USSR and its allies achieving a decisive victory in the event of war, using nuclear weapons to destroy NATO's armed forces, its urban-industrial centres and its communications. The planners do not seem to have asked themselves whether NATO's own use of nuclear weapons would have as devastating an effect on the Soviet bloc as the Warsaw Pact's plans had for the West. Although Khrushchev himself publicly asserted that East and West faced a choice between 'either peaceful co-existence or the most destructive war in human history', Soviet bloc preparations for war reflected the Marxist-Leninist premise that the final triumph of communism was historically predetermined, and that therefore the USSR and its allies would 'win' a nuclear war.[38]

Khrushchev's emphasis on nuclear strategy had other flaws. The USSR was strategically inferior to the USA, both in the production of strategic bombers and of ICBMs, and this gap in capabilities widened during Kennedy's presidency. As a result, Khrushchev ordered the deployment of a force of 40 medium-range nuclear missiles – protected and maintained by 44,000 troops – to Cuba. As a secondary factor the Soviet leader also wanted to defend Castro's regime from American pressure.[39] However, after the crisis of October 1962 not only was Khrushchev forced to order the withdrawal of the missiles (in return for an explicit American promise not to invade Cuba, and an informal promise to withdraw *Jupiter* missiles stationed in Turkey), but the US naval quarantine on Cuba demonstrated the limits of the USSR's ability to project power beyond its immediate frontiers. Both the Cuban missile crisis and Khrushchev's defence reductions alienated the Soviet party and military elite, contributing to his eventual overthrow in October 1964.[40]

the rise and fall of *détente*, 1963–79

By the 1970s, when the framework for superpower arms control negotiations was fully established the 'golden age' of nuclear strategy had passed.[41] The 'golden age' had begun both because the new world of cold war and nuclear danger demanded new thought, but also because of the widespread fear that the Eisenhower administration's massive retaliation policy was dangerously outmoded. This seemed to suggest that any attempt, however small, by the Soviet Union (or China) to encroach further into the 'free world' would be met by a massive nuclear response.

This golden age had concluded for a number of reasons. One was exhaustion: the key issues had been explored so fully that there was little left to dispute. Meanwhile the cold war antagonism that had made nuclear strategy a matter of such pressing concern appeared to have settled down following the crises over Berlin and Cuba in the early 1960s. Neither side now entertained thoughts of winning a nuclear war: deterrence was becoming institutionalised. Soon, along with the rest of the foreign policy establishment, the strategists were floundering. When it came to the first major conflict since Korea they had little to offer. Vietnam tainted anyone connected with cold war strategy. Meanwhile the nuclear specialists who had taken over from the first generation were more technical and more focused on the minutiae of nuclear arsenals (which had admittedly become much more complex by this time). This narrow focus continued until the abrupt end of the cold war at the end of the 1980s.

Strategy should respond to political conditions for it must reflect the objectives set by foreign policy. The USA's objectives were to contain what was presumed to be, with some evidence, a communist urge to expansion. The most dangerous moments of the cold war came as the points of containment were set. First in 1948–49 came Berlin, where the Soviets imposed a siege on the western outpost of West Berlin. In some ways this set the terms for the future, for the instinctive response was to hold to the status quo by keeping open the outpost, but not to go on the offensive by, for example, infringing Soviet rights in East Berlin and to put the onus on Moscow for further escalation. The ingenious strategy of an airlift met this requirement exactly and eventually it worked and the siege was lifted.[42]

By the time of Kennedy's assassination in November 1963 this straightforward, somewhat formulaic, analysis had come up against unanticipated geopolitical factors. The first was that the European allies interpreted the concept of flexible response quite differently to the United States. If Western Europe really was a vital interest of the USA then it should be defended as if it was part of the continental United States, that is through nuclear threats. This incidentally had the advantage of not requiring expensive investment in new conventional capabilities. Furthermore, as noted above, by the early 1960s it was clear that Khrushchev was exaggerating the scope of Soviet military power. Air reconnaissance and satellite imagery showed that there was a 'missile gap', but that it favoured the Americans. Before Kennedy realised this he had been forced to confront the obvious problem with flexible response, which was the anomalous position of West Berlin. Stuck in the middle of the GDR was a Western enclave which could not obviously be defended by conventional means. Kennedy's approach to Berlin concentrated again on the status quo. He stressed the position of West Berlin rather than allied rights in East Berlin and, with great misgivings, linked this to the nuclear weapons. As the Europeans suspected, Khrushchev was (in spite of his bluster) anxious to avoid war, and for both sides the construction of the Berlin wall in August 1961 represented an acceptable compromise.[43]

With the status of Cuba and Berlin confirmed there was no particular reason why the cold war need develop into a hot war. The effort over the coming decades was to reaffirm and consolidate this status quo, particularly in Europe. The strategic debate was concentrated during this period on whether or not there were ways to break the nuclear deadlock, as discussed above, but also on the possibility of developing a credible conventional defence of Europe. McNamara and his 'think-tank' protégés in the Pentagon had re-examined the Soviet order of battle, and concluded that the USSR's conventional supremacy was not as overwhelming as it appeared. NATO could therefore afford to bolster its ground and tactical air forces, enhancing its ability to defend itself without using nuclear weapons. However, once the intensity had been taken out of the Berlin issue, the Europeans had become even less interested in building up their conventional forces, and the experience of two world wars had left European powers less ready to contemplate another major land battle on their continent. The USA's allies were also sensitive about any action which might indicate the 'decoupling' of the American deterrent from Europe's defence. The French, for their part, were particularly determined to maintain a nuclear 'tripwire' in the event of a Warsaw Pact attack, and their opposition to 'flexible response' paralysed NATO's strategic review. After France's withdrawal from NATO's integrated military command in 1966, the alliance formally adopted 'flexible response' as part of MC14/3 (December 1967). NATO's plans for war were to resist a Warsaw Pact onslaught by conventional means and to delay the use of nuclear weapons – the controversial issue of how long a nuclear 'pause' would last was deliberately left unresolved. The alliance also prepared contingency plans for any Soviet bloc assault on its northern and southern flanks (respectively, Norway and the Eastern Mediterranean members, Greece and Turkey). What it did not do was actually back up 'flexible response' by increasing its conventional capabilities.[44]

During the course of the 'flexible response' debate the Kennedy and Johnson administrations expressed frustration at both the reluctance of allied governments to raise their defence spending, and the particular political inhibitions that rendered them wary of new conventional strategies. Much of this resulted from the special position of Germany, as the FRG's attitudes found echoes amongst their allies. Its topography ruled out defence in depth; its history ruled out preparing to mount conventional offensives; its division, and the example of Berlin, ruled out simply fortifying the inner-German border. Attempts to back up conventional firepower with even smaller and more tailored nuclear weapons met with distaste in many Western European countries. As Beatrice Heuser notes, NATO's European members tended to either fear that the Americans would provoke war by their reckless belligerence, or that they would abandon their allies rather than risk nuclear attack on their own homeland. Both these sentiments often arouse whenever disputes over the alliance's strategic planning arouse.[45]

It is worth noting here that as nuclear powers, both Britain and France developed their own approaches to deterrence. De Gaulle repeatedly declared that the USA could not be trusted to resort to the use of nuclear weapons to defend Western Europe. While the British were publicly as adamant that their US allies could be counted upon in the event of war, they privately considered British nuclear weapons to be an insurance against any decoupling of the US deterrent from NATO defence (the irony here being that from the late 1950s onwards the UK became increasingly reliant upon the transfer of nuclear technology, notably *Polaris*, from the USA). For both powers, their deterrent forces – though dwarfed by the superpower arsenals – were still significant as they nonetheless had the potential to inflict unacceptable damage to the USSR. British defence planners decided that the UK's nuclear force had to fulfil the 'Moscow criterion', and had to be sufficient at least to destroy the centre of the Soviet government. It was significant that while both Britain and France initially both built up strategic bomber forces, by the early 1970s both London and Paris had decided to replace these with a submarine-based deterrent, which was far less vulnerable to a Soviet first-strike.[46]

The fact was that NATO and the Warsaw Pact were becoming less vulnerable to a direct strike from the other and more vulnerable to internal dissension. During the 1960s France had challenged American hegemony in NATO but had failed to persuade any other members of the alliance to leave the integrated military command. Meanwhile the USSR could not take for granted the loyalty of its 'fraternal' European allies. Military power had been used to suppress the Hungarian revolution in October–November 1956 and Czechoslovakia's internal liberalisation in August 1968. With the nuclear balance dampening down any incentives to try to resolve the ideological division of Europe through military means, the question was always going to be one of which alliance would crack internally first, and what consequences this disintegrative process would have for Europe as a whole. Six months after the Warsaw Pact invasion of Czechoslovakia the then British Defence Secretary, Denis Healey, sombrely commented that future anti-communist uprisings in Eastern Europe could provoke a major Soviet military intervention which would destabilise continental security. This scenario became commonly regarded as the most likely cause of a third world war.[47]

Khrushchev's successor as General Secretary, Brezhnev, oversaw the rapid expansion of both the USSR's nuclear forces (including a submarine-based deterrent to match *Polaris*) and its conventional power. The first years of Brezhnev's tenure of power saw the modernisation of Soviet ground forces, bolstered by more sophisticated tanks and armoured personnel carriers for the motor-rifle divisions, and newer aircraft and helicopters for the tactical air force. The non-Soviet Warsaw Pact forces were also qualitatively upgraded. In a development which mirrored NATO debates on 'flexible response', Soviet military literature also began to envisage the prospects for 'limited war' – as opposed to all-out struggle between East and West – and the possibility of non-nuclear operations against the Western powers.[48] Developments in Soviet military power from 1965 to 1975 aroused NATO concerns that the USSR and its allies could launch a surprise attack (a 'standing start') on the alliance's central front. The nightmare for NATO commanders was that the Western powers would miss indicators of Warsaw Pact preparations for war until the day that Soviet tank columns poured across the inner German border. By 1970, it was clear that the Warsaw Pact was no longer a 'cardboard castle', but a fully-fledged, functioning military alliance.[49] The Brezhnev era also experienced a sudden increase in the USSR's surface and submarine fleets, which not only challenged the USA's global naval supremacy, but also posed a potential threat to the alliance's sea lines of communication between the USA and Europe.[50]

On the debit side, by the late 1960s the USSR also had to face the threat posed by an overtly hostile China. The schism between Moscow and Beijing derived from ideological differences, but military factors did also play a role, and the Soviets came to regret the ample assistance given to 'the new Mongol warriors with bombs in their quivers' (as the poet Yevgenii Yevtushenko depicted the Chinese). In March 1969 a border clash along the Ussuri river led to a series of battles along the Sino-Soviet frontier, raising the prospects of war between both communist powers. The USSR was obliged to bolster its forces in Central Asia and Siberia, raising them from 18 divisions in 1965 to 47 in 1982. The Soviets had to contend not only with the 4 million-strong People's Liberation Army (PLA), but also with a new nuclear threat. China tested its first atomic bomb in October 1964, and conducted a thermonuclear test three years later. During the course of the 1969 border clashes the Soviets apparently considered, but ruled out, a pre-emptive attack on the PRC's nuclear arsenal. When Chinese ICBMs entered service in 1980, their designated targets were in the USSR.[51]

Following the 1969 border clashes the Chinese perceived that the USSR was now their principal foe, and it was this calculation which contributed to the Sino-American rapprochement of the 1970s. The policy of *détente* which Brezhnev followed was therefore partly motivated by fears that the USSR would be isolated, and left to face both NATO and the PRC. However, the Kremlin also sought to stabilise the superpower arms race, as the USSR had by now achieved strategic parity with the USA.[52] Disarmament measures had been tried without success prior to the

Second World War, and attempts at the elimination of nuclear weapons during the late 1940s to early 1950s also proved impossible to achieve. As a consequence, the idea of arms control emerged. This depended on using the insights generated by deterrence theory to identify moves that if agreed between the two superpowers might stabilise their relationship and prevent an inadvertent slide into war. Of particular concern was a possible situation in which one side might fear that the other was about to launch a pre-emptive first-strike. The negotiations themselves, however, became the major forum for strategic discussion between the superpowers during the cold war, and became valued for that reason. Their tempo and mood was seen as a barometer for the wider political relationship.

US–Soviet strategic arms negotiations did bear fruit in 1972, with the Strategic Arms Limitation Treaty (SALT I) imposing restrictions on ICBM construction, and the ABM treaty prohibiting the further expansion of missile defence systems. The Soviets had deployed ABMs around Moscow in 1964, and during the late 1960s there was a bitter debate pitting the General Staff, which favoured nationwide missile defence, against party officials who balked at the cost and the potentially destabilising effects on the superpower military balance. Brezhnev's signature on the ABM treaty in 1972 represented a victory for the latter faction. Subsequent attempts to negotiate a second arms treaty, SALT II, foundered because of arcane disputes over the capabilities and characteristics of weapons systems, intense mutual mistrust between the superpowers, and the phenomenon which political scientists have dubbed 'the security dilemma'. The Soviets were aware that the SALT negotiations did not cover the USA's Forward Based Systems (such as nuclear-capable fighter-bombers within the NATO area) or the British and French nuclear forces, and so in 1977 the USSR deployed SS-20 missiles in Eastern Europe. This led the European NATO powers – notably the FRG and the UK – to request the stationing of US *Cruise* and *Pershing* missiles to counter the SS-20s. The consequence was a build-up of Intermediate-range Nuclear Forces (INF) which exacerbated East–West tensions and contributed to the 'second cold war' of the early 1980s.[53]

cold war strategies and the third world

As noted previously, the cold war coincided with the decolonisation of the European empires in Africa and Asia, a process which opened up the Third World to East–West competition, and which led to superpower intervention in 'proxy wars'. Successive US administrations were concerned by the instability of post-colonial governments. Their countries were at an early, pre-industrial stage of development and they faced many internal challenges, including from leftist groups, some of which were backed by Moscow (or Havana or Beijing). Khrushchev had proclaimed the USSR's support for 'wars of national liberation' in January 1961, while Mao had used the experience of the Chinese civil war to develop his own doctrine of guerrilla warfare. For Kennedy and his advisers, helping friendly governments meet the challenge posed by left-wing insurgents was the defining task of the next stage of the cold war. Here there was no body of innovative strategic literature to help. Kennedy found himself taking advice from colourful characters such as Edward Lansdale, who had assisted the Filipino government against the left-wing *Huk* rebels, or experienced British officers such as Robert Thompson, with his knowledge gained fighting communist guerrillas in Malaya. A body of counter-insurgency doctrine began to be developed but it lacked subtlety and overlooked the specific characteristics of individual insurgencies, shaped by local geography, history and social conditions. Unlike nuclear strategy which was conducted at a macro-level counter-insurgency strategy required attention to the micro-level.[54]

It had been assumed that counter-insurgency strategy would be tested in Latin America, but Cuban attempts to provoke revolution in South America came to naught – as was demonstrated by the heroic, but futile, death of Che Guevara in Bolivia in 1967. South-East Asia was quite a different matter. In Laos from 1959 to 1961 the *Pathet Lao* insurgency threatened to overturn the pro-American government in Vientiane, and Kennedy's advisers proposed a military intervention. Fortunately in this case there was a political solution based on a neutralist leader which Kennedy endorsed. In Vietnam there was no such option. The Americans were tied to Ngo Dinh Diem, a divisive figure whose corrupt and oppressive rule undermined the fight against the communists. Diem was assassinated at the start of November 1963, just before Kennedy, and at this point the Americans realised that they had to take main responsibility for a fight that was not going as well as they originally thought.[55]

In guerrilla warfare the objective of the insurgents is to play for time, while they build up their strength and sap that of the enemy. One approach, tried by American advisers to Diem's regime, was to win over Vietnamese 'hearts and minds', gaining the trust of the local people by promoting good works in order to leave the militants isolated, bereft of recruits and practical support. As that failed it was replaced by a tougher doctrine, which fitted more naturally with US military thinking, known as 'search and destroy'. This transition took place roughly about the same time that US troops became involved in combat operations in

South Vietnam (around the spring of 1965). The American war effort from 1965 to 1971 focused on eliminating the *Viet Cong* and deterring civilians from joining them. With militants who are able to work through civil society, however, the risk of this approach was that it caught many innocents at the same time, feeding local anger and thereby aiding the insurgency. It may be the case that poor tactics and doctrine can fuel a guerrilla campaign, but the corollary is not necessarily true. Good doctrine and tactics are not sufficient to make a hearts and mind strategy work, when used in support of an unpopular government. Harsher measures can work in certain circumstances – but again only in the context of a wider political process that meets the essential objective of any counter-insurgency strategy, which is to separate the militants from their potential constituency and sources of support. In the end, the Americans failed because they were never able to establish a regime in Saigon strong enough to beat the communists, and to be recognised by the South Vietnamese people as legitimate.[56]

After the defeat in Vietnam (which cost the USA 56,000 dead, with some 2 million Vietnamese killed) senior US commanders did not find it particularly fruitful to consider whether or not there were better ways to fight insurgencies. They concluded that it was best not to fight such conflicts at all. Accordingly they concentrated on preparing for major inter-state wars. In this context the most important aspect of Vietnam was the potential exhibited by new 'smart' bombs during the *Linebacker* air campaigns of 1972, when the US Air Force discovered that they could hit North Vietnamese targets with only a fraction of the effort required in the *Rolling Thunder* air campaign (1965–68). It was through exploring the potential of 'smart' weapons in the context of a land war with the Warsaw Pact during the late 1970s and early 1980s that US forces, particularly the army, revived their capabilities and morale.[57]

Soviet policy pronouncements on 'peaceful co-existence' did not preclude efforts by Moscow to undermine Western influence in the Third World by supporting 'progressive' regimes and 'wars of national liberation'. However, this policy had mixed results. Extensive Soviet arms supplies did not prevent Nasser's successor, Anwar Sadat, from aligning Egypt with the West during the late 1970s.[58] The USSR's military assistance to the Democratic Republic of Vietnam (DRV) and Cuba involved the obligation to support independent-minded allies whose own clashes with the USA had the potential to provoke a major East–West crisis. In their relations with the DRV from 1965 to 1975, the Soviets hoped to supplant Chinese influence in Hanoi and to advance the communist cause in South-East Asia, but they were also wary of risking a confrontation with the USA.

Throughout the Vietnam war Moscow consistently encouraged the DRV to negotiate with the USA, but the Soviets found that the volume of their arms supplies did not translate into political influence. In Cuba's case, Castro was more enthusiastic about supporting revolutions in Africa than Moscow was. During the Angolan civil war (1975–89), Cuban military aid to the MPLA regime preceded that of the Soviets, and Havana provided the bulk of the troops which saved the MPLA from being overthrown by their FNLA and UNITA rivals in the autumn of 1975.[59]

The USSR's military intervention in Afghanistan was viewed by American 'hawks' as part of a grand design to establish Soviet domination over South Asia and the Middle East. In fact, the Soviets sent troops to Afghanistan in December 1979 in order to overthrow a recalcitrant fellow communist leader (Hafizollah Amin) and to replace him with a more pliable figure (Babrak Karmal). Acting on the principle of the 'Brezhnev doctrine', the USSR intended to preserve the Afghan communist regime, which was beset by widespread popular revolt. However, the Soviet force sent to Afghanistan (known as the 40th Army, or the 'Limited Contingent') ended up being drawn into an inconclusive and costly guerrilla war against the *Mujahadin* guerrilla groups. Soviet 'scorched earth' tactics – which devastated the Afghan countryside, accounting for many of the 1 million Afghans killed during the war – served only to fuel popular hatred of the invaders and their client regime in Kabul. The 40th Army was unable to contain the *Mujahadin* – even at the height of the war the Soviet presence in Afghanistan never exceeded more than 120,000 troops (compared to over 500,000 US troops in Vietnam in 1968).[60] Not only were the Soviets overstretched by their need to maintain existing force levels facing NATO and China, but they were also ill-prepared for the challenges of an insurgency. An army configured for high-intensity combat operations in North-Western Europe or Manchuria was hardly suited to pursuing guerrillas across Afghanistan's predominantly mountainous terrain. The Soviets also failed because they were ideologically unable to accept that a 'progressive' regime could face a popular revolt, and were therefore unable to devise an effective counter-insurgency strategy which would gain popular acceptance of the Kabul regime's legitimacy.[61]

strategy and the end of the cold war, 1979–91

The 'second cold war' of the early 1980s enhanced NATO's fears of possible Warsaw Pact aggression in Europe, although on the other side the Soviets became increasingly concerned about qualitative improvements in the alliance's conventional forces. As far back as March 1968 General Otakar

Rytir, the Chief of the Czechoslovak General Staff, had informed his colleagues that the West's economic and technological supremacy would eventually translate into a military advantage. Rytir's comments proved to be prescient. From the late 1970s NATO commanders encouraged innovative thinking of their own on the conduct of large-scale operations, in conjunction with air power, encouraged by the possibilities opening up with the introduction of new sensors, communications and precision guided munitions (PGMs). The Arab–Israeli war of October 1973 demonstrated how anti-tank and anti-aircraft defences could impose crippling losses on an attacking force, a clear lesson for NATO armies worried about the Warsaw Pact's quantitative superiority in men and materiel. The development of PGMs, including *Cruise* missiles and laser-guided bombs, also enhanced NATO's capability to launch accurate air and missile strikes deep into the Warsaw Pact's rear. In 1987 Marshal Nikolai Ogarkov, the Chief of the Soviet General Staff, commented on the 'Revolution in Military Affairs' which had given the USA and its allies technological supremacy over the Warsaw Pact. Ogarkov's concerns showed that Soviet confidence in a victory against NATO was less assured.[62]

Given Eastern Europe's internal crises in 1956, 1968 and 1980–81, the reliability of the non-Soviet Warsaw Pact countries and their forces was also questionable. In Poland's case, the rise of 'Solidarity' from the summer of 1980 onwards was viewed in Moscow in much the same way as the Czechoslovak 'Prague Spring' had been interpreted – as an existential threat to Soviet hegemony over Eastern Europe as a whole. However, compared with 1968 the Kremlin was far less willing to use military force to crush 'counter-revolution' in Poland, knowing full well that the introduction of Soviet forces would lead to a national uprising. Although General Jaruzelski later defended the imposition of martial law in December 1981 on the grounds that it forestalled a far bloodier intervention by the USSR, Moscow had actually ruled out an invasion of Poland and was content to let the Polish army and security forces play the lead role in restoring internal order. However the 'Solidarity' crisis, and the ongoing political stalemate after December 1981, demonstrated that the status quo throughout Eastern Europe was a source of insecurity, rather than the opposite, for the USSR.[63]

Conservative American scholars have argued that the expansion of US defence expenditure during the 1980s was part of a conscious effort to force the Soviet economy to the brink of collapse, and to compel the USSR to reassess its policy of competition with the USA. This argument is heavily tainted by hindsight. Reagan's defence policy was based on the perception that previous administrations had underestimated the Soviet threat and that US military capabilities had deteriorated during the 1970s. His most ambitious idea, that of a space-based missile defence system (the Strategic Defense Initiative – SDI), was intended to render nuclear weapons obsolete. Furthermore, had the Reagan administration's intentions been to bankrupt the USSR then it was by no means guaranteed that the Soviets would peacefully concede that they had lost the arms race. Indeed, during the spring of 1983 Brezhnev's successor, Andropov, became convinced that the USA and his NATO allies were preparing for a nuclear war against the USSR, and he became convinced that NATO's *Able Archer* exercise, scheduled to take place later that year, was the precursor to a surprise attack on the Soviet bloc. Andropov's paranoia shows that it would not have required much for a hard-line Marxist-Leninist to misinterpret the motives behind the USA's military expansion, which could in turn have prompted a catastrophic decision by Moscow to destroy the threat of NATO 'aggression' with a prophylactic attack.[64]

However, after Gorbachev's accession in March 1985 the opposite happened. Soviet defence policy and military strategy underwent a profound and unprecedented revision which had consequences which the proponent of *glasnost* – let alone the CPSU's elite or Western governments – had not anticipated. To achieve the reconstruction (*perestroika*) of the Soviet economy, Gorbachev intended to reduce the burden of defence expenditure and convert a substantial portion of the military-industrial complex to civilian production. These objectives required improved relations with the USA and the NATO powers, and therefore influenced the withdrawal of the 40th Army from Afghanistan (February 1989) and significant concessions on arms control. In December 1987 Gorbachev and Reagan concluded the INF Treaty, which involved the removal and destruction of intermediate-range nuclear weapons from Western and Eastern Europe. The NATO–Warsaw Pact Mutual Balanced Force Reductions talks, deadlocked since their inception in 1973, were revived. These were concluded with the Conventional Forces in Europe (CFE) Treaty in November 1990, which led to the withdrawal of Soviet forces from Eastern Europe and force reductions for both NATO and the Warsaw Pact.[65]

Gorbachev's ideas on defence and security policy derived from advisers – notably Georgi Arbatov and Alexander Yakovlev – from the foreign policy institutes of the USSR's Academy of Sciences. The *instituchki* set about bridging the conceptual gap between 'military-political' and 'military-technical' doctrine, and much to the fury of senior officers they imposed in 1990 a military doctrine which abandoned any concept of an offensive against NATO, focusing the USSR's peacetime strategy on deterrence and its wartime aims as being territorial defence and war termination, rather than outright victory against any enemy. Gorbachev and his advisers also abandoned one of the main principles of Soviet foreign policy since 1945, namely the maintenance of the 'Socialist Commonwealth' in Eastern Europe. The Soviet leader concluded that in the nuclear age the *cordon sanitaire* along the USSR's western border was no longer vital to Soviet security. Gorbachev did not expect that the loosening of Soviet hegemony over Eastern Europe would lead to the revolutions of 1989 – he presumed that the region's communist regimes would survive by pursuing their own variants of *perestroika*. Nonetheless, the adoption of the 'Sinatra doctrine' (which enabled the USSR's clients to 'do things their way') not only condemned East European communism to oblivion, but it also led to the demise of the Warsaw Treaty Organisation, the unification of Germany within NATO, and the end of Soviet authority over the Eastern bloc.[66]

The consequences of Gorbachev's 'new thinking' for Soviet security policy were bitterly resented by the more hard-line party elite, as well as senior military and KGB officers, who interpreted the events of 1989–90 as a gain for the USSR's NATO adversaries. Believing that the fate of the USSR was at stake, the Defence Minister, Marshal Dmitri Yazov, and Sergei Akhromeyev (Ogarkov's successor as Chief of the General Staff) participated in the August 1991 coup. However, the Soviet armed forces were not an effective tool for the coup plotters. The military machine which had once inspired alarm in the West was crippled by draft-dodging, corruption, drug and alcohol abuse, ethnic strife and institutionalised bullying (known as *dyedovshchina*). The army was also drawn into suppressing nationalist dissent in both the Baltic states and the Caucasus. The officer corps was split – while Yazov and Akhromeyev participated in the 1991 coup, other senior officers (notably General Yevgenii Shaposnikov, the chief of the air force) aligned with Gorbachev and the Russian President, Boris Yeltsin. Soviet leaders from Lenin onwards recognised that the survival of the Soviet system depended on the party's control over the armed forces. The weakening of both party authority – and the cohesion of the armed forces themselves – contributed to the USSR's eventual disintegration.[67] In this respect, it is ironic that while for just over 40 years the Americans and their allies felt threatened by the USSR's military strength, it was Russia's *weaknesses* after 1991 that posed potential problems for Western security – whether this meant the possible transfer of nuclear weapons and fissile material to terrorist groups or 'rogue states', or the nightmare scenario of a violent collapse (made more credible after 1994 by the Chechen war) which could turn the Russian Federation into a 'Yugoslavia with nukes'.[68]

conclusions

During the 1980s the US military devised its 'air–land' doctrine in order to prepare itself for a war against the Warsaw Pact. In fact, this doctrine was tested not in Central Europe, but during the Gulf war of 1991 when, not long after the formal conclusion of the cold war, the United States found itself leading a multinational coalition to liberate Kuwait from Iraqi occupation. The 1991 Persian Gulf war was fought as a traditional conventional campaign, with air and land activity integrated and full use made of advanced weaponry to cripple Iraq's command, control and communications.[69] In later conventional campaigns there was equivalent success. Yet counter-insurgency techniques, along with peace support operations aimed at pacifying 'failed states' devastated by civil conflict, remained as problematic as they had been in Vietnam. During the 1990s nuclear strategy gained barely a mention as a matter of pressing concern: the issue was more about how to care for the arsenals while they were slowly dismantled and preventing their further proliferation to anti-Western states or terrorists.[70]

The legacy of the strategic thinking which took place in the universities and think-tanks was therefore limited. Because of the arcane and rarefied nature of so much discussion of nuclear strategy there was, apart from the odd occasion, very little discussion of the interaction between political conflicts and possible military operations using nuclear weapons. After the early 1960s all scenarios appeared far-fetched. Even during the crises of the early 1960s, over Berlin and Cuba, the political leadership took a very straightforward view of the meaning of any nuclear exchanges and paid little regard to the more nuanced concepts of how these might be conducted. During Berlin, for example, American policy-makers recoiled at the idea of launching a first strike against Soviet forces, even after a plausible demonstration of how it just might work, and in crisis games organised by one of the leading strategists, Tom Schelling, it became clear just how hard it was going to be actually to start a nuclear war. Faced with such a prospect the urge to find a political way out would be very strong.[71]

In fact by this time the strategists possibly had already performed their most useful function. Their success during the 1950s lay in explaining how even two sides engaged in a bitter struggle could still have a shared interest in avoiding mutual destruction, and how there were ways of exploring this common interest without ever denying the basic antagonism. This required an understanding of restraints and boundaries, a sensitivity to how defensive moves by one side could appear as threatening to the other, and an interest in forms of communication that relied on tacit understandings as well as official statements. In principle this line of thought had wider potential which Schelling in particular began to explore in the 1960s, but he like others was discouraged by Vietnam. As superpower negotiations became institutionalised with the arms control negotiations of the 1970s and 1980s, the nuclear specialists found themselves concentrating on second and third order issues.[72]

Interest in nuclear strategy persisted because NATO got itself in the position where it was over-reliant on nuclear threats because of the Warsaw Pact's advantages in conventional forces. The attempts to find ways round this problem, by either removing this reliance or rendering its threats credible, kept the nuclear specialists busy even though they faced severe political constraints in pushing forward their favoured prescriptions. The politicians were right to concentrate on holding the alliance together even though that limited fully preparations for a future war. In an otherwise stable political setting, alliance disarray always represented the most likely reason for a shift in the underlying balance of power. Although the dominant strategic theme during the cold war was deterrence this was not that difficult to achieve once there was the slightest risk of nuclear annihilation. Deterrence only appeared intellectually demanding once it took the form of explorations into what might happen if this risk was disregarded or was in some way transcended. Here at least there was a link to Clausewitz. As he once remarked: 'In war everything is simple, but the simplest thing is difficult.'[73]

notes

1. See, for example, Bernard Brodie (ed.), *The Absolute Weapon* (New York: Harcourt, Brace & Co, 1946) and *Escalation and the Nuclear Option* (Princeton, NJ: Princeton University Press, 1966); William Kaufman (ed.), *Military Policy and National Security* (Princeton, NJ: University Press, 1956); Hermann Kahn, *On Thermonuclear War* (Princeton, NJ: Princeton University Press, 1960); Thomas Schelling, *The Strategy of Conflict* (Cambridge, MA: Harvard University Press, 1960); and Albert Wohlstetter, 'The Delicate Balance of Terror', *Foreign Affairs*, 37:2 (1959). For an analysis of these works, and their impact on wider policy debates, see Lawrence Freedman, *The Evolution of Nuclear Strategy* (London: Macmillan, 1981; 3rd edition, 2003), and also Freedman, 'The First Two Generations of Nuclear Strategists', in Peter Paret (ed.), *Makers of Modern Strategy: From Machiavelli to the Nuclear Age* (Princeton, NJ: Princeton University Press, 1986), pp.735–78. On the strategists noted

above, see Fred Kaplan, *The Wizards of Armageddon: Strategists of the Nuclear Age* (New York: Simon & Schuster, 1983).

2. John L. Gaddis, *Strategies of Containment: A Critical Appraisal of American National Security Policy During the Cold War* (New York: Oxford University Press, 2005, 2nd edition), *passim*; David Rosenberg, 'The Origins of Overkill: Nuclear Weapons and American Strategy, 1945–1968', *International Security*, 7:4 (1983), pp.4–71; Melvyn Leffler, *A Preponderance of Power: National Security, the Truman Administration, and the Cold War* (Stanford, CA: Stanford University Press, 1992), *passim*; Saki Dockrill, *Eisenhower's New Look National Security Policy, 1953–61* (London: Macmillan, 1991); Lawrence Freedman, *US Intelligence and the Soviet Strategic Threat* (London: Macmillan, 1986) and *Kennedy's Wars: Berlin, Cuba, Laos and Vietnam* (New York: Oxford University Press, 2000); and Raymond Garthoff, *Détente and Confrontation: American–Soviet Relations from Nixon to Reagan* (Washington, DC: Brookings, 1994), *passim*.

3. A complete listing of the *Foreign Relations* volumes – as well as their contents – can be found online at <http://www.state.gov/r/pa/ho/frus/>. The National Security Archive's website is <http://www.gwu/edu/~nsarchiv/>.

4. John Baylis, *Ambiguity and Deterrence: British Nuclear Strategy, 1945–1964* (Oxford: Clarendon Press, 1995); Frederic Bozo, *La France et l'OTAN* (Paris: Masson, 1991), *passim*; John S. Duffield, *Power Rules: The Evolution of NATO's Conventional Force Posture* (Stanford, CA: Stanford University Press, 1995); Beatrice Heuser, *NATO, Britain, France and the FRG: Nuclear Strategy and Forces for Europe, 1949–2000* (London: Macmillan, 1997); and Jane Stromseth, *The Origins of Flexible Response: NATO's Debate over Strategy in the 1960s* (London: Macmillan, 1988).

5. See for example Christoph Bluth, *New Thinking in Soviet Military Policy* (London: RIIA 1990); John Erickson & E.J. Feuchtwanger, *Soviet Military Power and Performance* (New York: Archon, 1979); Matthew Evangelista, 'Stalin's Post-War Army Reappraised', *International Security*, 7:3 (1982–83), pp.110–38; Michael MccGwire, *Military Objectives in Soviet Foreign Policy* (Washington, DC: Brookings, 1987); Brian Ranft & Geoffrey Till, *The Sea in Soviet Strategy* (Annapolis, MD: Naval Institute Press, 1989); and Thomas W. Wolfe, *Soviet Power and Europe, 1945–1970* (Baltimore, MD: Johns Hopkins University Press, 1970), *passim*.

6. FRG Defence Ministry, 'Military Planning of the Warsaw Pact: A Study', *CWIHP Bulletin*, 2 (1992), pp.13–19; Gerhard Wettig, 'Warsaw Pact Planning in Central Europe: The Current State of Research', *CWIHP Bulletin*, 3 (1993), p.51; R. Craig Nation, *Black Earth, Red Star* (Ithaca, NY: Cornell University Press, 1992); Mark Galeotti, *The Age of Anxiety: Security and Politics in Soviet and Post-Soviet Russia* (London: Longman, 1995); David Glantz, *The Military Strategy of the Soviet Union* (London: Frank Cass, 1992); Robin Higham & Frederick W. Kagan (eds), *The Military History of the Soviet Union* (Basingstoke: Palgrave Macmillan, 2002); Vojtech Mastny, *The Cold War and Soviet Insecurity: The Stalin Years* (Oxford: Oxford University Press, 1996); William E. Odom, *The Collapse of the Soviet Military* (New Haven, CT: Yale University Press, 1998), *passim*; and Steven Zaloga, *Target America: The Soviet Union and the Strategic Arms Race, 1945–64* (Novato, CA: Presidio, 1993); Malcolm Byrne & Vojtech Mastny (eds), *A Cardboard Castle? An Inside History of the Warsaw*

Pact, 1955–1991 (Budapest & New York: Central European University Press, 2005), *passim.*

7. Carl von Clausewitz (trans. & ed., Michael Howard & Peter Paret), *On War* (Princeton, NJ: Princeton University Press, 1989), pp.80–1.

8. On the operational level, see Robert M. Citino, *Blitzkrieg to Desert Storm: The Evolution of Operational Warfare* (Lawrence, KS: University of Kansas Press, 2004). On the varying levels of war, see Edward Luttwak, *Strategy: The Logic of Peace* (Cambridge, MA: Harvard University Press, 2001), pp.93–167.

9. Brodie, *Absolute Weapon*, p.52. See also John Baylis & John Garnett (eds), *Makers of Nuclear Strategy* (London: Pinter Press, 1991).

10. See Barry Buzan, *Strategic Studies: Military Technology and International Relations* (London: Macmillan, 1987).

11. This term is based on the title of an unpublished book by James King.

12. For the recollections of one 'whizz-kid', see Alain Enthoven & K. Wayne Smith, *How Much is Enough? Shaping the Defence Programme, 1961–1969* (New York: Harper & Row, 1971). Stromseth, *Flexible Response*, pp.70–1.

13. UK Ministry of Defence, Defence Intelligence Service paper DIS(67)5(Final), *The Arab–Israeli War – June 1967*, June 1968, DEFE63/19(TNA). *Strategic Survey 1973–1974* (London: International Institute of Strategic Studies, 1974), pp.52–5.

14. Lawrence Freedman, *Deterrence* (Cambridge: Polity Press, 2004).

15. Kahn, *On Thermonuclear War*, *passim*. See also Sharon Ghamari-Tabrizi, *The Worlds of Herman Kahn: The Intuitive Science of Thermonuclear War* (Cambridge, MA: Harvard University Press, 2005).

16. Colin Gray, *Modern Strategy* (Oxford: Oxford University Press, 1999), pp.297–318; Richard Rosecrance, *Strategic Deterrence Reconsidered*, Adelphi Paper No.116 (London: International Institute for Strategic Studies, 1975).

17. Freedman, *Nuclear Strategy*, pp.342–77. Colin Gray, amongst others, tried to resolve this dilemma (with reference to US nuclear strategy in a war with the Soviets) in 'Nuclear Strategy: The Case for a Theory of Victory', *International Security*, 4:1 (1979), pp.54–87.

18. McGeorge Bundy, 'To Cap the Volcano', *Foreign Affairs*, 8:1 (1969), p.12. Freedman, 'Nuclear Strategists', p.735.

19. Lawrence Freedman, *Kennedy's War: Berlin, Cuba, Laos and Vietnam* (New York: Oxford University Press, 2000), pp.417–18.

20. On Nixon's 'madman' theory, see William Burr & Jeffrey Kimball, 'Nixon's Nuclear Alert: Vietnam War Diplomacy and the Joint Chiefs of Staff Readiness Test: October 1969', *Cold War History*, 3:2 (2003), pp.113–56.

21. Paul Lettow, *Ronald Reagan and His Quest to Abolish Nuclear Weapons* (New York: Random House, 2005).

22. Galeotti, *Age of Anxiety*, pp.35–7; William Taubman, *Khrushchev: The Man and His Era* (New York: Norton, 2003), p.503.

23. R.J. Crampton, *Eastern Europe in the Twentieth Century* (London: Routledge, 1994), pp.246, 297; Wolfe, *Soviet Power and Europe*, pp.42–4; Christopher Donnelly, *Red Banner: The Soviet Military System in Peace and War* (Coulsden: Jane's Information Group, 1988), pp.233–51.

24. Vojtech Mastny, '"We Are in a Bind": Polish and Czechoslovak Attempts at Reforming the Warsaw Pact', *CWIHP Bulletin*, 11 (1998), pp.230–49; Dennis

Deletant & Mihai Ionescu, *Romania and the Warsaw Pact, 1955–1989*, CWIHP Working Paper No.43 (2002).

25. Mark Kramer, 'The "Lessons" of the Cuban Missile Crisis for Warsaw Pact Nuclear Operations', *CWIHP Bulletin*, 5 (1995), p.59, 110–14; Douglas Selvage, *The Warsaw Pact and Nuclear Nonproliferation, 1963–1965*, CWIHP Working Paper No.32 (April 2001).

26. Condoleezza Rice, 'The Making of Soviet Strategy', in Paret, *Modern Strategy*, pp.648–76; Donnelly, *Red Banner*, pp.91–134; Stephen J. Cimbala, 'The Cold War and Soviet Military Strategy', *Journal of Slavic Military Studies*, 10:3 (1997), pp.25–37.

27. Phillip A. Karber & Jerald A. Combs, 'The United States, NATO, and the Soviet Threat to Western Europe', *Diplomatic History*, 22:3 (1998), pp.399–425; Evangelista, 'Stalin's Army', *passim*.

28. Nation, *Black Earth, Red Star*, p.170; David Holloway, *Stalin and the Bomb* (New Haven, CT: Yale University Press, 1994), pp.243–50. See also Zaloga, *Target America*, chapters 2–6.

29. Steven T. Ross, *American War Plans, 1945–1950* (New York: Garland, 1988); Vladislav Zubok & Constantine Pleshakov, *Inside the Kremlin's Cold War: From Stalin to Khrushchev* (Cambridge, MA: Harvard University Press, 1996), pp.52–3.

30. John Lewis Gaddis, *We Now Know: Rethinking Cold War History* (Oxford: Oxford University Press, 1997), pp.70–82. See also Sergei Goncharov, John Lewis & Xue Litai, *Uncertain Partners: Stalin, Mao and the Korean War* (Stanford, CA: Stanford University Press, 1993).

31. Leffler, *Preponderance of Power*, pp.403–6; Duffield, *Power Rules*, pp.34–47, 101–8. On East German rearmament, see Norman Naimark, *To Know Everything and to Report Everything Worth Knowing: Building the East German Police State, 1945–1949*, CWIHP Working Paper No.10 (1994), pp.19–24.

32. Richard Aldrich, *The Hidden Hand: Britain, America and Cold War Secret Intelligence* (London: John Murray, 2002), pp.326–33. William Stueck's *The Korean War: An International History* (Princeton, NJ: Princeton University Press, 1995), and *The Korean War in World History* (Lexington, KT: University of Kentucky Press, 2004), *passim*, are good introductory histories of this conflict.

33. Vojtech Mastny, *NATO in the Beholder's Eye: Soviet Perceptions and Policies, 1949–56*, CWIHP Working Paper No.35 (March 2002), pp.60–79. See also Mastny, *Reassuring NATO: Eastern Europe, Russia and the Western Alliance* (Oslo: Institut for Forsvarsstudier, No.5 1997), pp.22–6.

34. Dockrill, *Eisenhower's New Look National Security Policy*, pp.53–8; Maree-Anne Reid, 'A "Troublesome Coinage": Eisenhower, Dulles, and Massive Retaliation', *War Studies Journal*, 3:2 (1998), pp.3–29.

35. Freedman, *Kennedy's Wars*, pp.46–8, 107–10; Robert S. McNamara, *The Essence of Security: Reflections in Office* (London: Hodder & Stoughton, 1968), pp.52–9; McGeorge Bundy, *Danger and Survival: Choices about the Bomb in the First Fifty Years* (New York: Random House, 1988), pp.352–7.

36. Beatrice Heuser, *NATO*, pp.30–8; Baylis, *Ambiguity and Deterrence*, pp.245–50.

37. Steven Zaloga, 'Soviet/Russian Strategic Nuclear Forces', in Higham & Kagan (eds), *Military History of the Soviet Union*, pp.199–220; V.D. Sokolovsky

(trans. Raymond Garthoff), *Military Strategy* (London: Pall Mall Press, 1963), pp.13–17.

38. Petr Lunak, 'Planning for Nuclear War: The Czechoslovak War Plan of 1964', *CWIHP Bulletin*, 12–13, pp.289–98; Beatrice Heuser, 'Victory in a Nuclear War? A Comparison of NATO and WTO War Aims and Strategies', *Contemporary European History*, 7:3 (1998), pp.320–5.

39. Taubman, *Khrushchev*, pp.535–7; Timothy Naftali & Alexander Fursenko, *One Hell of a Gamble: Khrushchev, Castro, Kennedy, and the Cuban Missile Crisis, 1958–1964* (New York: Norton, 1999), *passim*. For an alternative view, see Richard New Lebow & Janice Gross Stein, *We All Lost the Cold War* (Princeton, NJ: Princeton University Press, 1994), pp.20–145.

40. Paul du Quenoy, 'The Role of Foreign Affairs in the Fall of Nikita Khrushchev in October 1964', *International History Review*, 25:2 (2003), pp.334–56; Matthew Evangelista, 'Why Keep Such an Army': Khrushchev's Troop Reductions, CWIHP Working Paper No.19 (1997); Christopher C. Lovett, 'The Soviet Cold War Navy', in Higham & Kagan (eds), *Military History*, pp.240–4.

41. See Colin Gray, *Strategic Studies and Public Policy: The American Experience* (Lexington, KT: University Press of Kentucky, 1982).

42. S.J. Ball, *The Cold War: An International History, 1947–1991* (London: Arnold, 1998); Zubok & Pleshakov, *Kremlin's Cold War*, pp.51–2.

43. John Gearson & Kori Schake (eds), *The Berlin Wall Crisis: Perspectives on Cold War Alliances* (Basingstoke: Palgrave Macmillan, 2002); Vladislav Zubok, *Khrushchev and the Berlin Crisis (1958–1962)*, CWIHP Working Paper No.6 (1993).

44. Francis Gavin, 'The Myth of Flexible Response: United States Strategy in Europe during the 1960s', *International History Review*, 27:4 (2001), pp.847–75; Sean Maloney, 'Fire Brigade or Tocsin? NATO's ACE Mobile Force, Flexible Response and the Cold War', *Journal of Strategic Studies*, 27:4 (2004), pp.585–613.

45. Heuser, *NATO*, pp.15–23; Stromseth, *Flexible Response*, pp.46–7, 121–50. See also Helga Haftendorn, *NATO and the Nuclear Revolution: A Crisis of Credibility, 1966–1967* (Oxford: Clarendon Press, 1996).

46. Heuser, *NATO*, pp.71–8, 95–110. UK Cabinet Nuclear Policy Committee meeting, PN(67)4th, 5.12.67, CAB134/3120(TNA). OPD(O)(67)16, *British Nuclear Weapons Policy*, 10.10.67, CAB148/81(TNA).

47. Transcript of speech by Healey at Munich, 2.2.69, PREM13/2568(TNA). This was the scenario outlined in the work of 'future history' written by General Sir John Hackett et al., *The Third World War* (London: Sidgwick & Jackson, 1978).

48. Odom, *Soviet Military*, pp.72–3; Mark O'Neill, 'The Cold War on the Ground, 1945–1981' and Christopher C. Lovett, 'The Soviet Cold War Navy', in Higham & Kagan (eds), *Military History*, pp.231–5, 244–6.

49. David Miller, *The Cold War: A Military History* (London: Pimlico, 2001), pp.38–9, 60–1; General J. Hackett (CinC NATO Northern Army Group – NORTHAG) to General J. Cassels (Chief of the General Staff), 21.12.66, DEFE13/635(TNA).

50. Barry Blechman, *The Changing Soviet Navy* (Washington, DC: Brookings, 1973). UK Delegation NATO to Foreign Office, No.2(Saving), 26.1.68, DEFE13/901(TNA).

51. Sergei Goncharenko, 'Sino-Soviet Military Co-operation', in Odd Arne Westad (ed.), *Brothers in Arms: The Rise and Fall of the Sino-Soviet Alliance 1945–63* (Stanford, CA: Stanford University Press, 2000), pp.141–64; John Lewis & Hua Di, 'China's Ballistic Missile Programs: Technologies, Strategies, Goals', *International Security*, 17:2 (1992), pp.9–10, 16–19; Lawrence Freedman, 'The Military Dimension of Soviet Policy', in Gerald Segal (ed.), *The Soviet Union in East Asia* (Boulder, CO: Westview Press, 1983), pp.88–101.

52. Report by four PLA Marshals to the Central Committee, 11.7.69, in Chen Jian & David Wilson (eds), '"All Under the Heaven Is Great Chaos": Beijing, the Sino-Soviet Border Clashes, and the Turn Toward Sino-American Rapprochement, 1968–69', *CWIHP Bulletin*, 11, pp.166–8; Geoffrey Roberts, *The Soviet Union in World Politics* (London: Routledge, 1999), pp.66–7.

53. Richard Crockatt, *The Fifty Years War: The United States and the Soviet Union in World Politics, 1941–1991* (London: Routledge, 2000), pp.227–9, 270–1. Garthoff's *Détente and Confrontation* provides the most comprehensive coverage of superpower arms control during this period. Zaloga, 'Nuclear Forces', in Higham & Kagan (eds), *Military History*, pp.210–11.

54. John Shy, 'Revolutionary War', in Paret (ed.), *Modern Strategy*, pp.838–62. Lansdale and Thompson express their own ideas in Edward Lansdale, *In the Midst of Wars: An American's Mission to South-East Asia* (New York: Fordham University Press, 1991); and Robert Thompson, *Defeating Communist Insurgency: Experiences from Malaya to Vietnam* (London: Chatto & Windus, 1972). See also Ian Beckett, *Modern Insurgencies and Counter-Insurgencies: Guerrillas and their Opponents since 1750* (London: Routledge, 2001), pp.95–109.

55. Freedman, *Kennedy's Wars*, pp.340–55; David Kaiser, *American Tragedy: Kennedy, Johnson and the Origins of the Vietnam War* (Cambridge, MA: Harvard University Press, 2000), pp.36–57, 150–85.

56. Robert Schulzinger, *A Time for War: The United States and Vietnam, 1941–1975* (Oxford: Oxford University Press, 1997); Kaiser, *American Tragedy*. The factors behind the US defeat are also covered in Marc Jason Gilbert (ed.), *Why the North Won the Vietnam War* (Basingstoke: Palgrave Macmillan, 2002).

57. Robert Pape, *Bombing to Win: Air Power and Coercion in War* (Ithaca, NY: Cornell University Press, 1996), pp.195–210. See also Mark Clodfelter, *The Limits of Air Power: The American Bombing of North Vietnam* (New York: Free Press, 1989); and Earl H. Tilford Jr., *Setup: What the Air Force Did in Vietnam and Why* (Maxwell AFB AL: Air University Press, 1991). Lawrence Freedman, *The Revolution in Strategic Affairs*, Adelphi Paper No.318 (IISS 1998), pp.21–7.

58. Alexander J. Bennett, 'Arms Transfer as an Instrument of Soviet Policy in the Middle East', *Middle East Journal*, 39:4 (1985), pp.745–74; Galia Golan, *Soviet Policies in the Middle East* (Cambridge: Cambridge University Press, 1990), pp.44–57, 82–3, 104–5.

59. Iliya Gaiduk, *The Soviet Union and the Vietnam War* (Chicago, IL: I.R. Dee, 1996), pp.57–72; Piero Gleijeses, 'Havana's Policy in Africa, 1959–76: New Evidence from the Cuban Archives', *CWIHP Bulletin*, 8–9 (1997); and Odd Arne Westad, 'Moscow and the Angolan Crisis: A New Pattern of Intervention', *CWIHP Bulletin*, 8–9 (1997), pp.5–38.

60. Mark Galeotti, *Afghanistan: The Soviet Union's Last War* (London: Frank Cass, 1995); Lester Grau (ed.), *The Bear Went Over the Mountain: Soviet Combat Tactics in Afghanistan* (London: Frank Cass, 1998).
61. Scott McMichael, *Stumbling Bear: Soviet Military Performance in Afghanistan* (London: Brassey, 1991); William Maley, *The Afghanistan Wars* (London: Palgrave Macmillan, 2002), pp.40–56.
62. Vojtech Mastny, 'Did NATO Win the Cold War?', *Foreign Affairs*, 78:3 (1999), pp.176–89. Comments by General Rytir at meeting of General Staff in Prague, 13.3.68, in '"We Are in a Bind"', p.244. Freedman, *Revolution in Strategic Affairs*, pp.27–8; Cimbala, 'Military Strategy', pp.41–6.
63. Saki Ruth Dockrill, *The End of the Cold War Era: The Transformation of the Global Security Order* (Hodder Arnold/Oxford University Press, 2005), pp.113–17, 125–6; Vojtech Mastny, *The Soviet non-Invasion of Poland in 1980/1981 and the end of the Cold War*, CWIHP Working Paper No.23 (1998).
64. For an example of the Reaganite view, see Norman Friedman, *The Forty Years War* (Annapolis, MD: Naval Institute Press, 2000), p.486. McCGwire, *Military Objectives*, pp.307–12; Raymond Garthoff, *The Great Transition: American–Soviet Relations and the End of the Cold War* (Washington, DC: Brookings, 1994), pp.135–41.
65. Robert Service, *A History of Twentieth Century Russia* (London: Penguin, 1998), pp.448–66; Raymond Garthoff, 'New Thinking and Soviet Military Doctrine', in Willard Frank & Philip Gillette, *Soviet Military Doctrine from Lenin to Gorbachev* (Westport, CT: Greenwood Press, 1992), pp.195–207.
66. R.J. Crampton, *Eastern Europe in the Twentieth Century* (London: Routledge, 1994), pp.407–8; Dockrill, *End of the Cold War Era*, pp.119–29; Heuser, 'Victory in a Nuclear War?', pp.324–6; Odom, *Soviet Military*, pp.119–23.
67. Stephen Blank, 'The Soviet Army in Civil Disturbances, 1988–1991', in Higham & Kagan (eds), *Military History*, pp.274–97; Galeotti, *Age of Anxiety*, p.57; Odom, *Soviet Military*, pp.47–8, 305–41.
68. Benjamin Lambeth, 'Russia's Wounded Military', *Foreign Affairs*, 74:2 (1995), pp.86–98. M.J. Orr, *The Current State of the Russian Armed Forces* (Camberley: Conflict Studies Research Centre, 1996). The 'Yugoslavia' analogy is taken from George J. Church's article 'Death Trap' in *Time Magazine*, 16.1.95.
69. For a good introductory text on the 1991 war, see Lawrence Freedman & Efraim Karsh, *The Gulf Conflict 1990–1991* (London & Boston: Faber & Faber, 1994), *passim*. See also Alex Danchev & Dan Keohane, *International Perspectives on the Gulf Conflict, 1990–1991* (London: Macmillan, 1994); and Bruce W. Watson et al., *Military Lessons of the Gulf War* (London: Greenhill, 1991).
70. The literature on post-1991 strategic issues is voluminous. Christopher Bellamy's *Knights in White Armour: The New Art of War and Peace* (London: Pimlico, 1997) provides a good introduction to the complexities of peace-keeping and peace enforcement in 'failed states'. For an analysis of rogue states and nuclear weapons, see Robert Litwak, *Rogue States and US Foreign Policy: Containment after the Cold War* (Baltimore, MD: Johns Hopkins University Press, 2000); and Peter Lavoy, Scott Sagan & James Wirtz (eds), *Planning the Unthinkable: How New Powers will use Nuclear, Biological and Chemical Weapons* (Ithaca, NY: Cornell University Press, 2000).

71. Freedman discusses Schelling's war-game in *Kennedy's Wars*, pp.101–2. See
    also Kaplan, *Wizards of Armageddon*, p.302.
72. Thomas Schelling, *Arms and Influence* (New Haven, CT: Yale University Press,
    1967), *passim*.
73. Clausewitz, *On War*, p.119.

6

economics

In the earliest accounts of the cold war, historians either largely neglected or over-emphasised economic factors. Written in the 1950s and 1960s at the height of the East–West confrontation, 'traditionalist' works on the cold war focused on the political and strategic causes of the cold war. Traditionalist historians blamed the expansionist foreign policy of the Soviet Union for the origins of the conflict. On the contrary, self-styled 'revisionist' historians argued that Soviet foreign policy was cautious and defensive. In their eyes, it was the economic 'open door' policy of the United States that led to the breakdown in cooperation between Washington and Moscow after the Second World War. The revisionists asserted that national economic interests drove US foreign policy and American intervention in Europe and East Asia could only be explained by Washington's quest to preserve capitalism and locate foreign markets for the country's burgeoning exports. In the 1980s and 1990s, however, a more complex picture of the economic dimension of the cold war emerged. Drawing on multinational archival sources, scholars began to set economic issues, such as trade and foreign assistance, within the context of the political, strategic and ideological aspects of the cold war. This research demonstrated that economics, ideology and security were inextricably linked with respect to both the origins and evolution of the East–West conflict. The aim of this chapter is to highlight the connection between the economic aspects and the security component of the cold war, as perceived by both the Western and Soviet blocs.

While many historians have emphasised the importance of the economic dimension of the cold war, as of this writing, there are only two comprehensive treatments of the subject. In 1989, Thomas J. McCormick, inspired by the writings of leading revisionist historian William Appleman Williams and the eminent sociologist Immanuel

Wallerstein, published a theoretically sophisticated overview of the rise and fall of American economic hegemony since 1945.[1] Almost a decade later, Diane B. Kunz also produced a history of US diplomatic history from an economic perspective. Basing her work on a range of primary and secondary sources, Kunz presented a detailed analysis of American international trade and monetary policy within the context of the East–West conflict.[2] The scholarship of McCormick and Kunz notwithstanding, a thorough global account of the economic dimension of the cold war has yet to appear. With the emergence of the 'post-revisionist synthesis' in the early 1980s, corporatist approaches to American diplomatic history pioneered by Michael J. Hogan demonstrated the influential role that business elites played in the making of US foreign policy.[3] Post-revisionist scholars drawing on links between national security and economics, moreover, sought to explain how American grand strategy in the cold war was underpinned by the necessity of ensuring economic strength at home and abroad. The new cold war historiography has developed the research of the post-revisionist school and a new generation of historians, with increasing access to primary sources in both Western and Eastern countries has begun to examine the economic aspects of the cold war from an international perspective.[4] Another key objective of this chapter, then, is to synthesise these major writings on the economic component of the post-Second World War superpower rivalry.

This chapter is divided into four sections. The first section concentrates on the economic origins of the cold war. It will examine the clash between the competing systems of capitalism and communism, the divergent economic aims of the United States and the Soviet Union for world economic order and the impact of the Marshall Plan on East–West tensions over Europe. The second section explores the role of Western and Eastern economic organisations during the cold war. Coverage is provided of the origins and evolution of COCOM (Coordinating Committee on East–West Trade) and the CMEA, also known as Comecon. The third section of the chapter traces the unsuccessful effort by the Nixon administration to use trade as a political lever for de-escalating the cold war through economic *détente* in the mid-1970s. This is followed with a discussion of the renewed East–West economic confrontation after the demise of *détente* during 1979–83. The chapter concludes with an evaluation of the economic developments that led to the end of the cold war from 1985 to 1991.

the economic origins of the cold war

The economic origins of the cold war lie with the competing perspectives of world order held by the United States and the Soviet Union after 1945.

It was the determination to defeat Hitler and prevent the emergence of German hegemony in Europe that brought together two powers with contrasting political and economic systems in an alliance of convenience during the Second World War. Once Nazi Germany and Imperial Japan had been defeated, however, Washington and Moscow began to pursue different paths towards economic reconstruction after the devastation wrought by the war.[5] The American vision was based on the tenets of liberal capitalism underpinned by democracy and political self-determination. The Roosevelt and Truman administrations envisaged a world economic order that would promote peace and prosperity through international financial stability, free trade and economic cooperation between nations. Conversely, Soviet economic plans were less ambitious. Striving for security against encirclement by the Western capitalist countries, Stalin aimed to build a political and economic sphere of influence in Eastern Europe of socialist nations loyal to the Kremlin. Inevitably, a clash occurred between American multilateralism and Soviet autarky, as both governments grew increasingly suspicious of the other's economic motivations, especially in Europe. By the late 1940s, two economic spheres of influence had emerged: a US-led community of capitalist nations and a Soviet-dominated bloc of subservient Eastern European communist governments.[6]

The American economic sphere evolved from a series of multilateral negotiations on international finance and trade. In 1944, a new international monetary system was conceived at a conference held at Bretton Woods, New Hampshire. The new financial arrangements provided for a system of fixed currency exchange rates, established a link between the dollar and gold at $35 an ounce and created two institutions, the IMF and the World Bank, to assist with national balance of payments difficulties and economic development. In 1948, a global trade regime was formed under the General Agreement on Tariffs and Trade (GATT). GATT was committed to the gradual reduction in the barriers to commerce between its members through a series of trade liberalisation rounds. The United States also drew on its vast economic power and resources to aid its allies in Western Europe with post-war reconstruction in the 1940s. In 1946, Washington provided Britain with a $3.75 billion low interest loan; from 1948 to 1952, the Truman administration provided $13 billion in economic and financial assistance to Western Europe under the European Recovery Program (ERP), known informally as the 'Marshall Plan'. In many ways, American efforts to create a multilateral world economic order were frustrated by the economic weakness of Western Europe and the ensuing cold war with the Soviet Union. By 1949, through careful nurturing by its European allies, Washington had embarked on three major initiatives – the Truman doctrine, the Marshall Plan and NATO – and found itself at the heart of a democratic community of capitalist nations.

Whereas the American economic sphere of influence was characterised by compromise, cooperation and shared mutual interests, the Soviet sphere was organised and managed through coercion. As the war was ending, Stalin turned to his Eastern European neighbours for reparations and bilateral trade agreements. Having extracted war reparations from Romania and Hungary, the Kremlin used barter agreements with the terms of trade tilted in favour of Moscow to obtain raw materials and machinery for economic reconstruction. The Soviet Union eventually signed bilateral barter agreements with several Eastern European countries during the course of 1945–46.[7] Mark Kramer estimates that the net outflow of raw materials, manufactured goods, equipment and machinery to the Soviet Union from Eastern Europe was valued in the region of $15–20 billion in the decade following the end of the Second World War.[8] Bilateral trade and joint stock company ventures supervised by Moscow enabled the Soviet Union to penetrate the economies of the Eastern European states.[9] By the end of the decade, however, Stalin had succeeded in imposing the Soviet command economy model on seven Eastern European nations. These countries were Bulgaria, Poland, Hungary, Albania, Czechoslovakia, Romania and the GDR.

The command economy model had three distinct features. First, the state directed, managed and owned the means of production. Decisions on resource allocation, investment and enterprise were determined solely by the government. Second, national economies were centrally planned; the communist parties set growth targets, allocated resources and monitored progress towards achieving the objectives of five-year plans. Finally, command economies were geared towards registering faster growth rates than their Western capitalist counterparts and central plans focused on the industrial sectors of chemicals, heavy machinery, iron, steel and electronics at the expense of agriculture and consumer goods.[10] How successful was the Soviet economic growth race against the West? Clearly, the growth rates of the command economies were commensurate with and, in some cases, higher than the levels achieved by the Western capitalist countries during the 1950s and 1960s. It has been calculated that by 1970 the combined Soviet and Eastern European centrally planned economies accounted for 30 per cent of world output.[11]

Economic tensions between the United States and the Soviet Union were evident in the immediate aftermath of the Second World War.

Truman refused a request for a $6 billion loan from Moscow in 1946 in response to Stalin's failure to adhere to the Yalta accords and latent expansionism in Eastern Europe.[12] Moscow, moreover, clashed with its wartime allies over the future of Germany. The three Western zones of the country administered by the United States, Britain and France were subsequently merged to form a powerful economic and political unit at the heart of Western Europe. In fact, the Western powers viewed the newly established FRG as the engine room for economic recovery in Western Europe, a key member of NATO from 1955 and a dynamic political force for the integration of the continent. The GDR, by contrast, was ruthlessly exploited by Moscow for raw materials and industrial goods after the war and became a satellite state of the Soviet Union in 1949. The economic cold war, however, broke out over the Marshall Plan. In strategic terms, the ERP was devised by the Truman administration to rehabilitate Europe and build a strong power centre as a bulwark against Soviet expansionism. American policy-makers also believed that the revitalisation of the Western European economies would also deter the rise of indigenous communist parties.[13] The Soviet Union and the Eastern European governments were invited by Washington to participate in the programme. But neither the Soviet Union nor its recently acquired client states were involved in the plan. This was due to two main reasons. First, the virulently anti-communist British and French governments blocked Soviet participation.[14] Stalin, moreover, was not prepared to comply with the conditions required of the recipient countries under the Marshall Plan, which he perceived as foreign interference in Soviet affairs. Even more dramatically, the Kremlin instructed Poland and Czechoslovakia, two Eastern European countries that had traditionally high levels of trade with the West, to withdraw from the ERP and forgo substantial allocations of assistance from the United States.[15] This was a significant event in the division of the continent.

In December 1947, the Truman administration approved restrictions on trade with the Soviet Union and its Eastern European satellites.[16] Washington implemented a strategic embargo on East–West trade through two export control lists – 1-A (strategic items) and 1-B (semi-strategic items) – in the summer of 1948. Governments participating in the ERP were also obliged to prohibit strategic trade and the transfer of technology to the Soviet bloc under the Mundt amendment to the Economic Cooperation Act of 1948. The Mundt amendment empowered the Marshall aid administrator to refuse delivery of goods under the ERP to countries engaged in strategic trade with the Soviet Union and Eastern Europe on the grounds of US national security. President Truman, moreover, ordered the Economic Cooperation Administration (ECA) to negotiate a multilateral strategic embargo with the Western European governments in August 1948.[17] The Soviet response to Washington's curtailment of East–West trade was to tighten Moscow's economic reins on Eastern Europe. In 1949, Stalin established an economic organisation, Comecon, dedicated to promoting trade between the socialist bloc countries.

cocom versus comecon: east–west trade strategies

A considerable body of literature now exists on the formative years of the Western strategic embargo against the Soviet Union and Eastern Europe. Over the past two decades, scholars have drawn upon declassified government documents on both sides of the Atlantic to present an accurate overview of the origins and evolution of the East–West trade group – COCOM – in the 1950s and 1960s.[18] Prior to the availability of archival sources, Gunnar Adler-Karlsson's path-breaking work on Western embargo policy during the cold war concluded that the United States dragged its reluctant allies into an export control programme through economic coercion.[19] Adler-Karlsson's claims have been largely refuted by evidence presented in government documents.[20]

The historiography of COCOM has highlighted three important themes in the making and execution of Western embargo policy against the Soviet bloc. First, the multilateral export control effort was organised primarily by the United States. Washington initially proposed the embargo and, together with Britain, shaped and drove the policy process in COCOM. Second, Washington and its European allies clashed over the content and scope of the embargo. The Americans wanted a comprehensive export control programme composed of strategic and industrial items; the Europeans sought to limit restrictions to trade in exports of high military potential. Finally, recent research has demonstrated the effectiveness of multilateral bargaining in the East–West trade group. Under British leadership, the European members of COCOM succeeded in tailoring the embargo to suit their economic interests and modified American demands for a more stringent export control programme.

The Truman administration looked to Britain for assistance in mobilising Western European support for an international embargo on exports to the Soviet bloc. The Labour government of Clement Attlee supported the strategic aims of the US embargo initiative, but was concerned that an overly restrictive trade policy towards Eastern Europe would deprive Britain of crucial raw material imports and export markets for industrial goods necessary for economic recovery after the Second World War. Other Western European countries shared London's sentiments regarding the benefits of non-strategic East–West trade for economic reconstruction. In fact, the majority of the Organisation for European Economic Cooperation (OEEC) countries were extremely reluctant to engage in what they perceived as economic warfare with the Soviet Union and East Europe. Britain, thus, found itself in an invidious position. On the one hand, London believed that strategic export controls were a necessary tool for waging the cold war; on the other, the Attlee government was keen to expand peaceful commerce with the Eastern European nations as a means of overcoming its chronic balance of payments problem and growing dollar gap with the United States.[21] In 1949, in partnership with France, Britain acted as the rope-bridge between the American and OEEC positions on East–West trade policy. With the formation of COCOM in January 1950, a compromise, facilitated by London and Paris, had been reached on a limited strategic embargo that would prevent technology transfer to the Soviet bloc, but would not impede commercial trade between Western and Eastern Europe.[22]

During 1950–53, relations between the United States and Western Europe in COCOM were characterised by friction and conflict. Although three international lists were created by the membership to administer the strategic embargo, Washington and its allies held fundamentally divergent perspectives over what constituted strategic goods. A particular bone of contention was a category of items termed 'dual-purpose' goods. Dual-purpose items were essentially goods that could be used for both military and commercial means. Whereas the OEEC governments viewed industrial exports as critical for commercial trade with Eastern Europe, the Americans insisted that dual-purpose items could be used by the Soviet Union for military production. As tensions between East and West heightened over the Korean war, the United States managed to secure an agreement with Britain and France to expand the number of industrial goods under embargo in December 1950. Relations in COCOM were strained when the US Congress passed legislation to impose sanctions against American allies violating the East–West trade embargo in October 1951. Truman, however, did not enforce the provisions of the Battle Act – which gave him discretionary power to suspend shipments of military aid to countries deemed to have exported strategic or dual-purpose goods to the Soviet bloc – and granted executive waivers to key American allies. Truman believed that suspending assistance would be counterproductive and only drive a wedge between the NATO governments, weakening mutual security.[23]

In August 1954, a major review of the international export control lists was undertaken in COCOM. The membership agreed to reduce by half the number of items under embargo in East–West trade. What accounts for this sudden change in policy? Historians have long debated the rationale behind the 1954 relaxation of the embargo. In particular, a debate materialised over President Dwight D. Eisenhower's role in pushing for the liberalisation of East–West trade.[24] The available evidence suggests that while Eisenhower was highly influential in the decision to relax the embargo, Churchill carefully prodded him in the direction of East–West trade liberalisation.[25] The embargo review was aimed chiefly at dual-purpose items and goods deemed to no longer have military or technological value to the Soviet Union. The strategic nature of the export control programme was retained, however, as the West prepared for the 'long haul': a period of tension short of conflict with Moscow.

The Europeans were not wholly satisfied with the August 1954 international export control list revisions. They continued to press the Eisenhower administration for a further relaxation of the embargo, especially with regard to restrictions on trade with the PRC. Since 1951, COCOM had maintained a more restrictive list of exports under control in trade with Beijing. Eisenhower, however, was reluctant to bring the China List into line with its Soviet counterpart given domestic hostility to trade with the PRC in the United States in the aftermath of the Korean conflict. Yet the British, French and Japanese governments, driven by commercial interests in the East Asian region, pushed for the abolition of the so-called 'China differential' during 1955–57. Washington, nevertheless, stonewalled their efforts. In May 1957, under increasing domestic pressure from parliament and the business community, the British Prime Minister, Harold Macmillan, unilaterally ended the 'China differential' by removing controls on the items on the China List. France and Japan immediately followed the UK's example. As a result, while the Europeans and Japan applied a similar list of restrictions in trade with the PRC and Soviet bloc, Washington's national embargo against Beijing was more severe than its Soviet bloc counterpart.[26] In the late 1950s and early 1960s, Britain began to question the role of COCOM in East–West trade. Privately, Macmillan called the continuing existence of the East–West trade group 'absurd'.[27] British negotiators in COCOM challenged the maintenance of export controls on technology that the Soviet Union had managed to acquire from other sources. They argued that in the era of *Sputnik* a strategic embargo on military and technological know-how was anachronistic.[28]

In contrast to COCOM, there is a dearth of archive-based accounts of Comecon. This is perhaps due to limited access to declassified documents in the former member states. Notwithstanding the lack of primary source material about Comecon, political scientists and economists have generated a sizeable literature on the group's strengths, shortcomings and various activities. Like COCOM, Comecon was a product of the economic cold war. It was created in January 1949 at the height of the East–West confrontation.[29] The initial membership consisted of the Soviet Union, Czechoslovakia, Poland, Hungary and Bulgaria. Albania joined in February; the GDR became a member of Comecon in 1950. The main objectives of Comecon were economic cooperation, technical and mutual assistance between a collective of socialist governments with planned domestic economies.[30] There has been considerable discussion in the literature as to the motivations behind Stalin's decision to create Comecon. For a number of scholars, the regime was an economic vehicle for consolidating the Kremlin's hold over its Eastern European satellites.[31] Still, others have argued that Moscow genuinely wanted to build an organisation to facilitate commercial contact between socialist states. The very nature of the planned economic process made trade between the Eastern European governments difficult. Comecon would therefore provide a framework for overcoming the obstacles of domestic protectionism and currency inconvertibility.[32] It has also been suggested that Comecon was formed in response to Western export controls on East–West trade. The formation of COCOM not only led to the disruption of historic trading links between Western and Eastern Europe, but also drove the socialist governments more firmly into the Soviet orbit. Comecon, therefore, can be viewed as a declaration of solidarity by the Eastern European governments against NATO in the emerging cold war conflict.[33]

During the course of the formative meetings of Comecon, the membership explored the possibility of creating a regional economic organisation. Delegates from the member states discussed strategies for developing a common economic plan for Eastern Europe that would increase growth and productivity and improve living standards in the member states. Yet, in the early 1950s, these efforts were frustrated by Stalin's determination to maintain an iron grip on his newly acquired sphere of influence. The Soviet leader was convinced that an autonomous organisation with supranational aspirations would constrain his ability to control the Eastern European governments. Such an organisation, he feared, could eventually act as a regional counterweight to Soviet economic power. Comecon, as a result, did not function as a mutual assistance regime during 1949–53. Instead, trade between the member governments was closely monitored and managed by Moscow through a series of bilateral agreements between the Soviet Union and its satellites.

As Adam Ulam has pointed out, Stalin basically used Comecon as a 'new piece of machinery for milking the satellites' for raw materials and machinery for Soviet industrial, agricultural and military production.[34]

It was only after Stalin's death in March 1953 that Comecon began to realise the objectives of the founding members.[35] After the Soviet invasion of Hungary in November 1956, General Secretary Nikita Khrushchev reconstituted Comecon with the goal of fostering higher standards of living in the member states and economic interdependence in the region. Significantly, the Moscow Declaration of 1957 committed the Comecon governments to a closer relationship with each other based on mutual respect, economic equality and recognition of national sovereignty. Undoubtedly, Comecon's golden era occurred in 1958–61. During a series of council sessions in 1957–58, the membership unveiled the 'transferable rouble' as a monetary device for overcoming the problem of currency inconvertibility in intra-Comecon trade. This initiative was followed with the inauguration of a goods pricing system in the CMEA designed to protect and insulate member governments from the vagaries of world market fluctuations. The most important development in the ten-year history of the CMEA was the Comecon Charter of December 1959, which committed the regime to the establishment of an 'international socialist division of labour'.[36]

In December 1961, Comecon released the 'Basic Principles of International Socialist Division of Labour'. The 'Basic Principles' called for the concentration of production processes in individual member states: some governments would focus on agricultural production, while others would specialise in industrialisation. To this end, it was hoped that the combined efforts of the members would ensure maximum growth in the agricultural and industrial sectors, raising living standards and increasing economic growth in the region. In the aftermath of the Berlin crisis, Khrushchev was keen to draw on specialisation in Comecon to bolster the GDR and create an economic rival to the FRG.[37] The Soviet leader proposed the establishment of a 'single planning organ' in November 1962 to facilitate the specialisation process. Khrushchev's attempts to transform Comecon into a supranational economic community, however, were thwarted by rising nationalist sentiment in Romania. The Romanian government believed that socialist economic integration was a direct threat to national sovereignty. The Romanians argued that the states themselves should reserve the right to select and organise national economic activities. While the integration project was shelved in the early 1960s, Comecon remained an important regional economic body in Eastern Europe during the 1960s. The bulk of foreign trade in the region was concentrated between the Comecon membership and new standing committees and joint ventures enhanced economic interdependence between the Soviet Union and Eastern Europe.

Why did the integration project fail? Three reasons account for the inability of Comecon to transform itself from a mutual assistance body into a supranational economic community. First, the socialist planning process, which was a key function of the state, proved a major obstacle to multilateral trade. The diverse planning apparatuses of the Comecon membership could only have been merged through either the adoption of market mechanisms or economic integration imposed by Moscow.[38] Second, Comecon acquired new members in the 1960s and 1970s including Mongolia, Cuba and Vietnam. The fact that these countries were geographically excluded from the Eastern European region made full integration in Comecon impossible. Even within Eastern Europe there remained huge disparities in terms of economic development, not least between the Soviet Union and its satellites. Finally, in the 1960s, many of the Comecon governments began to expand commercial contacts with Western countries as the international strategic situation improved and COCOM relaxed its restrictions on East–West trade. The Eastern European countries found that they could import consumer goods and high quality technology from the West that were essential for alleviating bottlenecks in their economies.

the rise and fall of economic *détente*

After Khrushchev's ouster from power in 1964, the new Soviet leadership continued to pursue peaceful co-existence with the West. There was general recognition within the *Politburo* that military confrontation with the United States should be avoided at all cost. Brezhnev favoured the traditional approach to Soviet foreign policy, which called for high levels of expenditure on defence and military production. The Soviet Premier, Alexei Kosygin, desisted from endorsing Brezhnev's policy and argued that the Soviet economy was lagging behind its Western counterparts in terms of technological innovation.[39] In Kosygin's view, the Soviet Union's deficiency in advanced technology could only be addressed through commercial contact with the Western states. Significantly, the annual growth rate of the Soviet economy had slipped from as high as 10 per cent in the 1950s to a figure of 5 per cent in the mid-1960s. Kosygin believed that transfers of Western technology could eliminate bottlenecks in the economy, expand growth and production levels and reverse Soviet economic decline.[40]

In the late 1960s, however, Brezhnev changed his mind. During a speech to the Twenty-fourth Party Congress in March 1971, the Soviet leader explained the motivations behind his decision to embark on a campaign to increase commercial contact with the Western capitalist countries. The so-called 'Peace Programme' announcement envisaged an improvement in political relations between Moscow and the West. As well as expanding foreign trade, Brezhnev indicated that the Soviet leadership was prepared to explore with the United States ways of slowing down the nuclear arms race.[41] This dramatic change in Brezhnev's thinking appears to have been motivated primarily by two factors. First, he desired to ensure the long-term economic and political survival of the Soviet Union. The procurement of Western technology, he thought, would allow for the modernisation of Soviet industry without wholesale domestic economic reform. International arms control, moreover, would improve the strategic climate of East–West relations and bolster Soviet national security. Second, *détente* with the United States would enable Moscow to gain international recognition for the Soviet Union's status as a superpower and its domination over Eastern Europe.[42]

Meanwhile, in the United States, Nixon and his national security adviser, Henry Kissinger, were disinclined to relax the strategic embargo.[43] Although both men recognised that the realities of American economic decline and parity in the nuclear arms race necessitated a more constructive relationship with Moscow, they viewed East–West trade as a strategic tool that could be used to extract concessions from the Soviet leadership. Given the Soviet leadership's desire for greater commercial contact with the West, Nixon and Kissinger viewed trade as a bargaining chip that could be exchanged for a lessening of cold war tensions, more restrained Soviet behaviour in the Third World and arms control negotiations.

East–West trade was discussed at the National Security Council (NSC) meeting of 21 May 1969. Nixon reaffirmed his opinion that trade liberalisation with the Soviet Union could only be linked to political concessions from Moscow. He discounted the argument that increased commerce between the two countries could be the basis of transforming the political situation in East–West relations.[44] In a directive following the NSC meeting, Nixon declared that the United States would only relax its strategic embargo against Moscow 'whenever there is sufficient improvement in our overall relations' with the Kremlin.[45] The Export Administration Act, which replaced the Export Control Act of 1949, granted the executive branch authority to fundamentally transform East–West economic relations and liberalise trade with the Soviet bloc. Yet, under Nixon's new directive, there was to be no change in US export control policy and Washington would prohibit the shipment of items 'contributing significantly to the military supporting industrial capability of the USSR and Eastern Europe regardless of foreign availability'.[46]

Nixon remained resolute in his determination to use trade as a bargaining lever with the Soviet leadership. He decided to 'defer any decision on new Administration initiatives to liberalise US trade policy towards the Communist Countries'. Nixon, furthermore, ordered that efforts by Congress to expand commerce with the Soviet bloc should be 'opposed only in a very low key way'.[47] The new US export control policy proved to be a remarkable reversal of the approach taken by preceding administrations. While Presidents Kennedy and Johnson had pushed Congress for trade liberalisation with the Soviet Union, the Nixon administration appeared to want to block efforts by the legislative branch to expand commerce with the communist nations. Nixon, furthermore, ignored American multilateral obligations in COCOM. Now that East–West economic relations had been designated an issue of high politics by the Nixon administration, Washington tended to operate independently of the multilateral regime on matters of trade and technology transfer. Nixon's unilateralism and failure to consult with the COCOM membership not only weakened the effectiveness of the international embargo, but also created tensions between the United States and its allies.

In a meeting with President Nixon on 29 September 1971, the Soviet Foreign Minister, Andrei Gromyko, signalled the Kremlin's interest in discussing East–West trade with the United States. Nixon told Gromyko that once the Vietnam war began to wind down 'all sorts of doors would be open' and Washington would be in a position to explore a commercial relationship with the Soviet Union. He did not give the Soviet foreign minister any assurances, but agreed to send Secretary of Commerce Maurice Stans to Moscow for informal talks with Prime Minister Kosygin.[48] Stans' discussions with Soviet officials revealed enthusiasm for Most Favoured Nation (MFN) status, bank credits, a relaxation of the US embargo and a joint agreement on scientific and technological cooperation. Nixon's reaction, though, was predictably cautious. He told the secretary of commerce that it remained imperative that the US 'attitude with respect to increasing trade with the Soviet Union be governed completely by the state of our political relations'. In short, Nixon would only consider the economic aspects of *détente* if the Soviet Union would play its part in lessening tensions in South-East Asia.[49]

The Stans visit did mark a significant change in Nixon's approach to East–West trade. During the Moscow summit in May 1972, Nixon and Brezhnev exchanged views on the possibilities of developing commercial trade contact between the two countries. Although the communiqué of the summit did not reveal any specific initiatives in the economic sphere, Nixon was receptive to further talks between American and Soviet officials on the issues of lend-lease debt, MFN status, bank credits and a possible trade agreement in the event that progress was made on arms control and Soviet restraint in South Asia. The communiqué committed the two leaders to establish a US–USSR Commercial Commission to deal specifically with East–West trade negotiations. After the Commission met in the summer, a trade agreement was signed on 18 October. The agreement conferred MFN status on Moscow, committed the two countries to $2.5 billion in bilateral trade over three years, provided for a lend-lease settlement of $722 million; and Export-Import Bank credits to the Soviet Union. This was undoubtedly the high point of economic *détente* in the early 1970s.[50] The superpower negotiations also fostered an improved international strategic situation, one of the political concessions Nixon's strategy of trade linkage strove to exact from the Soviets. Brezhnev, for his part, had gained access to advanced-industrial technology, consumer goods and bank credits that would assist in the modernisation and development of the Soviet economy.

In 1972–73, Washington and Moscow achieved major breakthroughs in arms control and the expansion of bilateral trade. There was also progress for Nixon in US relations with China. Rapprochement with Beijing paved the way for the removal of trade restrictions with the PRC.[51] But as trade increased with the communist countries, especially the Soviet Union, critics of Nixon's foreign policy began to question the merits of East–West trade liberalisation from a security standpoint. In March 1973, Senator Henry M. Jackson introduced an amendment to the Trade Reform Act, which contained the legislation required to approve the US–USSR trade agreement of October 1972, linking MFN to a more liberal Soviet policy towards Jewish emigration. Congressman Charles Vanik proposed a similar amendment in the House of Representatives further marring relations between the White House and Capitol Hill during 1973. The House subsequently passed the Jackson–Vanik amendment in December, much to the chagrin of Nixon and Kissinger.[52]

Evidently, Jackson and Vanik were using the issue of Jewish emigration to attack the Nixon administration's *détente* policy. Matters were complicated by an amendment sponsored by Adlai E. Stevenson III in the Senate in June 1974 to limit the amount of credit the Export-Import Bank could grant Moscow. Brezhnev and the *Politburo* were incensed by this development, as the Soviet Union, short of hard currency, required credits to trade with the West. The Jackson–Vanik amendment, nevertheless, produced a change in Soviet policy and Jewish emigration rose from 400 in 1968 to 35,000 in 1973. This did not satisfy Jackson's demands for a figure in the region of 60,000. As the Trade Reform bill threatened to derail *détente*, Kissinger managed to strike an agreement with Jackson on 18 October 1974. The outcome was a victory for the hawkish critics of *détente* in Washington. The bill was eventually passed in the Senate on 13 December with the Jackson–Vanik amendment; the new president, Gerald Ford, had no alternative but to sign the Trade Reform Act into law on 3 January 1975. This was the final straw for Brezhnev. On 13 January, the Kremlin announced that it was abrogating the October 1972 trade agreement with the United States.[53] Moscow's decision to pull out of the trade agreement sounded the death knell for economic *détente* and completely discredited Nixon and Kissinger's strategy of trade linkage domestically.

the role of economic factors in ending the cold war

Despite the limited availability of declassified government documents, much has been written about the renewed economic confrontation between the United States and the Soviet Union from 1979 to 1983. The literature has reached the following conclusions. First, the Carter and Reagan administrations reversed COCOM's commitment to the liberalisation of East–West trade embargo and reintroduced wide-ranging export restrictions along the lines of the strategic embargo that was implemented by the Truman administration. Second, relations between Washington and its allies deteriorated markedly in COCOM. During 1981–82, there was a palpable rift between the United States and leading Western European governments over the East–West trade embargo that had never been experienced throughout COCOM's 30-year history. Finally, American efforts to use the strategic embargo as an economic weapon against the Soviet Union were rendered ineffectual not only because of friction in COCOM, but also the Kremlin's success in circumventing the Western export control programme.

The Carter administration was deeply divided over the issue of East–West trade. Both the State and Commerce Departments pressed for an expansion in commercial trade with the Soviet Union and Eastern Europe. On the contrary, National Security Adviser Zbigniew Brzezinski and Secretary of Energy James Schlesinger believed that stricter controls were required on dual-purpose technology goods to the Soviet bloc. During 1977–78, the president sided with the more moderate position of Secretary of State Cyrus Vance and Secretary of Commerce Juanita Kreps, and adopted a policy of trade linkage towards Moscow. In return for Soviet restraint in the Third World and a respect for human rights, Carter offered Brezhnev increased commercial opportunities with the United States.[54] The president, however, abruptly shifted policy in December 1979 when the Soviet Union invaded Afghanistan. On 4 January 1980, Carter dented hopes for a more productive American–Soviet commercial relationship by tightening export controls on high technology, suspending grain shipments and calling for an international boycott of the Olympic games to be held in Moscow later in the year.[55]

Yet Carter miscalculated the response of American allies to the Soviet invasion of Afghanistan. Anxious to maintain East–West *détente*, the Western European governments were extremely reluctant to implement economic sanctions or intensify trade controls on trade with the Soviet Union.[56] The Carter administration's grain embargo was essentially a unilateral exercise that was costly to Washington from an economic and political standpoint. In economic terms, American–Soviet trade was reduced from $4.8 billion to $1.5 billion during the period the grain embargo was in force. This caused hardship among the American farming community and accentuated the US balance of payments deficit at a time when the domestic economy was in a deep malaise. Politically, the grain embargo increased Carter's unpopularity during an election year and, undoubtedly, alienated voters living in rural areas. What was more, Moscow was largely successful in accounting for the shortfall to its grain imports as a result of the American embargo. Defying Washington, Argentina, Australia and Canada willingly supplied the Soviet Union with millions of metric tons of grain.[57]

The Carter administration's experience with the grain embargo should have been a warning to Reagan regarding the futility of economic sanctions against the Soviet Union. Reagan, who had opposed the grain embargo, lifted the sanctions against Moscow in April 1981. In July, however, strongly influenced by the hard-line Defense Department, he began to pursue a more restrictive East–West trade policy, as part of an overall strategy of confrontation with Moscow. The Pentagon was convinced of the utility of strategic export controls as both a means of preventing the Kremlin from acquiring high-technology goods for military purposes and further weakening through trade denial the declining Soviet economy.[58] After martial law was imposed in Poland in December, Reagan implemented economic sanctions not only against the ruling regime in Warsaw, but also against the Soviet Union. The sanctions chiefly entailed the suspension of negotiations on a new grain agreement and the cancellation of export licences for high-technology goods destined for the Soviet bloc. There was much opposition to the sanctions in Western Europe and Japan. In a deal worth $10–15 billion, Western European firms had agreed to supply the Soviet Union with machinery and raw materials for the construction of a 5,000 km natural gas pipeline from Siberia to Ireland that would assist in supplying the continent's energy requirements for the next two decades.[59] The American sanctions therefore threatened to undermine the venture. Although Reagan did not manage to secure Western European support for the sanctions against Poland, the United States extended the COCOM embargo to incorporate critical technologies, computers and semi-conductors. The Reagan administration, moreover, was divided over the issue. Secretary of Defense Caspar Weinberger urged the president to widen the scope of the sanctions to the subsidiaries of American corporations and licensees in Western Europe. Secretary of State Alexander Haig, by contrast, wanted to avoid conflict with the Europeans and Japanese over East–West trade, which he argued would cause disunity in the Western alliance.

During a meeting of the advanced industrial countries in Versailles in June, Reagan attempted to bargain with his allies for tighter sanctions against the Soviet Union. In exchange for a multilateral agreement to limit export credits to Moscow, the pipeline project would not be subject to export controls. The Western Europeans, nevertheless, refused to accept Reagan's deal. In retaliation, the president announced on 18 June that the subsidiaries of American corporations based in Europe would now be subject to the December 1981 sanctions.[60] Reagan's action provoked outrage among Western European leaders; even the president's closest ally, Margaret Thatcher, denounced Reagan's resort to economic coercion as a clumsy attempt to press the Europeans to toe the American line. Ultimately, Reagan realised that Western disharmony was too high a price to pay for multilateral restrictions on trade credits to the Soviet Union. Having listened to more moderate voices in the administration, including the new Secretary of State, George Shultz, the president removed the economic sanctions on 13 November. The Western European governments did agree to more stringent East–West trade controls covering gas and oil technology, the standardisation and management of export credits, preferential assistance to the heavily militarised Soviet economy and an extension to the COCOM embargo.[61] But notwithstanding these European concessions, Reagan discovered the limitations of economic sanctions against the Soviet Union. While a more restrictive embargo did weaken the Soviet economy and prevent Moscow from obtaining dual-purpose high technologies, cold war export controls continued to be a source of friction in the Atlantic alliance.

By the early 1980s, the Soviet economy was in a parlous state. Annual growth levels fell from 5 per cent in the 1960s to 1.9 per cent during 1981–85. In 1986, Gorbachev proclaimed that the 'acceleration of the country's socio-economic development is the key to all our problems'.[62] He realised that in order to halt economic decline the Kremlin had to negotiate an end to the cold war. As well as *perestroika*, which involved restructuring of the domestic economy, Gorbachev sought to pursue *détente* with the United States and expand trade contacts with the Western industrial nations. According to Dale C. Copeland, Gorbachev's external strategy for stabilising the Soviet economy was informed by three objectives. First, the Soviet leader wanted to end the arms race with Washington. If an agreement on arms control could be concluded with the Reagan administration, Gorbachev hoped to significantly reduce military expenditure, which was running at a rate of about 20 per cent of Soviet GNP at the beginning of the decade. Second, Gorbachev was determined to convince Reagan not to proceed with the Strategic Defense Initiative (SDI). The Kremlin was anxious not to have to commit scarce capital resources to building a counterpart to the American space-based missile defence system. Finally, as the 'second cold war' began to thaw, Gorbachev began to urge the American president to relax restrictions on East–West trade and export credits to the Soviet Union. In similar vein to Kosygin in the mid-1960s, Gorbachev recognised the benefits of Western technology transfer for Soviet scientific and industrial development.[63]

The Eastern European countries also began to experience economic problems in the late 1970s and early 1980s. These problems were caused chiefly by indebtedness to Western banks and economic reliance on the Soviet Union. With regard to the former, Eastern European governments had borrowed heavily to fund trade and technology transfer from the Western industrial countries.[64] The governments blamed their economic plight on the failure of Comecon and Moscow's increasing exploitation of their resources. A considerable source of acrimony was the Kremlin's insistence in 1978 that the Eastern European members of Comecon increase their defence expenditure by 5 per cent. By and large the Eastern Europeans were opposed to Soviet militarisation during 1979–83 and welcomed the resumption of arms control talks between Washington and Moscow under Gorbachev. Some countries attempted to build economic bridges to the West. Hungary, for example, joined the IMF and World Bank in 1982.[65] Despite their indebtedness, the Eastern European governments oriented their economic strategy towards regional and international trade. An organisation in decline, Comecon ceased to be a major source of trade for its membership when the Soviet Union allowed the organisation to sign a reciprocal recognition agreement with the EEC in July 1985. Unwittingly, Comecon's demise was hastened by the negotiation of a series of trade agreements between the EEC and individual Comecon members. As Moscow released its political grip on the Warsaw Pact countries in July 1989, Hungary, Poland, Czechoslovakia, Romania and Bulgaria signed bilateral trade agreements with the European Commission.[66]

The signature of the INF Treaty in September 1987 proved to be the catalyst for a gradual expansion of East–West trade. Reassured by Gorbachev's commitment to arms control, the Reagan administration approved the removal of a number of highly significant dual-purpose items from the international embargo lists at a meeting of COCOM in January 1988. These items included exports related to computers and telecommunications equipment, goods that Washington had heretofore insisted should remain under control despite the protests of Japan and the Western European governments.[67] Gorbachev responded by withdrawing Soviet troops from Afghanistan and declaring Moscow's intention to participate actively in the world economy. While further restrictions on East–West trade were relaxed, it was apparent that the Soviet president had set his sights on achieving MFN status from the US Congress. MFN status for the Soviet Union, it will be recalled, was a victim of the fallout from the Jackson–Vanik amendment to the Trade Reform Act of 1975. In December 1989, Gorbachev pressed the new president, George H. W. Bush, for normalised trading relations between the United States and Soviet Union as part of a new post-cold war agenda for the superpowers.[68] At the Washington summit of April 1990, which prepared the ground for German reunification, the Soviet president told Bush that he could not return to Moscow without the economic benefits that would accrue from MFN status.[69] In less than a decade, American–Soviet relations were transformed from economic confrontation to cooperation. By the early 1990s, as the Soviet Union teetered on the brink of political and economic collapse, Gorbachev looked to the Kremlin's former adversaries for financial assistance and moral support.

conclusions

Economic factors played a critical role in the cold war. The East–West confrontation was caused by the divergent perspectives of world economic order held by the United States and the Soviet Union. Both powers strove to preserve and promote their economic and political systems within two ideologically opposed spheres of influence established in the aftermath of the Second World War. Washington and Moscow, moreover, devised and mobilised trade-based economic organisations during the formative years of the cold war. The US-led COCOM regime sought to restrict strategic trade and technology transfer to the Soviet bloc and the PRC. Comecon enabled the Kremlin to dominate the foreign commerce of its satellite states in Eastern Europe and access a ready source of raw materials for industrial and military production together with a marketplace for Soviet goods.

As East–West tensions eased in the late 1960s and early 1970s, the United States and the Soviet Union explored the possibility of increasing trade between the two blocs. This trade was perceived as beneficial to the West in terms of improving the strategic climate and crucial to the Warsaw Pact countries as a means of obtaining advanced technology to arrest the decline of the socialist centrally planned economies. While the Soviet invasion of Afghanistan triggered a new round of confrontation between Washington and Moscow in 1979, pressure on the Reagan administration from its Western allies and the assumption of power in the Kremlin by Gorbachev in 1985 were instrumental in the strategic shift from East–West economic conflict to cooperation. It is one of history's great ironies that the cold war ended and the Soviet Union collapsed not because of Western economic pressure in the form of trade denial and sanctions, but because of the failure of the centrally planned economic model and Gorbachev's unsuccessful attempt to integrate the Soviet command economy into the capitalist world system.

notes

1. Thomas J. McCormick, *America's Half-Century: United States Foreign Policy during the Cold War* (Baltimore, MD: Johns Hopkins University Press, 1989).
2. Diane B. Kunz, *Butter and Guns: America's Cold War Economic Diplomacy* (New York: Free Press, 1997)
3. The most influential corporatist work remains Michael J. Hogan, *The Marshall Plan: America, Britain and the Reconstruction of Western Europe, 1947–1952* (Cambridge: Cambridge University Press, 1987).
4. For three excellent recent examples stressing the intersection of economics and security during the cold war see Erin Mahan, *Kennedy, De Gaulle and Western Europe* (Basingstoke: Palgrave Macmillan, 2002); Hubert Zimmermann, *Money and Security: Troops, Monetary Policy and West Germany's Relations with the United States and Britain, 1950–1971* (Cambridge: Cambridge University Press, 2002); and Francis J. Gavin, *Gold, Dollars and Power: The Politics of International Monetary Relations, 1958–1971* (Chapel Hill, NC: University of North Carolina Press, 2004).
5. Thomas G. Paterson, *The Making and Unmaking of the Cold War* (New York: Norton, 1993), p.29.

6. John Lewis Gaddis, *We Now Know: Rethinking Cold War History* (Oxford: Oxford University Press, 1997), pp.28–39.
7. Thomas G. Paterson, *Soviet–American Confrontation* (Baltimore, MD: Johns Hopkins University Press, 1973), pp.102–5.
8. Mark Kramer, 'The Soviet Union and Eastern Europe', in Ngaire Woods (ed.), *International Relations since 1945* (Oxford: Oxford University Press, 1996), pp.111–12.
9. Robert A. Pollard, *The Economic Security Origins of the Cold War* (New York: Columbia University Press, 1985), p.36.
10. Philip Hanson, 'The Soviet Union', in Andrew Graham with Anthony Seldon (eds), *Government and Economies in the Postwar World: Economic Policies and Comparative Performance, 1945–85* (London: Routledge, 1990), pp.205–11.
11. Derek Aldcroft & Steven Moorewood, *Economic Change in Eastern Europe since 1918* (London: Edward Elgar, 1995), p.125.
12. Philip J. Funigiello, *American–Soviet Trade in the Cold War* (Chapel Hill, NC: University of North Carolina Press, 1988), pp.17–23.
13. Hogan, *The Marshall Plan*, pp.26–8 and 430–43.
14. David Reynolds, *Britannia Overruled: British Policy and World Power in the 20th Century* (London: Longman, 1991), p.175.
15. Robert Bideleux & Ian Jeffries, *A History of Eastern Europe: Crisis and Change* (London: Routledge, 1998), p.534.
16. 'Report by the National Security Council on the Control of Exports to the Soviet Union and Eastern Europe', 17.12.47, *FRUS 1948: IV*, p.512.
17. Telegram from Acheson to Certain Diplomatic Posts, 12.1.50, *FRUS 1950: IV*, p.147.
18. See Alan P. Dobson, *US Economic Statecraft for Survival 1933–1991: Of Sanctions, Embargoes and Economic Warfare* (London: Routledge, 2002); Ian Jackson, *The Economic Cold War: America, Britain and East–West Trade 1948–1963* (Basingstoke: Palgrave Macmillan, 2001), *passim*; and Michael Mastanduno, *Economic Containment: COCOM and the Politics of East–West Trade* (Ithaca, NY: Cornell University Press, 1992).
19. Gunnar Adler-Karlsson, *Western Economic Warfare, 1947–67: A Case Study in Foreign Economic Policy* (Stockholm: Almquist and Wiksell, 1968).
20. Jackson, *Economic Cold War*, pp.2–3.
21. Telegram from Gore-Booth, Foreign Office, to Coulson, UK Delegation to the OEEC, 25.1.49, UR727/45/48, FO371/77789(TNA).
22. Bent Boel, 'La France, les États Unis et la politique occidentale d'embargo, 1948–54', *Revue d'Histoire Diplomatique*, 1 (2001), pp.36–40; Ian Jackson, '"Rival Desirabilities": Britain, East–West Trade and the Cold War, 1948–51', *European History Quarterly*, 31:2 (2001), pp.270–4.
23. Jackson, *Economic Cold War*, pp.58–110.
24. Tor Egil Førland, '"Selling Firearms to the Indians": Eisenhower's Export Control Policy, 1953–54', *Diplomatic History*, 15 (1991), pp.221–44; Robert Mark Spaulding, '"A Gradual and Moderate Relaxation": Eisenhower and the Revision of American Export Control Policy, 1953–55', *Diplomatic History*, 17 (1993), pp.223–49.
25. John W. Young, 'Winston Churchill's Peacetime Administration and the Relaxation of East–West Trade Controls, 1953–54', *Diplomacy and Statecraft*, 7 (March), pp.425–48.

26. Shu Guang Zhang, *Economic Cold War: America's Embargo against China and the Sino-Soviet Alliance, 1949–1963* (Stanford, CA: Stanford University Press, 2001), pp.174–203.
27. Minute from Macmillan to Home, 9.2.62, UUE 10419/02, FO371/164505(TNA).
28. Outline of Foreign Office contribution to brief on Anglo-American talks on strategic controls, 10.5.61, M341/24, FO371/158074(TNA). Briefing Paper for Home, 30.6.61, M341/39, FO371/158074(TNA).
29. William V. Wallace & Roger A. Clarke, *Comecon, Trade and the West* (London: Pinter, 1986), pp.1–3.
30. Henry Wilcox Schaefer, *Comecon and the Politics of Integration* (New York: Praeger, 1972), pp.1–6.
31. Kramer, 'Soviet Union and Eastern Europe', p.112.
32. Josef M. van Brabant, *Socialist Economic Integration* (Cambridge: Cambridge University Press, 1980), pp.19–20.
33. Josef M. van Brabant, *Economic Integration in Eastern Europe* (London: Harvester Wheatsheaf, 1989), p.18.
34. Adam Ulam, *Expansion and Coexistence: Soviet Foreign Policy, 1917–1973* (New York: Holt, Rinehart & Winston, 1974), p.437.
35. Raymond Pearson, *The Rise and Fall of the Soviet Empire* (London: Macmillan, 1998), p.61.
36. Bideleux & Jeffries, *History of Eastern Europe*, pp.543–4.
37. R.J. Crampton, *Eastern Europe in the Twentieth Century* (London: Routledge, 1994), p.308.
38. János Kornai, *The Socialist System: The Political Economy of Socialism* (Oxford: Oxford University Press, 1992), pp.356–7.
39. Bruce Parrott, *Politics and Technology in the Soviet Union* (Cambridge, MA: MIT Press, 1983), pp.231–47.
40. Robin Edmonds, *Soviet Foreign Policy: The Brezhnev Years* (Oxford: Oxford University Press, 1983), pp.81–2.
41. Dale C. Copeland, 'Trade Expectations and the Outbreak of Peace: Détente 1970–74 and the End of the Cold War 1985–1991', in Jean-Mac F. Blanchard, Edward D. Mansfield & Norrin M. Ripsman (eds), *Power and the Purse: Economic Statecraft, Interdependence and National Security* (London: Frank Cass, 2000), pp.28–9.
42. Mike Bowker, 'Brezhnev and Superpower Relations', in Edwin Bacon and Mark Sandle (eds), *Brezhnev Reconsidered* (Basingstoke: Palgrave Macmillan, 2002), pp.91–2.
43. Henry Kissinger, *White House Years* (London: Phoenix Press edition, 2000), pp.151–3.
44. Dobson, *US Economic Statecraft for Survival*, pp.198–9.
45. 'National Security Decision Memorandum 15', 28.5.69, *FRUS 1969–76: IV*, pp.784–5.
46. Memorandum from Kissinger to Rogers, Laird and Stans, 23.4.70, *FRUS 1969–76: IV*, p.819.
47. 'National Security Decision Memorandum 99', 1.3.70, *FRUS 1969–76: IV*, p.840.
48. Editorial Note, *FRUS 1969–76: IV*, pp.877–8.

49. Memorandum of meeting between Stans and President Nixon, undated, *FRUS 1969–76: IV*, pp.887–9.
50. Raymond Garthoff, *Détente and Confrontation: American–Soviet Relations from Nixon to Reagan* (Washington, DC: Brookings, 1994), pp.342–6.
51. 'National Security Decision Memorandum 155', 17 February 1972, *FRUS 1969–76: IV*, p.357.
52. Richard W. Stevenson, *The Rise and Fall of Détente* (London: Macmillan, 1985), pp.161–2.
53. Garthoff, *Détente and Confrontation*, pp.506–12.
54. Funigiello, *American–Soviet Trade*, pp.190–2.
55. Dobson, *US Economic Statecraft*, pp.254–5.
56. Zbigniew Brzezinski, *Power and Principle: The Memoirs of the National Security Advisor, 1977–81* (New York: Farrar, Strauss & Giroux, 1985), pp.433–4.
57. Funigiello, *American–Soviet Trade*, p.193.
58. Mastanduno, *Economic Containment*, pp.236–8.
59. Bruce W. Jentleson, 'From Consensus to Conflict: The Domestic Political Economy of East–West Energy Trade Policy', *International Organization*, 38:4 (1984), pp.651–2.
60. Beverly Crawford, 'Western Control of East–West Trade Finance: The Role of US Power and the International Regime', in Gary K. Bertsch (ed.), *Controlling East–West Trade and Technology Transfer: Power, Politics, and Policies* (Durham, NC: Duke University Press, 1988), p.307.
61. Bruce W. Jentleson, 'The Western Alliance and East–West Energy Trade', in Bertsch (ed.), *Controlling East–West Trade*, pp.332–3.
62. Paterson, *Making and Unmaking of the Cold War*, pp.203–5.
63. Copeland, 'Trade Expectations and the Outbreak of Peace', pp.43–4.
64. Valerie Bunce, 'The Empire Strikes Back: The Evolution of the Eastern Bloc from a Soviet Asset to a Soviet Liability', *International Organization*, 39:1 (1985), pp.38–41.
65. Wallace and Clarke, *Comecon, Trade and the West*, pp.33–5.
66. Bideleux and Jeffries, *History of Eastern Europe*, pp.580–1; Anders Åslund, *Gorbachev's Struggle for Economic Reform* (London: Pinter, 1991, revised edition), pp.143–5.
67. Mastanduno, *Economic Containment*, pp.306–7.
68. George Bush and Brent Scowcroft, *A World Transformed* (New York: Knopf, 1998), p.227.
69. James A. Baker III with Thomas M. DeFrank, *The Politics of Diplomacy: Revolution, War and Peace* (New York: Putnam, 1995), p.254.

7
science and technology
christoph bluth

Following on from the Second World War, the cold war period was one of unprecedented progress in military technology. As Freedman and Hughes have noted, following the development of the first nuclear fission device entire new fields of science and engineering formed the basis of hitherto unimaginable military capabilities that provided the capacity to destroy virtually all life on earth in a very short period of time. The scale and the rapidity of technical developments, involving such fields as nuclear energy, advanced fuel technology, space research, inertial guidance, computers and electronics, aeronautics, radar technology, communications, optics, to mention but a few, required scientific and technical efforts on a national scale, involving substantial proportions of the scientific, engineering and industrial base.

This chapter will provide an account of the role of science and technology in the global conflict we call the cold war, and assess the manner in which technological progress affected the military competition between the superpowers. It also shows how the Soviet military-industrial complex developed to meet the challenge presented by American military technology.

the military-industrial complex

As the Soviet Union and the United States began to deploy strategic nuclear weapons in larger numbers it soon became evident that a strategic stalemate was emerging, whereby both sides would acquire strategic arsenals in excess of the requirements of 'assured destruction' while at the same time they would be able to retain an assured second-strike capability that would impose unacceptable risks on any first-strike scenario. Consequently a voluminous literature has discussed the factors that drove

189

the continued expansion and the increase in the technical sophistication of nuclear arsenals despite the emergence of 'mutual assured destruction'. One of the central concepts is that of the 'action–reaction phenomenon', a phrase coined by Robert McNamara, according to which the propensity of military planners to base themselves on 'worst-case scenarios' results in the procurement of greater forces than required, and inducing the other side to do the same in an increasing spiral. The continuous advancement in weapons technology provided additional momentum.

The consensus in the literature (which was not shared by significant sections of the political elite in the USA) was that the United States was the principal source of innovation in military technology and therefore responsible for driving the arms race, to the extent that the United States, in the words of Jerome Wiesner, was engaged in an arms race with itself. But the image of an unfettered arms race did not correspond to the reality of the development of strategic arsenals. There were examples of restraint (such as the modest pace of Soviet strategic arms deployment in the Khrushchev period), asymmetric responses (such as the Soviet failure to match the extent of the US strategic bomber force) as well as surges in deployment far in excess of the capabilities of the other side. Critics such as Albert Wohlstetter pointed out that the underlying assumption of the arms race paradigm may have been false or incomplete and that this explanation ignored a multitude of other factors affecting force planning. Thus strategic arms policy might not have been governed purely by external threats or the requirement of security, but that domestic factors may have played a decisive role. This argument focuses on the role of the armed services, the defence industries and the political elites and bureaucracies that constituted large and politically and economically powerful institutions, whose institutional interests demanded continuing large military expenditures. The construction of threat scenarios and technological progress were the instruments of this interaction of vested interests which resulted in the build-up of ever-increasing arsenals of weapons systems. Eisenhower coined the phrase 'military-industrial complex' to describe this phenomenon.

The Soviet Union was at a disadvantage because of its technological backwardness. Moreover, intellectual freedom is a fundamental prerequisite of scientific progress, while a strong economy provides the resources for research and development. The Soviet Union on the other hand could marshal resources on a large scale through the central planning system. Also, traditionally the Soviet education system had put far more emphasis on the sciences, producing excellent physicists, engineers and mathematicians. In response to the revolution in military affairs engendered by nuclear weapons and ballistic missiles the Soviet Union built up a vast military-industrial complex. Despite the hierarchical nature of the Soviet system, different interest groups also existed and thus interaction of institutions with their own vested interests was an important factor. The Khrushchev period was dominated by the attempt to restructure the Soviet economy by reducing investment in the heavy metal industries, relieving the manpower shortage in the economy by reducing military manpower and reallocating resources to light industry and agriculture. This policy resulted in considerable conflict inside the *Presidium* (as the *Politburo*, the central decision-making body of the CPSU, was known prior to 1966) and with sections of the military leadership, resulting eventually in Khrushchev's downfall. The public discourse in the Soviet Union, such as it was, differed greatly from that in the United States. In the USA continued arms spending and the procurement of new technologies and weapons systems was usually justified by general or specific threats. The Soviet leadership, although it often attacked the militaristic policies of the USA, never admitted any sort of military inferiority. During the Khrushchev period there were bombastic claims about Soviet capabilities that bore no relation to reality. These claims were part of a game of bluff in Khrushchev's diplomacy, but they also had the purpose to justify reducing conventional military forces even though Soviet strategic nuclear capabilities were relatively modest. In other words, Khrushchev tried to rein in the military-industrial complex and was not afraid to take on military leaders or the military industry in the process. Even though the Cuban missile crisis resolved any doubt about the question of whether or not the Soviet Union needed to develop strategic nuclear forces on a scale that could challenge the United States, Khrushchev reverted to his own priorities in 1963 after his main political rival, Frol Kozlov, was eliminated by a stroke. The ouster of Khrushchev the following year (supported, though not instigated, by the military leadership) resulted in a new deal whereby the military was granted significant autonomy in force planning and given resources for an all-round build-up in conventional and strategic nuclear forces.

The Soviet government controlled military industry through the Military-Industrial Commission (VPK – *Voenno-Promyshlenniya Kommissiya*), an agency of the Council of Ministers responsible for coordinating the various organisations in the military, the Party and the government involved with the procurement and production of weapons. The defence industries submitted their proposals to the VPK, where they were to be studied for their technical feasibility, production requirements and impact on other sectors of the economy. The VPK also considered funding, production and schedules. The decision by the VPK on any proposal would be subject to approval by the Council of Ministers. Military production took place in enterprises under various ministries such as the ministry of medium machine building (nuclear warheads) or the ministry of general machine building (ballistic missiles and space vehicles – these ministries were called state committees during part of the Khrushchev period). Missile design and development was carried out separately in the design bureaux (OKB: *Opytno Konstruktorskie Biuro*). Unlike in Western defence industries, design and production were separate, although the leading missile design bureaux headed by Sergei Korolyev, Mikhail Yangel and Vladimir Chelomei were linked with specific missile production plants (the Progress Plant in Kuibyshev, the Yuzhmash plant in Dnepopetrovsk and the Khrunichev plant in Fili respectively). Projects were often initiated by the design bureaux themselves, but they usually collaborated with research institutes under the ministries. Two research institutes in particular played a key role in the development of intercontinental ballistic missiles (ICBMs), the NII-88 in Kaliningrad near Moscow and the NII-4 MO (Scientific Research Institute-4 of the Ministry of Defence). The latter was a research institute of the Strategic Rocket Forces (RSVN) and coordinated its needs and requirements with the design and development of missiles. Although the design bureaux themselves initiated new projects, the military services initiated most of the requests for new or improved weapons systems. The General Staff played a key role in the weapons acquisition process. It did not usually initiate proposals for new weapons or give final approval for them. Its role was rather to review all proposals, fitting them in with overall procurement budgets and military policy, thus serving as a locus for the resolution of inter-service rivalry with regard to resource allocation.

During the cold war much of the academic literature reflected the view that in the Soviet Union weapons innovation and defence decision-making came from the top down, reacting to external forces, especially US initiatives, and that the rivalries between defence contractors, services and other vested interests were not relevant.[1] More recent analyses show that the opposite was the case.[2] Design bureaux had significant influence on weapons programmes, and the kinds of technologies to be pursued. There was considerable competition between these bureaux, and before a production decision was taken, prototypes produced by various designers were tested and several options fulfilling a certain mission requirement could be available. Given the requirement for a new weapon, the question of budgetary and materials allocation for its development of production thus arose in a climate where competition for resources was intense.

These issues were often resolved within the bureaucracy before a proposal reached the political leadership. Of course, at various times political leaders were proactive and interfered very directly in the decisions on weapons development, especially during the Khrushchev period. Moreover, in general the impact of US strategic capabilities on Soviet programmes is undeniable. But during the Brezhnev period the defence industries gained influence as a result of the technological challenges posed by the modernisation of strategic forces, the enormous resources lavished on the military-industrial complex and the weak leadership at the top that was easily swayed by internal lobbying. Consequently the defence industries managed to foist a range of different approaches to strategic arms development on a military that was rather reluctant to adopt all the various new complex weapons systems that were being developed, that were immensely difficult to manage and were based on conflicting approaches to nuclear strategy.

It is clear that the military-industrial complex in the Soviet Union acquired an increasing share of economic resources, to such an extent that even the Soviet government itself lost sight of how much it spent on the military. Thus it was a major factor in the decline of the Soviet system. The political mechanisms which kept defence spending under control, especially in Europe but even in the United States, did not operate in the Soviet Union and after Khrushchev the political leadership was unable to rein it in. Strategic and tactical nuclear forces were only a small part of the problem, accounting for a mere 7 per cent and 4 per cent respectively of military spending in 1951–90.[3] Many programmes became self-sustaining, as for example in the case of the air defence forces, which continued to be funded at a substantial level even after the bomber threat was replaced by the missile threat and the USA scaled down its air defence capabilities. The 'action–reaction' model therefore is insufficient to explain weapons programmes and force postures, which involved a complex web of competing vested interests and differing beliefs about the requirements of national security.

the beginning of the strategic nuclear confrontation

The first nuclear detonation carried out by the United States on 16 July 1945 and the subsequent bombings of Hiroshima and Nagasaki ushered in the nuclear age. As noted in Chapter 5, Stalin oversaw an all-out effort to develop the atomic bomb. The first Soviet nuclear device was detonated on 29 August 1949 in Semipalatinsk, in Kazakhstan, and on 12 August 1953 it tested a thermonuclear weapon.[4] Despite enormous efforts Stalin was unable to acquire the means to target the United States effectively. When he died in March 1953, the Soviet Union had less than a dozen bombs and the core of the long-range aviation force, the TU-4 bomber (a copy of the American B-29) did not have intercontinental range, whereas the United States could deliver 1,350 bombs at Soviet targets. During the 1950s the United States acquired a large stockpile of nuclear warheads and a substantial fleet of bombers of intercontinental range to reach targets in the USSR. The Soviet Union did put in place the infrastructure necessary for the mass production of nuclear weapons during the 1950s, but continued to experience severe technical problems with the development of engines for aircraft to deliver them at intercontinental range. Instead of competing with the United States in the deployment of strategic bombers, Khrushchev sought to rapidly change the perception of the strategic balance by moving the Soviet Union into the missile age. American fears of the emerging strategic nuclear capabilities of the Soviet Union were dramatically heightened by the Soviet launch of the first earth satellite (*Sputnik*) in October 1957, thus demonstrating to all the world that the Soviet Union possessed the technology to develop intercontinental ballistic missiles.

The American reaction to *Sputnik* demonstrated the success of Khrushchev's ploy. The United States had perceived itself as the nation leading technological development in the world, and thus the fact that the Soviets should be the first in space was a severe blow. Moreover, it raised questions about the scale of the potential threat represented by the USSR and America's readiness to meet it. Similar concerns were expressed in Europe. The truth of the matter was, of course, that US missile technology was already far in advance of Soviet technology and the USA could have launched a satellite if it had made a priority to do so.

The first-generation ICBM, the R-7 (the SS-6) which had been designed by Korolyev officially entered service on 20 January 1960, but was never deployed in more than token numbers. The R-7 was successful as a space launch vehicle, but was plagued with technical difficulties that made it unsuitable as a delivery vehicle for nuclear weapons – it used a highly unstable propellant which could not be stored (because Korolyev refused to use hypergolic fuels that could be stored at normal temperatures), making launching difficult and resulting in very low combat readiness. It took nearly 20 hours to prepare the missile for launch, and the maximum period for which it could be kept on alert was one day. Moreover, the guidance system, based on the German V-2, was not suitable for ranges of more than 160 miles. In order to achieve its projected accuracy of 5 miles from the target the position of the missile had to be tracked by ground radars and its flight control system would receive course corrections by radio every 20 seconds until it reached it final ballistic trajectory. Consequently the guidance system was subject to disruption by electronic interference. In addition to its technical weaknesses, the deployment costs (especially the cost of the launch complexes) was prohibitive.[5] For these reasons Khrushchev cancelled the construction of eight of the twelve launch pads at the R-7 base in Plesetsk, as well as those planned for other locations. Steven Zaloga suggests that another reason for the curtailment of the R-7 programme was the American U2 over-flights which meant that the location of the launch platforms could not be kept secret, rendering them vulnerable to pre-emptive attack by US bombers or ICBMs. By 1960 the Soviet Union had deployed a total of four ICBMs and 145 strategic bombers.[6]

The Yangel bureau, which proved itself with the development of intermediate range missiles such as the R-12 (SS-4), had been authorised in 1956 to study the development of ICBMs with storable fuels. By January 1958 the draft design of the first second-generation ICBM, R-16 (SS-7) was presented. The missile was designed to be launched within 30 minutes and it would be based on above-ground launch pads, whose construction would cost considerably less than those for the R-7. In October 1960 there was to be a test of the prototype. As the result of an accident which caused the second stage to fire, a massive explosion killed the first commander of the Strategic Rocket Forces, Marshal Mitrofan Nedelin, and a number of top engineers from Yangel's design team, although Yangel himself fortuitously escaped injury. After an accelerated programme of testing the missile finally entered service in 1962.

Despite the successful demonstration of its technology by being the first to test an ICBM and launch a satellite, the USSR fell very rapidly behind in the technological arms race. Whereas the Soviet focus on missile technology had in part been prompted by the technical problems associated with the development of bombers, the opposite was the case in the United States. The US Air Force (USAF), which became a separate service in 1947, opposed the development of ICBMs because it considered the strategic bomber as tried and tested technology that would improve even more in time and was a reliable platform to deliver nuclear weapons to targets in the Soviet Union. Atomic weapons were very heavy and the task of delivering one over thousands of miles seemed daunting, given that the trajectory of an intercontinental delivery vehicle would require it to rise up into space and re-enter the atmosphere. Even more important was the problem of accuracy; the V-2 had an average error of 4 miles. If this was extrapolated to a distance of 3,000 miles, the average error would be 60 miles. The scepticism was expressed by Vannevar Bush (one of the senior scientists in the US nuclear programme) who told the Senate Special Committee on Atomic Energy in 1945 when he stated his confidence that no one would know how to develop an accurate missile of intercontinental range for some time to come.[7]

The strategic bomber therefore became the platform for massive retaliation, and the USAF obstructed the development of ICBMs until 1954 when it became clear that long-range missiles were going to play an important role and that they should not become the preserve of the army. Even then a consensus took some time to emerge, as President Eisenhower himself stated in 1956 that he did not think much of ballistic missiles as weapons. Two missile systems were deployed in Europe, the USAF's *Thor* missiles based in Britain under dual key control and the Army's *Jupiter* in Turkey. The *Jupiter* was considerably more accurate than the *Thor* and was envisaged by the Army for tactical as well as strategic roles.[8] Future developments in the strategic arms competition were analysed in two reports submitted to the National Security Council, the Killian Report (1955) and the Gaither Report (1957). The former highlighted the lack of early warning systems and the vulnerability of strategic bombers and envisaged the emergence of strategic stalemate that might be impervious to further technological breakthroughs. It recommended the development of sea-launched missile systems alongside land-based ballistic missiles. The Gaither Report took a more alarmist view about emerging Soviet missile capabilities and considered the development of early warning capabilities, defences against ICBMs and nationwide shelters to protect the population. It envisaged a continuing race between offence and defence through technological innovation.[9]

We can identify several factors that propelled the US ICBM programme, none of which were decisive by themselves, but which had a cumulative effect. The first was the development of the hydrogen bomb, which permitted the miniaturisation of nuclear weapons, reducing the payload required. The second were the breakthroughs in inertial guidance and digital computing technology, that enabled the achievement of levels of accuracy acceptable for 'countervalue' attacks (and 'counterforce' missions later on). Other significant technical breakthroughs were the development of gas-accentuated bearings for gyroscopes that enabled missiles to be on permanent alert and solid propellants which allowed for very rapid launch. The third was the emergence of the Soviet missile programme and the perception of a missile gap. Strategic bombers were too slow to respond to an impending missile attack and became increasingly vulnerable to air defences.

As noted in Chapter 5, the missile gap turned out to be mythical. By 1962 the total number of nuclear warheads the USSR could deliver to the continental United States remained below 300. In contrast the United States could deliver in excess of 3,000 weapons using strategic bombers, and had deployed 183 ICBMs (*Atlas* and *Titan*). In addition nine *Polaris* submarines were equipped with 144 missiles. The *Atlas* and *Titan* ICBMs were quickly abandoned in favour of the solid-fuelled *Minuteman*. For the Kennedy administration, the low cost of the missile envisaged to be produced in significant numbers was an essential selling point. It was not only much smaller than its rivals, but its basing costs were so much lower than those of the larger liquid-fuelled ICBMs. By 1967 1,000 *Minuteman* and 54 *Titan II* missiles were deployed in underground silos.[10]

Although the Soviet missile programme created a major impetus for the development and deployment of long-range strategic missiles on the part of the US, the direct impact of Soviet capabilities or strategic requirements is unclear. The number of American ICBMs expanded very rapidly while Soviet deployments proceeded at a comparatively leisurely pace, and terminated when the expansion of the Soviet arsenal was at its height. The structure of the US strategic arsenal developed in quite a different way from that of the Soviet Union. In part this can be explained by inter-service rivalry; the large strategic bomber force made the USAF the dominant service when it came to nuclear war. The Navy pursued the *Polaris* programme primarily because of the emerging centrality of ballistic missile capabilities, and being left out would reduce the Navy to a marginal role. The strategic concept underlying the *Polaris* force – which in 1957 was projected to consist of 45 boats with 29 at sea at any time – was incompatible with the operational plan of the USAF's Strategic Air Command (SAC). Indeed, the coordinated, near simultaneous launch of all sea-based missiles located at distant places somewhere in the oceans was not feasible. Instead such a force would provide a more than adequate deterrent, capable of destroying all of the Soviet Union. Although the creation of such a substantial, invulnerable sea-based deterrent was later seen (especially by McNamara) as a significant strategic asset, the debate over ICBM vulnerability in the late 1970s to early 1980s highlighted the differing attitudes towards the role of the sea-based deterrent.

technology and nuclear strategy

The Kennedy administration moved away from the nuclear strategy of the 1950s to espouse a strategy of multiple options that could be adjusted to the challenge that was being faced. This meant an initial shift towards an explicit counterforce strategy, and the attack on Soviet strategic nuclear forces and related targets was the first of the five main options contained in the single integrated operational plan (SIOP). The USAF enthusiastically embraced the shift towards counterforce and city avoidance (giving rise to the fear that they were seeking a first-strike capability), partly in order to make its case for a new manned bomber, the B-70. The *Minuteman* ICBM was seen as a very effective weapon to attack cities, but too inaccurate and with a warhead lacking sufficient yield (0.4 megatons) for counterforce missions, especially when the Soviets began to deploy their missiles in hardened silos in 1963. The only missile in the US considered suitable for the counterforce role, the *Titan II* with a 9 megaton warhead and accurate to two-thirds of a nautical mile, was curtailed after limited deployment. The requirement for accuracy and counterforce capabilities was central to the United States Air Force Basic Doctrine of 1964. Since McNamara stopped the B-70 programme, the USAF had little choice but to apply its requirements to the ICBM programme. Still, the technical characteristics of the ICBM force the USA acquired in the 1960s was not considered to provide the capability to implement the strategic doctrine that was supposed to form the basis for operational planning. This situation drove the USAF to demand the highest level of accuracy possible for the successor to the *Minuteman*. The *Minuteman II* first deployed in 1966 had a higher yield warhead (1.2 megatons) and a circular error probable (CEP) of 0.26 nautical miles, with a much higher probability of destroying a Soviet missile silo. Ironically by this time the administration emphasised 'mutual assured destruction' and moved away from the notion of city avoidance and the stress on counterforce capabilities.[11]

Soviet nuclear strategy in the 1950s, which was developed in the context of an American commitment to 'massive retaliation', was preoccupied with the threat of an American surprise attack, especially from forward-based bombers and missiles in Europe. The establishment of the Strategic Rocket Forces in 1959 was accompanied by a revision in Soviet military doctrine announced by Khrushchev. In a speech before the Supreme Soviet in January 1960, the Soviet leader emphasised the irrelevance of conventional forces, placing a greater emphasis on the USSR's nuclear arsenal. Soviet military strategists envisaged a massive missile attack requiring virtually all forces in order to be successful, and since it appears unlikely that they were envisaging strikes at empty missile sites or bomber bases, this would point in the direction of pre-emption.[12] Pre-emption is, however, a technologically demanding strategy, requiring an effective counterforce capability. The alternative, launch-on-warning, is technically even more demanding, since it requires an efficient capability to detect the launch of nuclear missiles, an ICBM force with effective counterforce capabilities to eliminate the remaining enemy nuclear forces and the capability to have a large percentage of the force on a high alert status for the duration of a crisis at least, but perhaps over longer periods. The missiles must be designed so that they can be launched at very short notice.

The most significant constraints for operational planning in the early 1960s were most likely those imposed by early warning capabilities. The first Soviet early warning satellite was launched in 1967 (*Kosmos 159*), but even partial operational status for a satellite-based early warning system was not achieved until 1977. In the absence of Over-the-Horizon radar technology, warning time of an American missile attack would be very short – of the order of 10 minutes. During the mid- to late 1960s the Soviet primary early warning system consisted of two so-called *Hen House* radars north of Moscow. By 1970 a larger network consisting of seven such radars were deployed or under construction in the vicinity of Moscow, on the Baltic coast, the Kola Peninsula, near the Black Sea and in the southern part of the Soviet Union. The ballistic missile radars came on line as a fully integrated early warning system with links to the top leadership in 1971. This system would have provided tactical warning of an attack by US ICBMs of a maximum of 17 minutes (assuming the performance capabilities of US early warning radar systems), and much less of course of SLBMs launched from submarines closer to Soviet territory.[13]

The R-16 (SS-7) and R9 (SS-8) could not be launched in less than 20 minutes even if they were fuelled (the R-9 was Korolyev's second attempt at designing an ICBM, using the same fuel technology as the R-7) in anticipation of an attack. In practice, a launch-on-warning was not feasible, since the decision-times were too short. Under normal peacetime conditions, the level of alert of Soviet strategic forces was very low. For example, until the late 1960s nuclear warheads for strategic and tactical nuclear weapons were kept at storage depots some distance away from the delivery platforms. In order for a missile launch to occur, the warheads would have to be mated to the missiles. After having been armed, the missiles needed to be warmed for several hours. After that, there were further time-consuming preparations required.[14] Furthermore, as Berman and Baker have pointed out, this problem could not easily be overcome by having a large number of missiles on alert in a period of crisis:

[The] USSR's inability to maintain, without great expense, a large number of missiles on combat alert arose from the fact that the gyroscope in its guidance systems – necessary to induce stability in the missile – rotated on metal ball bearings, not on the gas-actuated bearings found on U.S. missile systems. The guidance system thus needed some time to warm up before a missile could be launched. And in any sustained period of holding a missile ready for immediate launching, the entire guidance system would fail because the ball bearings, which were mass produced to less than perfect tolerances, would fail under such continuing stress. If guidance systems could not be held on alert for more than 12 hours, and 10% of a force of ICBMs had to be put on alert each day, 20% of the guidance systems would have to be replaced on the first day and the entire force of ICBMs would be incapacitated after five days. Clearly, as its reliance on ICBMs increased, the USSR could not afford lengthy alert rates.[15]

In addition, missiles could not remain fuelled for more than 30 days. Indeed, a realistic appraisal must have led to the conclusion that the lack of early warning facilities and other technical problems might force the adoption of operational plans based on pre-emptive or even *preventive* strikes, in light of the vulnerability of Soviet ICBMs at the time. It was not until 1963 that the first missile silos became operational in the Soviet Union (the deployment of the R-16 in silos required the missile to be modified).

The shift in American defence policy in 1961 announced by the Kennedy administration and the resultant strategic missile programmes involving the *Polaris* SLBM and the fixed site *Minuteman* ICBM force changed Soviet targeting requirements. Kennedy's March 1961 speech projected the deployment of 600 *Minuteman* and this number was nearly doubled in his FY 1963 budget speech. The *Minuteman* were deployed in hardened silos from the outset and therefore required a hard-target kill capability which could only be achieved with much greater accuracy and a much larger number of missiles. The R-36 (SS-9), a successor to Yangel's R-16, was designed specifically to destroy US ICBM deployment areas.[16] Although it was the most accurate ICBM so far developed by the Soviet Union, and as a high yield weapon (maximum yield 18 megatons) was in principle suitable to attack hard targets, its large size meant that it could not be produced in large numbers rapidly enough to pose an effective counter against the emerging *Minuteman* force. It is believed to have been targeted principally at command and control facilities, and *Minuteman* launch control centres in particular.[17]

The main role in countering the large number of American *Minuteman* missiles was therefore given to the UR-100 (SS-11) designed by Chelomei's

OKB. It was more comparable to the *Minuteman* in size and payload. The R-36 was deployed at a constant rate of 42 missiles per year, levelling off at a total of 288 missiles, while 720 UR-100 (SS-11) ICBMs had been deployed by 1970; both missiles were deployed in hardened silos.[18] It is therefore apparent that the force posture which emerged by the end of the 1960s was geared to make a launch-on-warning policy operationally feasible. The trend towards launch-on-warning was confirmed by the scenario developed in a Soviet manual, *Design and Testing of Ballistic Missiles* by V.I. Varfolomeyev and M.I. Kopytov, where the United States strikes first. The first Soviet missile strike is a launch-on-warning. The manual also indicates a preference to launch as many ICBMs as possible during the first launch because of the threat to ICBM survivability by a coordinated American first-strike.[19] However, the capabilities to implement launch-on-warning did not exist at that time. In a study by the Yangel design bureau and the main research institute of the industry, TsNII-Mash, the doctrine of a pre-emptive strike which was favoured by Soviet military leaders was criticised because it contradicted the policy of the state never to use nuclear weapons first and was unlikely to prevent a massive American counter-strike. The study ruled out launch-on-warning as infeasible and recommended a doctrine of restraint, which was based on the concept of riding out an American attack. This would require Soviet strategic forces to have an assured second-strike capability and thus silos needed to be hardened; in view of increased accuracy the ICBM force would ultimately have to be mobile. Ustinov and therefore Brezhnev came out in favour of this approach, that was fiercely resisted by the Strategic Rocket Forces. It was not until the 1980s that launch-on-warning became feasible in principle.[20]

The issue of strategic defence was very controversial in the United States. Especially among Republicans who objected to the acceptance of strategic vulnerability there was strong support for ballistic missile defence. McNamara's preoccupation with constructing a stable strategic relationship with the Soviet Union was based on mutual assured destruction. Consequently the preservation of a secure second-strike capability became the main objective of strategic arms policy. ABMs would destabilise the strategic balance. The announcement by McNamara of plans for the deployment of the *Sentinel* system to provide an area defence against Chinese ICBMs was a classic case of bureaucratic politics, given that this was clearly a defence system without any significant capability against a threat that was yet to emerge. McNamara was under considerable pressure from Congress with regard to ballistic missile defence. The USAF was not keen on strategic defence (as opposed to new offensive systems), while the Navy and Army wanted an area defence system that would require a lot of investment and was not designed to protect the assets of the Air Force. The administration was practically forced to adopt an ABM system, so the outcome was a system designed to address the political pressures without abandoning the core objective of preserving strategic stability.[21] Similar considerations would shape the Clinton administration's programme for national missile defence in the 1990s under different circumstances. The Nixon administration decided to deploy *Safeguard* instead, a system that under the terms of the ABM Treaty was designed as a hard point defence to protect ICBMs. Such a system was more compatible with the notion of assured destruction as it was designed to protect a second-strike capability. Still, the continuing technical advantage of the offence over the defence resulted in the dismantlement of the *Safeguard* system soon after it was constructed.

the strategic build-up of the 1970s

The technological innovations in missile technologies in the late 1960s had a profound impact on the course of the strategic competition between the superpowers. The key factors were continuing advances in nuclear warhead technology (improvements in the weight to yield ratio), advances in inertial guidance resulting in significant increases in accuracy, and the technology of multiple independently-targetable re-entry vehicles (MIRV). All of these were embodied in the *Minuteman III* and they completely undermined the central purpose of SALT by permitting a substantial expansion of warheads even when the number of launchers remained fixed and were accompanied by a shift away from 'mutual assured destruction'. Initially there was opposition in the USAF to the substitution of a larger warhead with several smaller ones, partly because it weakened the argument for more missiles and might take resources away from the development of manned bombers. However, the existence of a significant new development programme, the potential for increasing the counterforce target list that required precise surgical strikes and the increased capacity of MIRVed missiles to penetrate ballistic missile defences won the day.[22]

The strategic debate in the Nixon administration was based on two contradictory developments: On the one hand, the loss of strategic superiority over the Soviet Union raised doubts about extended deterrence, on the other the development of new technological capabilities made the kind of flexible options considered during the McNamara period a more realistic possibility. Defense Secretary James Schlesinger was an ardent defender of 'war-fighting' strategies and counterforce capabilities. His doctrine of limit options which was embodied in the SIOP offered a menu of options in response to Soviet aggression, from the use of tactical nuclear forces to selective strategic strikes to an all-out strategic exchange as a final resort.[23] Thus the commitment to precision guidance and giving priority to military targets (especially nuclear assets) had become deeply entrenched at every level in the US military-industrial establishment.[24] The network of long-range radars and satellites for the detection of missile launches and nuclear detonations as well as the command and control system meant that all the elements of a 'launch-on-warning' or 'launch-under-attack' posture were in place.

The same technical trends could be observed in the development of the Soviet arsenal. The third generation of Soviet ICBMs, consisting mostly of the UR-100N (SS-19) with (360 missiles deployed) and the heavy R-36M (SS-18) (308 missiles, mostly deployed in an eight to ten warhead configuration)[25] gave the Soviet Union a substantial counterforce capability against the United States and thus radically transformed the Soviet strategic nuclear force posture. The UR-100N was developed by the Chelomei OKB and initially suffered from a design flaw that caused resonance oscillation in the missile's airframe after launch. This fault was only discovered after missiles had already been deployed in substantial numbers but was eventually corrected. The missile was highly accurate with a CEP (circular error probable) of 340 metres. The R-36M (SS-18) had a CEP of 430 metres. Key advances were made in fuel technology (allowing the MR-UR-100 (SS-17) and R-36M (SS-18) to be cold-launched), guidance systems (putting ICBM silos in the continental USA in reach of the UR-100N and the R-36M), and the development of MIRVs, which allowed a large expansion of the number of warheads deployed while keeping the number of launchers fixed as provided for by the SALT I agreement. The mid-1970s also saw the deployment of Soviet SLBMs of intercontinental range.[26]

It is important to note, however, that by comparison with US strategic forces, the Soviet ICBM force still suffered from significant technological disadvantages. Although the storable fuels used for the propulsion systems allowed the missiles to be launched within a very short period (4–8 minutes), it would have been preferable to use solid fuels which allow launch at the turn of a key and also deliver more power for a given volume. Two early solid-fuel ICBM designs, the RT-2 (SS-13) and the Temp-2-S (SS-16), were not very successful. The RT-2 was deployed in small numbers and the Temp-2-S not at all (although a two-stage version later became the intermediate range *Pioneer* (SS-20)). Soviet missile production complexes had difficulty with solid fuel technology. Another constraint on the use of solid fuels was the fact that because of their uneven rate of burn solid fuels require the missile to be equipped with a highly accurate inertial guidance system. However, the Soviets still had considerable problems with their guidance systems and therefore found it necessary to rely on liquid fuels.[27]

The structure of the Soviet third-generation ICBM force (including the surviving elements of the second generation) was such that it provided a versatile capability against a whole range of targets, including civilian and economic targets. It is quite evident nonetheless that the R-36M (SS-18) and UR-100N (SS-19) force was clearly designed to provide the capability to attack *Minuteman* silos. Apart from *Minuteman* silos, hardened command and control centres were also likely targets for this force. Important soft targets in the continental United States, such as strategic bomber fields, military headquarters and countervalue targets could be handled by single-warhead MR-UR-100 (SS-17) and UR-100N (SS-19) missiles. The UR-100 (SS-11) and the R-36M (SS-18) were also suitable for attacking long-range naval targets. The strategic force posture achieved by the end of the 1970s was in essence the partial achievement of capabilities which Soviet spokesmen claimed they possessed during the 1960s. In line with the new Soviet thinking that in the event of war the escalation to the strategic nuclear level ought to be avoided, it was essentially a posture of deterrence designed to guarantee an effective second-strike capability in order to sanctuarise Soviet territory. Thus we see an emphasis on reducing the vulnerability of ICBMs by hardening of silos and developing reload facilities for cold-launched missiles, increasing rapid launch capabilities, and early warning facilities. In continuity with Soviet military thought since the Second World War, the primary orientation of Soviet targeting was counter-military.[28]

icbm vulnerability and the rebirth of ballistic missile debate

During the 1970s ICBM vulnerability emerged as a key issue both in the United States and the Soviet Union as a result of the deployment of MIRVed ICBMs. The American fifth-generation ICBM, initially called MX and later dubbed *Peacekeeper*, was the culmination of the technological trends in the developments of strategic missiles in the USA. It had much greater throw-weight than the *Minuteman* which was light by comparison with Soviet missiles, was by far the most accurate missile yet and carried ten warheads. It was the ultimate counterforce weapon with a time-urgent hard-target kill capability that had no rivals. But the requirements for the MX were formulated at a time when mutual assured destruction and arms control dominated the strategic agenda. Ironically the weapon characterised by the Soviets as a first-strike weapon was advocated in terms of the provision of an assured second-strike capability. Alternatively the MX could have served as a bargaining chip in arms control. In the late 1970s, when the 'Committee on the Present Danger' (a conservative pressure group) warned against the Soviet threat of a first strike against ICBM silos that would eliminate US counterforce capabilities, the MX was advocated as the basis for a secure second-strike time-urgent counterforce weapon.[29]

The MX was not, however, intrinsically less vulnerable than the *Minuteman III*, so the public debate about this system focused on its basing mode. No politically acceptable solution to the problem of vulnerability could be found, however, so in the end a small force of MX (*Peacekeeper*) was deployed in silos. Despite the concerns about the 'window of vulnerability', however, this issue was less serious for the United States because its substantial and technically advanced sea-based deterrent gave it a secure second-strike retaliatory force. What the history of the development of the *Minuteman* and *Peacekeeper* missiles demonstrates is that the characteristics and capabilities of these weapons systems were partly due to dynamics of technical progress, and defined by the interaction between the armed forces, technological institutions and defence corporations. The political institutions seem to have had less impact, and often the outcome defied the initial preferences of political actors or even the leadership of the armed forces.

The structure of the Soviet strategic arsenal was quite different from that of the United States. By 1980 the Soviet Union had deployed 522 submarine-launched ballistic missiles (SLBMs) in a strategic mode. This represented less than 20 per cent of all strategic warheads deployed by the Soviet Union, whereas the United States had then more than 50 per cent of all its warheads deployed on SLBMs. A number of explanations have been advanced for this fundamental asymmetry in the strategic force postures. First of all, there is a greater naval tradition in the United States, whereas the Soviet Union was more of a continental power and emerged only recently as a global sea power. It is also evident that the Soviets had great difficulties in mastering the technologies required for submarine basing. There was a great asymmetry in submarine vulnerability – the less-sophisticated Soviet submarines were vulnerable to the extensive US anti-submarine warfare (ASW) network. On the other hand, the Soviets did not have the technical capabilities to locate and track the missile-carrying US submarines on station at any period of time. The peacetime deployment rate for Soviet submarines was very low (of the order of 15 per cent of submarines were on station at any given time, compared with 55 per cent of the US fleet). The Soviets were also concerned about the command and control problems posed by submarines, including the dangers of unauthorised launch. One can therefore discern a whole nexus of problems which explain the Soviet bias for ICBMs.

The fifth generation of Soviet ICBMs which emerged in the 1980s constituted an important step forward towards a truly modern missile force measured by the standards of American technology. The first successful solid-fuelled missile deployed by the Soviet Union was the intermediate-range SS-20 (or *Pioneer*). Both the SS-24 (RT-23UTTH) and the SS-25 (*Topol*) were solid-fuelled, thus enabling the quick alert rate and mobility which can only be achieved with the use of solid fuels. It is also clear that the Soviets had made important advances in inertial guidance systems. The accuracy of the SS-24 and SS-25 were 200 metres CEP – slightly better than that of the most accurate *Minuteman III* (220 m CEP), but not in the same class as the American MX *Peacekeeper* missile (100 m CEP).[30] The SS-24 was essentially the Soviet equivalent of the MX. Its throw-weight was slightly higher than that of the MX, and like the MX it carried ten MIRVed warheads. The yield of the warheads for the RT-23UTTH (SS-24) was 100 kilotons. A total of 89 were deployed both in silos, and in a rail-mobile mode with the Soviet view to ensure invulnerability through mobility. The SS-25 was a single-warhead missile deployed in silos or in a road-mobile mode and was the Soviet counterpart to the American *Midgetman* missile. (The *Midgetman* missile, however, was never fully developed.) Deployment began in 1985.

The general trends discerned in the Soviet strategic force posture as it emerged in the 1980s can be summarised as follows:

- Increasing progress in the mastery of the complex fuel and guidance technologies
- Reducing ICBM vulnerability through mobility
- The emergence of a genuine 'triad' of strategic nuclear forces with the development of a genuine intercontinental range bomber with air-launched cruise missiles (ALCMs) and a modern long-range SLBM force in addition to the land-based missiles.

All of these advances appeared to be threatened, however, by the announcement of SDI by Reagan in 1983, a new large-scale programme to build strategic defences and render nuclear weapons irrelevant. The

Soviet response went through two phases. At first SDI was considered as part of an effort to change the strategic balance and acquire a first-strike capability, and after Gorbachev came to power all his efforts in arms control were directed at defeating SDI. Eventually Soviet military leaders recognised that SDI was unlikely to affect Soviet strategic capabilities for some time to come. As Defence Minister Yazov stated in a meeting with the Polish leader, Jaruzelski, the threat was not from SDI, but from the application of new technologies to other military capabilities.

conclusions

The military dimension of the cold war was characterised by rapid technological advances that completely revolutionised warfare. A closer analysis of technological innovation and the development of the key technologies associated with strategic nuclear weapons systems confirms the consensus that the United States was usually the first to develop key technologies and apply them successfully to weapons systems. The list includes missile fuel technologies, guidance systems, satellite technology, radars and submarine propulsion. Although Soviet technology was usually a generation behind that of the USA, the USSR eventually mastered the key technologies needed to develop time-urgent hard-target strike capabilities and rival the American arsenal in quantity and to a significant extent in quality. It was in the area of conventional forces where a significant technological gap opened up in the 1980s that the Soviet Union had no hope of bridging.

Nevertheless, it could not be said that by the time the Warsaw Pact was dissolved that the Soviet Union had lost the military competition with the United States so that it could no longer defend its empire. The opposite was the case; there was a sufficient mix of conventional and nuclear weapons to deter an attack. Indeed, the possession of nuclear weapons did substantially resolve the problem of external security. If the 'security dilemma' had been the source of East–West tension, then the cold war should have ended with the acquisition of large nuclear arsenals. But the perpetuation of the East–West conflict (albeit in a manner which did not allow it to get out of control) was necessary for the Soviet power elites to preserve their own legitimacy and existence. The military-industrial complex grew to such an extent that the continued development of military technology and acquisition of weapons systems was central to the vested interests of a substantial portion of the societal and industrial elite. There is no doubt that the economic decline of the Soviet Union that contributed to the motivation for reform in the

Gorbachev period which led to the end of the cold war and the Soviet Union itself was in significant part due to the scale of resources devoted to military purposes.

notes

1. Matthew Evangelista, *Innovation and the Arms Race: How the United States and the Soviet Union Develop New Military Technologies* (Ithaca, NY: Cornell University Press, 1988); Michael McGwire, *Military Objectives in Soviet Foreign Policy* (Washington, DC: Brookings, 1987), *passim*.
2. Nikolai Sokov, *Russian Strategic Modernization* (Oxford: Rowman & Littlefield Publishers, 2000); Steven J. Zaloga, *The Kremlin's Nuclear Sword* (Washington, DC: Smithsonian Institution Press, 2002); Pavel Podvig (ed.), *Russian Strategic Nuclear Forces* (Cambridge, MA: MIT Press, 2001); Christoph Bluth, *Soviet Strategic Arms Policy Before SALT* (Cambridge: Cambridge University Press, 1992).
3. Noel Firth & James Noren, *Soviet Defense Spending: A History of CIA Estimates 1950–90* (College Station: Texas A&M University Press, 1998).
4. David Holloway, *Stalin and the Bomb* (New Haven, CT: Yale University Press, 1994), *passim*.
5. Steven Zaloga, *Target America: The Soviet Union and the Strategic Arms Race, 1945–64* (Novato, CA: Presidio, 1993), p.49; Podvig, *Strategic Nuclear Forces*, p.5.
6. Robert P. Berman & John C. Baker, *Soviet Strategic Forces* (Washington, DC: Brookings, 1982); Christoph Bluth, 'Defence and Security', in Martin McCauley (ed.), *Khrushchev and Khrushchevism* (London: Macmillan, 1987), pp.194–214.
7. Robert L. Perry, *The Ballistic Missile Decisions* (Santa Monica, CA: Rand Corporation, 1967).
8. Analysts distinguish between 'counterforce' and 'countervalue' targets. These refer respectively to the enemy strike forces (in particular nuclear missiles and aircraft), military installations and equipment, and civilian targets (cities, industrial centres). For more detail see Donald MacKenzie, *Inventing Accuracy: A Historical Sociology of Nuclear Missile Guidance* (Cambridge, MA: MIT Press, 1990).
9. Lawrence Freedman, *The Evolution of Nuclear Strategy* (London: Macmillan, 1981; 3rd edition, 2003), chapter 11.
10. Desmond Ball, *Policies and Force Levels: The Strategic Missile Program of the Kennedy Administration* (Berkeley, CA: University of California Press, 1980).
11. For more detail, see MacKenzie, *Inventing Accuracy*, *passim*.
12. V.D. Sokolovsky (ed., translated by Harriet Fast Scott), *Soviet Military Strategy* (New York: Crane, Russal & Company Inc., 1968). In this version those passages which only appeared in the second or third editions have been marked. In subsequent notes it is indicated which edition particular quotations have been taken from.
13. Bruce Blair, *The Logic of Accidental Nuclear War* (Washington, DC: Brookings, 1993), p.201.
14. Blair, *Accidental Nuclear War*, p.200.

15. Berman & Baker, *Soviet Strategic Forces*, p.88. The difficulties described by Berman & Baker were also referred to in the third edition of the Sokolovsky volume: 'The chief factor hampering an earlier attainment of high combat readiness in previous types of rockets was the time required for it to attain momentum and go over to the gyroscope system of missile guidance. The limited operational capability of the gyroscopes did not allow keeping them engaged during the entire time the missile was on combat alert.' Sokolovsky, *Soviet Strategy*, p.79. For more technical details, see Donald MacKenzie, 'The Soviet Union and Strategic Missile Guidance', *International Security*, 13:2 (1988), pp.5–54. MacKenzie's research indicates that a primary reason for the delay in the development of solid fuel missiles by the Soviet Union resides in the higher requirements imposed on the guidance systems by the uneven burning of solid rocket fuel.

16. This is asserted in Podvig, *Strategic Nuclear Forces*, p.127 and also represents the consensus of the Western literature. Zaloga casts some doubts on this due to the continuing problems relating to inertial guidance and the lack of satellite reconnaissance to reliably locate *Minuteman* complexes (Zaloga, *Target America*, p.111).

17. See for example McGwire, *Military Objectives*, p.486.

18. Berman & Baker, *Soviet Strategic Forces*, pp.116–24.

19. V.I. Varfolomeyev & M.I. Kopytov, *Design and Testing of Ballistic Missiles – USSR* (translated by the Joint Publications Research Service, JPRS-51810), (Washington, DC, 1970).

20. Zaloga, *Target America*, pp.137–9.

21. John Newhouse, *Cold Dawn: The Story of SALT* (New York: Holt, Rinehart & Winston, 1973).

22. Ted Greenwood, *Making the MIRV: A Study of Defense Decision-Making* (Cambridge: Ballinger, 1975).

23. Christoph Bluth, *Britain, Germany and Western Nuclear Strategy* (Oxford: Oxford University Press, 1995), chapter 7.

24. Terry Terriff, *The Nixon Administration and the Making of US Nuclear Strategy* (Ithaca, NY: Cornell University Press, 1995).

25. IISS, *The Military Balance 1988/89* (London: Jane's Defence Publishers, 1988); see also Berman & Baker, *Soviet Strategic Forces*, p.105; for comparison see Podvig, *Strategic Nuclear Forces*, *passim*.

26. Robbin F. Laird & Dale R. Herspring, *The Soviet Union and Strategic Arms* (Boulder, CO: Westview Press, 1984).

27. See Berman & Baker, *Soviet Strategic Forces*, chapter 3 and appendix B; MacKenzie, 'Strategic Missile Guidance', *passim*.

28. See Laird & Herspring, *Soviet Union and Strategic Arms*; see also McGwire, *Military Objectives*, appendix D.

29. Paul Nitze, 'Deterring our Deterrent', *Foreign Policy*, 25 (1976/77), pp.195–210; see also MacKenzie, *Inventing Accuracy*, chapter 4.

30. IISS, *Military Balance 1988/89*, *passim*.

8

intelligence

richard aldrich

In 1984, two leading scholars of international history, Christopher Andrew and David Dilks, described intelligence as the 'missing dimension' of most international history. They also argued that it should not be so, since persistent research in this area could uncover more reliable documentation than most people thought.[1] Almost two decades later, in the spring of 2002, the UK's Public Record Office launched a conference with the express purpose of re-evaluating the state of the study of intelligence. A range of scholars re-examined the 'missing dimension' and concluded that the subject of intelligence had largely been 'recovered', at least in the sense that it was no longer absent from the wider study of diplomacy and military affairs.[2] This reflected both an exponential growth of academic interest in the subject, and also the large-scale release of new documentation. Certainly, by 2002, few intelligence documents relating to the First or the Second World War remained closed to public inspection in Western archives.[3] However, the current state of the history of cold war intelligence is rather more uneven. Certain types of documentation have been released, but the majority of cold war intelligence material remains classified. More importantly perhaps, some intelligence issues have been integrated into the mainstream of academic writing on the cold war, but other aspects remain, at best 'semi-detached', receiving attention only from intelligence specialists.[4] While intelligence is certainly no longer 'the missing dimension', it perhaps remains the 'elusive dimension'.[5]

There are four reasons why the work of the intelligence services remains unevenly explored and imperfectly connected to the body of 'normal' cold war history. First, it has proved to be rather easier to write institutional histories of the particular intelligence services during the cold war than to show how intelligence connected with the business of policy-making. The challenge is demonstrating how, and how far, the work of the intelligence services made a difference, something which Robin Winks once usefully defined as the 'so what?' question.[6] Indeed, much of the writing on cold war intelligence might be divided into institutionalist history and contextualist history. Histories of particular institutions are plentiful.[7] By contrast, contextualist history which shows how intelligence impacted upon broader policy remains hard to find.[8] This is hardly surprising. Only a minority of intelligence officers interacted with the policy-makers and few policy-makers have recorded in detail how intelligence affected their work-a-day activities, either in their policy records or in their memoirs. Intelligence material is being declassified, indeed estimates have been released in great volumes, but precise documentation showing how this material affected policy is depressingly rare. More importantly, signals intelligence and satellite photography, the forms of intelligence that probably had the strongest impact on high level policy, remain the most highly classified. Until this changes there seems little chance of connecting up intelligence and policy in a really satisfactory way.[9]

Second, the work of the intelligence services varied greatly in its visibility. Intelligence gathering was a largely passive activity and was therefore easy to hide. Moreover, intelligence agencies that focused on human assets have continued to work vigorously to protect the identity of their agents. They know that a reputation for extreme secrecy with regard to the past will be helpful with recruitment in the future. By contrast, some of the other activities undertaken by intelligence agencies, especially covert action or special operations, which involved attempts to influence or shape the world were remarkably 'noisy'. Indeed, some covert actions were almost impossible to hide. Western aid to the *Mujahadin* in Afghanistan in the later 1980s was publicised even when it was still in progress. Accordingly, while we are still in the dark about much intelligence gathering – especially signals intelligence – many cold war covert actions have been identified and some have been quite well integrated into cold war history.[10]

This overlaps with a third explanation. The activities of the intelligence services, especially covert actions, seem to have interested students of the cold war in the Third World much more than elsewhere. This has sometimes gone hand in hand with a broadly critical outlook on the part of historians of the Southern hemisphere, many of whom have seen the activities of intelligence services (particularly those of the West) as the 'hidden hand' of a broader agenda of hegemony and dependency. Some writers have sought to use examples of covert action to suggest that the focus of the major powers was as much about North–South relations and the promotion of a liberal economic agenda, as it was about East–West rivalry. Whatever one's interpretative lens, there can be little doubt that at some point in the 1950s there was a deliberate shift in intelligence activity, and indeed cold war strategy as a whole towards the Third World.[11] It was not just that the Bandung Conference of 1955 illuminated the growing importance of these new states in the international system. It was also that underdeveloped countries seemed to offer the intelligence services more scope for success than the 'frozen front' of cold war Europe, where agent running and 'listening in' was proving hard work against improved security measures.

Finally, our understanding is uneven because we continue to know much less about Soviet intelligence than we do about the West. There have been fortuitous insights here, notably in the early 1990s when some authors charmed their way into KGB archives with the assistance of Russian co-writers. In addition, redacted versions of *Venona* signals traffic have been released. Most helpfully a number of former KGB officers have tried to set out the record of their organisation and one in particular, Vasili Mitrokhin, brought with him extensive notes from the archives.[12] Some East and Central European states have opened their domestic security archives.[13] However, we still know much less about Moscow than we do about Washington and if anything that imbalance is becoming greater by the year. In particular we know very little about how Soviet intelligence, often very good intelligence from well-placed human sources, impacted on policy-making in Moscow.[14]

Overall, cold war intelligence services present a complex picture that varies both geographically and functionally. At one end of the spectrum our understanding of covert action in the Third World is not only extensive, it has also been thoroughly integrated into the wider history of the cold war. By contrast, our understanding of how intelligence impacted upon policy, and especially how signals intelligence impacted on East–West relations during key events, such as the Berlin crisis of 1958–61 or the invasion of Czechoslovakia in 1968, remains minimal. This uneven picture is also perhaps a legacy of different styles of policy-making. For some countries, like Britain, intelligence was closely woven into the fabric of the core executive, but for countries like France and Germany, the intelligence services remained somewhat on the periphery of government. In the United States, the intelligence services gradually drew alongside the policy-making agencies, at times making policy in their own right. The intelligence services in Moscow also had a tendency to become over-mighty subjects, but exactly how the Soviet machine worked remains largely opaque.

covert action

Covert action or, in British parlance, 'special operations' is now well understood. From the mid-1950s, both the CIA and the KGB devoted considerable attention to covert action. It has been persuasively argued that this was a manifestation of 'muscle-bound superpowers', capable of fantastic destruction, yet reduced to near impotence through the logic of deterrence. As many have observed, the more frustrated Washington felt about being unable to turn its military power into foreign policy advantage, the more it resorted to covert action. In other words the relatively stable military balance that developed during the 1950s rendered 'backdoor' advantage through coups or wars of liberation increasingly attractive.

The first 25 years of the cold war represented the 'Golden Age' of covert action. In the United States this trend was perhaps reinforced by a strong paramilitary culture inherited from the wartime Office of Strategic Services. The CIA acquired its own air-force in the early 1950s and this process reached its apogee with semi-secret armies in areas like Thailand, Laos and Tibet during the late 1960s. Thereafter, American enthusiasm for covert action began to oscillate. During the 1970s covert action was reined in as a direct result of the Church Committee Congressional hearings and a general collapse in American confidence that followed the Watergate scandal, the 'oil shock' of 1973 and defeat in Vietnam. Covert action was much frowned upon by Stansfield Turner, Jimmy Carter's DCI (Director of Central Intelligence), and had become a dying art form by the late 1970s. However, in the early 1980s it was revived under Ronald Reagan who had pledged, even on the electoral hustings, to 'unleash the CIA'. It was not long before Reagan's entourage were embroiled in Iran–Contra and a further wave of Congressional restrictions followed. One of the reasons that we understand this area reasonably well is that the 'diet and binge' nature of American covert action, punctuated by official inquiries, has revealed much to historians. Underpinning this curious oscillation is the eternal battle between Congress and the White House for control of foreign policy generally and war-making in particular. This aspect has been succinctly characterised by John Prados who has characterised covert action as 'the President's secret wars'.[15]

CIA covert actions in the Third World have not always presented an edifying spectacle. During 1953, the British and Americans worked together to overthrow the left-leaning Premier of Iran, Dr Mohammed Mossadeq, and to restore the exiled Shah, thereby toppling a popular nationalist regime in favour of a cowardly figure who they themselves referred to sarcastically as 'Boy Scout'. The Shah feared the foreign secret services that sponsored him almost as much as he feared his political opponents. Too afraid to partake in the coup, he hid in a luxury hotel in Italy until he was called forward to assume power. However, he received a lesson in the potential importance of secret services and once in place, the hallmark of his regime was the prominence of SAVAK, his uncompromising security police.[16]

The following year a further coup in Guatemala displaced the popular Arbenz government. The debate continues as to whether the allegiances of Jacobo Arbenz were socialist or communist; however, new evidence seems to suggest that in both Iran and Guatemala, American policy was driven more by security concerns than by economic interest. Both coups revealed to Washington that remarkably little covert activity was required to overthrow governments. Arbenz fell because Guatemala's army refused to fight a battle that they would have undoubtedly won, given that the US-backed opposition forces were minuscule. By the mid-1950s covert action seemed an increasingly attractive instrument for handling awkward situations in the Third World, especially for applying pressure to troublesome neutrals. Sometimes the purpose of operations was coercion rather than complete regime change, as in the case of Indonesia in 1958.[17]

It is now clear that both Britain and the United States were willing to eliminate some of their opponents in the Third World. Particularly eye-catching have been the declassified documents relating to American operations to assassinate Castro – no less than 13 attempts in all. Although this is not news – the Church Committee hearings of the 1970s gave us the story in outline – the detailed material is startling. Some attempts were farcical and involved poison tablets that were initially tested on monkeys and which were hopefully destined for Castro. Other efforts involved a fountain pen designed to inject poison. Agents were sent to Cuba with this material, but who, if anyone, encountered this nasty material remains unclear. Further ineffectual efforts continued under Kennedy.[18]

Britain was not inactive, attempting to liquidate the leaders of insurgencies in Malaya and then Cyprus during the 1950s. Eden reportedly called for Nasser's extermination on an open telephone line while Macmillan's circle expressed themselves about Nasser in only slightly more guarded terms.[19] Perhaps the best-documented example is an Anglo-American planning document for a 1957 coup in Syria, codenamed 'Operation *Straggle*'. Recently uncovered by Matthew Jones in the papers of the British Minister of Defence, Duncan Sandys, its language is uncompromising:

In order to facilitate the action of the liberative (sic) forces, reduce the capabilities of the Syrian regime to organize and direct its military actions, to hold losses and destruction to a minimum, and to bring about desired results in the shortest possibly time, a special effort should be made to eliminate certain key individuals. Their removal should be accomplished early in the course of the uprising and intervention and in the light of circumstances existing at the time. Those who should be eliminated are Sarraj, Bizri and Khalid Bakdash.[20]

Materials of this kind do not surface often, but arguably when they do, they reveal much about the texture of British and American policy in the Middle East.

Unsurprisingly, some of those writers who have examined CIA or SIS covert action in the Third World have often adopted a 'New Revisionist' perspective. While few writers have judged covert action in the Third World to be a success, the critique ranges widely from those with an area studies perspective who have particular issues about a country they have studied closely, such as Iran,[21] to those who wish to portray covert action as a generally mendacious style of interaction with the Southern hemisphere.[22] Some of this writing can be a little shrill. However, some of the more persuasive critiques have focused on the manner in which the intelligence services have supplied large quantities of light weapons to preferred factions in many parts of the world.[23] The lingering question is, once a country like Angola or Afghanistan had been subverted or destabilised, how was it to be re-stabilised? A number of countries in Asia and Africa are still struggling with this question.[24]

'New Revisionism' has also characterised important work on covert action in Western Europe and North America. In 1999 Frances Stonor Saunders published *Who Paid the Piper?*, a path-breaking account of the CIA's cultural warfare programme. Although revisiting a subject that was already known to some specialists, the new details about the funding of Western intellectuals and artists through CIA fronts were compelling. Saunders painted a remarkable picture of a shadowy battle between East and West that extended to ballet, music and science. Although Saunders' view of a puppet-master relationship between the intelligence services and their protégés is now contested by most historians, her work remains influential. Cultural historians have since been extremely active in unravelling the detail of such activities by both the CIA and Britain's IRD (Information Research Department). Their findings, discussed in greater detail in Patrick Major and Rana Mitter's chapter, show how

American cultural projection was not only designed to deal with Soviet competition but also wavering Western European attitudes towards American world leadership. Washington's determination to show that the United States produced great art and great literature formed part of an effort to convince the populations of Bonn, Paris and Rome about its fitness for world leadership. Covert action in Europe, no less than in Africa and Asia, had a complex agenda that extended beyond the bilateral tensions of the cold war.[25]

Bilateral conflict was nevertheless there. Substantial covert operations of a paramilitary type were launched into Eastern Europe during the first ten years of the cold war, alongside a growing struggle for dominance of the airwaves. These activities are often described as 'roll-back' operations, intended to prize away some of the satellite states, and inspired to some degree by Yugoslavia's defection from the Soviet bloc in 1948.[26] The best known example is the ill-fated series of operations into Albania in 1949 and 1950. Within both Washington and London, policy-makers were divided over the wisdom and purpose of these sort of adventures and it is clear that Eisenhower eventually judged them too risky.[27] Washington and Whitehall were divided about the underlying purpose of these operations. Some were genuinely committed to liberation. Others saw the effort merely as an attempt to keep the Soviets off balance and never entertained serious hopes of overthrowing communism in any Eastern bloc country. Yet others, in the military, were thinking in terms of preparations for a future conventional war in Europe which would require guerrilla operations in the East and stay-behind groups or *Gladio* networks in the West. Most studies conclude that these activities helped to encourage Hungary down the road to an unsuccessful rising in 1956.[28]

At least some of these operations were also about deception. Both British and American officials were seeking to incite conflict within communist ruling circles and even to smear politicians in Eastern Europe with the taint of collaborating with the West. This represented an attempt to encourage Stalin's existing suspicions of his own loyalists across Eastern Europe. There is certainly no indication that these activities prompted Stalin's famous purge, which was already taking shape in 1948. However, it is likely that Western activities sought to accelerate this exercise in self-destruction. It will still be some time before the precise shape of cold war covert action can be mapped. However, it is hard to escape the conclusion that the intelligence services were often at the gritty edge of cold war fighting.[29]

counter-insurgency and regime support

In 1961 Khrushchev famously declared that while nuclear war was not an option, the Soviets would prevail through wars of liberation. Both East and West invested considerable amounts of intelligence resource into supporting and protecting the regimes of their protégés across Asia and Africa. For the British and the French, the issue of counter-insurgency merged seamlessly with the business of a fighting retreat from empire and the boundaries between cold war and contracting colonialism were certainly were not clear. In Malaya, the British were up against communist guerrillas whom they wrongly believed to be taking orders from Moscow or Beijing. In Cyprus, the British struggled unsuccessfully to convince the Americans that the Greek guerrillas demanding unification with the mainland were 'communistic'. In London there were ongoing discussions – never fully resolved – as to whether Britain's clandestine apparatus should be mostly focused on the cold war or else employed against anything that might be perceived as anti-British.[30]

More than any other area of the cold war, it was perhaps within the operational realm of counter-insurgency that getting intelligence right could make a difference. In Malaya and the Philippines during the late 1940s and early 1950s, relatively small insurgencies allowed intelligence officers the rare luxury of climbing the learning curve, albeit it was climbed slowly. Good intelligence could allow the application of more selective military force and therefore encourage cooperation from the local population. Surrendered guerrillas in particular played a major part in the Malayan campaign and began a British tradition of using turned guerrillas or 'pseudo-gangs' against the enemy, a technique that would be employed later in Kenya, Cyprus and copied again by the Selous Scouts in Rhodesia.[31] The approach taken in Malaya was not the only model. Harsher approaches were used by the French in Algeria and Indochina, or by the Portuguese in Africa, in which intelligence gathering made use of torture. The extent of these abuses is only now becoming clear.[32]

The Vietnam war ensured that for more than a decade the CIA's largest sphere of operations was South-East Asia. Here efforts were made to apply lessons learned from elsewhere, not least by Ed Lansdale in the Philippines. Yet the experience of applying intelligence to counter-insurgency in South Vietnam was different to that enjoyed by the British and the French in imperial territories. In Vietnam there could be no pretence of working for stability as a stepping stone to an eventual transfer of power. Instead the requirement was to work though the local regime and indeed the local intelligence service. This provided its own special frustrations.

Eastern bloc experiences were remarkably similar. During the 1960s and the 1970s these services undertook a degree of role specialisation. The Romanians and the Bulgarians were given some responsibility for covert action, while the East Germans specialised in security intelligence support to friendly Third World countries. This specialisation also reflected the impressive language training programmes carried out by the communist intelligence services. These were so many teams from the GDR's security service (the MfS, or *Stasi*) attached to pro-Soviet leaders in Africa that they were given the nickname 'The new Afrika Korps'. The *Stasi* were especially active in the Yemen, Ethiopia and Angola.[33]

In Afghanistan, the KGB provided a degree of intelligence support to the government of Prince Muhammad Daud (1973–78) and several of Daud's ministers had significant contacts with the KGB. After the Soviet invasion in December 1979, Moscow devoted considerable efforts to expanding the indigenous Afghan communist security service, KhAD. There was widespread use of torture and assassination, and KhAD was quite effective in penetrating Western-backed *Mujahadin* groups in their training camps. Given the need of the *Mujahadin* to continually recruit new volunteers, this sort of penetration was unavoidable.

Remarkably, the KGB employed the same sorts of 'pseudo-gang' operations that had been developed by the West in campaigns as far apart as Malaya, Kenya and Cyprus. The KGB oversaw numerous 'false flag' military operations inside Afghanistan during the 1980s. The purpose of these operations was for Soviet-trained Afghan guerrilla units to pretend to be anti-Soviet *Mujahadin* rebels in order to generate confusion and to allow the KGB to identify genuine rebels for concerted attacks. Mitrokhin notes that by early 1983, there were some 86 KGB-trained 'false bands' in action throughout Afghanistan. One of the frequently reported aspects of the war in Afghanistan during the 1980s was the serious *Mujahadin* infighting and it now seems likely that some of this was generated by groups that were operating on behalf of the KGB and their local protégés. This in turn may have contributed to the fierce civil war fought in Afghanistan in the mid-1990s. Afghanistan, in many respects, sums up a wider experience in the realm of intelligence support to both insurgency and counter-insurgency in the Third World.[34]

human intelligence

Historians have tended to downplay the importance of human intelligence, or the use of espionage agents. Some have gone so far as to assert that there is no evidence of any major political or military decision being reported by an agent in such a way as to allow the other side to take effective counter-action.[35] This reflects perhaps a natural reaction against some of the more improbable claims made by popular writers in this field.[36] Classically, two kinds of arguments have been advanced here. First, it has been suggested that the West was relatively unsuccessful at recruiting and running spies inside the extremely secure environment of communist states. Second, while the Soviets and their Eastern bloc allies were the undoubted masters of running agents inside the Western government, and especially in European capitals such as Bonn, their own decision-making bureaucracies were simply too dysfunctional to make effective use of the high-grade information that was obtained. This reflected not only the corrupt and ineffective nature of communist governments, but also the ideological prism through which some of the material was viewed.[37]

Moscow's paranoia seems to have extended even to its top agents. At the end of the Second World War, some of the most effective operators who had worked inside Nazi-occupied Europe were recalled to Russia to face bizarre disciplinary tribunals and periods of imprisonment that reflected Stalin's anxiety about double-agents and penetration. A number of figures from the fabled *Rote Kapelle* or 'Red Orchestra' spent the early cold war period in prison and might have remained there but for the death of Stalin. These problems did not end in 1953 and suspicion later extended to the KGB's star agent Kim Philby, whose access in both London and Washington perhaps rivalled any agent before or since. In his own memoirs he portrays himself as a senior KGB intelligence officer, but the sad reality was that Philby was under strong suspicion from some sections of the KGB and, after his defection in 1963, was kept in semi-isolation in Moscow. Although rehabilitated in the 1980s he never rose above the humble rank of agent.[38]

The experience of Western espionage against the Eastern bloc was arguably rather different. Running agents inside secure police states proved to be extremely hazardous. Although the subject remains little discussed, agents for the most part suffered imprisonment or execution in significant numbers. This was also true of 'third country' recruitments, made in third countries like India or Indonesia where it was easier to approach communist officials. However, once the people were back inside the Eastern bloc, few operated with impunity for any extended period of time. Even more hazardous were the border-crossing operations undertaken during the Korean and the Vietnam wars. In both these conflicts hundreds of agents were despatched and few lasted more then a week.[39] Those running agents in Korea speak of the depressing loss rates and the strong suspicions that those few who remained active and came up on the radio net had actually fallen under communist control. William Colby launched numerous teams into North Vietnam during his first tour as CIA station chief in Saigon and all were caught.[40]

Undeniably, several 'star' recruitments were made by the West during the cold war. However, most historians have concluded that while their information was useful it remains hard to show how it changed policy in any significant way. Perhaps the most closely discussed case is that of Colonel Oleg Penkovsky, a GRU officer recruited by Britain's SIS (more popularly known as MI6) in the 1950s who enjoyed access to elevated circles in Moscow and who worked on Soviet missile systems. Substantial claims have been made with regard to the impact of his espionage in relation to the Cuban missile crisis. However, while Penkovsky's intelligence about Soviet missile systems helped to confirm the absence of a so-called 'missile gap', allowing Kennedy to act with more confidence during the ensuing crisis, Penkovsky was no longer operative by October 1962.[41] During the Cuban missile crisis the key information came from U-2 overhead reconnaissance flights. This did not reflect a lack of agents on the ground in Cuba – far from it – the CIA processed thousands of reports from hundreds of agents and sub-agents during the crisis. However, as recently declassified materials reveal, the problem was that many of these reports seemed to contradict each other and evaluation was extremely difficult. By comparison overhead photography appeared to offer unambiguous information.[42]

In the latter part of the cold war, the most impressive Western recruitments were probably Oleg Gordievsky and Vasili Mitrokhin, each of whom brought a treasure trove of information to the West. Remarkably, while still in place as the KGB head of station in London, Oleg Gordievsky briefed Thatcher before her meeting with Gorbachev in December 1984. By and large however, the recruitment of KGB officers proved more useful in the narrow world of 'spy against spy' and does not seem to have had much impact on policy. Spy activities could impinge on the world of diplomacy. Edward Heath's decision to expel over a hundred Soviet diplomats from London in 1971, codenamed 'Operation Foot', is perhaps the most obvious example. This had resulted from the defection of a KGB officer called Oleg Lyalin, who revealed some of the more unpleasant aspects of KGB contingency planning for war with the West.[43]

While the assessments of the significance of human agents has been largely downbeat some qualifications need to be advanced. Spies clearly made a real impact in the realm of technical intelligence gathering and, indirectly upon arms racing. The Eastern bloc may have been clumsy in its efforts to use political or diplomatic intelligence, however its efficacy in the realm of exploiting military-technical 'kleptionage' was remarkable.[44] The most important instances of technical espionage probably relate to nuclear weapons. It is now clear that the wartime atomic programme at Los Alamos was badly penetrated by figures such as Klaus Fuchs, Ted Hall and a cast of more minor characters. The Soviet Union detonated an atomic bomb in late August 1949, some three or four years earlier than Western intelligence had predicted. The revelations of the espionage of Klaus Fuchs shortly after this event sealed the connection in the public mind between espionage and the early Soviet acquisition of the atomic bomb.[45] The connections between espionage, weapons development and policy are potentially complex. While some suggested that Stalin's acquisition of the bomb lent him the confidence to launch the Korean war, this is not universally accepted. Other have argued that Stalin did not expect the United States to defend Korea and so would have invaded anyway without the need for atomic parity. Some have argued that espionage may have shortened Soviet bomb development by as much as two years, while others have suggested that access to Western atomic plans resulted in the Soviets taking a 'wrong turn' by abandoning promising indigenous approaches to atomic weapons, in favour of the cruder, but proven designs employed at Hiroshima.[46] Intriguingly, it has now been suggested that the espionage conducted by Klaus Fuchs may have contributed to the origins of the Soviet hydrogen bomb project. Either way, it is clear that many aspects of Western nuclear developments were an open book to Soviet scientists.[47]

A further area in which human agents were clearly important was in the stealing of codes and cyphers. During the cold war the effectiveness of the secure communications of developed countries became extremely good. Fully electronic systems, frequency hopping and online ciphering ensured that the high-grade communications of the major powers were mostly unbreakable even with the aid of high-power computers. As a result the attraction of 'pinching' codes and cyphers, perhaps by recruiting an embassy cipher clerk, or by using an agent to plant a bug in a cipher room, was considerably greater.[48] Equally, it seems likely that during the 1970s and 1980s figures such as Geoffrey Prime in Britain and John Walker in the United States managed to compromise some hard-won gains in the realm of 'SIGINT' and resulted in the Soviets tightening their communications security.[49]

molemania and the security state

Human agents may have had only limited impact upon policy but they did much to expand the cold war 'security state'. Revelations of their activities had a significant impact on the security climate at several different levels. At the official level, anxieties about 'moles' led to the tightening of procedures relating to the security screening of personnel. In the West this meant detailed background checks or 'positive vetting'. At the political level the repercussions were was most visible in the antics of Senator Joseph McCarthy and the HUAC (House Un-American Affairs Committee). At a wider societal level, revelations about the work of moles and spies contributed to the remarkable growth of the public profile of the intelligence services. In the early 1950s, the public knew little about espionage, but by the late 1960s the public understood that the cold war was a battle fought largely by the intelligence services. Sheila Kerr has suggested that one of the most important consequences of the defection of figures such as Philby, Burgess and Maclean was their impact on public perceptions as to who was winning or losing the cold war. In response to this, the CIA, and later the SIS, began to develop public relations departments to manage their public profiles and indeed their history.[50]

In the West, the initial trigger for security anxieties was a series of revelations about agents connected to atomic espionage. The atomic dimension added greatly to both public anxiety and private concern by officials. Igor Gouzenko, a defecting Soviet cipher clerk, brought the atomic espionage of the British scientist Allan Nunn May to public attention in 1946 and anxiety was heightened by the Fuchs case in 1950. The United States made it clear to Britain that the introduction of positive vetting, which involved background checks for all those with access to sensitive information, was a condition of continued cooperation. Pressure from Washington ensured that this was introduced as almost the last act of a departing British Labour government in 1951. However, British officials resisted the exhortations of the Americans that the polygraph should be introduced at locations such as GCHQ.[51]

In the United States, political reactions to Soviet espionage were volatile. Diverse American groups seized on the problem of Soviet espionage and subversion with the intention of making this a major public issue. This included the China Lobby, a group who were concerned to identify those diplomats responsible for the 'loss of China' to communism in the late 1940s and for what they believed was an excessively generous settlement with Stalin at Yalta. Amateur witch-hunting resulted in the blacklisting and persecution of hundreds of artists, musicians, actors, playwrights and teachers because of left-liberal views or because of their participation in anti-fascist activities in the 1930s. These lamentable episodes have been documented in some detail. Harder to measure was the undoubted 'chilling out' of a spectrum of left-liberal political activity in the United States during the 1950s because of anxieties about the consequences of expression of such opinions.

The activities of Senator McCarthy and committees through which he briefly operated were political rather than official. Perversely, they had a detrimental effect on some of the new agencies set up to fight the cold war. Some of the best and brightest officers recruited by the CIA in the late 1940s were liberals who had been ardent opponents of fascism in the 1930s and supporters of Roosevelt's New Deal politics. A good example was Cord Meyer, a rising star in the CIA who had succeeded Tom Braden as head of the CIA's International Organisations Division. A former advocate of world-federalism, he fell under suspicion and was fortunate that McCarthy did not terminate his career. Many employees of Radio Liberty and Radio Free Europe, with whom he cooperated, also came under persistent pressure from McCarthy.[52]

Intelligence officers sometimes defected, with serious repercussion for the intelligence services themselves. Although the intelligence services were designed – as their name implies – to provide a 'service' to other parts of government, there was also a sense in which the war of 'spy against spy' had developed its own momentum by the 1960s. The discovery of high-level moles such as Donald Maclean, Guy Burgess, Kim Philby and George Blake had prompted a belief that one of the most valuable things that KGB defectors might provide was knowledge of who else was secretly working for Moscow. Unfortunately, genuine defectors were accompanied by false defectors and by those who exaggerated their knowledge for reasons of personal vanity. During the 1960s and 1970s this led to periods of 'super-molehunting', exemplified by the CIA's counter-intelligence chief, James Jesus Angleton. The zealous security activities of Angleton all but paralysed the activities of the CIA section working against the Soviet Union for almost a decade. The Western powers also set up an allied super-molehunting group called CAZAB in which security officers from countries such as Canada, Australia, Britain, New Zealand and the United States pursued especially sensitive investigations. Peter Wright was at the centre of CAZAB activities and published his *Spycatcher* memoirs in order to vent his personal conviction that Roger Hollis, Director General of the British Security Service (MI5), was a Soviet agent. This was not the case. However, it is not hard to imagine the sort of difficulties presented by the fact that some officials believed this might be a possibility.[53]

It was only in the 1990s that historians were offered the prospect of resolving some of these troubling issues. Salvation came from partial insights into the Soviet archives, and also from the releases of sanitised *Venona* signals intelligence material.[54] Towards the end of the Second World War the US Army's cryptanalytic service began to have success in breaking into Soviet intelligence radio traffic. The reason for this was Soviet inefficiency. Their intelligence services used a communication system that depended on sheets of enciphering material called 'One Time Pads' which, as the name implied, should only be used once. However, the Soviets began to re-use their material, making their communications vulnerable. American inroads into Soviet intelligence traffic were partial, but sufficient to identify major agents, including Fuchs and Maclean.

For Americans, the declassification of *Venona* offered to resolve questions of some importance. After all, the guilt or innocence of figures such as Julius Rosenberg or Alger Hiss had, for some decades, assumed an almost theological significance in American political life. For the right, they were examples of the aggression of Soviet communism, for the left they were martyrs to an American security state that had been running out of control. Gaddis has observed that the new evidence against these sorts of characters is now 'conclusive' and that in this area the study of cold war espionage is 'shifting from the realm of speculation to the reality of the archives'. He adds that the multiple volumes that have appeared on the subject of Soviet espionage in America, drawing on both American and Soviet materials, now allow us to 'triangulate' the subject and so provide an 'excellent basis' for reassessing the role of Soviet espionage in early cold war history.[55]

These new intelligence archives have resolved some specific questions of guilt. They have also contributed to interpretations that might be regarded as 'New Traditionalism' that focus on large-scale nefarious Soviet activities that were underway inside the United States both before and after the Second World War.[56] 'New Traditionalism' has a certain attractive logic. After the United States had won the cold war what could be more natural than winning the battle for cold war history? Soviet undercover activities, including the widespread covert funding of communist parties around the world, were indeed extensive and unpleasant. However, the battle for cold war history is not yet done, partly because *Venona* material is problematic, being heavily sanitised to protect the identities of further spies and therefore promoting controversy. This sanitisation has lent the area of *Venona* history a curious 'Whodunit' atmosphere, with some of the lengthy arguments about who best fits the 'clues' in the *Venona* text.

Moreover, excessive confidence in this new material can lead even the best historians to say more than they really know.[57]

John Gaddis, for example, has asserted that 'the Rosenbergs were spies' and that the evidence for this is 'conclusive'.[58] Rejoinders to this statement have not been slow in arriving. More cautious historians have observed that while Julius Rosenberg's guilt is now clearly established, evidence suggesting that his wife, Ethel, was active in espionage is completely absent. While she may well have known of her husband's activities, there is little to suggest that she was involved in anything more than underground communist political activity. Indeed, it appears that Ethel was arrested primarily to put pressure on Julius and that, even on the eve of his execution, the FBI were trying to ascertain whether she was cognisant of her husband's espionage.[59]

Problems of this sort are disconcerting, since Julius and Ethel Rosenberg constitute two of the highest-profile espionage cases in cold war history. No less troubling are the assertions of historians that the KGB was too efficient and disciplined to exaggerate its work in recruiting agents and so never reported innocent contacts as recruited agents. Clearly, most of those named in *Venona* traffic or in KGB files in Moscow were indeed agents, but can we be sure about all of them? As Tim Weiner has rightly observed, intelligence officers reporting to headquarters 'tend to exaggerate the number and importance of the agents they have recruited'. If KGB officers in the field did not inflate some of their achievements then they are unique in the annals of secret service history. It is more likely that the KGB's reporting of agent recruitment was patchy, just like its communications procedures. We may not be completely certain about agent identities even after the KGB and GRU files are fully opened in Moscow, and this will not be anytime soon.[60]

Some areas of consensus are emerging. Wisely, most revisionist historians working on internal security have accepted that *Venona*, together with new material from the Moscow archives, has indicated a vast scale of Soviet espionage together with substantial connections between this and the American Communist Party.[61] Revisionists have meanwhile turned their attention more specifically to McCarthy and to the FBI. Athan Theoharis, a life-long sceptic of the value of the FBI, has asked the obvious question. Given the fact that some FBI counter-espionage personnel had access to the wonders of *Venona*, and given that there was so much Soviet espionage activity in America, why did FBI agents catch so very few spies? Theoharis answers his own question by asserting that the FBI wasted much of its time harassing black activists, gays, pacifists, environmentalists and anyone else perceived as being distant from the political mainstream. Theoharis is unlikely ever to write much that is favourable to the FBI. However, it has to be conceded that there is now a vast body of documentation on FBI repression of 'fringe' groups during the cold war. Much of the FBI's domestic security activity was repellent.[62]

Although Theoharis' question about *Venona* is a good one, it has several answers. One of these relates to the very secret nature of the intercept material. The FBI could not use it in court for fear of compromising the source. Accordingly, once a spy had been identified, they had to be kept under surveillance until they could be caught 'red handed' in an act of espionage or else they had to be confronted in the hope that the shock would prompt a confession. Fuchs, for example, confessed at length. However, some important figures, including the American atomic spy Ted Hall, decided to protest their innocence and, in the absence of other evidence, escaped prosecution even though their guilt was clear to the authorities.[63]

Alongside these historical issues there are also some puzzling historiographical questions. Given the vaunted importance of these revelations, why have mainstream cold war historians not taken more interest in *Venona*? The answer perhaps lies in the disappointing mediocrity of the newly revealed Soviet agents. There were certainly numerous Soviet agents inside the United States and in most other Western countries. However, so many of them were clerks, corporals, school teachers, lab technicians, even taxi-drivers. Since the uncovering of John Cairncross in 1990, no further major-league cold war spies have come out of the woodwork. Philby had taught us to think of Soviet spies in the West as giants, but the revelations of the last 20 years have produced what looks like an army of pygmies.

overhead reconnaissance

In contrast to human espionage, it is not difficult to identify the manner in which overhead reconnaissance changed the nature of the cold war. The growth of this area of intelligence-gathering was driven by three factors. First, espionage efforts by human agents working into the Eastern bloc had proved to be ineffective and also costly in terms of lives. Second, bombers and rockets were the main means of delivery for nuclear weapons and some of these high-priority intelligence targets were eminently visible from the air. Third, the development of arms control initiatives during the 1950s and 1960s increased the demand for accurate weapons estimates.

Overhead reconnaissance moved through several overlapping phases, from traditional over-flights with conventional aircraft, though a phase of high-flying unconventional aircraft such as the U-2 spy-plane and quickly onwards to the era of satellite platforms which arrived in the 1960s. During the late 1940s it appears that Britain carried out some over-flights of communist countries, but the United States refrained from this practice because the State Department feared diplomatic incidents. The advent of Soviet atomic power increased the appetite for such flights and in 1951 a British *Canberra* aircraft, one of the first of its type, reportedly made a flight over Soviet rocket test ranges. The United States then joined this activity, flying its own missions and contributing the RB-45C four-engined jet aircraft which allowed the RAF to reconnoitre targets deep inside the Soviet Union again in 1952 and 1954.[64]

By the mid-1950s, the US Air Force was operating a wide range of over-flight and perimeter flight programmes for the purpose of both photo-reconnaissance and electronic eavesdropping. Remarkably, during a seven-week period in the spring of 1956 the US Air Force launched Project *Home Run* which involved no less than 156 missions over Soviet Siberia, including one operation that involved a flight by a whole formation of US aircraft.[65] American government historians have taken the line that all these flights were authorised by Eisenhower or his subordinates in a proper manner. However, other evidence suggests that the White House was worried by these Air Force activities. Partly for this reason Eisenhower turned the main reconnaissance effort over to the CIA.[66]

Spy-flights were revolutionised in 1956 with the arrival of the CIA's high altitude U-2 aircraft. Flying at over 55,000 feet, the U-2 could then cruise with impunity over the Soviet Union, providing the first significant window on Soviet strategic capability.[67] Admirers of the U-2 have claimed much for its achievements, insisting that it helped to destroy the myth of Soviet strategic superiority, the so-called 'bomber gap', and allowed Eisenhower to rein in those who were pressing for massive increases in American defence spending. This claim is not unfounded, but has probably been exaggerated. The U-2 could not provide the depth of coverage that Eisenhower needed to be certain that the 'bomber gap' did not exist, although it did much to reinforce his natural scepticism. Moreover, for security reasons, Eisenhower could not share the limited evidence from the U-2 flights with his most vociferous critics in Congress.[68]

Eisenhower was conscious that the Soviets were struggling to bring U-2 invulnerability to an end and each flight beyond 1959 involved greater risk. The eventual shoot-down of a U-2 aircraft piloted by Gary Powers in 1960 brought public embarrassment and terminated a long-awaited

East–West summit in Paris. Two years later, the loss of a U-2 during the Cuban missile crisis provided a potential flash-point. These anxieties were soon superseded when another U-2 briefly strayed into Siberia during the same period of tension. Because of the existing high state of alert during the Cuban missile crisis the subsequent combination of errors and automatic procedures during this episode perhaps constituted one of the most precarious moments of the cold war. While over-flights provided a great deal of strategic intelligence, the aircraft losses were politically damaging and at times quite dangerous.[69]

This 'hot' period of U-2 incidents stands in direct contrast to the 'cooler' era of satellite reconnaissance that followed hard on its heels. Indeed, almost as soon as the first U-2 was launched it was recognised that its period of operational utility over the Soviet Union would be short. The U-2 continued to be used in many other locations during the 1960s and 1970s, especially the Middle East where it supported the work of the United Nations in enforcing ceasefires. However, from 1963 the task of providing photo coverage of the Soviet Union was undertaken by the *Corona* satellite system. The moment when a *Corona* satellite delivered its first payload of photography was a genuine turning point in the cold war. The first *Corona* mission over the Soviet Union provided more photography than had been gathered by all the previous U-2 over-flights put together.[70]

Satellites were of crucial importance in opening the door to serious strategic arms control. The connection between arms control, verification and technical espionage was underlined by Eisenhower's 'Open Skies' proposal as early as 1958.[71] Overhead photography by satellites was not a panacea and each country soon developed drills designed to foil the work of these space sentinels. Nor were satellites as effective in supporting efforts at conventional force reduction as they were in assisting strategic arms talks. Nevertheless, for the last three decades of the cold war they provided substantial reassurance. They also played a key part in the immediate post-cold war build-down of strategic arsenals. In the 1990s, as the complements of missiles on submarines was lowered in support of arms reductions, the missile hatches of the submarines in dock would be left open so that passing satellites could count the increasing number of empty tubes.

Working in tandem with satellites were a range of curious ground stations conducting some of the more baroque intelligence operations of the cold war designed to assess the scale of atomic arsenals. In many cases these were seismic listening stations that picked up ground shocks from nuclear tests. Other facilities attempted to measure minute amounts of gas released by the production of particular atomic isotopes, thereby indirectly measuring Soviet bomb production. Some of these stations were secretly located inside diplomatic premises unknown to the host country. Each major protagonist developed a small, specialist and highly secretive 'atomic intelligence service'. Although these obscure agencies were small, their contributions were significant and they were accorded the highest priority by policy-makers.[72]

signals intelligence

Signals intelligence (or SIGINT) remains the most secretive aspect of cold war espionage and was probably the most important. What is certain is that the SIGINT agencies were leviathans. During the latter stages of the cold war, the US SIGINT agency, or the National Security Agency (NSA), probably directed close to 100,000 people who were either its own staff, or allocated to its support. In Britain, the equivalent organisation, GCHQ, was superintended by the Foreign Office. Yet GCHQ enjoyed a budget larger than that of the Foreign Office and often superintended as many, if not more, personnel.[73]

Although there were some successes in reading Soviet traffic immediately after the Second World War, this was brought to a halt during the late 1940s by the activities of the Soviet agent William Weisband. Working as a sergeant in the US Army signals intelligence organisation, he was recruited by the Soviets and 'blew' some important work, including *Venona*. The Soviets could not prevent the Americans from continuing to work on messages already captured and recorded, but Soviet cipher security improved markedly. Indeed, for much of the cold war the cipher systems of the major powers remained sophisticated and hard to break even with the application of enormous computer power. Although the West had begun to make advances with various Soviet systems during later decades of the cold war, it is thought that human espionage by the Soviets undermined some of these fresh advances.[74]

This did not mean that the major powers did not listen in to each other's communications. A great deal of effort was devoted to monitoring low level voice traffic, especially from military operations and exercises. Efforts were also made to measure precisely the types, directions and volumes of traffic emitted at particular periods, even if the actual text could not be read. This in turn allowed each side to watch for signs of unusual activity which might preface an attack. In short, one of the major functions of SIGINT monitoring, especially in locations such as Germany, was a kind of unilateral confidence-building measure. It would have been very hard for either side to prepare to mount a major attack without generating some signals noise. SIGINT provided a reasonable level of reassurance that nothing dramatic was happening on either side of the inner-German border and at several other points of tension around the world.[75]

During the 1950s and 1960s, Western communications analysts also kept themselves busy with neutral and even allied communications. These could be more useful than material from the Warsaw Pact. During the 1960s, the British were more interested in the thoughts of West German policy-makers in Bonn than with their East German equivalents. London wished to know about Bonn's likely reaction to any move to recognise the GDR and about Bonn's views of Britain's attempts to join the EEC. Across Europe, a major challenge for Britain and the United States was to try to ensure that the communications of other NATO states were secure enough to prevent the Soviets from reading them, but not so secure that their Anglo-Saxon allies could not read them. Britain and the United States were also keen to discourage the development of a sophisticated European cryptographic industry.

Accordingly, signals intelligence was related to the less glamorous world of COMSEC or communications security, the practice of defending one's own communications from hostile attack and making sure that embassies were free of electronic 'bugs'. These had become more numerous with the advent of transistors and miniaturisation. There were plenty of bugs to be found. During the first two decades of the cold war the Americans uncovered some 160 bugs in their Eastern bloc embassies and consulates. This culminated in a major discovery in May 1964 of a large number of hitherto undetected bugs in its Moscow embassy. It was clear that much of what had been said during the last few years had been closely followed by the Soviets. However, they were puzzled by the fact that when they reviewed the sequence of some recent negotiations, they could not identify where foreknowledge of American negotiating positions had made a difference to Soviet behaviour.[76]

If the communications of the developed countries were hard to read during the cold war, the playground for signals intelligence was the Third World where cipher security and telephone security was often weak. The work of capturing, processing and analysing the resulting volume of communications prompted the English-speaking powers to continue their wartime pattern of cooperation on signals intelligence. Between 1942 and 1948 a number of agreements and memoranda were exchanged giving rise to an intelligence alliance referred to as 'UKUSA'. This agreement divided the world up into spheres of responsibility for both collection and analysis, typically with the British taking a significant role in Africa and the Canadians focusing on northern Europe and the northern Soviet Union.

One of the primary British contributions to this alliance was what the Americans referred to as 'residual empire', a network of bases, often on remote islands and locations secured as part of post-colonial settlements that provided the ground-stations for collection. Retention of these ground-stations was important and became a policy issue in itself. The determination of London and Washington to retain their listening stations on Cyprus contributed in no small degree to their policies towards the protracted conflict on that troubled island. Exactly which communications were intercepted from Cyprus has not yet been revealed, but one account mentions how soldiers from Britain's 9 Signals Regiment listened in to the shouts of Israeli and Egyptian tank crews as they battled it out during the Yom Kippur war of 1973.[77]

conclusions

One of the great puzzles for cold war historians and for cold warriors alike, was why, given the vast sums spent on intelligence gathering, the intelligence services were nevertheless often caught napping by major events. During the first five years of the cold war, Western intelligence seems to have missed the coming of the Tito–Stalin split of 1948, misdated the first Soviet atomic bomb by between three and four years and was completely surprised by the invasion of Korea. The Soviets did little better, even suggesting that the Marshall Plan was part of a desperate search by the United States for new markets that prefigured the impending collapse of Western capitalism.

The record of the analysts did not improve much with time. The United Stated failed to second-guess the nefarious activities of its British and French allies at Suez in 1956, believing instead that the intense military build-up in the region pointed towards a coming confrontation between Israel and Jordan. In Vietnam, the US Army was taken by surprise by the Tet Offensive in 1968. In the same year the British Joint Intelligence Committee (JIC) insisted that the Soviets would not invade Czechoslovakia despite a volume of evidence to the contrary. The invasion of the Falklands was missed in 1982, prompting a major British post-mortem. Most remarkably of all perhaps, the end of the cold war was second-guessed by enterprising journalists but missed by secret services, both large and small. The end of the cold war did not mean the end of intelligence mishaps, since the same leviathans missed the Iraqi invasion of Kuwait in 1991, the Pakistani nuclear test of May 1998 and were badly wrong about Iraqi weapons stocks in both 1991 and 2003.

Many of these 'failures' related to the issue of surprise attack. In fairness to the intelligence services, they were always painfully conscious of the special problem of surprise. Some of the key impediments were identified by one of the founding fathers of intelligence analysis, Sherman Kent, in his pioneering work, published in 1951. Three decades later, the CIA were funding comparative work by the renowned political scientist, Richard Betts, in an attempt to identify exactly what made surprise events so difficult to predict or warn against. Three types of problem beset the analytical chain.[78] First was the problem of modelling or stereotyping. In a world of infinite detail a certain amount of presumption about what certain indicators mean was essential in order to draw meaning from a vast ocean of collected data. One of the most obvious examples of this is 'rational actor presumption', suggesting that leaders will not behave in improbable ways. Analysis is about joining up the dots. When the dots are not numbered, analysts are inclined to see the pattern that they have seen before or a pattern of behaviour that seems reasonable. Analysts are therefore temperamentally inclined to see the normal and to be sceptical about the suggestions that something unusual or irrational is happening.

Second was the problem of intelligence bureaucracy. By the 1960s intelligence bureaucracies had themselves become so large that they formed a barrier between the field collector and the policy-maker. The United States boasted no less than 13 intelligence agencies around Washington's beltway and the US Director of Central Intelligence had become a referee in what was sometimes referred to as the 'Beltway War'. The compilation of a US National Intelligence Estimate was often a process of negotiation between agencies with different views or different bureaucratic ownership. The process was vulnerable to either dilution through comprise or undue influence by dominant coalitions fielded by the Department of Defense. As a result, so called 'high-level' estimates could prove to be remarkably dull and failed to inform, or even attract the attention of, busy policy-makers. Members of the NSC rarely read them, even in summary.

The most impermeable barrier to intelligence-informed policy was probably the policy-makers themselves. By their nature those who achieved senior positions were intolerant of advice that did not suit their wishes. Existing policies had often resulted from intricate negotiations within bureaucratic or political circles and so leaders were not always receptive to challenges from 'independent' intelligence experts who wished to identify awkward facts or even suggest a different hierarchy of priorities. This was illustrated during the Vietnam war, when there was a serious erosion of the boundary between analysts and policy-makers. Moreover, a divided intelligence community allowed policy-makers to pick the particular estimates which conformed most closely to what they wanted to believe. Lyndon B. Johnson and his circle preferred more optimistic military intelligence and discounted the civilian agencies, which were more sceptical.[79]

Sherman Kent had always argued that intelligence-producers should be insulated from the pressures of policy-makers. He envisaged cold war intelligence in a semi-academic role, providing objective and independent advice that might implicitly challenge policy. This idealist vision was probably right. However, over the four decades of the cold war and beyond, intelligence increasingly fitted an opposing definition of intelligence that was more 'realistic'. This was one developed by the Pentagon and conceived of intelligence as a form of support to existing policy and strategy. In short, intelligence was becoming a function of command. While this trend continued – both during and after the cold war – performance was bound to remain mediocre at best. Moreover, while the intelligence analysts were mostly keen to emphasise the limits of intelligence and the contingent nature of their predictions, consumers often chose to strip away any words of qualification where it suited them. Again this was a phenomena that continued to be visible well beyond the end of the cold war.[80]

notes

1. Christopher Andrew & David Dilks (eds), *The Missing Dimension: Governments and Intelligence Communities in the Twentieth Century* (London: Macmillan, 1984), pp.1–5. The phrase was coined by Sir Alexander Cadogan.
2. O. Hoare (ed.), *British Intelligence in the Twentieth Century: A Missing Dimension?* (London: Frank Cass, 2002). This was also a special issue of the journal *Intelligence and National Security*, 17:1 (2002).
3. The most obvious exception is the archive of Britain's Secret Intelligence Service (MI6) which remains closed for the period beyond 1909.
4. Some historians have given very little attention to intelligence of any kind, see for example: M.J. Hogan, *Cross of Iron: Harry S. Truman and the Origins of the National Security State* (Cambridge: Cambridge University Press, 1999); Melvyn Leffler, *A Preponderance of Power: National Security, the Truman Administration, and the cold war* (Stanford, CA: Stanford University Press, 1992), *passim*.
5. The historiographical literature on cold war intelligence is now substantial. See for example: Christopher Andrew, 'Intelligence and International Relations in the Early Cold War', *Review of International Studies*, 24:3 (1998), pp.321–30; J. Ferris, 'Coming in from the Cold: The Historiography of American

Intelligence, 1945–1990', *Diplomatic History*, 10:1 (1995), pp.87–116; John L. Gaddis, 'Intelligence, Espionage and Cold War Origins', *Diplomatic History*, 13:2 (1989), pp.191–213; D.C. Watt, 'Intelligence and the Historian: A Comment of John Gaddis', *Diplomatic History*, 14:2 (1990), pp.199–204; Raymond Garthoff, 'Foreign Intelligence and the Historiography of the cold war', *Journal of Cold War Studies*, 6:2 (2004), *passim*.

6. Gaddis, 'Intelligence, Espionage and Cold War Origins', pp. 191–213.

7. In the UK and the USA this might be connected with the popularity of historical institutionalism as an approach over several decades.

8. A third category of intelligence literature might be intelligence biography and memoir. I have tried to draw out the distinction between contextualist and institutionalist approaches more fully elsewhere; see R.J. Aldrich, 'Grow Your Own: Cold War History and Intelligence Supermarkets', in Hoare (ed.), *British Intelligence*, pp.135–52. A good example of contextualist history is C.M. Andrew, *For the President's Eyes Only: Secret Intelligence and the American Presidency from Washington to Bush* (London: HarperCollins, 1995).

9. We are beginning to see some post-war SIGINT history, but this is more about dogged research than generous declassification. The best example is perhaps Korea. See M. Aid, 'US Humint and Comint in the Korean War [Part I]: From the Approach of War to the Chinese Intervention', *Intelligence and National Security*, 14:4 (1999), pp.17–63; 'American Comint in the Korean War (Part II): From the Chinese Intervention to the Armistice', *Intelligence and National Security*, 15:1 (2000), pp.14–49.

10. The literature is vast. Recent examples include: M.J. Gasiorowski & M. Byrne (eds), *Mohammad Mosaddeq and the 1953 Coup in Iran* (New York: Syracuse University Press, 2004); N. Cullather & Piero Gliejeses, *Secret History: The CIA's Classified Account of its Operations in Guatemala, 1952–1954* (Stanford, CA: Stanford University Press, 1999); A.R. Kahin & G. McT. Kahin, *Subversion as Foreign Policy: The Secret Eisenhower and Dulles Debacle in Indonesia* (New York: New Press, 1995); J.K. Knaus, *Orphans of the Cold War: America and the Tibetan Struggle for Survival* (New York: Public Affairs, 1999).

11. Saki Dockrill, *Eisenhower's New Look National Security Policy, 1953–61* (London: Macmillan, 1991), pp.169–70.

12. For recent non-*Venona* material see particularly Christopher Andrew & Oleg Gordievsky, *KGB: The Inside Story* (London: Hodder & Stoughton, 1990); Christopher Andrew & Vasili Mitrokhin, *The Mitrokhin Archive: The KGB in Europe and the West* (London: Penguin, 1999), *passim*; Nigel West & Oleg Tsarev, *The Crown Jewels: The British Secrets Exposed by the KGB Archives* (London: HarperCollins, 1997); A. Weinstein & G. Vasiliev, *Haunted Wood: Soviet Espionage in America – The Stalin Era* (New York: Random House, 1999).

13. See for example, Denis Deletant, *Communist Terror in Romania: Gheorghiu-Dej and the Police State, 1948–1965* (New York: St Martin's Press, 1999). A great deal of new material from central and eastern Europe was presented in 2005 at a conference organised by the Norwegian Institute for Defence Studies in Oslo, 'Intelligence in Waging the Cold War: NATO, the Warsaw Pact and the Neutrals, 1949–90'.

14. See Michael Parrish, 'Soviet Espionage and the Cold War', *Diplomatic History*, 25:1 (2001), pp.105–20.

15. John Prados, *Presidents' Secret Wars: CIA and Pentagon Covert Operations from World War II through the Persian Gulf* (Chicago, IL: Ivan R. Dee, 1996), *passim*.

16. J.A. Bill, 'America, Iran and the Politics of Intervention, 1951–1953', in J.A. Bill & Wm. R. Louis (eds), *Musaddiq, Iranian Nationalism and Oil* (London: I.B. Tauris, 1988), pp.286–7.

17. Cullather & Gliejeses, *Secret History*; *passim*; Kahin & Kahin, *Subversion as Foreign Policy*; K. Conboy & J. Morrison, *Feet to the Fire: CIA Covert Operations in Indonesia, 1957–1958* (Annapolis, MD: Naval Institute Press, 2000). For Gaddis's most extended treatment of the CIA is in the context of the Third World, see *We Now Know: Rethinking Cold War History* (Oxford: Oxford University Press, 1997), pp.166–72.

18. Andrew, *For the President's Eyes Only*, pp.250–4; Lawrence Freedman, *Kennedy's Wars: Berlin, Cuba, Laos and Vietnam* (New York: Oxford University Press, 2000), pp.149–52.

19. Richard Aldrich, *The Hidden Hand: Britain, America and Cold War Secret Intelligence* (London: John Murray, 2002), pp.444, 479, 483, 505, 581. The definitive account of efforts against General Grivas in Cyprus is R. Holland, *Britain and the Revolt in Cyprus, 1954–59* (Oxford: Oxford University Press, 1998), pp.312–13.

20. Mark Jones, 'The "Preferred Plan": The Anglo-American Working Group Report on Covert Action in Syria, 1957', *Intelligence and National Security*, 19:3 (2004), p.408.

21. Bill & Louis, *Musaddiq, Iranian Nationalism and Oil*, pp.10–12.

22. Chalmers Johnson, *Blowback: The Costs and Consequences of American Empire* (New York: Metropolitan Books, 2002).

23. See for example J. Stockwell, *In Search of Enemies* (New York: W.W. Norton, 1978), pp.266–8.

24. On Angola see the excellent coverage of CIA and mercenary activity in Piero Gleijeses, *Conflicting Missions: Havana, Washington, and Africa, 1959–1976* (Chapel Hill, NC: University of North Carolina Press, 2002), *passim*; on Afghanistan see, Steve Coll, *Ghost Wars: The Secret History of the CIA, Afghanistan and bin Laden, from the Soviet Invasion to September 10, 2001* (New York: Penguin Press, 2004), *passim*.

25. H. Laville, *Cold War Women: American Women's Organisations in the Cold War* (Manchester: Manchester University Press, 2002); Hugh Wilford, *The CIA, the British Left and the Cold War* (London: Frank Cass, 2003), *passim*; W. Scott Lucas, *Freedom's War: The US Crusade Against the Soviet Union, 1945–56* (New York: New York University Press, 1999), *passim*.

26. G. Mitrovich, *Undermining the Kremlin: America's Strategy to Subvert the Soviet Bloc, 1947–56* (Ithaca, NY: Cornell University Press, 2000). See also S.J. Corke, 'Bridging the Gap: Containment: Covert Action and the Search for the Missing Link in American Cold War Policy, 1948–53', *Journal of Strategic Studies*, 20:4 (1997), pp.45–65.

27. Dockrill, *Eisenhower's New Look*, pp.149–67; Robert Bowie & Richard Immerman, *Waging Peace: How Eisenhower Shaped an Enduring Cold War Strategy* (Oxford: Oxford University Press, 1998), pp.135–7, 160, 169–71, 219–20.

28. For a discussion of the New Revisionism in the studies by Lucas and Mitrovich see S.L. Rearden, 'The Cold War: How the Winner Won', *Diplomatic History*, 25:4 (2001), pp.707–12.
29. Mitrovich, *Undermining the Kremlin*, pp.9–10. Recent documentation on this subject was released in the UK at DEFE 28/43,(TNA).
30. S.L. Carruthers, 'A Red Under Every Bed? Anti-communist Propaganda and Britain's Response to Colonial Insurgency', *Contemporary Record*, 9:2 (1995), pp.294–318.
31. Frank Kitson, *Gangs and Counter-gangs* (London: Faber & Faber, 1986); R.R. Daly, *Selous Scouts Top Secret War* (Alberton, SA: Galago, 1982).
32. French approaches are related frankly in a recent memoir by General Paul Aussaresses, *Services Spéciaux, Algérie 1955–1957* (Perrin, 2001).
33. Melvin Croan, 'A New Afrika Korps?', *The Washington Quarterly*, 3:1 (Winter 1980), p.31.
34. Vasili Mitrokhin, *The KGB in Afghanistan*, CWIHP Working Paper No. 40 (2002). See also his article 'KGB Active Measures in Southwest Asia in 1980–82', *Cold War International History Bulletin*, 14:15 (2003–04), pp.193–204.
35. Garthoff, 'Foreign Intelligence', p.30.
36. The hyperbolic title of a recent book about Penkovsky by J. Schecter & P. Deriabin, *The Spy Who Saved the World: How a Soviet Colonel Changed the Course of the Cold War* (New York: Scribner's, 1992), is an indication of what serious historians are reacting against.
37. Christopher Andrew & J. Elkner, 'Stalin and Foreign Intelligence', *Totalitarian Movements and Political Religions*, 4:1 (2003), pp.69–94.
38. Andrew & Gordievsky, *KGB: Inside Story*, pp.24–6, 544–5.
39. M.E. Haas, *The Devil's Shadow: UN Special Operations During The Korean War* (Annapolis, MD: Naval Institute Press, 2000); K. Conboy & D. Andrade, *Spies and Commandos – How America Lost the Secret War in North Vietnam* (Lawrence, KS: University of Kansas Press, 2000).
40. John Prados, *Lost Crusader: The Secret Wars of CIA Director William Colby* (Oxford: Oxford University Press, 2003).
41. Len Scott, 'Espionage and the Cold War: Oleg Penkovsky and the Cuban Missile Crisis', *Intelligence and National Security*, 14:4 (1999), pp.23–48.
42. Timothy Naftali & Alexander Fursenko, *One Hell of a Gamble: Khrushchev, Castro, Kennedy, and the Cuban Missile Crisis, 1958–1964* (New York: Norton, 1999), *passim*. The problem of assessing and validating the myriad human sources come through especially clearly in M.S. McAuliffe (ed.), *CIA Documents on the Cuban Missile Crisis – 1962* (Washington, DC: CIA History Staff, 1992).
43. Operation *Foot* is well-documented in *Documents on British Policy Overseas*, Series III, Volume I: *Britain and the Soviet Union, 1968–1972* (London: HMSO 1998).
44. K. Macrakis, 'Does Effective Espionage Lead to Success in Science and Technology? Lessons from the East German Ministry for State Security', *Intelligence & National Security*, 19:1 (2004) pp.52–77.
45. David Holloway, *Stalin and the Bomb* (New Haven, CT: Yale University Press, 1994), *passim*; J. Albright & M. Kunstel, *Bombshell: The Secret Story of America's Unknown Atomic Spy* (New York: Times Books, 1997).

46. Parrish, 'Soviet Espionage', pp.107–8; B. Cathcart, *Test of Greatness: Britain's Struggle for the Atom Bomb* (London: John Murray, 1994).
47. Michael S. Goodman, 'Grandfather of the Hydrogen Bomb? Klaus Fuchs and Anglo-American Intelligence', *Historical Studies in the Physical Sciences*, 34:1 (2004), pp.1–22.
48. See for example, L. Headley & W. Hoffman, *The Court-Martial of Clayton Lonetree* (New York: Henry Holt & Co., Inc., 1989).
49. D.J. Cole, *Geoffrey Prime: The Imperfect Spy* (London: Robert Hale, 1998); R.W. Hunter, *Spy Hunter: Inside The FBI Investigation of the Walker Espionage Case* (Annapolis, MD: US Naval Institute Press, 1999).
50. S. Kerr, 'The British Cold War Defectors: The Versatile, Durable Toys of Propagandists', in R.J. Aldrich (ed.), *British Intelligence, Strategy and the Cold War, 1945–51* (London: Routledge, 1992), pp.111–41.
51. Peter Hennessy, *The Secret State: Whitehall and the Cold War* (London: Penguin, 2002), pp.90–8.
52. Cord Meyer, *Facing Reality: From World Federalism to the CIA* (Lanham, MD: University Press of America, 1980), pp.60–84.
53. Tom Mangold, *Cold Warrior: James Jesus Angleton: The CIA's Master Spy Hunter* (New York: Simon & Schuster, 1991).
54. E. Breindel & H. Romerstein, *The Venona Secrets: The Soviet Union's War II Espionage Campaign Against the United States and How America Fought Back* (New York: Basic Books, 2000); R.L. Benson & M. Warner (eds), *VENONA: Soviet Espionage and American Response, 1939–1957* (Washington, DC: National Security Agency/Central Intelligence Agency, 1996); J.E. Haynes & H. Klehr, *Venona: Decoding Soviet Espionage in America* (New Haven, CT: Yale University Press, 1999); A. Weinstein & A. Vasiliev, *The Haunted Wood: Soviet Espionage in America – the Stalin Era* (New York: Random House, 1999).
55. John L. Gaddis, 'Out of the Woodwork', *Times Literary Supplement*, 30.4.99, pp.10–11.
56. J.E. Haynes, 'The Cold War Debate Continues: A Traditionalist View of Historical Writing on Communism and Anti-communism', *Journal of Cold War Studies*, 2 (2000), pp.76–115.
57. C.G. Cogan, 'Review Article: In the Shadow of Venona', *Intelligence and National Security*, 12:3 (1997), pp.190–5; H.B. Peake, 'OSS and the Venona Decrypts', *Intelligence and National Security*, 12:3 (Autumn 1997), pp.14–34.
58. Gaddis, 'Out of the Woodwork', *passim*.
59. Parrish, 'Soviet Espionage', pp.115–16.
60. Tim Weiner, 'Soviet Spies: Did They Make a Difference?', *World Policy Journal*, 16:1 (S2002), pp.101–2.
61. See especially E. Schrecker, *Many are the Crimes: McCarthyism in America* (Princeton, NJ: Princeton University Press, 1998); E. Schrecker, 'Soviet Espionage on American, TV: The VENONA Story', *Diplomatic History*, 27:2 (2003), pp.279–82.
62. Athan G. Theoharis, *Chasing Spies: How the FBI Failed in Counterintelligence but Prompted the Politics of McCarthyism in the Cold War Years* (Chicago, IL: Ivan R. Dee, 2002). See also Anthony Summers, *Official and Confidential: The Secret Life of J. Edgar Hoover* (New York: G.P. Putnam's, 1993); C. Gentry, *J. Edgar Hoover: The Man and the Secrets* (New York: W.W. Norton, 1992).

63. On the problems of using *Venona* to catch spies see Christopher Andrew, 'The Venona Secret', in K.G. Robertson (ed.), *War, Resistance and Intelligence* (London: Macmillan, 1998), pp.203–25.

64. J. Crampton, 'Russian Photo-shoot', *Air Pictorial*, August 1997, pp.38–41.

65. W.E. Burrows, *By Any Means Necessary: America's Secret Air War in the Cold War* (New York: Farrar, Straus & Giroux, 2001).

66. Paul Lashmar, in his study *Spy-Flights of the Cold War* (London: Sutton Books, 1996), has asserted that some USAF officers hoped to use intelligence flights to provoke the Soviet Union into a shooting-match. These assertions are contested by US government historians, see for example C. Hall & J. Neufeld (eds), *United States Air Force In Space, 1945 to the Twenty First Century: Proceedings, Air Force Historical Foundation Symposium* (Washington, DC: USGPO, 1993).

67. The best account of the U-2 is Chris Pocock's study, *The U-2 Spyplane: Towards the Unknown – A New History of the Early Years* (Atglen, PA: Schiffer Military History, 2000).

68. P.J. Roman, *Eisenhower and the Missile Gap* (Ithaca, NY: Cornell University Press, 1995). For a sceptical view of the value of strategic intelligence analysis in informing weapons policy in the 1970s see D. Dunn, *The Politics of Threat: Minuteman Vulnerability in American National Security Policy* (London: Macmillan, 1998).

69. S. Sagan, *The Limits of Safety: Organisations, Accidents and Nuclear Weapons* (Princeton, NJ: Princeton University Press, 1993); S. Sagan, 'Nuclear Alerts and Crisis Management', *International Security*, 9:4 (1985), pp.99–139.

70. K.C. Ruffner, *Corona: America's First Satellite Program* (Washington, DC: CIA History Staff, 1995); J.E. Lewis, *Spy Capitalism: Itek and the CIA* (New Haven, CT: Yale University Press, 2002).

71. Susan Schrafstetter & Steven Twigge, *Avoiding Armageddon: Europe, the United States, and the Struggle for Nuclear Non-Proliferation, 1945–1970* (New York: Praeger, 2004).

72. Steven Twigge & Len Scott, *Planning Armageddon: Britain, the United States and the Command and Control of Western Nuclear Forces, 1945–64* (London: Harwood, 2000).

73. Seymour Hersh, 'The Intelligence Gap', *The New Yorker*, 29.11.99. More generally see James Bamford, *The Puzzle Palace: America's National Security Agency and Its Special Relationship with GCHQ* (London: Sidgwick & Jackson, 1983); Nigel West, *GCHQ: The Secret Wireless War, 1900–86* (London: Weidenfeld & Nicolson, 1986); Matthew Aid & Cees Wiebes (eds), *Secrets of Signals Intelligence During the Cold War and Beyond* (London: Frank Cass, 2001).

74. Matthew Aid, 'The National Security Agency and the Cold War', in Aid and Wiebes (eds), *Secrets of Signals Intelligence*, pp.35–6.

75. Michael Herman, *Intelligence Power in Peace and War* (Cambridge: Cambridge University Press, 1993).

76. 'The Walls Have Ears', *Newsweek*, 1.6.64. I am indebted to Matthew Aid for further information.

77. Geoffrey Robertson, *The Justice Game* (London: Chatto & Windus, 1998), pp.104–34.

78. Sherman Kent, *Strategic Intelligence for World Policy* (Princeton, NJ: Princeton University Press, 1949); Richard Betts, *Surprise Attack: Lessons for Defense Planning* (Washington, DC: Brookings, 1983).
79. James Wirtz, 'Intelligence to Please? The Order of Battle Controversy during the Vietnam War', *Political Science Quarterly*, 106:2 (1991), pp.239–63.
80. P. Mescall, 'A Creature of Compromise: The Establishment of the DIA', *International Journal of Intelligence and Counterintelligence*, 7:3 (1994), pp.251–74. The debate over the relationship between analysts and policy-makers continues, for the most recent iteration see the thoughtful essays by C.A Medina and S.R. Ward in *Studies in Intelligence*, 46:3 (2002).

9
culture

patrick major and rana mitter

Cultural history became a major field in modern history at around the time of the fall of the Berlin wall in 1989.[1] The study of cold war cultural history has been pioneered instead by scholars from other disciplines, above all literary and film studies. Traditional historians may find some of their approaches, for instance the great attention to genre or to postmodernism, not strictly relevant to their own interests, but for a conflict which was more a war of words than a shooting war, culture cannot easily be ignored. A body of work has indeed begun to emerge, most of it highly America-centric as will become evident, but an interim overview is now possible. Besides a stock-taking of recent scholarship, and in particular of high-profile issues such as the CIA's cultural politics, we would also like to encourage new research into specific areas hitherto overlooked, above all East Asia. We also offer a more detailed outline of how popular culture can be used to chart the double-edged impact of culture in a cold war context.

the cultural cold war versus cold war culture

First, it is worth briefly examining one particular area of definitional difference which has emerged in new writing on the cold war: that between the 'cultural cold war' and 'cold war culture'. There has not yet been a great deal of historiographical literature which addresses these two as separate phenomena, not least because the idea of culture as a field of interpretation of the cold war is still less dominant than that of elite politics (although growing). Nonetheless, the difference is important. By 'cultural cold war', academic studies have usually meant something rather specific: cultural diplomacy between the blocs, and within them, in areas outside what is ostensibly the direct state and governmental ambit, whether in the field of high culture (literature, the arts, music) or popular culture (television, pop and rock music, films). Cultural diplomacy, which will be followed up in more detail below, is clearly an important, but delimited area of investigation. Nevertheless, the state often remains the prime mover in such approaches.

By contrast, the notion of a 'cold war culture' has a more anthropological sense, relating to the less specific but wider-ranging concept that everyday social existence may have been shaped by the global dynamics of the cold war.[2] Necessarily more nebulous than the 'cultural cold war', the idea that there is some sort of cross-bloc matrix of signification (culture, in other words, as a system of interlocking meanings) is a potentially fruitful one which deserves further attention from social and cultural historians. Recent approaches suggest the impossibility of conceiving one's identity without reference to an outside 'other'. Since Edward Said, alterity has become a major component of cultural history.[3] It is odd, therefore, that in a situation when the political 'other' was literal, relatively little has been written on cold war orientalism.[4] By the same token, we are just beginning to witness the counter-concept of 'occidentalism', whereby both those east of the iron curtain, as well as Western Europeans championing a third way, understood and misunderstood America.[5] Outside enemy figures also encouraged a willingness to see surrogate 'enemies within'. The McCarthyite purges were directly mirrored by the last Stalinist show trials of the early 1950s, suggesting the mutually-reinforcing social disciplinary uses of cold war identities.

This idea of a cold war culture, a system of meaning and behaviour shaped by the dynamics of the conflict that emerged in the late 1940s, has been the subject of considerable attention in the US history field in recent years.[6] The editors of *Rethinking Cold War Culture*, Peter Kuznick and James Gilbert, have argued for a suggestive set of key turning-points and factors that shaped the cold war as social history. These factors include changes in demographics, the new capacity of the population for physical movement, and the impact of McCarthyism, with the Korean conflict acting as an important juncture. Their judgement of the cold war's effects on the culture of the post-war USA is that it was primarily 'psychological', but that it was also capable of cooptation and subversion by social groups (such as women) who could adapt the seeming rigidity of the cold war to their own ends.[7] However, at least one of the authors included in their collection is not convinced about the uniqueness of the cold war as a period of historical analysis: Leo P. Ribuffo argues that the cold war was in fact not significantly new in its political dynamics.[8]

The agenda suggested by this volume (among others), the linking of the worlds of foreign policy and domestic social history, has only recently begun to blossom. One of the most complex and original examples of how this type of history is being written is Jeremi Suri's *Power and Protest*. Suri examines the global rise of *détente* in the 1960s, but rather than taking a more traditional international historian's view of the issue, he argues for a 'convergent response to *détente*' that had a social origin in domestic political developments, which in turn gave rise to an 'international language of dissent'.[9] Suri's analysis is remarkably transnational, taking on board not only the USA, but also European nations and even China's Cultural Revolution, and concludes with an argument that 'The Cold War, more than anything else, created a remarkable conjuncture among societies in the 1960s' in fields 'cultural, political, and diplomatic'; 'foreign policy,' he concludes, 'is also social policy'.[10] Although Suri's book is still relatively recent, its twin agendas of combining international with social history, as well as demanding a cross-cultural field of study, seems certain to stimulate further research.[11]

One sub-field, which has still been working out from the centre to a large extent, but wishes to 'culturalise' International Relations studies, is the linguistic deconstruction of leadership rhetoric.[12] Such approaches analyse the metaphors employed by world leaders to expose underlying mentalities and thus feed into the 'constructivist' school of diplomatic history, which questions the perfect rationality of decision-making espoused by so-called 'realists'. The Ivy League masculinity of the Kennedy administration and the liberal missionary zeal of its leader have been put forward as important for Democrat internationalism,[13] or the sporting metaphors of his predecessor for the competitive ethos of world leaders.[14] Khrushchev famously applied his down-to-earth peasant proverbs to international relations ('If you start throwing hedgehogs under me, I shall throw a couple of porcupines under you'), which also had the function of defusing tensions. East German vocabulary was unwittingly coloured by memories of trench warfare in the First World War: enemies had to be 'rolled up', positions had to be 'retaken'. Jeffrey Brooks has tested the press speak of Stalinism,[15] and the bureaucratic language of the GDR has been briefly analysed from a party perspective[16] as well as the mania for abbreviations which became unintelligible to West Germans.[17] A bottom-up approach to the deconstruction of language is likely to reveal further cold war usages which slipped into the popular vocabulary, from 'commies' to 'critical mass', from '*blat*' to '*Bückwaren*'.[18]

Part of the distancing which has enabled such new approaches, and one which demands a high degree of introspection from historians themselves, has resulted from the conceptual tools of the discipline itself coming under closer historical scrutiny.[19] Recent intellectual histories have examined ways in which some of the big ideas of the later twentieth century, many of which have since been taken for granted, were themselves partly the product of the cold war. The concepts of totalitarianism[20] and modernisation theory[21] have been contextualised as attempts to discredit and support East and West respectively. The history of 'area studies', itself an invention of the cold war, has also begun to reveal the institutional backing behind certain projects.[22] Think-tanks such as the Rand Corporation mediated between the university world and government, and academics often provided scientific respectability for enemy stereotypes.[23] The field of mass communication studies was yet another product of research sponsored by the Pentagon for military purposes.[24] Indeed, cold war academics do not have to go very far to find evidence that ideas have a very specific social and political context!

the cultural cold war: the congress for cultural freedom (ccf)

Some of the most powerful debates in recent work on the cultural cold war have been in the field of high culture. Central among the themes addressed by this scholarship is the record of the CCF and its British offspring, *Encounter* magazine. The CCF's record has not been remembered kindly by all. It remains an article of faith among many on the left that the revelation of CIA funding for *Encounter* rendered that publication a mere stooge of American imperialism, although it is remembered more fondly by many on the moderate left and right. A substantial account, partly memoir, by a participant in the CCF's activities, Peter Coleman, betrays in its title (*The Liberal Conspiracy*) the slightly shamefaced, yet defiant, irony with which members of the non-communist left associated with its activities regarded the CCF after the end of the cold war.[25]

The academic argument about the CCF has, in just a few years, exposed a variety of viewpoints. Although it has been the subject of controversy, the most significant point of reference for the debate has been Frances Stonor Saunders' *Who Paid the Piper?*[26] Based on impressive archival as well as interview materials, Stonor Saunders gives both a substantial and extremely well-written narrative account of the CCF's formation and downfall, as well as interpreting its history in a way that is not unsympathetic, but ultimately critical. Individual figures, such as the CIA agent Michael Josselson who was instrumental in the development of the CCF, are described as complex and human figures, but ultimately,

Stonor Saunders declares, the CCF project and *Encounter* magazine must be considered fatally flawed because of their support from undeclared CIA funds.

This thesis has come under attack. David Caute argues that, 'Unfortunately, the relentless pursuit of exposure – who paid the piper? – ... has resulted in a lopsided view of cultural activity and what inspires it': in other words, that the idea that the source of funding for the CCF's activities was sufficient to condemn its output cannot stand. 'Despite Zhdanov and despite McCarthy, sincere conviction lay at the root of most cold war cultural production.'[27] More willing to accept the Stonor Saunders thesis, but still critical of it, is Hugh Wilford, who argues that British intellectuals, at least, 'used *Encounter* as much as it used them'. He goes on to say that, 'It might well have been the case that the CIA tried to call the tune; but the piper did not always play it, nor the audience always dance to it.'[28] While both Caute and Wilford take issue with Stonor Saunders, the repeated references to 'the piper' suggest that her argument has had a significant impact. A further angle on the controversy is that of Giles Scott-Smith, who draws on Scott Lucas's idea of 'state-private networks' to interpret the CCF in terms of 'transnational social elites' and to adopt the wider model of 'culture' it addresses. Taking a Gramscian approach, Scott-Smith argues that its attempts to form a hegemonic culture were not, per se, a malevolent idea, but that 'a hegemony has to adapt to succeed' and that this meant that the CCF was doomed when it failed to reorient itself in the world of the 1960s, so different from that of the 1950s.[29]

David Caute's work, *The Dancer Defects*, mentioned above, does not simply have the interpretation of the CCF's activities in its sights. Caute notes with regret that the preponderance of work on the cultural cold war addresses a highly US-centred set of themes, with 'centres of Americocentricity' keeping one bloc hermetic, and scholars of Russian studies in the West likewise refusing to look outside their own field. 'It's a cold war,' he notes, 'which features Arthur Miller and Ralph Ellison but not Sartre and Camus, not Simonov and Havel, not Brecht ... and Wajda.'[30] As Caute suggests, the problem is not merely that scholarship on the cultural cold war (and cold war culture) outside the USA is less rich, but rather that the work that exists does not move cross-culturally and transnationally.

One of the most valuable elements of Caute's analysis is his transnational approach to the question of cultural rivalry, in which the USA championed modernism and the 'avant-garde' as 'the talisman of political virtue' precisely because the USSR hated modernism with such a passion. Yet artistic achievement was clearly not lacking in the Eastern bloc, as the examples of Brecht, Shostakovich and the Bolshoi ballet showed: rather, the Soviet bloc's often rather crude attempts to bludgeon Western audiences into dislike for the 'decadent' aspects of the West gave rise to ridicule rather than sympathy.[31]

culture and the cold war in east asia

One area where new work is emerging to analyse the cultural cold war as well as cold war culture is not just with respect to the Eastern bloc in Europe (as lamented by David Caute), but in the non-European world. East Asia is one obvious focus, yet, just as the US side of cold war culture has been far more analysed than the Soviet side, so the Japanese side of the Asian divide has been much more closely examined than the Chinese or Korean. Some of this is the inevitable product of the relative openness of Japan's post-war democracy as opposed to the dictatorships of the People's Republic of China, Taiwan, and South and North Korea. However, most of the work on the most obvious aspect of post-war cold war culture in Japan, the trauma of the atomic bomb, lies more in the literary and cultural studies field than the comparative historical, although the work of Yoshikuni Igarashi, for instance, shows how the two can be combined with great sophistication.[32] The understandable desire to examine what was unique about Japan's encounter with nuclear warfare – that is, the fact that it remains the only nation to have suffered an atomic attack in wartime – made it harder to move into areas of cross-cultural comparison, for instance, the ways in which the dynamics of the cold war had shaped the shared histories of Japan, Korea and China in the post-1945 environment.

New trends in the writing of history and historiography have opened up fresh vistas in the last few years. One of the most intractable problems in doing comparative work on the Eastern bloc was the closed nature of communist-era records, something suddenly changed by the events of 1989–91. While China has not had the kind of regime change which brought about such major changes in access to Eastern European and Russian archives, the thaw in the study of Chinese history has meant that the early People's Republic period is now open for study as a historical topic in its own right. Local archives remain more accessible than national ones, but nonetheless, an empirically rich examination of the 1950s, linking local society to wider national policies and trends, is now a key trend in the study of the early Mao period, with the Cultural Revolution of the mid-1960s now providing the kind of barrier point that 1949 previously marked.[33] The democratisation of Taiwan and South Korea also means that archival study of the cold war era is now possible and flourishing. Only North Korea, for the moment, remains a field that is much more difficult to penetrate.[34]

What questions may emerge from the new cold war historiography in East Asia? The comparative work on East and West Germany, parts of a nation-state united by language but divided by ideology, offers points of comparison both for China/Taiwan and for North and South Korea. Just as both Germanies were the products of a very different response to the legacy of Nazism and defeat, so both China and Korea found themselves split ideologically, although in neither case was there a West German-style liberal democracy, but rather states that were defined by their adherence to or abhorrence of communism. However, both Chinas and Koreas were heirs to their turbulent pre-war past, with the legacy of war and ideological division shaping their highly confrontational post-war politics. When examining how cold war culture shaped East Asia, the divisions between the East Asian states bear significant comparison with the European case. The other similarity, again worthy of further analysis, is the way in which the early cold war saw a reversal of who was the enemy: in Europe, the (West) Germans and Soviets swiftly swapped places in Western eyes, whereas the Chinese and Japanese carried out the same reversal in Asia. Of course, the view from the West was not the only worthwhile vantage point, and the far more ambivalent view that the Chinese, Japanese and Koreans held of each other during the cold war cannot be interpreted simply in terms of 'friends' or 'enemies'.

Nor is the cultural cold war missing from the East Asia front. The analysis of Japanese literature and popular culture in terms of 'nuclear fear' has been a mainstream topic of discussion for some time.[35] Ibuse's *Black Rain* (1965) became the classic Japanese novel of the first atomic bombing and the problem of remembrance for the *hibakusha* or survivors. While work on the Chinese and Korean sides of the question is still in a much earlier state of development, the rich seam of fiction and film in both nations on, for instance, the Korean war, makes the analysis of cold war influences on East Asian high cultural production a necessary field of scholarly development.[36]

cold war cultures: the case of popular culture

Besides battles over high culture, which were a reflection of Americans' inferiority complex in the face of European traditions harking back hundreds of years, popular culture became another cold war area of contestation. This was not so much official cultural policy as articulated by Voice of America, the BBC, Radio Moscow or the CCF, but part of the unofficial expansion of the 'culture industry', as Adorno and Horkheimer were to label it in 1944.[37] This is a slightly less instrumentalised version of Scott Lucas's concept of the state–private network, whereby US government co-opted sections of the private sector into a propaganda struggle 'conducted not just by the Government through judicial and executive measures but by "private" groups and individuals keeping their own houses in order. This was a war not for territory or profit but for a culture.'[38] We would add the caveat, nevertheless, that popular culture was an area of relative autonomy from the state. Whereas Caute and Scott-Smith rightly point out that the individual writer or composer was capable of artistic integrity, the business interests so closely connected with popular cultural production had their own profit-related agendas. As will also become clear, popular culture created economic dependencies in the Eastern bloc which militated against ideological purity, and contributed to the corruption of 'real existing socialism'.

Since popular culture was chiefly associated with the United States, it was also viewed, even at the time, as a form of cultural imperialism, challenging the values of both cold war allies in Western Europe, as well as permeating the iron curtain and provoking a two-pronged Eastern strategy of proscription and appropriation. For some this was a symptom of modernity and almost unstoppable; for others it was specifically American and mobilised significant political resistance. Consequently, there has been a great slew of work since 1989 on Americanisation and its discontents. Europeans often viewed consumerism as a form of mass conformity which would rob them of their purported individualism, encapsulated in the battle against 'Coca-colonisation'.[39] Much of this work has focused on France,[40] but a growing body is emerging on Germany,[41] and a large synthetic work on the whole European experience has just appeared.[42] The democratising aspects of American culture prompted some profound soul-searching among the French intellectual elite.[43] The battle for national culture was also capable of uniting the most unlikely political bedfellows, such as communists and Gaullists in 1940s France. Or it could be highly selective: Jean-Luc Godard's films reveal a cultural love of American *film noir*, a term coined by the French, but a contempt for US militarism, just as Jean-Paul Sartre opposed segregation but loved black jazz. Culture therefore maps onto the political landscape in often counter-intuitive patterns.

It is also now recognised that even Russia was penetrated to some extent by Western-style popular culture, if studies on the 1980s are anything to go by.[44] 'Material culture' studies have also begun to examine the limited socialist consumerism which took place chiefly in the 1960s in the Eastern bloc more generally.[45] There is also a corpus of work on the specific influence of popular music in Eastern Europe,[46] but also locally in the Soviet Union[47] and the GDR.[48] The Eastern bloc's second best-known American in the 1970s, after the President, was allegedly Dean Reed, an expatriate American singer who also made his name in socialist spaghetti westerns.[49] Communist cultural officials initially echoed the objections of the Frankfurt School (chiefly Adorno and Horkheimer) that popular music was a manipulation of the masses by corporate capitalist interests, but the prominence of oppressed African-Americans and the growth of an anti-establishment counter-culture softened their stance in the 1960s. The growing financial constraints in the East meant a further loosening of ideological prescriptions. By the late 1980s concerts by politically acceptable Western rock musicians such as Bruce Springsteen were taking place there, in the GDR case to raise hard currency through televisation rights.[50]

Much attention has also been focused on ways in which popular culture might have been used to propagandise home audiences in the United States. Alan Nadel has suggested that a domestic form of 'containment' was at work within American culture, even in 'sword and sandals' biblical epics; or that progressive politics could be found in more unlikely publications such as *Playboy*.[51] Suzanne Clark, reading post-war literature, concludes that a literary 'national realism' wrote non-whites and women out of a warrior-based narrative of the times.[52] Robert Corber does something similar for the position of homosexual men.[53] This is part of a trend to make manifest 'hidden' cold war messages in everyday cultural artefacts of the era.[54] Familiar products such as the western film thus become metaphors for conflict.[55] Yet, often enough these studies are heavily based on text-criticism and authorial interpretation, with little recourse to empirical verification of audience responses to such texts. The challenge for cultural historians of the cold war, therefore, is to combine the imagination of such approaches with some attempt at a grounding of culture in the socio-economic realities of the period. Paying more attention to reception of culture will also help to obviate the current dangers in assuming that cultural messages were consumed with the meanings with which they were transmitted. Eastern cinema audiences may have been paying just as much attention to background clothes and cars as to the main plot. And as the head of the British Board of Film Censors reported rather dispiritedly on London audience reactions to the Soviet wartime epic, *The Fall of Berlin* (Chiaureli, 1949): 'No one, in fact, seemed to mind that Russia was depicted as the hero of the Second World War; people enjoyed the spectacle and rejected the propaganda. It was a box office success.'[56] Popular culture had a habit of biting back at those trying to control it.

Propagandists had long recognised the value of popular culture as a ready-made medium of mass communication. Even the Nazi propagandist Joseph Goebbels had realised that effective indoctrination was best packaged in an entertaining format, and was a great admirer of Hollywood for conveying political themes via the human interest story.[57] The 'grammar' of popular fiction and film usually demands an identification figure and the division of the world into simple binary opposites, both important ingredients in friend/foe propaganda. But this was a two-edged weapon which could be wielded both by governments and their critics. We would suggest two major tropes within popular culture: the conversion narrative and the subversion narrative. By conversion narrative is meant a story designed to convert a reluctant public to make the sacrifices on the home front necessary for the global cold war effort. It usually features a sceptical protagonist or antagonist who rehearses the known counter-arguments, but is gradually persuaded of the value of mobilisation in a good cause and becomes a true believer. The message often involved rousing a passive, consumerist public which had somehow 'gone soft' after the privations of the Second World War, suffering from what Philip Wylie would call 'momism', a feminisation of society, in contrast to the supposed virility of the Soviet 'other'. Subversion narratives, on the other hand, questioned authority, suggesting that the national security state had begun to assume a momentum of its own and to treat society as a means to an end. The sympathies of the audience or reader were therefore no longer with the government but with the private citizenry or the lone vigilante.

Generally speaking, early American conversion narratives carried a conservative message, reflecting a retrenchment in media politics in the late 1940s and early 1950s. Film, for instance, witnessed a conservative shift away from the inter-war experimentalism and radicalism of the New Deal era. In 1946 Hollywood's future head of the Motion Pictures Producers' Association, Eric Johnston, warned that 'We'll have no more *Grapes of Wrath*, we'll have no more *Tobacco Roads*, we'll have no more films that treat the banker as villain.'[58] Johnston himself was an enforcer of the wartime media control apparatus, which wished to extend its lease on life into the post-war period. The movie industry itself soon famously became the object of scrutiny of the House Un-American Affairs Committee (HUAC), when in 1947 the 'Hollywood Ten' screenwriters and directors were forced to testify on alleged subversion in the American film industry.[59] The result was the *de facto* blacklisting of 'un-American' radical writing talent and the informal censorship of film content to conform to patriotic and conservative motifs. By the mid-1950s the American film industry was even the object of a covert scheme, 'Militant Liberty', to inject freedom motifs into its movies, supported by directors and actors such as John Ford and John Wayne.[60] Scholars outside the USA have begun to examine the degree of politicisation of their own industries. In the case of Great Britain Tony Shaw concludes that this was less intrusive, but that an informal network did exist of 'ministerial overtures, either directly with "friendly" producers or directors', or through the film censorship board, or funding and information control.[61] In the Eastern bloc research has just begun, but it is clear that Zhdanov's campaign in 1948 represented a cultural crackdown against 'cosmopolitanism' and Western influences. Stalin took a personal interest in film scripts,[62] as did the East German Ministry of Culture. What is also evident in the GDR, at least, is that crypto-market forces began to compete with political correctness, to the extent that the film industry became increasingly dependent on 'apolitical' film treatments of classic novels and fairytales which could be exported to generate revenue.[63] State control of culture and leisure, even in the East, tended to wane as the cold war went on.[64]

At the height of the cold war, however, even the United States was not averse from politicising its popular culture. During the McCarthyite investigations Wayne himself had already starred as *Big Jim McClain* (Ludwig, 1952), a film praising the work of the HUAC fight against communist infiltration of the unions and suggesting that those pleading the fifth amendment were in fact all communists. The telling location of the investigation in Hawaii, and Wayne's reverential visit to the hulk of the USS *Arizona*, a victim of Pearl Harbor, remind the audience that pre-emptive action is permissible this time around. The conversion narrative faced a particularly difficult task, however, in persuading the public that informing on neighbours was an honourable duty. The classic film treatment of this dilemma was Elia Kazan's *On the Waterfront* (1954), in which whistle-blowing against corrupt union officials became a metaphor for naming names before HUAC. The fight against communism recruited the most unlikely auxiliaries. *Film noir* thrillers even witnessed petty criminals, such as the pickpocket anti-hero of *Pickup on South Street* (Fuller, 1949), turning their skills to the advantage of the FBI. Hoover himself clearly saw the value of using the movie industry for good public relations.[65]

Yet by the late cold war it had become almost axiomatic in popular culture that the intelligence services themselves were the enemy. One can follow this trajectory of conversion to subversion in the spy thriller, for instance. Ian Fleming's James Bond started off battling the Soviet SMERSH, but by 1961 Fleming had decided to tone down the political background by introducing the criminal organisation of SPECTRE.[66] This was a tendency reinforced by the Bond films in which, as often as not, as in *Diamonds Are Forever* (1971), a criminal-terrorist third force holds the world to ransom, forcing a temporary alliance between the superpowers. This reached a peak in 1977 in the film version of *The Spy Who Loved Me*, where Bond teams up with his (female) KGB counterpart, Major Amasova, in a form of intelligence *détente*. Such depictions welcomed cold war bipolarity as a stabilising force. Yet both the literary and film Bond represented a spy with whom the audience was still meant to identify, whereas other treatments were far more questioning. Graham Greene had already poked fun at the intelligence services in *Our Man in Havana* (1958; filmed in 1959 by Reed), suggesting that a salesman was capable of deceiving his handlers by passing off diagrams of vacuum-cleaner parts as atomic secrets. More serious in intent was John le Carré, who made his breakthrough in 1963 with *The Spy Who Came In from the Cold*. In his early novels, although it is suggested that the intelligence services of both East and West employ equally underhand techniques, the ends justify the means for MI6. The later le Carré was far more condemnatory of the West. In a less cerebral way, fellow British spy author Len Deighton attacked the establishment values of the intelligence community, but was still patriot enough in his *Hook, Line and Sinker* trilogy (1988–90) to suggest that the fall of the Berlin wall had been engineered by British secret agents. In this case, however, reality had overtaken fiction, forcing Deighton to add layer after layer of retrospective (and rather unconvincing) justification for the MI6 *deus ex machina*.[67]

Little work has been done on this sort of popular culture on the other side of the wall. Nevertheless, the East Germans also understood the value of popularising their own spies. In 1963 the film *For Eyes Only: Streng Geheim* (Veiczi) depicted a clean-cut *Stasi* agent behind enemy lines in southern Germany, secretly gathering the West's alleged plans to invade the East. It obeys many of the conventions of early Western conversion narratives. The agent manages to convince a defected Czech operative, who presents the case for the easy life in the West, to return with him to the East; the Americans are all portrayed as decadent, sunglasses-wearing exploiters of the local population, including their womenfolk. East German television audiences were also treated to another hero of the 'invisible frontier' in the shape of Achim Detjen, an undercover agent working in Bonn. Some young East Germans were moved enough by his exploits to cite him as a reason for joining the *Stasi*.[68] Yet the partisanship of the hero figures in the GDR could reach such proportions as to become counter-productive. The reader's report for the GDR's most famous spy thriller, *Der Gaukler* (1978) by Harry Thürk, a fictionalised version of the Solzhenitsyn case, complained that friend and foe imagery was too crass: 'the black only gets blacker, the white whiter'.[69] Readers would hardly be able to credit that the defection of such a high-ranking dissident had all been the work of the Western intelligence services. Thürk was thus asked to tone down the omnipotence of the CIA in his drafts of the novel. The GDR's other prolific thriller writer, Wolfgang Schreyer, initially pleased the Ministry of Culture with tales aimed against the CIA's interventions in Central America and South-East Asia. By the 1980s, however, he was beginning to use his manuscripts for coded critiques of bureaucracy under socialism, to the extent that publishers felt obliged to shun this previous bestseller. Finally, in frustration, Schreyer turned to publishing one short story in the West, unaware that it would be syndicated to *Playboy* magazine, much to the anger of his local Communist Party.[70]

The theme of paranoia was also one which science fiction films picked up on, often literalising the notion of a fifth column. Following conservative science fiction author Robert A. Heinlein's *The Puppetmasters* (1951), which had giant sluglike aliens attaching themselves to the nervous systems of unwitting hosts, movies such as *Invaders from Mars* (Mackenzie, 1953) showed everyday citizens, including policemen, being taken over by alien beings. The theme was more famously repeated in *It Came from Outer Space* (Arnold, 1953) and *Invasion of the Bodysnatchers* (Siegel, 1956), in which citizens who outwardly looked normal, carried a dark inner secret. Yet, as Peter Biskind has shown, such films require careful unpacking to reveal a liberal or conservative bias in the filmmaker.[71] Arnold's aliens prove to be benign; whereas Siegel's are more threatening. The cultural historian must pay close attention to where the audience is being asked to place its loyalties: with the forces of corporate 'big government', in the shape of police, soldiers and scientists, or with the maverick individual. The subversion narrative was increasingly to side with the individual and to depict the government not as part of the solution, but part of the problem. As we shall see, however, this individualism was to experience a further subdivision into anarcho-liberal and conservative-vigilantist variants.

The transition from the 'anodyne to terror' as Paul Boyer has put it,[72] can likewise be traced in nuclear films.[73] Initially, the armed forces continued the wartime tradition of cooperating with Hollywood to produce a patriotic message about war readiness. *Strategic Air Command*

(Mann, 1955) recalls James Stewart, himself a real airforce veteran and thus assured of audience sympathy, to active duty against the selfish protests of his wife.[74] Likewise, *Invasion USA* (Green, 1952) converts a self-indulgent late-night cocktail bar crowd who cannot take the cold war seriously. By the finale, however, after a hypnotic premonition of a future under communism, even the most hardened hedonist, including the heroine, who only a month ago 'wanted a mink stole – I thought it was important', has come to realise that she must do her bit; she heads for the nearest blood bank. The same can be said of public information films sponsored by the Federal Civil Defense Administration (FCDA), in which the main enemy appeared to be apathy. Shorts such as *The House in the Middle* (1954) suggested that keeping properties tidy and well-painted would make them more resistant to the thermal blast of nuclear attack! Therefore, even housework and DIY became part of the national defence effort.[75] Popular novelists such as Philip Wylie, himself an adviser to the FCDA, produced similar parables on readiness, comparing the fates of two fictional Midwest towns to show the perils of not taking civil defence seriously in his 1954 *Tomorrow!*[76]

It did not take long, however, for film to start to parody these patriotic jeremiads. Indeed, one of the drawbacks of popular culture, from a propagandist's point of view, is the tendency for the formula to try to outdo itself in each successive outing; the line between the sublime and the ridiculous is a narrow one, and parody was effectively built into the genre. A film such as Kubrick's *Dr. Strangelove* (1963) could hardly have been more different from *Strategic Air Command* in satirising the dangers of rampant militarism. The filmscript itself was taken from a serious thriller, but Kubrick decided that black comedy was the only way of doing justice to the horrors of nuclear warfare. The 1960s witnessed other satirical takes on the cold war. Joseph Heller's 1961 novel *Catch 22* suggested a corrupt military-industrial complex, and its film version in 1970 by Mike Nichols could be seen as a parable for Vietnam and the futility of bombing. Likewise, Robert Altman's *M*A*S*H* (1970) transported representatives of the counter-culture back in time to the Korean war, in what was a thinly disguised version of Vietnam. Yet it could be argued that the culture industry itself was partially able to tame these subversive tendencies. In the *M*A*S*H* television spin-off, which ran from 1972 to 1983, anarchists such as Trapper John were soon replaced by more sober characters, and the figure of the corrupt reservist, Colonel Blake, gave way to the more avuncular Colonel Potter.[77]

1960s subversion narratives had tended to champion the liberal cause against authority. Yet a more conservatively tinted version of anti-authoritarianism emerged in the 1970s and above all the 1980s. On this reading, the Federal government itself was viewed as the front for a conspiracy against the American people, or was guilty of betraying them. Films such as *Capricorn One* (Hyams, 1978) indulged conspiracy theorists who had suggested that the Moon landings had been faked, to suggest a Mars mission in which government plays an elaborate hoax on the public. The film's depiction of a state-within-a-state of black helicopters and secret service personnel became common currency in later films. The classic of the genre, with an unambiguous conservative revisionist agenda, was certainly Rambo, whose second outing in *First Blood II* in 1985, supported conspiracy theorists claiming that the government had abandoned its missing GIs in Vietnam. Sylvester Stallone now provided a fantasy, asking 'Do we get to win his time?'; the answer from Reagan, posturing for a more muscular foreign policy, was an emphatic yes. By this point the subversion narrative was being officially endorsed by the government itself. But all of these, including the crassly anti-communist *Red Dawn* (Milius, 1984), in which teenage American freedom fighters engage in guerrilla warfare against an imaginary Russo-Cuban occupation, reflected the resurgent anxieties of the second cold war of 1979–85. In a microcosm of the shifts from the 1950s to the 1960s, this was in turn followed by a period of celluloid *détente* as Gorbachev appeared on the scene in the mid-1980s. The mood lightened in films such as *Red Heat* (Hill, 1985), in which Schwarzenegger's tough Moscow militiaman helps combat organised crime alongside James Belushi's more laid-back Chicago cop. Or in Robin Williams' comedic depiction of Vladimir Ivanoff, the loveable defector in *Moscow on the Hudson* (Mazursky, 1984).

There has also been work on the shifting politics of comic books.[78] Sex and violence were the unacceptable face of American comics in the mid-1950s, but many continued the patriotic wartime trend of 'golden age' comics, led by Captain America in 1941 who defied isolationism to become an early internationalist in the fight against Hitler. In the immediate aftermath of the Second World War there were not quite so many overtly political themes, although the Korean war did cater for some war stories.[79] Yet the superpowers needed superheroes, and the fantastic forces of nature unleashed by the atom led to a spate of 'silver age' superheroes in the 1960s from Marvel Comics. This generation of superheroes managed to harness the forces of nature to an unreflective moral crusade for good. There were also several overtly cold war superheroes such as Iron Man, who was even prepared to lend a hand against the 'Red Barbarian'.[80] More interestingly perhaps, in the second cold war of the 1980s, a darker and more subversive alternative comic variant emerged in the form of the graphic novel. Frank Miller pioneered the anti-superhero with a sinister new, vigilantist Batman, in which the issue of nuclear war was tackled head-on.[81] The British text-writer Alan Moore took this disaffection to new heights, from a more identifiably leftist perspective, in his *Watchmen* (1986–87), in which America's superheroes have become superannuated and corrupt, in an alternative future in which the USA has won the Vietnam war and President Nixon still rules.[82] Thatcherism also became the subject of a dark allegory in Moore's *V for Vendetta*, which was set in a totalitarian, crypto-fascist future Britain.[83]

The question remains here of whether Hollywood directors and producers, but also comic book writers, were simply following the changes in the political climate, or were a driving force capable of shaping public opinion. Future research will perhaps show how rapidly the culture industry could respond to political changes of climate. Were some film scripts and novel drafts rejected at certain points as inopportune? How closely were they matched to shifts in public opinion? Since popular culture was consumed by millions, despite its apparent superficiality or frivolity, by sheer dint of numbers it was a powerful social force. Scholars such as Stonor Saunders have suggested a high degree of manipulation. Yet we should be wary of thinking that all popular culture followed a state-driven agenda. The exploitation movie, the low-budget B-movie production, often simply took a situation – be it organised crime, nuclear warfare, or climate change – then applied a formula.[84] The chief motive of doyens of exploitation cinema such as Roger Corman was to make money.[85] They realised that audiences liked to be frightened. This was the cold war as *grand guignol*, which may, in itself, have helped to defuse tensions. But what seems undeniable is that popular culture exploited the cold war as much as cold warriors used the culture industry. It provided the ultimate thrill of potential nuclear extinction. The spy novel was also capable of giving the illusion that even the most humdrum office clerk might secretly be doing vital work (and therefore be more attractive to the opposite sex). We hope that it is also clear, nonetheless, that some popular culture, certainly by the late 1960s, had matured and was capable of profound statements on the conflict. A sceptical generation of filmmakers, bestseller-writers, graphic artists and popular musicians learned to use culture to describe the deep sense of alienation which the cold war had engendered. Neither of these tendencies, exploitation schlock-horror, or anti-authoritarian critique, was what the (high) cultural cold warriors necessarily intended. Yet it would be one way of reading a semi-autonomous 'cold war culture' as set out above.

At the same time, future research must examine the ways in which Western popular culture penetrated the iron curtain, but also prompted a homegrown communist popular culture which attempted to act as an antidote to the headier capitalist concoctions. Radio was perhaps the chief transmitter of Western ideas and trends. Although the Soviet Union was heavily jammed, much of Eastern Europe had relatively ready access to the ether. Much of the existing literature focuses on the more obviously propagandistic branches of broadcasting and on spoken-word radio.[86] Yet in the GDR, at least, the most listened to station among youths was the pop broadcaster, Radio Luxembourg, receiving sack-loads of East German listeners' mail before the wall. If they did not have tape-recorders, East German rock fans were capable of phonetically transcribing the lyrics of English songs from the radio. The East German agit-prop authorities had also taken to broadcasting 'forbidden' popular music to attract Western soldiers on the GDR's *Freiheitssender 904*. It then proved impossible to stop other East Germans tuning in, resulting in the GDR setting up its own youth station, *DT-64*. Despite the *Politburo*'s best efforts, this too broke East Germany's own rules by broadcasting a majority of its output in English. The study of popular culture outside of its American heartland promises, therefore, to be highly instructive for the former Eastern bloc. A greater geographical diversification will also help to avoid a replication in the academic sphere of the sort of 'cultural imperialism' of which America was accused at the time. As we have shown, this is beginning to happen for some areas of Eastern Europe; but the other East, East Asia, remains largely *terra incognita*, apart from the odd, but welcome exception. Expanded methodological horizons through popular culture, as well as high culture, will also help to bring the 'people' more sharply into focus in a history of the cold war. In a period as heavily mediatised as the cold war, in which television came to shape popular perceptions to an unprecedented degree,[87] cultural history is also social history.

conclusions

The cultural turn in cold war history does also have profound implications for how we regard the outcome of the cold war. Was it the result of missiles and moles, or shopping baskets and creeping modernisation? Joseph Nye has suggested that 'soft power', a government's ability to spread its values in a form of Gramscian cultural hegemony, is just as important as hard military and economic power in asserting national interests. According to Nye: 'Long before the Berlin Wall fell in 1989, it had been pierced by television and movies. The hammers and bulldozers would not have worked without the years-long transmission of images of the popular culture of the West that breached the Wall before it fell.'[88] cold war leaders had realised this, whereas the current Bush administration has apparently unlearnt this lesson. Cultural cold warriors were aware from the start that culture was an attractive propaganda proposition, precisely because it was perceived by many to be *apolitical*. With growing access to the files, historians can, of course, show that behind the scenes this was anything but the case. Yet whereas it might be concluded that in the realm of high culture, the cultural cold war was stalemated, or resolved itself around differences between modernism and traditionalism which cut across the iron curtain, in terms of popular culture it was a very uneven contest. The profit motive driving Hollywood and Motown, Marvel Comics and Pan Paperbacks, was always going to produce more, and often better, than in the East. There, governments literally could not afford to go beyond satisfying the people's needs to addressing their aspirations. Too much desire was a bad thing. In the broader perspective, therefore, the cultural cold war can be seen as an early stage in the process of globalisation, in which not only the nation-state, but a bloc-wide system, was unable to withstand the transnational pressures of consumer capitalism. This, in turn, has profound implications for how we do cold war history. Foreign policy, military and intelligence establishments will no doubt remain at the centre of the jigsaw, but will now be joined by a much larger array of pieces: from broadcasters to public intellectuals, from film reviewers to television viewers and radio-listeners, from rock stars to amateur musicians, and even the ordinary shopper and conspiracy theorist in the street. In short, in order to move beyond the cold war's sites of cultural production to the sites of reception, we need to embrace the 'state–public network'.

notes

1. Emblematic is Lynn Hunt (ed.), *The New Cultural History: Essays* (Berkeley, CA: University of California Press, 1989).
2. Lisle A. Rose, *The Cold War Comes to Main Street: America in 1950* (Lawrence, KS: Kansas University Press, 1999).
3. Edward Said, *Orientalism* (New York: Pantheon, 1978).
4. Christina Klein, *Cold War Orientalism: Asia in the Middlebrow Imagination, 1945–1961* (Berkeley, CA: University of California Press, 2003).
5. Ian Buruma & Margalit Avishai, 'Occidentalism', *The New York Review of Books*, 17.1.02, pp.4–8.
6. A review essay on cross-bloc approaches to the socio-cultural history of the cold war is Patrick Major & Rana Mitter, 'East is East and West is West?: Towards a Comparative Sociocultural History of the Cold War', *Cold War History*, 4:1 (2003), pp.1–22.

7. Peter J. Kuznick & James Gilbert (eds), *Rethinking Cold War Culture* (Washington, DC: Smithsonian Institution Press, 2002), pp.3–12.
8. Leo P. Ribuffo, 'Will the Sixties Never End? Or Perhaps at least the Thirties? Or Maybe even the Progressive Era? Contrarian Thoughts on Change and Continuity in American Political Culture at the Turn of the Millennium', in Kuznick & Gilbert (eds), *Cold War Culture*, pp.201–23.
9. Jeremi Suri, *Power and Protest: Global Revolution and the Rise of Détente* (Cambridge, MA: Harvard University Press, 2003), pp.2–3.
10. Suri, *Power and Protest*, pp.262, 265.
11. A similar approach on Soviet foreign policy has been taken by Ted Hopf, *Social Construction of International Politics: Identities and Foreign Policies, Moscow, 1955 and 1999* (Ithaca, NY: Cornell University Press, 2002).
12. Lynn Boyd Hinds & Theodore Otto Windt, *The Cold War as Rhetoric: The Beginnings, 1945–1950* (Westport, CT: Praeger, 1991); Francis A. Beer & Robert Hariman (eds), *Post-Realism: The Rhetorical Turn in International Relations* (East Lansing, MI: Michigan State University Press, 1996); Martin J. Medhurst et al., *Cold War Rhetoric: Strategy, Metaphor and Ideology* (Ann Arbor, MI: Michigan State University Press, 1997); Emily S. Rosenberg, '"Foreign Affairs" after World War, II: Connecting Sexual and International Politics', *Diplomatic History*, 18 (1994), pp.59–70; Shawn J. Parry-Giles, *The Rhetorical Presidency: Propaganda and the Cold War, 1945–1955* (Westport, CT: Greenwood, 2001).
13. Robert D. Dean, *Imperial Brotherhood: Gender and the Making of Cold War Foreign Policy* (Amherst, MA: University of Massachusetts Press, 2003).
14. Christian G. Appy, 'Eisenhower's Guatemalan Doodle, or, How to Draw, Deny, and Take Credit for a Third World Coup', in Appy (ed.), *Cold War Constructions: The Political Culture of United States Imperialism, 1945–1966* (Amherst, MA: University of Massachusetts Press, 2000), pp.183–213.
15. Jeffrey Brooks, *Thank You, Comrade Stalin!: Soviet Public Culture from Revolution to Cold War* (Princeton, NJ: Princeton University Press, 1999).
16. Alf Lüdtke & Peter Becker (eds), *Akten, Eingaben, Schaufenster: Die DDR und ihre Texte* (Berlin: Akademie, 1997).
17. Birgit Wolf, *Sprache in der DDR: Ein Wörterbuch* (Gruyter: Berlin, 2000).
18. '*Blat*' was the Russian black market 'economy of favours'; '*Bückwaren*' were literally 'stoop goods', which the shopkeeper had to retrieve from under the counter.
19. Jessica C.E. Grienow-Hecht, 'Shame on US? Academics, Cultural Transfer and the Cold War: A Critical Review', *Diplomatic History*, 24 (2000), pp.465–94.
20. Abbott Gleason, *Totalitarianism: The Inner History of the Cold War* (Oxford: Oxford University Press, 1995).
21. Michael E. Latham, *Modernisation as Ideology: American Social Science and 'Nation Building' in the Kennedy Era* (Chapel Hill, NC: North Carolina University Press, 2000), *passim*; David C. Engerman et al. (eds), *Staging Growth: Modernization, Development, and the Global Cold War* (Amherst, MA: University of Massachusetts Press, 2003).
22. Christopher Simpson (ed.), *Universities and Empire: Money and Politics in the Social Sciences during the Cold War* (New York: New Press, 1998).
23. Ron Robin, *The Making of the Cold War Enemy: Culture and Politics in the Military-Industrial Complex* (Princeton, NJ: Princeton University Press, 2001).

See also Rebecca S. Lowen, *Creating the Cold War University: The Transformation of Stanford* (Berkeley, CA: University of California Press, 1997).

24. Christopher Simpson, *Science of Coercion: Communication Research and Psychological Warfare, 1945–1960* (New York: Oxford University Press, 1996).

25. Peter Coleman, *The Liberal Conspiracy: The Congress for Cultural Freedom and the Struggle for the Mind of Postwar Europe* (London & New York: Macmillan, 1989), *passim*.

26. Frances Stonor Saunders, *Who Paid the Piper?: The CIA and the Cultural Cold War* (London: Granta Books, 1999), *passim*; published in the United States under the title *The Cultural Cold War: The CIA and the World of Arts and Letters*.

27. David Caute, *The Dancer Defects: The Struggle for Cultural Supremacy during the Cold War* (Oxford: Oxford University Press, 2003), p.617.

28. Hugh Wilford, *The CIA, the British Left and the Cold War* (London: Frank Cass, 2003), pp.289, 301.

29. Giles Scott-Smith, *The Politics of Apolitical Culture: The Congress for Cultural Freedom, the CIA, and Postwar American Hegemony* (London: Routledge, 2002), p.165. On state–private networks, see W. Scott Lucas, *Freedom's War: The US Crusade Against the Soviet Union, 1945–56* (New York: New York University Press, 1999), *passim*.

30. Caute, *The Dancer Defects*, p.615. Jean-Paul Sartre (1905–1980) and Albert Camus (1913–1960) were two of France's most renowned existentialist intellectuals, but while Sartre retained a residual sympathy for Marxism Camus renounced his support for communist ideology. Konstantin Simonov (1915–1979) remains renowned as one of Russia's best wartime and post-war poets. Bertold Brecht (1898–1956), the German playwright, remained a convinced communist throughout much of his life and resided in the GDR in his final years. However, the June 1953 rising in Berlin shook both his faith in communism, and his respect for the East German leadership. The Czech playwright Vaclav Havel (1936–) became a leading dissident during the 1970s, and was imprisoned by the Prague regime. After the 'Velvet Revolution' of 1989 he became Czechoslovakia's first (and last) post-communist president. The Polish film director Andrzej Wajda (1926–) attracted worldwide renown for his work, which profited from the comparatively liberal cultural atmosphere of post-1956 Poland. His trilogy of war films, *Pokolenie* (A Generation), *Kanal* (Canal) and *Popiol I Diamenty* (Ashes and Diamonds) established his reputation internationally.

31. Caute, *Dancer Defects*, p.11; Volker Berghahn, *America and the Intellectual Cold Wars in Europe: Shepard Stone between Philanthropy, Academy and Diplomacy* (Princeton, NJ: Princeton University Press, 2001), *passim*.

32. Yoshikuni Igarashi, *Bodies of Memory: Narratives of War in Postwar Japanese Culture, 1945–1970* (Princeton, NJ: Princeton University Press, 2000).

33. The field is growing almost month by month, but representative works include Neil Diamant, *Revolutionizing the Family: Politics, Love and Divorce in Urban and Rural China, 1949–1968* (Berkeley, CA: University of California Press, 2000), and Judith Shapiro, *Mao's War Against Nature: Politics and the Environment in Revolutionary China* (Cambridge: Cambridge University Press, 2001).

34. On Korea, see Charles K. Armstrong, 'The Cultural Cold War in Korea', *Journal of Asian Studies* (2003); and Sheila Miyoshi Jager, 'Women, Resistance, and the Divided Nation', *Journal of Asian Studies* (1996).

35. John Whittier Treat, *Writing Ground Zero: Japanese Literature and the Atomic Bomb* (Chicago, IL: Chicago University Press, 1995); Mick Broderick (ed.), *Hibakusha Cinema: Hiroshima, Nagasaki and the Nuclear Image in Japanese Film* (New York & London: Kegan Paul International, 1996).

36. First inroads are being made, for instance Tina Mai Chen, 'Internationalism and Cultural Experience: Soviet Films and Popular Chinese Understandings of the Future in the 1950s', *Cultural Critique*, 58 (2004), pp.82–114.

37. Theodor W. Adorno & Max Horkheimer, 'The Culture Industry: Enlightenment as Mass Deception', in *Dialectic of Enlightenment*, trans. John Cumming (London: Verso, 1997), pp.120–67. Hollywood was one of the chief targets, which predigested its cultural output, thereby allegedly denying the audience a critical input.

38. Lucas, *Freedom's War*, p.93.

39. Mark Pendergrast, *For God, Country and Coca-Cola: The Unauthorized History of the World's Most Popular Soft Drink and the Company that Makes It* (London: Phoenix, 1993).

40. Richard F. Kuisel, *Seducing the French: The Dilemma of Americanization* (Berkeley, CA: University of California Press, 1993); Denis Lacorne et al. (eds), *The Rise and Fall of Anti-Americanism: A Century of French Perception* (London: Macmillan, 1990).

41. Reinhold Wagnleitner, *Coca-Colonization and the Cold War: The Cultural Mission of the United States in Austria after the Second World War* (Chapel Hill, NC: University of North Carolina Press, 1994); Ralph Willett, *The Americanization of Germany, 1945–1949* (London: Routledge, 1989); Reiner Pommerin (ed.), *The American Impact on Postwar Germany* (Providence RI & Oxford: Berghahn, 1995); David F. Crew (ed.), *Consuming Germany in the Cold War* (Oxford: Berg, 2003).

42. Victoria de Grazia, *Irresistible Empire: America's Advance through Twentieth-century Europe* (Cambridge, MA: Belknap, 2005).

43. Brian Rigby, *Popular Culture in Modern France: A Study of Cultural Discourse* (London: Routledge, 1991).

44. Adele Marie Barker (ed.), *Consuming Russia: Popular Culture, Sex, and Society since Gorbachev* (Durham, NC: Duke University Press, 1999); Victor Ripp, *Pizza in Pushkin Square: What Russians Think about Americans and the American Way of Life* (New York: Simon & Schuster, 1990).

45. David Crowley & Susan E. Reid (eds), *Style and Socialism: Modernity and Material Culture in Postwar Eastern Europe* (Oxford: Berg, 2000).

46. Timothy W. Ryback, *Rock Around the Bloc: A History of Rock Music in Eastern Europe and the Soviet Union* (Oxford: Oxford University Press, 1990); Sabrina P. Ramet, *Social Currents in Eastern Europe: The Sources and Meaning of the Great Transformation* (Durham, NC: Duke University Press, 1991).

47. Artemy Troitsky, *Back in the USSR: The True Story of Rock in Russia* (London: Omnibus, 1987); Thomas Cushman, *Notes from Underground: Rock Music Counterculture in Russia* (Albany, NY: State University of New York Press, 1995).

48. Uta G. Poiger, *Jazz, Rock and Rebels: Cold War Politics and American Culture in a Divided Germany* (California Press, 2000); Michael Rauhut, *Beat in der Grauzone: DDR-Rock 1964–1972: Politik und Alltag* (Berlin: links, 1993).

49. Reggie Nadelson, *Comrade Rockstar: The Search for Dean Reed* (London: Chatto & Windus, 1991).
50. Michael Rauhut, *Schalmei und Lederjacke: Udo Lindenberg, BAP, Underground: Rock und Politik in den achtziger Jahren* (Berlin: Schwarzkopf, 1996), pp.128–78.
51. Alan Nadel, *Containment Culture: American Narratives, Postmodernism and the Atomic Age* (Durham, NC: Duke University Press, 1995).
52. Suzanne Clark, *Cold Warriors: Manliness on Trial in the Rhetoric of the West* (Carbondale, IL: Southern Illinois University Press, 2000).
53. Robert J. Corber, *In the Name of National Security: Hitchcock, Homophobia and the Political Construction of Gender in Postwar America* (Durham, NC: Duke University Press, 1993) and *Homosexuality in Cold War America: Resistance and the Crisis of Masculinity* (Durham, NC: Duke University Press, 1997).
54. See also Klein, *Orientalism*, pp.191–222, for musicals and modernisation.
55. Stanley Corkin, *Cowboys as Cold Warriors: The Western and US History* (Philadelphia, PA: Temple University Press, 2004).
56. Roberts to Strang (FO), 29.1.52, FO1110/528(TNA).
57. Eric Rentschler, *The Ministry of Illusion: Nazi Cinema and its Afterlife* (Cambridge, MA: Harvard University Press, 1996).
58. Lary May, *The Big Tomorrow: Hollywood and the Politics of the American Way* (Chicago, IL: University of Chicago Press, 2000), p.177.
59. Gordon Kahn, *Hollywood on Trial: The Story of the Ten Who Were Indicted* (New York: Arno, 1976).
60. Stonor Saunders, *Who Paid the Piper?*, pp.284–7.
61. Tony Shaw, *British Cinema and the Cold War* (London: I.B. Tauris, 2000), p.195.
62. Sarah Davies, 'Soviet Cinema in the Early Cold War: Pudovkin's *Admiral Nakhimov* in Context', in Mitter and Major (eds), 'Across the Blocs: Cold War Cultural and Social History', special issue of *Cold War History*, 4:1 (2003), pp.49–70.
63. Sean Allan & John Sandford (eds), *Defa: East German Cinema, 1946–1992* (Oxford: Berghahn, 1999).
64. Anne White, *De-Stalinisation and the House of Culture: Declining State Control over Leisure in the USSR, Poland and Hungary* (London: Routledge, 1990).
65. Richard G. Powers, *G-Men: Hoover's FBI in American Popular Culture* (Carbondale, IL: Southern Illinois University Press, 1983).
66. Jeremy Black, *The Politics of James Bond: From Ian Fleming's Novels to the Big Screen* (New York: Praeger, 2001), p.49.
67. Patrick Major, 'Coming in from the Cold: The GDR in the British Spy Thriller', in Arnd Bauerkämper (ed.), *Britain and the GDR: Relations and Perceptions in a Divided World* (Berlin, 2002), pp.339–52.
68. Personal communication of Jens Gieseke to the author.
69. Günther Claus, 'Verlagsgutachten', 14.2.78, Bundesarchiv Berlin (BAB), DR-1/5432, fos. 270–5.
70. Duty, 'Verlagsgutachten', 11.8.86, BAB, DR-1/2193, fos. 245–55.
71. Peter Biskind, *Seeing Is Believing: How Hollywood Taught Us to Stop Worrying and Love the Fifties* (London: Pluto, 1984), pp.101–59.
72. Paul Boyer, *By the Bomb's Early Light: American Thought and Culture at the Dawn of the Atomic Age* (Chapel Hill, NC: North Carolina University Press, 1994, 2nd edition), p.122.

73. James F. Shapiro, *Atomic Bomb Cinema: The Apocalyptic Imagination on Film* (London: Routledge, 2002), esp. pp.141–68.
74. Peter J. Kuznick & James Gilbert, 'US Culture and the Cold War', in Kuznick & Gilbert (ed.), *Rethinking Cold War Culture*, p.1.
75. For more on this see Laura McEnaney, *Civil Defense Begins at Home: Militarization Meets Everyday Life in the Fifties* (Princeton, NJ: Princeton University Press, 2000).
76. Philip Wylie, *Tomorrow!* (New York: Holt, 1954). See also David Seed, *American Science Fiction and the Cold War: Literature and Film* (Edinburgh: Edinburgh University Press, 1999), pp.14–24.
77. Richard A. Schwartz, *Cold War Culture: Media and the Arts, 1945–1990* (New York: Checkmark Books, 1998), pp.190–1. Schwartz is an invaluable reference source.
78. Bradford W. Wright, *Comic Book Nation: The Transformation of Youth Culture in America* (Baltimore, MD: Johns Hopkins University Press, 2001).
79. William W. Savage, *Commies, Cowboys, and Jungle Queens: Comic Books and America, 1945–1954* (Hanover, CT: Wesleyan University Press, 1998).
80. Marvel Comics, *The Essential Iron Man*, vol. 1 (New York: Marvel, 2000).
81. Frank Miller, *Batman: The Dark Knight Returns* (New York: DC Comics, 2002, reprint).
82. Alan Moore & Dave Gibbons, *Watchmen* (New York: DC Comics, 1986–87).
83. Alan Moore & David Lloyd, *V for Vendetta* (New York: DC Comics, 1988–89).
84. Eric Schaefer, *Bold! Daring! Shocking! True!: A History of Exploitation Films, 1919–1959* (Durham, NC: Duke University Press, 1999).
85. Roger Corman, *How I Made a Hundred Movies in Hollywood and Never Lost a Dime* (New York: Random House, 1990).
86. Walter L. Hixson, *Parting the Curtain: Propaganda, Culture and the cold war, 1945–1961* (London: Macmillan, 1997); Arch Puddington, *Broadcasting Freedom: The Cold War Triumph of Radio Free Europe and Radio Liberty* (Lexington, KT: University of Kentucky Press, 2000).
87. Michael Curtin, *Redeeming the Wasteland: Television Documentary and Cold War Politics* (New Brunswick, NJ: Rutgers University Press, 1995); Nancy E. Bernhard, *U.S. Television News and Cold War Propaganda, 1947–1960* (New York: Cambridge University Press, 1999).
88. Joseph S. Nye, *Soft Power: The Means to Success in World Politics* (New York: Public Affairs, 2004), p.49.

10
decolonisation and empire

john kent

The transitions that the world has undergone, and is still undergoing since 1945, have seen a new interest in 'empire'. Since the end of the cold war the unilateral exercise of American power under the second Bush administration in particular has been included in the 'empire' debate.[1] The fact that some conservative American commentators are beginning to regard the idea of an American empire and the exercise of American power with a degree of satisfaction and pride has distracted attention from the ways in which the old European empires were dismantled after 1945 and the changes that were thus produced. Although authors like Michael Doyle continue to analyse the roles of maritime empires,[2] land-based empires of former days now play a more prominent role in imperial literature. The rise and decline of great powers and their empires is more connected to hard power factors – military and economic power – and the nature of European decolonisation and soft power elements have been marginalised.

Paradoxically this has been done more with regard to the cold war, and in misleading orthodox ways, than with an emphasis on the accompanying decline of twentieth-century European empires. Despite the fact that the transfer of power, in the sense of political and administrative control, was generally accompanied by a French and British desire to retain influence – a lesser manifestation of power – ideology and ideas have been underplayed. In other words decolonisation was initially connected to a wish to continue exercising power on the international stage as geo-strategic concepts intermingled with the ideology of the cold war and concerned policy-makers grappling with the ending of European empires. As the early cold war began transforming the international system, and before the more aggressive US policy began in 1948, decolonisation was only partially in evidence. It was only later in the decolonisation process in the 1950s and 1960s that the exercise of power, regarded more and more as influence through the usage of a softer form, came to dominate and the cold war became more intimately connected to decolonisation. This process was primarily a phenomenon associated with the British and French (although each were influenced by very different colonial and imperial traditions as well as by different administrative practices) and the British aim was also to gain a special place in the American empire, unlike the French.[3]

Both the United States and the Soviet Union during the wartime alliance had been opponents for different reasons of European empires and the possession of colonies. Autarchic trading blocs were not welcomed by American capitalism whatever their ideological hue but such sentiments applied specifically to colonies were disappearing even before Franklin D. Roosevelt's death in April 1945.[4] In recent history, the informal empire of the United States, along with that of the Soviet Union, have been linked to the elements of hard power that preceded the cold war years in which the European empires collapsed. The standard hard power framework analysed in the cold war has been one of a bipolar competitive world of the superpowers with their nuclear weapons and arms acquisition. As such with less emphasis on soft power, the superpowers can be more aptly compared with the old pre-war empires in terms of their acquisition of territories and political domination. When it comes to the processes that produced the abandonment of European empires after the Second World War the hard power explanation of decolonisation and cold war is certainly less persuasive and re-enforced by the collapse of the Soviet Union. During the latter stages of decolonisation the role of empires, the British in particular, was much less defined by the means of control and the exploitation of resources as features of power. Imperial powers are now having to adjust to a relative lack of such hard power capabilities.

Even as early as the end of the Second World War, empires, in their most obvious forms of economic exploitation and political domination, that were projecting 'power in the world' were no longer regarded as acceptable parts of the international system. They therefore had to contribute to increasing the state's power and status within the international community in some other way – influence in less tangible and concrete forms. Yet they were to some extent reprieved by the onset of the cold war, even if the latter is interpreted primarily as an ideological conflict, as opposed to a geo-strategic battle featuring nuclear weapons and economic resources. The debates over the nature and meanings of empires and European decolonisation are clearly associated with and inseparable from the cold war world which had to deal with the new states produced by the ending of European colonialism. In this situation it was not just a relationship between the imperial states and those that they ruled, which had existed on a basis of political subordination (colonialism), that was having to find a new relationship. The cold war world was one in which the relationship between the imperial states and the superpowers was also reflected in the nature of the state system itself and the changes the cold war produced. Whether decolonisation was merely a footnote to the cold war is therefore a very pertinent question.[5]

The early cold war itself, in orthodox explanations, has been defined simply as a response to the Soviet geopolitical challenge and misrepresented as a response to a Soviet military threat which was never perceived at the time.[6] NATO was never designed to meet a Soviet attack by protecting Western Europe through the deployment of conventional forces in a military alliance. Western policy-makers saw alliances as a means to meet the ideological challenge through political organisation. Empire, whatever the associations with military and economic strength, became at the same time part of this political and ideological challenge involved in the pursuit of the cold war. How one defines these international developments in an increasingly globalised and decolonising world after the Second World War depends very much on how one defines twentieth-century European empires. (Just as the definition and use of the term 'Third World' in relation to the global system depends on perceptions of how the system operates in relation to the cold war.[7]) The ideological questions asked by the cold war (which system or bloc were the countries emerging from colonial rule freely going to choose to align with) then became linked to ending the colonial relationship between rulers and ruled. And, crucially, to how this new relationship could replace the hard power, in military and economic terms with which it had been associated in the past. For the Europeans this had been significantly reduced, relative to the USA, by the war and that power loss would have to be replaced by other forms of influence that could satisfy, or be represented as satisfying, the requirements of the cold war. In that way the old imperial roles could serve to represent power in international terms through the prestige, status or influence that could no longer just be defined by hard power criteria or the exercise of an outmoded form of political or economic domination. The legacy of empire would have to fulfil a cold war role, using military deployments of a lesser kind, not to deal with hot war threats, but to prevent any destabilisation of the capitalist system or undermining of Western interests and values.

In that sense the old terminology of empire which applied to the nineteenth-century European empires has become less appropriate for the debates about cold war and decolonisation. Yet 'hegemony, 'unilateralism' and other terminology defining the nature of the global distribution of power are equally unhelpful. Old imperial terms such as 'assimilation', 'association' and even 'indirect rule' are also not relevant to the collapse of the Soviet empire. Nevertheless it should always be remembered that during the cold war the concept of 'colonialism', and in particular its relationship to decolonisation or the ending of formal administrative controls, was always distinct from the concept of 'imperialism' broadly defined as the projection of power in the world. And as the British empire was transformed into a Commonwealth and the nature of Britain's relations with its former dependencies radically changed, the ambitions or pretensions of Britain to remain a great global power remained or were arguably strengthened. Whether this could be best expressed through the decolonisation process or by continuing to conduct military operations and station troops in various parts of the world was yet to be determined in a cold war context.

It was a question of trying to retain global status as a world power while abandoning empire through decolonisation. In a cold war world which produced its own ideological requirements these same requirements might be used as a screen for more traditional imperial positions of regional influence. This was the cold war road the British were to travel down with particular emphasis on their informal empire in the Middle East. Here the transfer of political authority had largely taken place before 1945 and the close relationship between cold war, empire and global influence should not therefore be much of a surprise. Even less so if one defines the cold war as an ideological struggle over cultural and socio-economic systems, which aimed to win the hearts and minds of the people in the world's newly independent states. This aim and its political realisation was of course part of the British justification for an overseas presence and the retention of global power status. It enables us to understand how a declining imperial power was affected by, and still able to influence the international system when its far flung possessions were demanding the freedom which communism threatened to remove.

The Second World War had proved to be the most crucial event in undermining European rule and in transforming global power relations. Its onset had caused consternation and fear amongst governments and elites in Europe. The fears of British Conservative leaders, such as Neville Chamberlain, concerned the domestic consequences of a major war. It was considered that a price would have to be paid for the cost of social reform by conservative elites if the British empire was forced to fight, and for the next 40 years that price proved to be considerable.[8] Yet appeasement was adopted for many reasons, including the exposure of the imperial bluff long played by Britain with its possessions in East Asia and the Pacific. Another related economic reason put forward by the Prime Minister was the actual financial cost expected to be borne by the British taxpayer of preventing chaos and disorder in areas under British colonial rule. In each case the non-negotiable issues were the socio-economic order at home and the importance for global power and influence of the British empire abroad. Internationally the latter could be compared to the British upper classes being fundamentally important to the British way of life in national terms. In the event both the national and international were seen as coming under threat after the war when the Allied failure to agree on the power political concessions and compromises needed for an agreed post-war international order led to tensions and disagreements by 1946. These then produced confrontation and cold war animosity on both sides from 1948 onwards.[9] The position of the British Commonwealth in strategic terms had consequently to be preserved in new ways. These now became linked to the ideological challenges of the cold war and the anti-colonial movements which made decolonisation unavoidable.[10]

This breakdown of the Grand Alliance and the emergence by 1948 of the 'war fought by all means short of international armed conflict' significantly affected the ideological changes experienced by empires.[11] Initially the main hope had been that the standing of the British empire, or Commonwealth, as it became known, could be preserved through cooperation with the USA and the Soviet Union. Empires and spheres of influence could then be preserved under a cooperative framework embodying the security arrangements needed to prevent another world war.[12] But doubts grew between 1946 and 1948 about achieving this and reconciling the Big Three's perceptions of their vital interests within it. A 'new' Commonwealth and a United Nations based on internationalism that would enable the hard power problems of the former empire to be subsumed within a new international order also disappeared. And with it the hope that decolonisation *and* a 'global power' role for Britain could thereby be accommodated in a cooperative international order.[13]

In a sense that also had implications for the viability of the British strategy that developed in the 1930s preceding the outbreak of war. The need to avoid internal colonial disturbances in Africa, the Caribbean and Palestine in particular produced the initial, hesitant embrace of significant change for the colonies, as opposed to the white Dominions, in Whitehall.[14] The British colonial empire soon became seen as having to follow, in the larger colonies at least, the path previously taken by the

Dominions. This would refashion the means by which influence in the Empire/Commonwealth was remade and presented to fulfil the status and prestige needs of a liberal world power. In part this was a response to the difficulties many colonies had experienced during the Depression and in part a reflection of liberal feelings within the Colonial Office. Most of all it was also a response to the challenges threatening Britain's world position at the head of what was still a great empire of considerable geographic spread. If the position of the British Empire/Commonwealth was to be retained after the war then it would be necessary to avoid the expenditure on troops to deal with the revolts that had been occurring in various parts of the empire.[15] The colonial empire was now expected to provide, not so much the manpower and resources, but a source of prestige and influence that a refashioned colonial relationship, with help from Treasury funds, would provide. It would embody development to meet colonial needs, and self-government, if not complete independence, would be prepared for.

Ten years later the problem of the cold war and the preservation of British power produced a more acute problem. It had not been fully faced when the wartime assumption had been that some form of international great power cooperation would continue. Hence the British reaction to the Indian demands for self-government which was not only conditioned by the Prime Minister's personal experience of India in the inter-war years,[16] but by the fact that the concessions made to Indian nationalists were made before the cold war had become an entrenched characteristic of the international scene.[17] Prior to this it was easier to abandon a possession where influence could be linked to a new 'internationalist' global role in the hope of great power cooperation. Unfortunately after India was promised independence, the domestic threat to the socio-economic order in Western Europe was now radical enough to threaten more than social reform. And it was more potent internationally as the ideology of Soviet communism was backed by the hard power of a major victorious state. It is the author's view that the two threats have been conveniently but misleadingly conflated by historians just as the possession and subsequent loss of a colonial empire has been conflated with the loss of British power. And while the former was a policy, albeit often expressed on the right in a reluctant acceptance of the inevitable, the latter was never accepted, either at Suez or with Tony Blair's determination to maintain a 'pivotal global (not European) role' for a twenty-first-century Britain.[18]

The development of a new imperial role after 1945 embodied such liberal concepts as economic and social development and welfare and the preparation of less developed colonial people for self-government in the modern post-war world. It was only one aspect of the transfer of power and the end of empire, and not exclusive to Britain. The abandonment of world power status which a global role had provided was quite another and a more difficult challenge for policy-makers to confront. However for the British, global influence on the world stage was going to be based *faute de mieux* on less tangible concepts than economic or military power by the use of concepts such as prestige. Thus power in the words of one senior official would not be 'represented by money and troops alone', but by 'what the rest of the world thinks of us'.[19] This was quite a different matter for a declining power eager to cling to a pivotal role in the world to provide. Thus in order to understand the relationship of cold war to British decolonisation it is necessary to distinguish the ending of colonial rule from an acceptance of a loss of prestige and world power status. The latter was not seen as the inevitable result of the former and in areas on informal empire like the Middle East, however, 'power' was defined. The loss of status was only accepted, if at all, with extreme reluctance and after the cold war in the 1950s had been used as a screen to try and conceal it prior to the Suez debacle.[20]

The French were in a rather different position regarding their world role that had previously been based on colonial possessions. They had entered the Second World War with the hope that their colonies would compensate for the superiority of Germany in manpower and resources and emerged from it with a particular attachment to those African territories which had fought for the Free French. Under de Gaulle in 1945–46 the French were equally taken by such concepts of prestige or *gloire* (equivalent to the British *raison d'être* of world power status), but the Second World War had left them very little in terms of either hard power or prestige. Influenced by French traditions of assimilation they developed a concept of empire based less on the idea of decolonisation and more on the *de jure* abolition of colonies. The French possessions in their overseas empire would become part of a newly created French Union along with metropolitan France. As the colonies became parts of overseas France, equality in name, but not in substance, would be granted. At the same time individual indigenous inhabitants would receive the empty promise that they too could become citizens of the 'one and indivisible French republic' through in effect assimilation on an individual basis into the newly created French Union. These indigenous inhabitants would be offered social and economic reforms and the territories of overseas France would receive a not insubstantial amount of money in development aid from metropolitan France.[21]

Unfortunately at the end of the war the French failure to satisfy the demands of Ho Chi Minh and Vietnamese nationalists, eager for full independence, immediately produced an armed conflict in 1946. It was a conflict which revealed the limited impact of the French Union in enhancing French prestige outside Europe. The French problem in Indochina was soon interpreted by the Truman administration as very much part of a cold war struggle in Asia, and one which lacked an economic resource rationale and failed to offer a strategic benefit for the West (or for the French) in any hot war. Yet the strength of the armed resistance of the nationalist movement in Vietnam, although quickly affecting the global situation as well as the future of the French Union, produced a French reaction which contrasted with the British responses to anti-colonial movements in South Asia, if not in Malaya.

Not only were the key British decisions on Asia taken in the hopeful atmosphere of the immediate post-war world, but the Middle East (in the perceptions of the British empire that were dominant amongst British policy-making elites) had already replaced India in importance during the inter-war years.[22] In addition, the full scale of the British metropolitan need for imperial resources to assist with economic recovery was not fully appreciated until 1947. The latter was a hard power factor that produced a conflict between the liberal requirements of decolonisation and the resource needs of European post-war recovery which the British had to meet through increased economic exploitation of the colonies.[23] This did not meet the pre-war need to portray the empire in liberal, progressive, development and welfare terms. Planning to influence world market prices for the benefit of colonial producers ran headlong into the problems for European recovery of the dollar gap.[24] This produced a clear contradiction between maximising colonial production to earn dollars or replace goods purchased by Britain in the dollar zone, and the need to prevent surplus British production increasing colonial access to consumer goods for the benefit of producers.[25] Hence the greater importance of a political commitment to self-government if Britain's continuation as a world power was to be justified in ways that replaced the image of an exploitative colonialism. Inevitably the emphasis now had to be put on the development of the political relations between Britain and anti-colonial elites in those territories, like the Gold Coast (now Ghana),[26] which were leading the way towards self-government. If British influence was to be retained then the process of decolonisation and the transfer of power would have to meet the political rather than the economic criteria desired by the developing anti-colonial movements.

And there remained those geo-strategic areas of the British empire where no power was to be transferred.

The Middle East was one such area at the end of the 1940s, because apart from the colonies of Aden and Cyprus and the shore of the Gulf, in the greater Levant area cooperation in the transfer of power could no longer lead to a new form of British influence. The relationship embodying British influence had to be reflected in military bases and close cooperation with or domination of indigenous elites, many of whom were not representative of the local population. Yet the regional influence this produced was still a crucial element of British power in the world. As the 1950s began this power could not be easily sustained by military capabilities that were declining.

In the Soviet empire Stalin had always been preoccupied with the consolidation of his own and the Soviet state's power. The Soviet leader did not have to worry about the nuances of an imperial role for the Soviet empire. Yet for the American leadership, whatever the nature of the American empire that had emerged by the end of the war, their attitudes to the concept were conditioned by the cold war. Their first priority required the rebuilding of Western Europe and it was only with events in South-East Asia and Indochina, particularly after 1948, that the United States turned its attention to other areas of the globe. Africa had been perceived initially as playing a useful contributory role in cold war Europe's reconstruction, and the United States only developed a distinct policy for Black Africa in 1952.[27] One year later a more independent policy towards the Middle East was adopted in the wake of the rise of Mossadeq in Iran in 1951 and Dulles's tour of the region in 1953.[28] Whatever importance is attached to the idea of a growing and informal US empire has often been associated with the material rewards available in Middle East. On the other hand for the Americans the cold war generally had gradually become more of an ideological conflict since 1948. Hence their concern with decolonisation and the future of the former European colonies, which grew as their attainment of self-government and a 'responsible' place in the cold war ideological alignment appeared more necessary for the West's winning of the global 'hearts and minds' battle.

This American shift of emphasis followed the debate that developed in the wake of NSC-68 under first Truman and then Eisenhower, and the Soviet atomic and later hydrogen bomb explosions. Crucial to both was the devising and then the questioning of a more aggressive, but ideological, American cold war strategy that had developed since the issuing of NSC-7 in 1948.[29] Covert action aimed at subverting communist rule in Eastern Europe and the USSR was becoming riskier as the dangers of a hot war being produced by the aggressive pursuit of the cold war increased in the thermonuclear age. As the difficulties of undermining the Soviet Union or its satellite empire in Eastern Europe increased, former non-self-governing territories and those on the verge of independence assumed greater cold war importance, irrespective of the communist success in China at the end of 1949.

Assisting this shift was the growing American realisation that the commitment to 'development' in the Afro-Asian world could not simply be left to Europeans. The implementation of purely European development plans, even if assisted by Point Four aid instigated by the Truman administration, was inevitably to bring accusations of imperialism, exploitation and neo-colonialism.[30] This was becoming increasingly damaging in the cold war world of the 1950s. The spotlight was therefore put more firmly on the nature and progress of decolonisation precisely because of these changes in the cold war environment.[31] One immediate dilemma that American governments faced, and were to continue to face, was instantly obvious. Cooperation with the European colonial powers was an essential requirement of NATO. Even if the political purpose and value of the organisation is emphasised as it should be, (rather then its military role), there was an obvious contradiction between avoiding European unhappiness with an anti-colonial US role and meeting the ambitions of newly emerging colonial elites. The latter were eager to follow in American footsteps and break free from the constraints on their political freedoms imposed by colonialism.

In 1950 it was clear that the same American pressure that was placed on the Dutch (the USA even considered withdrawing Marshall aid) to prevent the suppression of so-called nationalist forces in Indonesia could now not be so easily applied elsewhere.[32] Nor could the Eisenhower administration rely on economic largesse to replace demands for political change as the British had already discovered. If the British in the Gold Coast were therefore willing to adopt a strategy of placating nationalists by seizing the initiative in taking the steps that would gradually replace colonial rule with self-government or independence, others in the early 1950s were not. While the Portuguese and the French remained committed to the pretence that colonialism had in effect been superseded, no one, least of all the anti-colonial leaders in Indochina and North Africa, was prepared to believe them. For the Portuguese, even though the challenge did not come until the 1960s, economic benefits from trade, combined with emigration from Portugal, made the fascist elites in Lisbon eager to cling on to the colonies of Mozambique, Guineé and Angola in the face of anti-colonial movements. Once again assimilation and social reform in the colonies, because they did not herald the adoption of self-government which might take the sting out of communist attacks on Western imperialism, were unacceptable to the Americans. The exploitative and unequal relationship that European empires seemed to represent could no longer be hidden for the Portuguese by the cold war. Although for the next two decades this did not prevent attempts by Lisbon to do just that and point to the stability allegedly produced by the rule of capitalist states.[33]

It was of course always difficult for the USA to deny that dissatisfaction with colonial rule contained more than an element of truth however much the Western colonial powers might point to the benefits brought by colonialism. Dulles, not one prepared to go against the American traditions of freedom and anti-colonialism, initially sought to square the circle by arguing that for cold war reasons the comparison between colonialism and communism should be advantageous.[34] Unfortunately not only had few colonial people become aware of the benefits of colonialism, even fewer had suffered at the hands of communism. The idea of the Third World, a term first coined by Alfred Sauvy in 1952, seemed to imply not just a quest for an alternative to the first and second worlds but 'to be something' to the solidifying cold war global alignments. It was also implied and argued that, like their French predecessors in the third estate, the members of the Third World had experienced some sort of subservience and a denial of rights. The Third World was exploited in the same way as the nobility and religious orders had exploited the third estate and its destiny was therefore a revolutionary one that rejected all forms of imperialism. In the cold war context the success of decolonisation had to avoid any such radicalism.

Under Eisenhower, the cold war and any attempt to avoid siding with the Afro-Asians required that self-government become a *sine qua non*, to the annoyance of the French who were not offering it in the early 1950s. The US determination to push for the granting of self-government, or at least an acknowledgement that those under French rule were moving toward such a goal, was played out first in Morocco and Tunisia. Support for the political movements led by 'moderate' indigenous leaders came from both the Americans and the United Nations. Despite the fact that the war in Algeria broke out in November 1954, the progress begun by the then Premier, Pierre Mendes-France, in North Africa was soon extended to other parts of overseas France.[35] The *loi cadre*, embodying this in the form of representative assemblies in the overseas territories, was conceived in 1955 and implemented in 1956. As this occurred, the French, in a process that the Portuguese were later to follow with limited success, tried time and again to persuade the Americans that a continued European presence was desirable for cold war reasons and the cohesion of the Atlantic alliance. The British too, or at least the Foreign Office, were not averse to playing the communist card to avoid international interference through the United Nations.[36] Yet by 1956 they had convinced Dulles that by organising 'responsible' collaborators they would implement the transfer of power successfully. Colonialism of the liberal British variety would serve as an excellent preparation for entry into the modern cold war world so enabling the USA and the colonial powers to work towards the same ends in Africa.[37]

In West Africa things appeared to be going smoothly there for British decolonisation and its US cold war supporters despite the obvious dilemma which the crux of the problem revealed. Crucial to any commitment to self-government and independence was the timing of the transfer of power. This became more problematic as the cold war became more significant for the future of the Third World. If power was transferred too slowly there would be time for the radicalisation of anti-colonial movements as the more moderate leaders proved unable to deliver the political goods. This fear of losing control of the burgeoning nationalist or anti-colonial movements was a strong one in the United States as well as in Britain. On the other hand the converse problem was transferring power too quickly. If that proved to be the case, independence in an unprepared new state ran the risk of heralding instability and economic or political disorder which could be exploited by communism.[38]

In the Middle East the Americans became generally unconvinced that a European presence would provide the influence necessary to ensure that instability was not the precursor of radical nationalism which in turn might lead to communism. In the Middle East the issue was ensuring that those who had received power in the past continued in the early and mid-1950s to use it for the maintenance of British influence and prestige. Ostensibly, the military base in the Suez Canal Zone and the Baghdad Pact existed to meet the cold war needs of the British in military strategic terms, the reality was somewhat different. Given the lack of hard power military capabilities, the status and prestige they gave to the Britain came from the apparent justification they provided for a leading British regional role. The distinctions between informal empire with its emphasis on power, global roles and ideology, and the colonial practices of decolonisation remained important in understanding the British empire in different regions of the globe in the 1950s.

The battle for the leadership of the Middle East initially centred on Britain and Egypt and eventually culminated in the traumatic debacle of

Suez and the temporary rupture it produced with the United States. The positive contribution or otherwise of colonial territories was becoming less important for Britain's world role and global influence, however defined, than relations with the United States. Attempts to justifying the benefits of colonialism and decolonisation were of little or no value after 1956. This was to continue to be the case in the 1960s. At the end of the decade it was to be the withdrawal from East of Suez that produced division and some consternation about the implications for Britain's world role. By then the critical cold war role of the United States had overshadowed the regional roles of old imperial actors. In a sense Suez had been of less significance for the future of the British Commonwealth than for the future of British relations with the United States. From the 1950s the cold war was used to justify the maintenance of British power, now based more and more on British prestige. At the same time ensuring that Britain's weakness in terms of military strength was not exposed and that Britain's ability to impose its will on other countries remained key imperial and cold war goals even after Suez ended its regional leadership.

Yet paradoxically the interpretations given to strategy, security and geopolitics associated with individual dependencies in the 1950s remained a key consideration especially in the Middle East even when they could produce no tangible effect on the implementation of operational plans. An understanding of this requires an accurate analysis of hard power in the cold war that changed in the early 1950s. The ability of the decolonising British to rely on strategic bases to implement a given military strategy was no longer reflecting the realities which the conduct of military operations required. In the Middle East the ability to defend the Northern Tier, the ostensible barrier whose defence would allegedly contain the Soviet Union was in fact a facade involving nuclear deception plans directed against the fellow signatories of the Baghdad Pact.[39] The reality was that any Soviet military advance could not be halted but the requirements of British influence and status as a world power could endeavour to use the cold war as justifying a position in the region by providing the main rationale for its defence, however meaningless these were in operational terms.[40]

Suez removed the possibility of an Anglo-French *entente* distancing the two colonial powers from the United States. The British concluded that any world role had to be played in conjunction with the United States, not as a fully independent power but as a fully dependent one that would use the term 'interdependence' to mask this reality.[41] France, on de Gaulle's return to power in 1958, instead looked more to Europe and a leading French role within it affecting global politics, and the bipolar division of the globe. De Gaulle turned from empire to seeking influence through a leading role in Europe to change the global alignments of which the cold war was as integral part. French status would be boosted by the erosion of the two blocs and the development of a more nuanced realignment of global power and influence. Hence the granting of full independence to the majority of French overseas possessions by 1960. The French empire had nothing to offer France's world role in the 1960s and nothing to contribute to the modernisation of the French economy – rather the reverse.[42] France would achieve greater international status after decolonisation by having a key impact on Europe and through that on the bipolar world. It would enable France to play a more decisive international role by weakening the blocs and withdrawing from the military structures of NATO. This would promote *détente* between East and West and France's importance in a settlement of the German problem would bring Europe, led by de Gaulle and the French, to greater global prominence in a transformed Western alliance.[43]

As French decolonisation came to embody more of a European focus for the means of achieving a greater global impact, Britain by contrast was to remain obsessed with a non-European focus in its perceptions of a desired place in the cold war world. Despite the retreat from East of Suez that followed the main stages of decolonisation, British plans after Suez continued to focus on how best to be perceived as a world power with global rather than European status. For the British their world role formerly embodied solely in the liberal British empire now became embodied in the United States, and for both Harold Macmillan and later Harold Wilson the term 'interdependence'. Today Blair prefers to describe the same dependence as Britain's pivotal world role.

It was fortunate for the process of decolonisation, as opposed to the definition and manifestation of a British world role, that Dulles's approach after 1955 was so positive. The American Secretary of State saw great virtue in the sensible preparation for the self-government and independence of the colonies as viable new states.[44] There was a slight hiccup after his death when the USA became convinced in late 1959 that the British were going too slowly with the process of transferring power in the Central African Federation.[45] The problems of multi-racialism as a preferred solution to African majority rule seemed temporarily to have stalled the steady progression to meeting the demands of the indigenous African people. It was, however, put back on track by the commitment to African majority rule in Kenya at the Lancaster House Conference in January 1960 and by Macmillan's 'winds of change' speech to the South

African Parliament the following month. Thus Washington's concerns were eased by the shift from 'multi-racialism' and 'partnership' to a policy which was 'non-racial' and which the 'winds of change' embodied in preparing the final stages of British decolonisation.[46] From London's perspective, the decolonisation process in Africa was complicated by the pace and timing of the progress of still dependent territories in the face of inter-racial problems, and secondly the means by which the West should seek to retain the sympathy and support of newly independent states in Africa and to prevent them being 'subverted by Soviet influence'.[47] The non-racial 'winds of change' and the concession of the principle of African majority rule effectively sealed the fate of the Central African Federation before the Monkton Report undermined its feasibility even further by recommending African majority rule in Northern Rhodesia (Zambia) later in 1960.[48]

By then the two main cold war crises of the latter stages of the main European decolonisation process that the US government had to face were both in evidence. The first was in the Belgian Congo (now the Democratic Republic of Congo) in 1960, when, on the achievement of independence, the weaknesses of the fledgling state were quickly exposed. If there were any lingering doubts in the Macmillan government about delaying the preparations for self-government as opposed to getting out before being embroiled in the ghastly mess the Congo became they were quickly dispelled. As Iain Macleod, the British Colonial Secretary, described it, the problem was now 'to achieve an orderly transfer of power to the Africans without losing the confidence of the Europeans'.[49] The new Congo government had tried to develop a sense of Congolese nationalism to supersede the regional rivalries that had been increased by the sudden and rapid Belgian transfer of power. With most of the Congo's financial reserves expatriated to Belgium[50] and no time for the independent government to prepare either an appropriately trained administrative cadre or a suitably trained African army, it was only a matter of days after independence that Belgian troops were sent in to restore order. For the Americans in particular the issue was the establishment in the eyes of the world of a viable African state in the Congo to confirm the success of Western methods in transferring power. These should be for the benefit of the Africans rather than for their former masters, but carried out in ways that would ensure that all doors to Soviet communist or radical socialist influence remained firmly closed. The old link between empire and cold war was again in evidence if no longer linked to benefiting the British position in the world. For the British, the Congo and its cold war implications reinforced the need to abandon empire in Central Africa before its world position was damaged. The cold war aim was now to avoid the delay that preparations for self-government and the retention of influence threatened to produce when the problems of racialism or left-wing ideas threatened stability in Central Africa.

The cold war dimension was made more problematic by the secession of the Congo's mineral rich province of Katanga with the help of expatriate Europeans and the staff of the *Union Miniere de Haut Katanga*. The United Nations was called in by the new Congolese government of Patrice Lumumba, outraged by the reappearance of Belgian troops, but was soon nervous about ending the secession of Katanga through the use of military force. When, as a result, Lumumba appealed for Soviet help and began to receive Russian transport aircraft, the African cold war fat was in the fire. It took three years of American diplomacy in liaison with the UN, accompanied by murder, mass killing, inter-African wrangling and bitter European hostility to the UN as well as prolonged negotiations in Africa and Europe, before the Kennedy administration succeeded in bringing the secession to an end. It stuck firmly to its policy of creating viable African states free from European colonialism and Soviet communism despite British and French doubts, yet it was a pyrrhic victory for the success of decolonisation in Africa.

The other cold war crisis faced by the administration began in neighbouring Angola in 1961. It took 13 years before progress in decolonising the Portuguese empire was subsequently made with the coup in Lisbon. During this period the role of the UN in pushing for the ending of colonialism and the acceptance of the principle of self-determination was again in evidence, if less controversially. The UN resolution of December 1960 condemning colonialism as a denial of human rights and calling for the immediate transfer of power was passed with the support of the Kennedy administration. Although this was not welcomed by all government officials, the United States then also supported a specific resolution in March 1961 calling for Portugal to introduce reforms in Angola that would enable the indigenous people to exercise their right of self-determination.[51] The Kennedy administration firmly believed that the outcome of the cold war would be significantly determined by how the United States was able to influence the choices made by the emerging nations now independence was seen as both inevitable and desirable. Even the renewal of the Azores Base agreement (military arrangements for hot war), which Kennedy did not wish to jeopardise, did not derail the commitment to self-determination and a successful transfer of power as part of American cold war aims.

The importance of winning the hearts and minds of Angolans emerging from the European decolonisation process as opposed to the importance of using a military base in the Azores again reflects two different understandings of the cold war. Military power and the securing of overseas bases of strategic significance is a prerequisite of hot war which is linked to, but far from constituting the essence of cold war. For the Africanists in the State Department in particular, who were influential in the Kennedy administration, the ideological battle and the contrasting ways of life were what constituted the essence of the cold war. For the United States in 1961, therefore, Africa was the most important battleground for hearts and minds. For the Europeanists, Berlin and the NATO conventional deployments were seen as more important. These two opposing views embody the hard power realist views on the cold war expressed through arms races and military alliances to maintain 'security' or geo-strategic interests. Critics of realism at the other end of the spectrum see the cold war in terms of ideologies, propaganda, psychological warfare and other forms of soft power.

The Portuguese left few stones unturned in their effort to convince the Americans that their policies of demanding change in Portuguese colonial policy, and the abandonment of Angola and Mozambique, would help communism and be fatal for Western interests. The Portuguese Foreign Minister, Franco Nogueira, told the US ambassador that not only was Angola more important than Berlin, but that the Portuguese were prepared to face a third world war to retain their African colonies.[52] The rationale for the Portuguese resistance to decolonisation was neither strategic nor military nor even based on an ideological struggle. Portugal defined itself as a nation needing colonial possessions to provide economic opportunities for its citizens who were settling more in the colonies after the Second World War. And more importantly the Portuguese needed to overcome perceptions of Portugal's inferior status as a weak and relatively impoverished European power.

At the start of the 1960s as Britain entered the final phase of decolonisation, uppermost in policy-makers' minds was the dependent relationship with the United States that would maintain a world role for Britain. It was now producing divisions within the Macmillan government over what that role would mean in hard power terms. Could Britain afford to play an important military role out of the NATO area and still devote resources to the Commonwealth by stationing troops in many non-European areas? Could the abandonment or weakening of a NATO role in order to emphasise a world role that required deploying forces East of Suez be compatible with American ideas on the conflict with the

Soviet Union and China and the maintenance of stability in the less developed world? This was the question addressed by the Macmillan and Home governments still determined on the maintenance of a world role as power was transferred.

In 1960 Macmillan's thoughts on how to do this in a cold war situation still reflected the longstanding dilemma of a declining power – is it necessary to cut commitments or can this be avoided by repeated cost-cutting measures that spread deployments more thinly? With the formation of NATO this had been considered as involving effective operations in both a major hot, a limited hot and a cold war. In addition there was the provision of nuclear weapons as symbols of British power and their use in Europe if the deterrent failed. Operational deployments would justify and contribute to British influence/prestige as a world power with or without a colonial empire. Macmillan saw some value in reducing overseas out-of-area (the area covered by NATO) limited war capabilities and replacing them by forces for police-type operations and internal security. The arguments against this considered the adverse impacts on the sterling area and the latter's political contribution to British influence which the Foreign Office was well aware of.[53] The issue soon ceased to be a choice essentially between a world role and European one, if it ever had been, despite the failed application for the EEC in 1961 and the increasing loss of the colonial empire.

Avoiding a choice between Europe and a world role was made easy by the request of the Kennedy administration during the Berlin crisis for a troop build-up in Europe which ended the hope that a reduction in the British Army on the Rhine (BAOR) could be used to reinforce an overseas presence. The Conservative government was inclined to emphasise the importance of its 'East of Suez' commitments in defending Western interests overseas. This view was expressed by the Defence Secretary, Peter Thorneycroft, and by the Chief of the Defence Staff, Lord Mountbatten, who believed it was 'only in this world wide influence, the heritage of Empire, that we can hope and should try to maintain our special position in the Anglo-Saxon community and in the world'.[54] As the Macmillan government neared its end, the support for a world role was clear even if British deployments in support of it were more in question. The colonial empire had now become much more of an awkward problem which had to be got rid of in the most convenient way that would not damage Britain's international position. Equally problematic had become the importance of Britain's European role in contributing to this world role. The means to be employed to ensure that Britain could wield influence in Washington to obtain that support remained unclear.

As in 1948 the main advocate of the importance of a European role in doing this was the Foreign Office, but the government of Sir Alec Douglas-Home (Macmillan's successor) was reminded in 1964 that Britain was the only country that had a presence in all parts of the world.[55] Yet it never became a simple choice between Europe and the world because of what could be done to maximise the appearance of power. Should Britain consider becoming a more important European power to persuade the United States that it should be listened to? But by retaining its Commonwealth connections, now the colonial empire was largely gone, expressed in out-of-area military commitments would it not be more useful to Washington in cold war terms? The other factor was decolonisation becoming more about how Britain could escape from a post-imperial role embodying financial assistance for the smaller island colonies, especially in the Caribbean.[56] When the Labour government assumed office the problem was still white settler opposition and the existence of an 'independent' white ruled Southern Rhodesia. This was soon to be prove an intractable problem to escape easily from when British world power status was proving more difficult to maintain in the changing cold war as resources for military deployments were harder to stretch.

Most important in this realisation was the Confrontation with Indonesia (1963–66) and its costs. Stemming from the formation of Malaysia which incorporated Borneo, Malaya and Singapore, the British attempted to restrict the communist tendencies in Singapore but retain the use of defence facilities there at a lower cost.[57] Almost immediately it proved an initial disaster and provided for the loss of facilities at a considerable cost. Indonesian opposition to Malaysia centred on accusations of neo-colonialism and ensured that rather than saving money while retaining commitments, Britain would have to bear the burden of confronting Indonesia in a low-intensity war with around 20,000 troops. When the Labour government assumed office in October 1964 it immediately confronted the necessity of ending Confrontation in order to deal effectively, 20 years too late, with reducing British defence commitments in line with rational economic priorities. The determination to retain a significant degree of prestige and status on the international stage had been a feature of decolonisation in redefining Britain's relationships with non-self-governing areas outside Europe. In the past it had overridden sensible economic choices about the maintenance of commitments helped by the cold war and irrespective of decolonisation.

The whole issue of an overseas presence and world power, now that decolonisation was in its final stages by 1965, would have to be tackled by the Labour government of Harold Wilson. The Prime Minister initially had personal and deep rooted prejudices in favour of the Commonwealth and a world role for Britain. In May 1965 he told Rusk he would rather pull troops out of Germany than pull any out of the Far East.[58] The USA, which had been supportive of both decolonisation and British involvement in Europe, now had in Vietnam a more emotive commitment to cold war competition in the Third World, and the Johnson administration encouraged London to retain its 'East of Suez' commitments. Britain was also committed before 1966 to the maintenance of its unique commitment to Aden and the Gulf over and above the enormous and growing importance of Kuwait for its sterling reserves. Yet Wilson was to become disillusioned with the Commonwealth.[59] The Commonwealth had certainly changed as the 1960s progressed after the formation of the Secretariat and the departure of the South Africans in 1961.

However Britain was not like France in confronting a situation where economic strength, cold war priorities and French world power status required a new commitment to Europe and the rejection of empire. The British approach under Macmillan, and later, was to seek world power status through combining a role in Europe with its former imperial traditions that were eventually deemed to provide a 'pivotal world role'. Certainly while the retreat from Aden and East of Suez at the end of the 1960s was in a sense 'decolonisation plus', this apparent turn away from the world and its regions outside Europe was now refashioned. New ways short of choosing Europe *or* the world, involved using Europe *and* the world for expressing British influence in new ways. Even a past British presence in parts of the less developed world could still claim to embody influence, because of experience, and prestige centred on 'special' links with the United States (interdependence) and an important role in, but not as an integral part of, Western Europe. Wilson may have reversed his initial Commonwealth preference dictating military deployments and prioritised NATO when telling Rusk in 1966, before he applied again to join the Common Market the following year, he would prefer to keep troops in Germany if the cost issues with the Germans could be overcome.[60]

The increasing economic difficulties inclined the new Labour government to pursue steps, with the Defence Review and White Paper of 1966, such as the decision to abandon Aden and to reduce the UK's military capabilities for overseas intervention. For a number of MPs, and civilian and military officials, the gradual retreat from 'East of Suez' was difficult to accept, as it undermined both the policy of 'interdependence' with the Americans and constituted a loss of British prestige. However, the devaluation crisis of November 1967 led the Cabinet to reluctantly decide to order the complete withdrawal of British forces from the Middle East and East Asia by 1971. It can, however, be argued that while the UK's foreign and defence policy was henceforth focused upon Europe, successive British governments could not envisage completely surrendering Britain's world role. The UK's intervention in Oman (1970–76), the Falklands conflict (1982) and the Blair government's commitment of British forces to Sierra Leone (2000) and the US-led interventions in Afghanistan and Iraq show that to some degree the traditions of both 'interdependence' and the imperial legacy still persist in Whitehall.[61]

conclusions

If the cold war had been useful in the 1950s in slowing the pace of decolonisation and loss of hard power in the Middle East it had precisely the opposite effect in South-East Asia during the later 1960s. Yet as has been argued it was never a choice between world and European roles but how the global role could best be retained through British influence which could no longer depend on the deployment of British forces. If Britain had pulled militarily out of non-European areas under Labour, despite pressure from Washington with its own desires on how Britain's global position could best serve American interests, this mirrored US policy on decolonisation. Washington aimed to ensure that its strategy in the cold war was supported by European decolonisation and then also to ensure, which proved much more difficult, that the use of military force in and out of Europe was equally useful. A later Labour leader, even though the cold war had ended, was to put token military force *faute de mieux* back East of Suez with unedifying consequences. The attempt was again to maintain the facade of a pivotal global role through helping the United States.

After the debacle of Suez in 1956, empires became less and less important and more and more difficult to reconcile with a British cold war role, as soon became evident in South-East Asia. Europe was looming ever larger but as a factor to be integrated into the means chosen to remain a world power, not as a means to replace Commonwealth and empire as a source of power and influence in hard or soft terms. Once British requirements of replacing formal colonial controls but still maintaining world power status in the cold war world are better understood and disaggregated, the Europe/wider world alternative becomes more complex. On the one hand, using the legacies and traditions of empire/Commonwealth to fulfil a global role through expenditure on defence out of area had to be compared with what Europe could provide in terms of influence with the Americans to produce the facade of British world power. A global role would combine the contribution to NATO in Europe, emphasised by the Foreign Office, with a commitment to an out-of-area role despite the significance of the withdrawal from East of Suez. It was not an 'either/or' choice but more one of tinkering with developments that might be prioritised or emphasised within a framework committed to both.[62] As in the reassessments after Suez, the EEC applications of 1961 and 1967, decolonisation and even in the retreat from East of Suez in 1968, there was support for a world role *and* for a European role that would help provide it.

Decolonisation or negotiating 'the orderly end of empire' was one of the main achievements highlighted by a Foreign Office review of policy overseas in the 1960s.[63] The reappraisal of Britain's role in the world was one of the results of that process in the cold war which remained linked to, but very different from, military strategy and its translation into operational deployments. This reappraisal was another milestone which the Foreign Office paper drew attention to. Meaningless deployments were catching up with Britain which could ill afford a full scale military conflict with Indonesia. Yet at the start of the decolonisation process the Foreign Office remained firmly committed to a world role and to a European and Atlanticist emphasis for British foreign policy.

These roles could never be retained through the perception of an 'either/or' choice between the old imperial projection of power and the new economic strength that might be developed and translated into political influence in Europe. Britain could in the 1960s, as today, so it was erroneously believed, only remain a world power by combining a European role with one that built on Britain's history and experience in areas way beyond Europe. Only through that combination could Britain convince the United States of its important and distinctive role in the world and thereby wield influence in Washington. Accepting the wishes of the United States at the expense of Britain's own interests could not yet in the 1960s be guaranteed, as the Anglo-American arguments and ill feeling demonstrate. Compared with the loss of Empire the loss of a global role for military power, however insubstantial, was always harder to contemplate. This was the context in which the Labour government discussed the abandonment of a military role East of Suez and the political influence that might be attached to it in the cold war.

notes

1. Andrew J. Bacevich, *American Empire* (Cambridge, MA: Harvard University Press, 2002) looks at the empire in the context of the historical development

of American power, and Dominic Lieven, *Empire: The Russian Empire and its Rivals* (London: John Murray, 2000) deals with empire more broadly but in the modern context of land-based empires in Europe and Asia rather than in the contemporary context of declining maritime powers which accompanied the rise to domination of the American empire. But see pp.17–26 for an introduction to the modern debate.

2. Michael W. Doyle, *Empires* (Ithaca, NY: Cornell University Press, 1991).

3. The initial British desire to retain power and influence after the Second World War and which lasted until October 1949 has been neglected in colonial and cold war historiography. See John Kent, *British Imperial Strategy and the Origins of the Cold War* (New York & Leicester: Leicester University Press, 1993), *passim*.

4. For the anti-colonialism of the Roosevelt administration see Wm Roger Louis, *Imperialism at Bay: The United States and the Decolonisation of the British Empire* (Oxford: Clarendon Press, 1977).

5. The question was first posed to me by Ronald Hyam at a seminar with participants from the British Documents on the End of Empire when it was in its early stages and the Soviet Union had only recently collapsed. See Ronald Hyam, 'The Primacy of Geopolitics: The Dynamics of British Imperial Policy 1763–1963', *Journal of Imperial and Commonwealth History*, 27:2 (1999).

6. J. Kent & J.W. Young, 'Britain the Third Force and the Origin of NATO: In Search of a New Perspective', in B. Heuser & R. O'Neill (eds), *Securing Peace in Europe* (London: Macmillan, 1992); and J. Kent & J.W. Young, 'The Western Union Concept and British Defence Planning 1947–48', in R. Aldrich (ed.), *British Intelligence Strategy and the Cold War* (London: Routledge, 1992).

7. The term was first coined in 1952 and during the subsequent years has been regarded as 'inappropriate' with the underdeveloped, developing, undeveloped and less developed world meeting the different political criteria.

8. See Wolfgang Mommsen & Lothar Kettenacker (eds), *The Fascist Challenge and the Policy of Appeasement* (London: Allen & Unwin, 1983).

9. The date of the cold war's onset is highly controversial, but for the 1948 argument see John W. Young & John Kent, *International Relations since 1945: A Global History* (Oxford: Oxford University Press, 2004), pp.121–6.

10. See John Darwin, *Britain and Decolonisation: The Retreat from Empire in the Post-War World* (London: Macmillan, 1989), chapters 1 and 2, for the impact of the war on the challenges to British colonial rule.

11. For the critical period of 1945–46 in which this occurred see Kent, *Imperial Strategy*, chapter 3.

12. The reasons for the failures which were evident by February 1946 remain a matter of dispute but are clearly connected to different perceptions of the new international order and the bases for cooperation involving the mutual recognition of power political interests with the ideological rhetoric stemming from differing socio-economic and political systems.

13. Attlee's hopes and aspirations for a cooperative world were first brought out by R. Smith & J. Zametica in 'The Cold Warrior: Clement Attlee Reconsidered 1945–47', *International Affairs*, 61:2 (1985). Since then there have been numerous criticisms of his policies for the empire in the Middle East as utopian or unrealistic. For a less critical approach see Kent, *Imperial Strategy*, *passim*.

14. Stephen Constantine, *The Making of British Colonial Development Policy 1914–1940* (London: Frank Cass, 1984), p.237.
15. Constantine, *Colonial Development Policy*, p.243.
16. Attlee had been a member of the Simon Commission and had contributed to a minority report urging more rapid transition to independence.
17. Howard Brasted, Carl Bridge & John Kent, 'Cold War, Informal Empire and the Transfer of Power: Some "Paradoxes" of British Decolonisation Resolved?', in Michael Dockrill (ed.), *Europe in the Global System, 1938–1960* (Bochum: Universitatsverlag Dr. N. Brockmeyer, 1995), pp.11–30.
18. This word derives from the Strategic Defence Review of 1998. This is available online on the Ministry of Defence (MoD) website, <http://www.mod.uk/issues/sdr/index.htm>.
19. Minute by Sir Pierson Dixon, 23.1.52, FO 371/96920(TNA).
20. On Suez see W. Scott Lucas, *Divided We Stand* (London: Hodder & Stoughton, 1991), and for British attitudes to Egypt from 1945 to 1956 see Kent (ed.), *British Documents on the End of Empire Project (BDEEP). Egypt and the Defence of the Middle East Series B Volume 4* (HMSO 1998), especially Part 1, Introduction.
21. FIDES (the *Fonds d'Investissement pour le Développement Economique et Social*) was created in April 1946.
22. R.F. Holland, *In Pursuit of Greatness: Britain and the World Role, 1900–1970* (London: Fontana, 1991).
23. See especially D.K. Fieldhouse, 'The Labour Governments and the Empire Commonwealth 1945–1951', in R. Ovendale (ed.), *The Foreign Policy of the British Labour Governments, 1945–1951* (Leicester: Leicester University Press, 1984).
24. The dollar shortage meant Britain was desperate to encourage colonial producers to provide goods otherwise obtainable in the dollar zone and to encourage direct exports to that region. At the same time they were restricting consumer imports to the colonies from dollars that colonial exporters earned for the sterling area.
25. Fieldhouse, 'Empire Commonwealth', *passim.*
26. R. Rathbone (ed.), *BDEEP. Ghana Series B Volume 4* (HMSO, 1992), Part I, pp.xliv–xlvii.
27. J. Kent, 'US Reactions to Empire, Colonialism and Cold War in Black Africa 1949–1957', *Journal of Imperial and Commonwealth History*, 33:2 (2005).
28. *FRUS. The Near and Middle East Vol IX, Pt I, 1952–54* (USGPO, 1986), pp.1–167.
29. For the American pursuit of an aggressive ideological 'crusade' after NSC-7 in 1948 see W. Scott Lucas, *Freedom's War: The US Crusade Against the Soviet Union, 1945–56* (New York: New York University Press, 1999); and G. Mitrovich, *Undermining the Kremlin: America's Strategy to Subvert the Soviet Bloc, 1947–56* (Ithaca, NY: Cornell University Press, 2000), *passim.*
30. The association between cold war non-alignment and the desire to escape from oppressive colonial rule was enshrined at Bandung, Indonesia, in 1955.
31. Regional Policy Statement on Africa South of the Sahara prepared by the Bureau of Near Eastern, South Asian and African Affairs, 29.12.50, in *FRUS V, 1950* (USGPO, 1976), p.1587.
32. See Nicholas Tarling, *Britain, South East Asia and the Onset of the Cold War 1945–1950* (Cambridge: Cambridge University Press, 1998), pp.211–36, 280–95, for the two Dutch police actions.

33. For Portugal and cold war in the 1960s and 1970s see Norrie MacQueen, *The Decolonisation of Portuguese Africa* (London: Longman, 1997), and John Marcum, *The Angolan Revolution*, Vol. 2: *Exile, Politics and Guerrilla Warfare 1962–76* (Cambridge, MA: MIT Press, 1981).

34. Memorandum by US Representatives on Trusteeship Council, Mason Sears, 'U.S. Policy on Colonial Issues', 18.8.53, *FRUS III 1952–54*, (USGPO, 1979), pp.1162–3.

35. I am indebted to Ryo Ikeda for information on the French in North Africa.

36. See David Goldsworthy, 'Britain and the International Critics of British Colonialism, 1951–56', *Journal of Commonwealth and Comparative Politics*, 29 (1991).

37. US National Archives, RG59, CDF 611.70, 1955–59, Box 2513 Memorandum by the Office of African Affairs, 'US Problems in Africa', 17.2.56.

38. This dilemma briefly became a problem when Central Africa problems were being considered early in 1959.

39. In nuclear terms, 'UK representatives are authorised to state that the existing UK plans for the theatre in war are based on the availability of nuclear weapons from H hour, and that these would be available in support of operations under the Baghdad Pact.' Unfortunately the UK did not have any weapons which could be deployed in the theatre for use by Canberras and was not expected to have before 1959. Moreover, the USA would not agree to deploy nuclear forces in support of the Baghdad Pact. Therefore 'it is the primary concern of existing deception plans for the Middle East to cover up this nuclear deficiency by portraying a nuclear capability for our fore in the theatre now'. See JP(56)10(Final) 18.1.56, DEFE5/34(TNA).

40. For the deficiency in the conventional forces that were available see COS(55)49, 4.3.55, DEFE5/57(TNA).

41. Michael Middeke, 'Britain's Global Military Role, Conventional Defence and Anglo-American Interdependence after Nassau', *Journal of Strategic Studies*, 24:1 (2001), pp.143–64.

42. J. Marseille, *Empire Colonial et Capitalisme Francais: histoire d'un Divorce* (Paris: Editions Albin Michel, 1984).

43. Frederic Bozo, *Two Strategies for Europe: De Gaulle, the United States, and the Atlantic Alliance* (Lanham, MD: Rowman & Littlefield, 2001), pp xi–xii.

44. USNA RG59 CDF 611.70 1955–59 Box 2513, Memo of Conversation between Dulles and Selwyn Lloyd (UK Foreign Secretary) and officials Bermuda 23.3.57.

45. Record of US/UK meeting on the future of Africa 23.11.59, FO371/137977.

46. The speech delivered to the South African parliament on 3 February 1960 is in DO 35/10570 and printed in *BDEEP*, Series A, Volume 4, Part I, R. Hyam & Wm Roger Louis (eds), *The Conservative Government and the End of Empire 1957–64* (2000), pp.162–74; H. Macmillan, *Pointing the Way 1959–1961* (1972), pp.473–82 and A.N. Porter & A.J. Stockwell (eds), *British Imperial Policy and Decolonisation*, Vol. 2: *1959–1964* (1989), pp.522–31.

47. FO 371/137972 memo 'Africa in the Next Ten Years', report of official committee, June 1959. Reprinted in part in *BDEEP*, Hyam and Louis (eds), *Conservative Government*, p.123.

48. Cmnd.1148, *Report of the Advisory Commission on the Review of the Constitution of Rhodesia and Nyasaland*, October 1960 (HMSO, 1960).

49. CPC1(61)2 Minutes of the Colonial Policy Committee 6.1.61, CAB134/1560(TNA). Hyam & Louis (eds), *Conservative Government*, pp.184–7.

50. Key details on this are in USNA RG 59 CDF 855a Box 2061 Brussels to SD 30 March 1960; Leopoldville to SD 13 Apr 1960; CDF 755b Box 1832 Leopoldville to SD 7 Apr 1960.

51. For a review of the developments in US–Portuguese relations since March under Kennedy see USNA RG59 CDF 753b Box 1818 Memo by GC McGhee 20.4.62.

52. JFK Library (Boston MA), NSF Country Series Angola Box 5 Lisbon to SD 11.7.61.

53. The Foreign Office was particularly keen on the political value of the sterling and the 1960 Future Policy Study had deemed keeping sterling strong 'the necessary condition for maintaining our place in the world'; CAB129/100 C(60)35 24.2.60, CAB129/100.

54. Michael Middeke, *Britain's Interdependence Policy and Anglo-American Cooperation on Nuclear and Conventional Force Provision, 1957–1964* (PhD thesis, London School of Economics, 1999), pp.204–6.

55. T. Bligh to Home 11.2.64, PREM11/4794(TNA). Cited in Middeke, *Interdependence Policy*, p.291.

56. See S.R. Ashton & D. Killingray (eds), *BDEEP Series B Vol 6, The West Indies* (HMSO, 1999).

57. David Easter, *Britain and the Confrontation with Indonesia, 1960–1966* (London: I.B. Tauris, 2004).

58. S.R. Ashton & Wm Roger Louis (eds), *BDEEP Series A Vol V Pt I, East of Suez and the Commonwealth 1964–1971* (HMSO, 2005), p.xxxiv.

59. Ashton & Louis (eds), *BDEEP*, p.xxxi.

60. Ashton & Louis (eds), *BDEEP*, p.xxxviii.

61. P. Gordon Walker to H. Wilson 23.11.65, PREM13/1216(TNA).

62. For a discussion on the choice see Saki Dockrill, *Britain's Retreat from East of Suez: The Choice between Europe and the World* (Basingstoke: Palgrave Macmillan, 2002), chapter 8. For the views of Gordon Walker see Ashton & Louis (eds), *BDEEP*, p.xxxvii.

63. For a discussion on the choice see Saki Dockrill, *Britain's Retreat from East of Suez: The Choice between Europe and the World* (Basingstoke: Palgrave Macmillan, 2002).

select bibliography

useful websites

Cold War International History Project website: <http://www.cwihp.org>
Foreign Relations of the United States (Washington, DC: US Government Printing Office, 1960–2005): <http://www.state.gov/r/pa/ho/frus/>
National Security Agency: <http://www.nsa.gov/>
National Security Archive: <http://www.gwu.edu/~nsarchiv/>
Parallel History Project for NATO and the Warsaw Pact: <http://www.isn.ethz.ch/php/>
UK National Archives: <http://www.nationalarchives.gov.uk/>

international system

Baylis, John & Steve Smith (eds), *The Globalization of World Politics* (Oxford: Oxford University Press, 2001, 2nd edition)
Booth, Ken & Steve Smith (eds), *International Relations Theory Today* (Cambridge: Polity Press, 1995)
Booth, Ken & Michael Cox & Tim Dunne (eds), *Empires, Systems, and States: Great Transformations in International Politics* (Cambridge: Cambridge University Press, 2002)
Bull, Hedley, *The Anarchical Society: A Study of Order in World Politics* (London: Macmillan, 1977).
Crockatt, Richard, *The Fifty Years War: The United States and the Soviet Union in World Politics* (London: Routledge, 2000)
Deutsch, Karl W., *The Analysis of International Relations* (Hemel Hempstead: Prentice Hall, 1968)
Dockrill, Saki Ruth, *The End of the Cold War Era: The Transformation of the Global Security Order* (London & New York: Hodder Arnold & Oxford University Press, 2005)
Gaddis, John Lewis, *The Long Peace: Inquiries into the History of the Cold War* (New York & Oxford: Oxford University Press, 1987)
Gillingham, John R., *European Integration, 1950–2003: Superstate or Market Economy?* (Cambridge: Cambridge University Press, 2003)
Huntington, Samuel, *The Clash of Civilisations and the Remaking of World Order* (New York: Simon & Schuster, 1996)
Katzenstein, Peter, *Small States in the World Economy* (Ithaca, NY: Cornell University Press, 1985)

Keohane, Robert O. & Joseph S. Nye, *Power and Interdependence: World Politics in Transition* (Boston, MA: Little, Brown, 1977)

Krasner, Stephen (ed.), *International Regimes* (Ithaca, NY: Cornell University Press, 1983)

Mastny, Vojtech, *The Cold War and Soviet Insecurity: The Stalin Years* (Oxford: Oxford University Press, 1995)

Mazower, Mark, *Dark Continent: Europe's Twentieth Century* (London: Penguin, 1998)

Morgenthau, Hans, *Politics among Nations: The Struggle for Power and Peace* (New York: Knopf, 1986, 6th edition)

Nye, Joseph, *Soft Power: The Means to Success in World Politics* (NY: Public Affairs, 2004)

Reynolds, David, *One World Divisible: A Global History since 1945* (London: Penguin, 2000)

Ruggie, John G., *Constructing the World Polity: Essays on International Institutionalisation* (London: Routledge, 1998)

Slaughter, Anne-Marie, *A New World Order* (Princeton, NJ: Princeton University Press, 2004)

Waltz, Kenneth, *Theory of International Politics* (Reading, MA: Addison-Wesley, 1979)

Westad, Odd Arne (ed.), *Reviewing the Cold War: Approaches, Interpretations, Theory* (London: Frank Cass, 2000)

national security

Chang, Gordon H., *Friends and Enemies: The United States, China, and the Soviet Union* (Stanford, CA: Stanford University Press, 1990)

Chen Jian, *Mao's China and the Cold War* (Chapel Hill, NC: University of North Carolina Press, 2001)

Dumbrell, John, *A Special Relationship: Anglo-American Relations in the Cold War and After* (New York: Macmillan, 2001)

Gaddis, John Lewis, *Strategies of Containment: A Critical Appraisal of American National Security Policy During the Cold War* (New York: Oxford University Press, 2005, 2nd edition)

Garthoff, Raymond, *Détente and Confrontation: American–Soviet Relations from Nixon to Reagan* (Washington, DC: Brookings, 1994).

Hanhimäki, Jussi M., *The Flawed Architect: Henry Kissinger and American Foreign Policy* (New York: Oxford University Press, 2004)

Hopf, Ted, *Social Construction of International Politics: Identities and Foreign Policies, Moscow, 1955 and 1999* (Ithaca, NY: Cornell University Press, 2002)

Katzenstein, Peter J. (ed.), *The Culture of National Security: Norms and Identity in World Politics* (New York: Columbia University Press, 1996)

Leffler, Melvyn P., *A Preponderance of Power: National Security, the Truman Administration and the Cold War* (Stanford, CA: Stanford University Press, 1992)

Medhurst, Martin J., et al., *Cold War Rhetoric: Strategy, Metaphor and Ideology* (East Lansing, MI: Michigan State University Press, 1997)

Nye, Joseph, *The Paradox of American Power: Why the World's Only Superpower Can't Go It Alone* (New York: Oxford University Press, 2003)

Ouimet, Matthew J., *The Rise and Fall of the Brezhnev Doctrine in Soviet Foreign Policy* (Chapel Hill, NC: University of North Carolina Press, 2003)

Vaisse, Maurice, *La grandeur: politique étrangere du General de Gaulle, 1958–1969* (Paris: Fayard, 1999)

Westad, Odd Arne (ed.), *The Fall of Détente: Soviet–American Relations during the Carter Years* (Oslo: Scandinavian University Press, 1997)

ideology

Carew, Anthony, *The International Confederation of Free Trade Unions, International and Comparative Social History, 3 and Index* (NY & Bern: P. Lang, 2000)

Carew, Anthony, *Labour under the Marshall Plan: The Politics of Productivity and the Marketing of Management Science* (Detroit, MI: Wayne State University Press, 1987)

Carew, Anthony, *Walter Reuther, Lives of the Left Index* (New York & Manchester: Manchester University Press, 1993)

Filippelli, Ronald, 'Luigi Antonini, the Italian-American Labor Council, and Cold War Politics in Italy, 1943–1949', *Labor History*, 33:1 (1992), pp.102–25

Filippelli, Ronald, *American Labor and Postwar Italy, 1943–1953* (Stanford, CA: Stanford University Press, 1989)

Guasconi, Maria Eleonora, *L'altra Faccia Della Medaglia. Diplomazia Psicologica E Sindacale Nelle Relazioni Italia–Stati Uniti Durante La Prima Fase Della Guerra Fredda (1947–1955)* (Messina: Rubbettino, 1998)

Kirby, Diane, *Religion and the Cold War* (Basingstoke: Palgrave Macmillan, 2002)

Latham, Michael E., *Modernisation as Ideology: American Social Science and 'Nation Building' in the Kennedy Era* (Chapel Hill, NC: North Carolina University Press, 2000)

Lucas, W. Scott, *Freedom's War: The US Crusade Against the Soviet Union, 1945–56* (New York: New York University Press, 1999)

Morgan, Ted, *A Covert Life: Jay Lovestone, Communist, Anti-Communist, and Spymaster* (New York: Random House, 1999)

Rathbun, Ben, *The Point Man: Irving Brown and the Deadly Post-1945 Struggle for Europe and Africa* (Washington, DC: Minerva Press, 1996)

Romero, Federico, *The United States and the European Trade Union Movement, 1944–1951* (Chapel Hill: University of North Carolina Press, 1992)

Zubok, Vladislav, 'Gorbachev and the End of the Cold War: Perspectives on History and Personality', *Cold War History*, 2:2 (2002), pp.61–100

alliances

Bozo, Frederic, *Deux Strategies pour l'Europe: de Gaulle, les Etats-Unis, et 'l'alliance atlantique'* (Paris: Plon, 1996)

Buszynski, Leszek, *SEATO: Failure of an Alliance Strategy* (Singapore: Singapore University Press, 1983)

Byrne, Malcolm & Vojtech Mastny (eds), *A Cardboard Castle? An Inside History of the Warsaw Pact, 1955–1990* (Budapest: Central European University Press, 2005)

Cleveland, Harla, *The Transatlantic Bargain* (New York: Harper & Row, 1970)

Gati, Charles, *The Bloc That Failed: Soviet–East European Relations in Transition* (Bloomington, IN: Indiana University Press, 1990)

Kaplan, Lawrence S., *The United States and NATO: The Formative Years* (Lexington, KT: University Press of Kentucky, 1984)

Kaplan, Lawrence S., *NATO Divided, NATO United: The Evolution of an Alliance* (Westport, CT: Praeger, 2004)

Mastny, Vojtech (ed.), *A Cardboard Castle: An Inside History of the Warsaw Pact* (Budapest & New York: Central European University Press, 2005)

Melandri, Pierre, *Incertaine alliance: Les Etas-Unis et l'Europe, 1973–1983* (Paris: Publications de la Sorbonne, 1988)

Nelson, Daniel N., *Alliance Behaviour in the Warsaw Pact* (Boulder, CO: Westview Press, 1986)

Persson, Magnus, *Great Britain, the United States, and the Security of the Middle East* (Lund, Sweden: Lund University Press, 1998)

Remington, Robin A., *The Warsaw Pact: Case Studies in Communist Conflict* (Cambridge, MA: MIT Press, 1971)

Schmidt, Gustav (ed.), *A History of NATO: The First Fifty Years*, 3 vols (Basingstoke: Palgrave Macmillan, 2001)

Smith, Mark, *NATO Enlargement during the Cold War: Strategy and System in the Western Alliance* (Basingstoke: Palgrave Macmillan, 2000)

Westad, Odd Arne (ed.), *Brothers in Arms: The Rise and Fall of the Sino-Soviet Alliance, 1945–63* (Stanford, CA: Stanford University Press, 2000)

strategy

Beckett, Ian, *Modern Insurgencies and Counter-Insurgencies: Guerrillas and their Opponents since 1750* (London: Routledge, 2001)

Dockrill, Saki, *Eisenhower's New Look National Security Policy, 1953–61* (Basingstoke: Macmillan, 1996)

Duffield, John S., *Power Rules: The Evolution of NATO's Conventional Force Posture* (Stanford, CA: Stanford University Press, 1995)

Freedman, Lawrence, *The Evolution of Nuclear Strategy* (Basingstoke: Palgrave Macmillan, 2003)

Freedman, Lawrence, *Kennedy's Wars: Berlin, Cuba, Laos and Vietnam* (New York: Oxford University Press, 2000)

Friedman, Norman, *The Forty Years War* (Annapolis, MD: Naval Institute Press, 2000)

Colin Gray, *Modern Strategy* (Oxford: Oxford University Press, 1999)

Heuser, Beatrice, *NATO, Britain, France and the FRG: Nuclear Strategy and Forces for Europe, 1949–2000* (London: Macmillan, 1997)

Higham , Robin & Frederick W. Kagan (eds), *The Military History of the Soviet Union* (Basingstoke: Palgrave Macmillan, 2002)

Luttwak, Edward, *Strategy: The Logic of Peace* (Cambridge, MA: Harvard University Press, 2001)

Odom, William E., *The Collapse of the Soviet Military* (New Haven, CT: Yale University Press, 1998)

Paret, Peter (ed.), *Makers of Modern Strategy: From Machiavelli to the Nuclear Age* (Princeton, NJ: Princeton University Press, 1986)

Schelling, Thomas, *The Strategy of Conflict* (Cambridge, MA: Harvard University Press, 1960)

economics

Bertsch, Gary K. (ed.), *Controlling East–West Trade and Technology Transfer: Power, Politics, and Policies* (Durham, NC: Duke University Press, 1988)

Blanchard, Jean-Mac F. & Edward D. Mansfield & Norrin M. Ripsman (eds), *Power and the Purse: Economic Statecraft, Interdependence and National Security* (London: Frank Cass, 2000)

Gavin, Francis J., *Gold, Dollars and Power: The Politics of International Monetary Relations, 1958–1971* (Chapel Hill, NC: University of North Carolina Press, 2004)

Jackson, Ian, *The Economic Cold War: America, Britain and East–West Trade, 1948–1963* (Basingstoke: Palgrave Macmillan, 2001)

Kunz, Diane B., *Butter and Guns: America's Cold War Economic Diplomacy* (New York: The Free Press, 1997)

Parrott, Bruce, *Politics and Technology in the Soviet Union* (Cambridge, MA: MIT Press, 1983)

Shu Guang Zhang, *Economic Cold War: America's Embargo against China and the Sino-Soviet Alliance, 1949–1963* (Stanford, CA: Stanford University Press, 2001)

science and technology

Ball, Desmond, *Policies and Force Levels: The Strategic Missile Program of the Kennedy Administration* (Berkeley, CA: University of California Press, 1980)

Berman, Robert P. & John C. Baker, *Soviet Strategic Forces* (Washington, DC: Brookings, 1982)

Bluth, Christoph, *Soviet Strategic Arms Policy Before SALT* (Cambridge: Cambridge University Press, 1992)

Evangelista, Matthew, *Innovation and the Arms Race: How the United States and the Soviet Union Develop New Military Technologies* (Ithaca, NY: Cornell University Press, 1988)

Holloway, David, *Stalin and the Bomb* (New Haven, CT: Yale University Press, 1994)

MacKenzie, Donald, 'The Soviet Union and Strategic Missile Guidance', *International Security*, 13:2 (1988), pp.5–54

Podvig, Pavel (ed.), *Russian Strategic Nuclear Forces* (Cambridge, MA: MIT Press, 2001)

Schwarz, Stephen I. (ed.), *Atomic Audit: The Costs and Consequences of US Nuclear Weapons since, 1940* (Washington, DC: Brookings, 1998)

Zaloga, Steven, *Target America: The Soviet Union and the Strategic Arms Race, 1945–64* (Novato, CA: Presidio, 1993)

intelligence

Aldrich, Richard, *The Hidden Hand: Britain, America and Cold War Secret Intelligence* (London: John Murray, 2002)

Andrew, Christopher & Oleg Gordievsky, *KGB: The Inside Story* (London: Hodder & Stoughton, 1990)

Andrew, Christopher & Vasili Mitrokhin, *The Mitrokhin Archive: The KGB in Europe and the West* (London: Penguin, 1999)

Andrew, Christopher & Vasili Mitrokhin, *The KGB and the World* (London: Allen Lane, 2005)

Collm, Steve, *Ghost Wars: The Secret History of the CIA, Afghanistan and Bin Laden, from the Soviet Invasion to September, 10, 2001* (London: Penguin, 2004)

Dorril, Stephen, *MI6: Fifty Years of Special Operation* (London: Fourth Estate, 2001)

Garthoff, Raymond, 'Foreign Intelligence and the Historiography of the Cold War', *Journal of Cold War Studies*, 6:2 (2004), pp.21–56

Hennessy, Peter, *The Secret State: Whitehall and the Cold War* (London: Penguin, 2002)

Prados, John, *Presidents' Secret Wars: CIA and Pentagon Covert Operations from World War II through the Persian Gulf* (Chicago, IL: Ivan R. Dee, 1996)

culture

Berghahn, Volker, *America and the Intellectual Cold Wars in Europe: Shepard Stone between Philanthropy, Academy and Diplomacy* (Princeton, NJ: Princeton University Press, 2001)

Caute, David, *The Dancer Defects: The Struggle for Cultural Supremacy during the Cold War* (Oxford: Oxford University Press, 2003)

Klein, Christina, *Cold War Orientalism: Asia in the Middlebrow Imagination, 1945–1961* (Berkeley, CA: University of California Press, 2003)

Major, Patrick & Rana Mitter, 'East is East and West is West?: Towards a Comparative Sociocultural History of the Cold War', *Cold War History*, 4:1 (2003), pp.1–22

Stonor Saunders, Frances, *Who Paid the Piper?: The CIA and the Cultural Cold War* (London: Granta Books, 1999)

Smith, Giles Scott & Hans Krabbendam (eds), *The Cultural Cold War in Western Europe, 1945–1960* (London: Frank Cass, 2003)

Shaw, Tony, *British Cinema and the Cold War* (London: I.B. Tauris, 2000)

Suri, Jeremi, *Power and Protest: Global Revolution and the Rise of Détente* (Cambridge, MA: Harvard University Press, 2003)

Wilford, Hugh, *The CIA, the British Left and the Cold War: Calling the Tune?* (London: Frank Cass, 2003)

empires and the third world

Bacevich, Andrew J., *American Empire* (Cambridge, MA: Harvard University Press, 2002)

Dockrill, Saki, *Britain's Retreat from East of Suez: The Choice between Europe and the World* (Basingstoke: Palgrave Macmillan, 2002)

Gleijeses, Piero, *Conflicting Missions: Havana, Washington, and Africa, 1959–1976* (Chapel Hill, NC: University of North Carolina Press, 2002)

Kent, John, *British Imperial Strategy and the Origins of the Cold War* (New York & Leicester: Leicester University Press, 1993)

Kyle, Keith, *Suez: Britain's End of Empire in the Middle East* (London: I.B. Tauris, 2003)

Lieven, Dominic, *Empire: The Russian Empire and its Rivals* (London: John Murray, 2000)

MacQueen, Norrie, *The Decolonisation of Portuguese Africa* (London: Longman, 1997)

Maley, William, *The Afghanistan Wars* (Basingstoke: Palgrave Macmillan, 2002)

Schulzinger, Robert, *A Time for War: The United States and Vietnam, 1941–1945* (Oxford: Oxford University Press, 1997)

Sherwood, Elisabeth D., *Allies in Crisis: Meeting Global Challenges to Western Security* (New Haven, CT: Yale University Press, 1990)

Stuart, Douglas T. & William T. Tow, *The Limits of Alliance: NATO and Out-of-Area Problems since 1949* (Baltimore, MD: Johns Hopkins University Press, 1990)

index

Printed in the United States
126583LV00001B/55-78/P